Trade Secrets and Intellectual Property

Trade Secrets and Intellectual Property

Policy, Theory and Comparative Analysis

Second Edition

William van Caenegem
Luc Desaunettes-Barbero

Wolters Kluwer

Published by:
Kluwer Law International B.V.
PO Box 316
2400 AH Alphen aan den Rijn
The Netherlands
E-mail: lrs-sales@wolterskluwer.com
Website: www.wolterskluwer.com/en/solutions/kluwerlawinternational

Sold and distributed by:
Wolters Kluwer Legal & Regulatory U.S.
920 Links Avenue
Landisville, PA 17538
United States of America
E-mail: customer.service@wolterskluwer.com

ISBN 978-90-411-8664-5

e-Book: ISBN 978-90-411-8671-3
web-PDF: ISBN 978-90-411-8672-0

About the Authors

Dr William van Caenegem is a Professor of Law at Bond University, Queensland, Australia. He is the author of *Intellectual and Industrial Property Law* published by LexisNexis (4th edition) and the lead author of *Intellectual Property in Australia* by LexisNexis (7th edition). He published *Intellectual Property and Innovation* with Cambridge University Press and *Trade Secrets and Intellectual Property: Breach of Confidence, Misappropriation and Unfair Competition* (1st edition) with Kluwer Law International. He holds a Doctoral degree from Cambridge University (UK) and is a Law graduate of the University of Leuven in Belgium. He is an Honorary Visiting Professor at the University of Gothenburg and has also taught (*inter alia*) at Ghent and Paris (Sorbonne No 1 & No 2) universities. He has undertaken extensive comparative and policy work in IP law, including in relation to trade secrets and employee mobility. He lectures in Intellectual Property (IP) law and the law of Evidence.

Dr Luc Desaunettes-Barbero is a researcher and lecturer at UClouvain, Belgium. His research agenda primarily focuses on IP, addressing issues related to trade secrets, such as justification and comparative analysis; patent law, particularly concerning the European Unitary Patent Package, the patentability of de-extinct species, the proportionality of injunctive relief, supplementary protection certificates (SPCs), and standard essential patents (SEPs); and copyright law, especially the impact of AI technologies.

Additionally, his work encompasses broader questions, including the legal appropriation of and access to data, the effects of internationalization (e.g., Trade-Related Aspects of Intellectual Property Rights (TRIPS) flexibility clauses) and European integration (e.g., the impact of harmonization and the role of the European Court of Justice), as well as the relationship between IP protection, sustainability, and fundamental rights more generally. Beyond IP law, he actively engages with competition law, having published two comprehensive monographs on Articles 101 and 102 of the Treaty on the Functioning of the European Union (TFEU). He is also expanding his research to address legal issues arising from the platform economy, including the legal handling of ratings and reviews and the challenges posed by disinformation.

In addition to his research activities, Dr Desaunettes-Barbero is also involved in teaching at several universities, notably in Belgium (UClouvain), France (CEIPI at the University of Strasbourg and Sciences Po Strasbourg), Germany (MIPLC Munich), and Portugal (NOVA University Lisbon).

Table of Contents

About the Authors v

Acknowledgements xiii

CHAPTER 1
Introduction and Background of Trade Secrets Protection 1
§1.01 This Work 1
§1.02 Background 2
§1.03 Trade Secrets from an Innovation and Commercial Perspective 4
§1.04 Trade Secrets from a Doctrinal Perspective 6
§1.05 Harmonization in IP and Related Areas 8
§1.06 The Broader Context of Rights 10
§1.07 Comparative Trade Secrets Law 12
§1.08 The Intrinsic Significance of Trade Secrets 14
§1.09 The Adequacy and Appropriateness of Legal Protection 15
§1.10 The Public Domain and Development 17
§1.11 The Following Chapters 18

CHAPTER 2
Property, Propriety and Policy 19
§2.01 Introduction: Policy and Doctrine 19
[A] Property in Information? 21
[B] IP, Crime, and Property 26
§2.02 Some Economics of Trade Secrets 27
[A] Lemley: Trade Secrets as IP in the US Context 30
[B] The Property Rationale in English Law 34
[C] Risch: The Centrality of Cost Reduction 36
§2.03 A Behavioural and Socio-Legal Approach 41
§2.04 A Doctrinal Approach 44
[A] Focus on the Nature of Remedies 44

[B] Bone's Radical Take: No Law of Trade Secrets 47
§2.05 The Privacy Rationale 53
§2.06 Conclusions 55

CHAPTER 3
International Standards 61
§3.01 Introduction 61
§3.02 From Paris to TRIPS 62
[A] The Paris Convention: First Step Towards an International Standard 62
[B] Article 39 TRIPS: First Explicit International Obligation to Provide Legal Protection of Undisclosed Information 62
[C] TRIPS Negotiations: Tensions Concerning the Nature and Inclusion of Trade Secret Protection 63
[D] TRIPS Approach to Trade Secret Protection 64
[E] Treaty Standards, Domestic Implementation and Transborder Trade 69
§3.03 Other International Provisions Including the EU Trade Secrets Directive 71
[A] Free Trade Agreements Incorporating an Obligation to Protect Trade Secrets 71
[B] The European Trade Secret Directive 72
§3.04 Systemic Differences 73
[A] Remaining Relevance of Common Law Versus Civil Law Distinctions? 73
[B] Fundamental Rights 74
[C] Law and Equity 76
[D] Cases, Statutes and the Role of the Courts 77
§3.05 Global Doctrinal Differences 78
[A] Equity Versus Tort 79
[B] The Different Levels of Statutory Intervention 80
[C] The Unequal Application of the Criminal Law 81
§3.06 Doctrinal Similarities 83
[A] Property Rights in Trade Secrets Not Recognized 83
[B] The Level of Secrecy Required Is Not Absolute 85
[C] Trade Secrets Law Is Default Law 85
[D] Complexity and Uncertainty Is Best Resolved by Contract 86
§3.07 Concluding Comments 87

CHAPTER 4
The Common Law Approach: The English Law System 89
§4.01 Introduction to the English Approach 89
§4.02 Elements of the Modern Action 94

§4.03 Implementation of the EU Trade Secrets Directive in the UK: Trade Secrets (Enforcement, Etc.) Regulations 2018 99
[A] Introduction 99
[B] Recent Developments and Decisions Concerning the Regulations 101
§4.04 Industrial Espionage in English Law 102
[A] Impropriety or No Impropriety, What Is Impropriety? 106
§4.05 The Role of Statute and Criminal Law in England and Similar Jurisdictions 111
§4.06 Conclusions 113

Chapter 5
The Common Law Approach: The United States 115
§5.01 Introduction 115
[A] The Emergence of Trade Secrets Law in the US 116
[B] The Impact of the US Constitutional System on the Development of Trade Secret Law 121
§5.02 Unfair Competition and Other Actions 123
[A] Unfair Competition 123
[B] The Other Relevant Causes of Action 125
[C] Misappropriation and INS 129
§5.03 Civil Law Protection 130
[A] Background of the UTSA 130
[B] Origins of UTSA Trade Secrets' Definition 131
[C] Conditions Pertaining to Confidentiality and Value of Information 132
[D] Evidence of Measures to Protect Secrecy 134
[E] Impropriety 136
[F] Inevitable Disclosure 139
[G] The Defend Trade Secrets Act 141
[H] Some Characteristics of Litigation in the US 142
[I] Extraterritoriality of US Law 143
§5.04 The Criminal Law 147
§5.05 Conclusion 150

Chapter 6
The European Trade Secret Directive 151
§6.01 Introduction: Context of the Directive and Influence of US Law 151
§6.02 EU Competency, Legal *Instrumentarium* and Scope of the Directive 153
[A] EU Competency and Decision to Rely on a Directive 153
[B] No Harmonization of Criminal Protection 155
[C] No harmonization of the Relationship Between Employer and Employee 156

[D] Minimum Harmonization and the (Limited) Potential for More Far-Reaching Protection 158
[E] Overview of the National Transpositions 158
§6.03 Subject Matter: Replica of the TRIPS Definition 160
[A] Origin, Logic and Impact 160
[B] Importance of Case Law and Implications of the Current Lack of CJEU Decisions 162
[C] Requirements 163
[1] Secrecy 163
[2] Economic Value 166
[3] Reasonable Protection Measures 168
§6.04 Misappropriation 170
[A] Direct Infringers: Unfair Competition Versus Proprietary Approaches 170
[B] Third Parties and Infringing Goods 172
[C] Reverse Engineering: Lawfulness at the Mercy of Contract 174
§6.05 Enforcement and Proportionality Test 176

Chapter 7
Civilian Approaches: France 179
§7.01 Introduction 179
[A] Historical Background 179
[B] Some General Comments on the French System 180
§7.02 Civil Law: Extra-contractual Protection 181
[A] From the Praetorian Establishment of a Protection System Based on Unfair Competition … 181
[1] Unfair Competition Law and the Law of 'Parasitic Misappropriation' 181
[2] Notion of '*Savoir Faire*' and Fault Before the Transposition 184
[3] Comparative Points Concerning the French Approach Prior to the Transposition of the Directive 186
[B] … to the Transposition of the European Directive 187
[1] Legal and Political Context of the 2018 Reform 187
[2] Overview of the Transposition 187
[3] The Flawed Transposition of the Proportionality Test by the French Legislator 189
§7.03 Civil Law: Contractual Protection of Trade Secrets 189
[A] Transfer of *Savoir-Faire* 189
[B] Employment Contract and Confidentiality Clauses 191
[1] Legal Duty Inherent in the Employment Contract 191
[2] Express Confidentiality Clauses 192
[3] Use of Information after Termination of the Contractual Relationship 193

[C] Non-competes 194
[1] General Regime 194
[2] The Requirement of Consideration 199
§7.04 Criminal Protection 202
[A] Secrets de Fabrique 202
[B] General Criminal Law: Theft of Information 'as Such'? 203
[C] Receiving and Handling Stolen Information? 206
[D] Abus de Confiance 207
[E] The Reform Projects Aimed at Adopting Transversal Criminal Protection 207
[1] The 'Projet De Loi Carayon' 207
[2] The Reform Attempt During the Transposition of the Directive 208
§7.05 Conclusions 209

Chapter 8
Civilian Approaches: Germany 211
§8.01 Introduction 211
§8.02 Situation under the Unfair Competition Law (UWG) Before the Transposition of the European Directive 212
[A] Generalities and Comparative Elements 212
[B] Subject Matter: A Definition Forged by Case Law 212
[C] Criminal Protection under Articles 17 and 18 of Former UWG 214
[D] Civil Protection under Article 3 UWG and 823, 826 BGB 216
§8.03 The Trade Secret Act (*GeschGehG*) and Transposition of the European Directive 218
[A] The 2019 Trade Secret Act: Context and Generality 218
[B] The Definition of Trade Secrets in Article 2 *GeschGehG*: A German Recipe 219
[C] Definition of Lawful and Unlawful Behaviour: Transposition of the Directive with Minimal Adjustments 221
[D] The Lawfulness of Reverse Engineering: A Paradigm Shift 222
[E] Enforcement and Proportionally: The German Approach to the Balancing Test of the European Directive 223
[F] Criminal Law: Reshaping to Ensure Coherence with the Civil Law Framework 224
§8.04 Employment and Non-competes: Remaining Areas of National Law 227
[A] Employment and Extra-contractual Protection of Trade Secrets 227
[B] Contractual Obligations During and after Employment 228
[C] Non-compete Agreements in German Law 230
§8.05 Conclusion 232

CHAPTER 9
Trade Secrets and Employees 235
§9.01 Introduction 235
§9.02 Relevant Areas of Law and the Use of Knowledge after Termination 237
§9.03 Know-How and Trade Secrets in the English Law Tradition 241
§9.04 Contractual Devices 244
[A] Confidentiality Clauses 244
[B] Non-compete Clauses 245
§9.05 Assessment and Reform of the Law 251
[A] Non-competes: To Regulate or Not? 253
[B] Judicial Power to Rewrite Non-compete Clauses? 253
[C] Prescriptive Statutory Standards 256
[D] Rendering Non-competes Unenforceable by Statute? 258
[E] Strict Adherence to Principle? 259
[F] Legitimate or Protectable Interests 260
[G] Know-How as a Category of Information Protectable by a Restraint? 262
§9.06 Conclusion 265

CHAPTER 10
Conclusions: Global Convergence or Global Confusion? 267
§10.01 A Global Doctrinal Patchwork 267
§10.02 Persistent Fundamental Differences at the Global Level Despite Evidence of Rapprochement 271
§10.03 Does Harmonizing mean Strengthening Trade Secrets Protection? 274

Index 277

Acknowledgements

My thanks go to Anja Kramer of KLI for her patience and perseverance in relation to this book project. I would also like to thank my co-author Luc Desaunette-Barbero for his hard work and cooperation on this book, which results in part from our interesting discussions on complex and controversial topics. My thanks also to family, friends, my co-author Luc and colleagues who have patiently supported me throughout the long and sometimes arduous process of research, writing and editing.

William van Caenegem

I would like to express my gratitude to William van Caenegem for his trust and for asking me to contribute to this second edition. It has been a pleasure to collaborate with him and engage in lively discussions about the evolution of trade secret protection. I also want to thank Alain Strowel, whose crucial role as a facilitator in the research community made this collaboration possible. Finally, I want to extend a heartfelt thanks to my family for giving me the time I needed to write these pages.

Luc Desaunettes-Barbero

CHAPTER 1

Introduction and Background of Trade Secrets Protection

§1.01 THIS WORK

This work highlights the different approaches to the protection of trade secrets across civil law and common law jurisdictions and further examines doctrinal and policy issues from a comparative perspective. The book focuses on the European Union (EU) and its member countries, with a closer look at France and Germany on the one hand and at countries with an English law system (as adopted in Australia, Canada, etc.) and the United States of America (US) on the other hand. Although there are multiple different approaches to trade secrets law around the world, these jurisdictions are chosen to illustrate the unfair competition, equitable breach of confidence, and statutory and tortious approaches that figure prominently in the debate about appropriate trade secrets protection. They also represent different choices in relation to the application of the criminal law, and in the underlying policy goals and theoretical dimension of the legal status of trade secrets. In recent times, the United Kingdom (UK), France and Germany have more closely approximated their relevant laws by implementing the EU Trade Secrets Directive, although some important differences remain.

In every country, trade secrets issues arise most prominently in the post-employment period, where previous employers often attempt to use the law of trade secrets to prevent former employees from using knowledge acquired on the job. Their purpose is to stymie competition, and the question arises as to what extent such use of the law to achieve this goal should be considered legitimate. They also revert to contractual devices such as confidentiality clauses and non-compete agreements for this purpose. These aspects of the law are considered most closely in this work, in particular, because there has also been some regulatory movement in the area of non-competes in a number of jurisdictions (the UK, US and Australia, for instance). By contrast, the protection of regulatory data is not considered any further.

The aim of this work is not to conclude whether one or another approach is more effective. Rather, it illustrates that jurisdictions grapple with similar factual and fundamental policy issues but attempt to resolve them from different jurisprudential perspectives. Trade secrets cases are often difficult because they require decision-makers to resolve the tension between opposing principles and policy goals, such as the right to work and to conduct business, the fundamental freedoms of communication on the one side, and the right to protection of significant commercial assets and the fundamental rights to property or privacy on the other side. In practice, the judicial implementation of these legal systems also generates practical difficulties of proof and maintenance of confidentiality during the proceedings.

Trade secrets are not truly a form of intellectual *property*: in fact, the beneficiaries are not granted an *erga omnes* exclusive right to their secrets. They, therefore, require very careful management and precautionary legal action: once a trade secret has escaped into the public domain, it cannot be restored to its 'owner'. Those issues of management become even more challenging when business is conducted across multiple jurisdictions, and the latter compete to provide the legal environment most conducive to transnational investment. In comparison with areas of Intellectual Property (IP) law such as patents and copyrights, there is very little in the way of international standards or harmonization in trade secrets law, although the EU Trade Secrets Directive has now brought member-country civilian laws substantially into line with the US approach. This adds to the unique challenges of developing and understanding this multi-faceted area of law, which is often a fallback or last resort when commercial dealings and relationships go wrong.

§1.02 BACKGROUND

Despite their economic relevance,[1] trade secrets law has been the orphan child of IP scholarship, although, in more recent times, there has been an increasing interest in the topic.[2] This lack of interest is partly because, although commonly treated as such, it

1. *See* Richard C. Levin et al., 'Appropriating the Returns from Industrial Research and Development' (1987) 3 *Brookings Papers on Economic Activity* 783, 793-796 https://doi.org/10.2307/2534454, with the conclusion based on an empirical study comparing the relative importance of several means of protection within the US manufacturing industry, that 'Secrecy, though not considered as effective as lead time and learning advantages, was still considered more effective than patents in protecting processes.' *See also* Wesley M. Cohen, Richard R. Nelson & John P. Walsh, 'Protecting Their Intellectual Assets: Appropriability Conditions and Why US Manufacturing Firms Patent (or Not)' (2000) *NBER Working Paper Series 7552*, 9-10; Najib Harabi, 'Appropriability of Technical Innovations an Empirical Analysis' (1995) 24(6) *Research Policy* 981, 984 https://doi.org/10.1016/0048-7333(94)00812-4; Katrin Hussinger, 'Is Silence Golden? Patents Versus Secrecy at the Firm Level' (2006) 16(8) *Economics of Innovation and New Technology* 735 https://doi.org/10.1080/10438590500510467.
2. *See, e.g.*, Rochelle C. Dreyfuss & Katherine J. Strandburg (eds), *The Law and Theory of Trade Secrecy: A Handbook of Contemporary Research* (Edward Elgar Publishing, 2012); Tanya Aplin, Lionel Bently, Phillip Johnsnon & Simon Malynics, *Gurry on Breach of Confidence: The Protection of Confidential Information* (Oxford University Press, 2nd ed, 2012); Tanya Aplin, 'Recent Developments in Commercial Confidentiality' (2010) 15(2) *Media and Arts Law Review* 1 https://doi.org/10.4324/9780203060605-8; Hogan Lovells International LLP, 'Report on Trade

arguably does not form part of IP law at all.[3] Trade secrets law tends to fall in the cracks between various legal regimes, such as IP, torts, unfair competition and equity.[4] Trade secrets are also difficult to verify, document accurately and measure – unlike patents, for instance, which supply a vast source of readily available recorded and organized data for empirical analysis.[5]

Another difficulty for trade secrets research is that the global legal picture has long been fluid, multifarious and opaque. Trade secrets law lies at the complex intersection between other regimes, in particular, labour law, unfair competition law, equity, contract and criminal law. Many of its most crucial legal questions cannot be resolved without recourse or regard to these other legal regimes, to such an extent that some scholars have questioned the need for a separate trade secrets regime at all.[6] In countries where unfair competition is the framework for trade secrets protection, arguably no separate trade secrets law exists, and the same can be said in the English law tradition where the action for breach of confidence is but one aspect of equity.[7] However, the disparate European approaches which nonetheless tended to see trade

Secrets for the European Commission' (Study on Trade Secrets and Parasitic Copying (Look-alikes)), 13 January 2012, http://ec.europa.eu/internal_market/iprenforcement/docs/trade/Study_Trade_Secrets_en.pdf ('Lovells Report'). At time of writing the Report was not available at this link or any other official link; the Report is held on file by the authors. *See also* Michael Risch, 'Why Do We Have Trade Secrets?' (2007) 11 *Marquette Intellectual Property Law Review* 1-59; Yuval Feldman, 'The Expressive Function of Trade Secret Law: Legality, Cost, Intrinsic Motivation, and Consensus' (2009) 6(1) *Journal of Empirical Legal Studies* 177-212 https://doi.org/10.1111/j.1740-1461.2009.01141.x; Ansgar Ohly, 'Reverse Engineering: Unfair Competition or Catalyst for Innovation?' in Wolrad Prinz zu Waldeck, et al. (eds), *Patents and Technological Progress in a Globalized World* (Springer, 2008) 535-552; Friedman, D., Landes, W.M. & Posner, R.A., 'Some Economics of Trade Secret Law' (1991) 5(1) *Journal of Economic Perspectives*, 61-72 https://doi.org/10.1257/jep.5.1.61; Luc Desaunettes-Barbaro, *Trade Secrets Legal Protection: From a Comparative Analysis of US and EU Law to a New Model of Understanding* (Springer, 1st ed., 2023).

3. Although the concept of 'property' is always problematic when it comes to intellectual assets, it is particularly so when trade secrets are concerned.
4. Between labour laws, IP law, contract law, unfair competition law, equity, competition law, etc.
5. However, in terms of where policy analysts and policy makers direct their interest, trade secrets law does not have the attraction of patents law. There is no large empirical data set of filings, applications, registrations, etc., to underpin mathematically and statistically significant analysis and conclusions. Trade secrets are by nature difficult to uncover, identify, catalogue, quantify and value. Nonetheless, patent data can throw some light on trade secrets issues as is discussed in the chapters on employee trade secrets and know-how. Trade secrets are often associated with patented inventions, so that where there is a patent, there is usually a trade secret. But since there is no register or the like of the latter, we cannot easily identify the extent and value of such secret knowledge and information. Nor can we catalogue its inherent nature, since other than being of commercial value and not in the public domain; anything can be protected as a trade secret, whether technical or commercial in nature.
6. Bone states that: '[T]rade secret law is merely a collection of other legal norms – contract, fraud, and the like – united only by the fact that they are used to protect secret information. Neither the fact that a trade secret is information nor the fact that it is secret provides a convincing reason to impose liability for a nonconsensual taking. Trade secret law in this sense is parasitic: it depends on a host theory for normative support.': Robert G. Bone, 'A New Look at Trade Secrets Law: Doctrine in Search of Justification' (1998) 86(2) *California Law Review* 241, 245 https://doi.org/10.2307/3481134.
7. Note that the Lovells Report (*see* above n 2) deals with two unfair competition issues, slavish imitation and trade secrets misuse.

secrets law through the lens of fair competition have now been displaced by a separate statutory regime that nevertheless has echoes of unfair competition tort law.[8]

Trade secrets law contrasts starkly with the established and distinct IP regimes that attract much scholarly, legislative and international attention. Fairly detailed and binding international treaties have resulted in IP regimes that are in fundamental respects homogenous and instantly recognizable for lawyers from all jurisdictions. By contrast, regulatory data supplied to governments is the only category of trade secrets that has attracted some more detailed and prescriptive global standards.[9] The World Trade Organization (WTO) or The Agreement on Trade-Related Aspects of Intellectual Property Rights (TRIPS) requirement of protection for 'undisclosed information' is minimal and not understood to mandate a particular legal regime; there is a complex relationship with the unfair competition article in the Paris Convention (Article 10bis). Nonetheless, as the recent initiative of the European Commission (EC) that resulted in the EU Trade Secrets Directive illustrates, legal differences in the protection of trade secrets can have a negative impact on the development of cross-border business relationships. The Commission was concerned that the lack of harmony in trade secrets law might hamper trade within the EU, and from this concern developed a uniform model now adopted in all EU Member States.[10]

§1.03 TRADE SECRETS FROM AN INNOVATION AND COMMERCIAL PERSPECTIVE

Despite voluminous writings on the topic, there is some doubt about patents as a proxy for innovation, as the great increase in patent filings around the industrialized world has not been matched by a concomitant rise in Research and Development (R&D) investment. In any case, patent data offers a less-than-complete picture, as companies often avoid applying for patents. They have strategic drawbacks, prominent among which is the fact that published patent specifications reveal otherwise secret knowledge to rivals. Even if competitors do not always derive useful technical information from patent disclosures, they can at least learn about the direction of a rival firm's innovation efforts and draw useful inferences concerning commercial strategies. Further, whereas the patent monopoly is limited in time, secrecy can be maintained indefinitely without any knowledge spilling over to competitors.

There are sometimes compelling reasons to patent, for example, because it is not practically possible to commercialize a new technology without revealing it to the public; because it is easy to reverse engineer it; or because there is a clear risk that rivals will arrive at the same innovation independently before long. Patents may also be

8. Via its reliance on US law as a model, which itself is rooted in unfair competition law (?).
9. *See* further below, Chapter 3.
10. European Commission, Report, European Commission Conference of 29 June 2013, 'Trade Secrets: Supporting Innovation, Protecting Know-How' 2, 15; Directive (EU) 2016/943 of the European Parliament and of the Council of 8 June 2016 on the Protection of Undisclosed Know-how and Business Information (trade secrets) Against Their Unlawful Acquisition, Use and Disclosure [2016] OJ L 157/1.

attractive as they are not so subject to the risk of disastrous failure as trade secrets protection can be. For example, monetary remedies rarely provide adequate compensation for the catastrophic loss of value from a premature disclosure of a trade secret. Firms additionally have strategic reasons to patent which include the purpose of cross-licensing, disrupting competition by the threat of litigation, and attracting risk capital.

But often secrecy is considered more practical and cheaper, since although secrecy measures entail costs, a patent portfolio is much more expensive to acquire and maintain. In many industries, innovative firms will combine secrecy and patent strategies to maximize efficiencies. There is limited empirical data concerning firms' preferences for patents over trade secrets, but our intuition tells us that secrecy is far more commonly relied upon than patenting. It is the natural first call where new information or knowledge has been generated. In fact, a patent can only be obtained for an invention that is new and presents an inventive step at the time of filing, which means, de facto, that a patent can only be obtained for information that qualifies as a trade secret in the first place. Besides, relying on trade secrets law does not require active deliberation or choice, as a firm can usually fall back on it when the need arises, as long as secrecy has been maintained in some demonstrable way. The law of trade secrets tends to be weak, so reliance on it in practice amounts to adopting a self-help strategy (hiding information) with some soft legal underpinnings. It amounts to nothing like the monopoly rights in a patent, highly legalistic and very precisely and extensively documented.

However, although perhaps weak, the reach of trade secrets law is wide. Many commercially significant innovations cannot be captured by patenting because that legal regime extends to technological innovation only. TRIPS links patents to technology, and in recent times, the courts have reigned in any tendency to extend patents into theoretical knowledge and discovery (in the biotech field) or into the service industries, commercial strategies, business ideas and management techniques.[11] By contrast, trade secrets protection extends to valuable commercial as well as technical data (such as business plans, supplier data, price information, client data, etc.), at least as long as they remain invisible and can be particularized. On one view, trade secrets protection extends not just to information but to the private sphere.[12] Nonetheless, it is a form of protection that is always vulnerable to legitimate intelligence gathering by competitors – unlike patents where competitors, no matter how they arrive at the same information, are prohibited from exploiting it during the patent term.

We know there is much inventive and innovative commercial and technological activity and much new knowledge created, which patent specifications do not reveal. In this light, it is difficult to gauge to what extent patent data is a reliable proxy for innovation as a whole. Furthermore, due to low legal standards, patentable inventions

---

11. *See, e.g., Welcome Real-Time SA v. Catuity Inc* (2001) 113 FCR 110; *Bilski v. Kappos*, 561 US 130 S. Ct. 3218 (2010); *Grant v. Commissioner of Patents* (2006) 154 FCR 62.
12. *See* above n 2.

require a mere scintilla of inventiveness,[13] so that many patentable inventions are of little real significance in terms of visible or resulting innovations.[14] Many firms invest more in strategic rather than in genuinely innovative activities, in mapping applications to their competitive positions by building patent portfolios, participating in patent pools, etc.[15]

A further significant fact that sometimes disappears from view in the midst of all the patent number-crunching is that real invention is and remains a human activity. Machines, such as AI solutions, are just tools (albeit very powerful ones) that serve these human activities. Even if their capabilities are constantly increasing, the fact remains that an AI algorithm, however powerful, only offers solutions because a human being asks it to do so in the first place.[16] Therefore, it is most often the confluence of human knowledge, human ability and human communication in the workplace that generates innovation. The human activities of thought, inference, logic and inspiration are more closely connected with trade secrets than with patent law. Knowledge is born first in the human mind, where it remains secret until it is revealed by being expressed in some form. Whereas the public-good characteristics of information are often alluded to, what is commonly overlooked is that new knowledge is of human origin and, therefore, initially private and not public. Only when an individual decides to reveal it does it display public-good characteristics, whereupon the law of trade secrets naturally frames that individual's relevant rights and obligations, whether against the background of equity, unfair competition, tort, statute or quasi-property.

§1.04 TRADE SECRETS FROM A DOCTRINAL PERSPECTIVE

Trade secrets law is not only interesting from an innovation policy perspective but also in terms of the doctrines of IP and associated areas of law. Non-proprietary regimes

13. *See* Harold Potts, 'The Definition of Invention in Patent Law' (1944) 7(3) *Modern Law Review* 113 https://doi.org/10.1111/j.1468-2230.1944.tb00974.x; *Lockwood Security Products Pty Ltd v. Doric Products Pty Ltd* (2007) 235 CLR 173.
14. Inventiveness is not normally a standard examined by the patent office when an application is filed, so that many patents that are in fact granted would failed the test if fully investigated in terms of inventive step.
15. *See* Kurt Brekke & Odd Straume, 'Pharmaceutical Patents: Incentives for Research and Development or Marketing?'(2009) 76(2) *Southern Economic Journal* 351 https://doi.org/10.4284/sej.2009.76.2.351; Jinheng Feng, 'When a Shield Becomes a Sword: Regulating Abusive Patent Litigation in the Context of Competition' *Bond University* (online) 16 June 2022, https://research.bond.edu.au/en/studentTheses/when-a-shield-becomes-a-sword-regulating-abusive-patent-litigatio.
16. The contrary view (that machines are capable of patent-relevant invention) having been rejected in a series of decisions in different jurisdictions, such as *Commissioner of Patents v. Thaler* [2022] FCAFC 62; *Thaler v. Comptroller-General of Patents, Designs and Trademarks* [2023] UKSC 49; and J 0008/20 (Designation of inventor/DABUS) 21 December 2021 (EUIPO). We accept that some argue that AI has a capacity analogous to human inventiveness and creativity. To some extent, this depends on how human intelligence and inventiveness are defined. For a more detailed consideration of some of these issues, *see* Francina Cantatore & William van Caenegem 'Is AI Capable of Original Creativity? A Critical Discussion of the Real Impact of AI on IP Regulation' (2023) 3(3) *Australian Intellectual Property Journal* 163. However, inventive activity itself is only triggered by a human impulse, and any AI solution remains a tool.

such as breach of confidence, misappropriation, unfair competition, unjust enrichment and fiduciary duties govern information, knowledge and reputation at the edges and in the interstices of IP law. Alternatively, they constitute the unifying underpinnings of the proprietary regimes: their position as an alternative or complementary source of obligations and liabilities is consistently controversial.

Consideration of a default regime like trade secrets law, therefore, triggers thinking about the proper contours and extent of proprietary claims to intellectual assets. What does 'property' really mean in the context of intellectual rather than physical goods? What is the utility of property concepts in relation to knowledge and information? Are or should property rights be extended to cover trade secrets?

A review of trade secrets law also triggers thinking about the proper contours of any regime of unfair competition law because that was the relevant legal regime in many civilian jurisdictions and remains so in some.[17] This approach conceives of misuse of a trade secret as a species of unfair competition against the original progenitor of the information concerned. By contrast, courts have rejected such a tort in the common law jurisdictions, most firmly in countries which are more closely aligned with English law.[18] In the US, it has had more resonance, without being wholeheartedly embraced there either.[19] To some extent, the common law shows reluctance because a remedy for something as ill-defined as 'unfair competition' threatens to destabilize the finely balanced spectrum of IP laws.

But in truth, in many civilian jurisdictions, the relationship between unfair competition and IP *sensu stricto* is not settled either. If the legislators have carefully and continuously crafted a regime comprising different proprietary rights in intellectual assets, what is the relative merit of a broad unfair competition tort? Further, how can unfair competition law be controlled to 'fit in' and coexist with IP? Is it better to reject unfair competition so that all market actors know with precision where they stand being that recovery is limited to IP remedies? Are property rights 'better' in any case since they promise more certainty about the contour of rights? Or can complex fact scenarios be parcelled into facts relevant to liability in one regime and other facts relevant to another regime? The new departure in the EU and its Member States, which has turned away from unfair competition as a suitable remedy for trade secrets abuses,

17. For instance, in China, the Anti-unfair Competition Law of the People's Republic of China remains the main source of trade secrets protection. *See also* in Japan, the *Unfair Competition Prevention Act* (Act No 47 of 1993) (UCPA).
18. *See Mogul Steamship Co v. McGregor Gow & Co* (1889) 23 QBD 598, 625-626; *Victoria Park Racing and Recreation Grounds Co Ltd v. Taylor* (1937) 58 CLR 479; *Moorgate Tobacco Co Ltd v. Philip Morris Ltd (No 2)* (1984) 156 CLR 414; *Cadbury Schweppes Pty Ltd v. The Pub Squash Co Ltd* [1981] RPC 429; *L'Oreal SA v. Bellure NV* [2007] EWCA Civ 968. *See also* Tom Alkin, 'Should There Be a Tort of "Unfair Competition" in English Law?' 2008 3(1) *Journal of Intellectual Property Law & Practice* 48 https://doi.org/10.1093/jiplp/jpm209.
19. *See* for instance Lauren M. Gregory, 'Hot Off the Presses: How Traditional Newspaper Journalism Can Help Reinvent the Hot News Misappropriation Tort in the Internet Age' (2010-2011) 13 *Vanderbilt Journal of Entertainment and Technology Law* 577; Bruce D. Brown, 'Hot News on the Hot Seat' (2012) 29(1) *Communications Lawyer* 18; Victoria Smith Ekstrand, *News Piracy and the Hot News Doctrine: Origins in Law and Implications for the Digital Age* (LFB Scholarly Publishing, 2005).

tends to reflect a turn towards a more proprietary approach and away from principles of fairness.

Nonetheless, the trade secrets law continues to illuminate critical arguments in the broader debate concerning property and unfair competition.[20] But in fact the English law has had its own rather analogous regime, being rather broad and flexible but based on evaluating conduct against standards of good faith rather than fairness: equity, which includes breach of confidence. That regime is now augmented by the regulatory approach which transposes the EU Trade Secrets Directive (which entered into force before Brexit). Here also, the proper extent and unitary basis of equitable remedies is constantly under debate.

Consequently, the analysis of trade secrets law is fundamental to dissecting IP as a whole, in particular the relative positions of general liability regimes (whether more tort or equity) and proprietary regimes. This issue is further considered in the next Chapter.

§1.05 HARMONIZATION IN IP AND RELATED AREAS

The issues raised above are further complicated by the low level of global harmonization of trade secrets law. Unlike other areas of IP, the TRIPS provisions are not very prescriptive, with little detail concerning how the required protection of 'undisclosed information' is to be achieved.[21] Article 39 TRIPS suggests unfair competition as the dominant norm. However, a certain uncertainty in the dogmatic classification of trade secret protection is also evident in the Agreement: despite this apparent preference for an unfair competition approach, Article 39 is still part of a section on the 'availability, scope and use of intellectual property rights', while intellectual property rights (IPRs) are clearly defined in the preamble as 'private rights'.

The unfair competition approach is also no longer the preferred path in many civil law countries, some, in particular in Europe, having adopted a sui generis statutory regime.[22] There have been major recent changes in trade secrets law, for instance, in Japan, the US and the EU and its Member States.[23] Nonetheless, much of the protection of undisclosed information will, in reality, be based on contract rather

20. As a default remedy, it does not only concern the area of trade secrets but also extends to the protection against product and image imitation. In particular, it emerges in the debate concerning protection against imitation without consumer deception – should the law intervene if the imitator, by some reckoning, achieves an unfair competitive advantage or uses unfair tactics to compete? In particular, should that be the case where IP law has not or does not grant the initial party exclusive rights, as for instance in a registered design? In terms of European as opposed to EU law, in 2021 the law in Norway, for instance, was also amended to reflect the EU Trade Secrets Directive. *See* Åse Røynestad Konsmo, 'The Trade Secrets Directive: Norway' (2019) 3 *Les Nouvelles – Journal of the Licensing Executives Society* 207; *Norwegian Trade Secrets Act* 2021.
21. *See* further below, Chapter 3.
22. For instance, Sweden has an Act dealing specifically with the protection of trade secrets. *See* the *Protection of Trade Secrets Act* (Sweden) No 1990:409; alternatively, *Act on the Protection of Trade Secrets (1990:409)* (1990).
23. *See* United Kingdom Intellectual Property Office, 'The Economic and Innovation Impacts of Trade Secrets' *United Kingdom Government* (online) 19 April 2021, https://www.gov.uk/

than the general law, but of course, this in turn is partly due to the uncertainty of the default law.

Nonetheless, there is a growing realization that where companies undertake business across different jurisdictions and hire personnel governed by distinct regimes, variable rules concerning trade secrets impact investment decisions, structuring of multinational businesses and hiring policies.[24] Governments are increasingly aware that ineffective trade secrets protection will deter certain kinds of foreign direct investment (FDI) and will also place a break on cross-border trade and commercial agreements.[25] Governments have recently also given increased attention to the connection between mobility of persons and the mobility of tacit knowledge, in particular in the sphere of non-compete agreements.[26] As indicated above, within the EU, the importance of trade secrets protection has come to the Commission's attention, as it has in Member States. This has resulted in major changes in the EU states. However, at the global level, only the protection for regulatory data has seen any significant movement since the time of the Paris Convention, and there seems little appetite to do more.

In fact, in some of its aspects, trade secrets law trends towards greater regulatory competition and divergence. This was particularly the case in the US, where some of the states are inclined to reduce trade secrets protection by way of non-compete clauses in employment contracts, whereas others have tended towards greater non-compete enforceability. Courts in different states observe different legal standards, which are

---

government/publications/economic-and-innovation-impacts-of-trade-secrets/the-economic-and-innovation-impacts-of-trade-secrets. Japan revised its Unfair Competition Act in 2018, providing civil and criminal remedies for trade secrets: *see Unfair Competition Prevention Act* (Act No 47 of 1993) which now imposes significant criminal penalties for the violation of trade secrets under Art. 21.

24. For a practical account *see* Kim Daria, 'Protecting Trade Secrets under International Investment Law: What Secrets Investors Should Not Tell States' (2016) 15(2) *The John Marshall Review of Intellectual Property Law* 228 https://doi.org/10.2139/ssrn.2754006. For a more theoretical analysis, *see*, Asli Leblebicioglu & Ivan Kandilov, 'Trade Secrets Protection and Foreign Investment'. Available at SSRN: https://ssrn.com/abstract=4770611 or http://dx.doi.org/10.2139/ssrn.4770611.

25. *See* Andrew Beckerman-Rodau, 'Choice Between Patent Protection and Trade Secret Protection: A Legal and Business Decision' (2002) 84 *Journal of the Patent and Trademark Office Society* 371, 376; Shubha Ghosh, 'Open Borders, the US Economic Espionage Act of 1996, and the Global Movement of Knowledge and People' (2010) 21(1) *King's Law Journal* 1 https://doi.org/10.1080/09615768.2010.11423691; Belay Seyoum, 'The Impact of Intellectual Property Rights on Foreign Direct Investment' (1996) 31(1) *Columbia Journal of World Business* 50 https://doi.org/10.1016/s0022-5428(96)90006-x; Beata Smarzynska Javorcik, 'The Composition of Foreign Direct Investment and Protection of Intellectual Property Rights: Evidence from Transition Economies' (2004) 48(1) *European Economic Review* 39 https://doi.org/10.1016/s0014-2921(02)00257-x.

26. In the United States, *see* Federal Trade Commission, 'Non-compete Clause Rule' *Federal Register* (online) 5 July 2024, https://www.federalregister.gov/documents/2024/05/07/2024-09171/non-compete-clause-rule. *See also* Daniel Pasternak & Laura Lawless, 'Federal Court Enjoins Federal Trade Commission's Rule Prohibiting Non-Competition Agreements (US)' *Squire Patton Boggs* (online) 3 July 2024, https://www.employmentlawworldview.com/federal-court-enjoins-federal-trade-commissions-rule-prohibiting-non-competition-agreements-us/#:~:text=In%20January%202023%2C%20the%20US,non%2Dcompetition%20arrangements%20with%20workers.

thought to have certain policy implications. However, the promulgation of the Non-compete Clause Rule (Final Rule) by the Federal government purports to create a uniform standard for all of the United States: a complete ban reflecting the existing Californian approach.[27] By comparison in Australia, New South Wales is said to have a more employer-friendly regime than other states.[28] Within the EU there has been a considerable variety of legal regimes applying to non-competes, from the highly prescriptive German model to the largely case-based French and common law approaches.[29]

§1.06 THE BROADER CONTEXT OF RIGHTS

The broader regulatory context also impacts the national configuration of trade secrets law. In particular, some jurisdictions recognize both a basic right to privacy and a constitutional right of freedom of expression and communication, whereas these protections are absent from the English common law tradition. That informs both the scope of protection – in the English law world extending beyond commercial secrets to encompass also personal data under the broad umbrella of 'confidential information' – and the mechanism whereby the balance between significant policy goals (competition and openness versus private communications and trust) is struck. Historically, in the English tradition, there is no express external counterweight, such as freedom of speech: for any action for breach of confidence, the balance is struck endogenously.[30] In most other jurisdictions, including those considered in this work, freedom of speech (or communication or information or the press) is expressly guaranteed. That reality impacts the equation: any legal restraint, based on trade secrecy, that impedes communication of information must be weighed up against the potential affront to freedom of speech that it constitutes. In terms of private information, since there is traditionally no separate tort of invasion of privacy, the action for breach of confidence deals with misuse of personal information as best it can in the common law tradition. Contrastingly, in civil law jurisdictions and in the US, a separate action for invasion or breach of privacy is available. The interest in maintaining a protected personal sphere is seen as fundamental and warranting tailored protection per se, irrespective of any communication that vests another party with an obligation of confidence.

Another contextual issue concerns the relationship with contract: until recently, in the English tradition, the prevalence of contract left little room for an independent area of trade secrets law to develop coherently. Only in *Coco v. A N Clark (Engineers)*

27. Although there are legal and constitutional concerns about the rule's validity. *See* above n 26.
28. New South Wales' *Restraints of Trade Act 1976* makes judicial amendment and thus enforcement of non-competes that protect trade secrets easier.
29. *See* further below, Chapters 6 and 7.
30. In this sense, this area of law has some parallels with the torts of libel and defamation. For instance, in Australia, there is only a limited right of political discussion acts as an external counterweight to the interests of a plaintiff in protecting reputation. *Theophanous v. Herald & Weekly Times Ltd* (1994) 182 CLR 104; *Stephens v. Western Australian Newspapers Ltd* (1994) 182 CLR 211.

Ltd,[31] did the English common law expressly recognize that an action for breach of confidence lies independently of contract. In most commercial relationships, the treatment of trade secrets is in reality of course governed by express or implied contractual terms. Within employment contracts also, the question of confidentiality is often dealt with expressly. Normally, a contract prevails over the general law, and, therefore, in commercial situations, recourse to the general law is often unnecessary or secondary. However, public domain information cannot be turned into a trade secret by contractual *fiat* and, therefore, contract and trade secrets law are closely intertwined and employ very similar factual tests.[32] There are also important situations in which recourse to contract is clearly unavailable or else rather artificially constructed, specifically where information is exchanged in pre-contractual negotiations and where information is used by employees after their departure. Thus, trade secrets law remains important, despite it often being pre-empted by the existence of a contractual obligation or remedy.

Furthermore, litigated trade secrets matters are often effectively disposed of at the interlocutory or preliminary injunction stage. Here, legal issues concerning trade secrets protection (the strength of the case) are important but not determinative by themselves. The balancing test which also encompasses the 'balance of convenience' is undertaken at the preliminary stage in all jurisdictions.[33] Importantly, matters very often rest with the court's discretionary decision at that stage, as Rowe points out:

> Unlike most civil cases, the majority of trade secret misappropriation cases begin in injunctive mode. Thus, in addition to filing a complaint, a trade secret plaintiff will often seek a temporary restraining order against a defendant, and a preliminary injunction hearing will be set for about ten days later. This is significant because the preliminary injunction hearing serves as a filter that influences not only the procedure of the case, but also the manner in which the case is evaluated by the court, thus ultimately having a large impact on the outcome. Although the availability of preliminary injunctions could itself be seen as a negative tool, the mere threat of which could silence a defendant or cause her to settle, the overall effect in trade secret litigation may instead be positive because, when properly applied, the preliminary injunction inquiry places a higher burden on the plaintiff.[34]

There is some difficulty in evaluating the truth of Rowe's conclusion as the legal and evidentiary issues are usually not fully ventilated at the preliminary stage.[35]

31. [1969] RPC 41. Although preceded by the Australian decision in *Ansell Rubber Co Pty Ltd v. Allied Rubber Industries Pty Ltd* [1967] VR 37.
32. *Maggbury Pty Ltd v. Hafele Australia Pty Ltd* (2001) 210 CLR 181.
33. Although the precise test may differ; in Australia *see ABC v. O'Neill* (2006) 227 CLR 57; in Europe, *see* generally Trade Secrets Directive Art. 11, for the transposition in France Art. L152-3 Code de Commerce and for the transposition in Germany § 20 Gesetz zum Schutz von Geschäftsgeheimnissen (GeschGehG).
34. Elizabeth A. Rowe, 'Trade Secret Litigation and Free Speech: Is It Time to Restrain the Plaintiffs?' (2009) 50 *Boston College Law Review* 1425, 1446.
35. Rowe also makes the interesting point that the risk that defendants who are being sued disclose the secret acts as a restraining influence on plaintiffs. *Ibid.*, 1450. She also points out that the costs of litigation are high, particularly in the US which she comments that, 'On average it costs more than $700,000.00 to litigate a trade secret case through trial, and that average can easily

However, what is significant here is that tests other than 'does the plaintiff establish every element of the action' play a determinative role in many trade secrets disputes. Trade secrets law sits within this broader procedural and strategic context.

A further contextual question relates to control over knowledge as between employees and employers, which is a central issue in a majority of trade secrets cases. Here, trade secrets law coexists with the law relating to the ownership of inventions. Patent law on the whole determines that employers own inventions made by an employee in the course of their employment. Significant is when the invention was made (either during the term of employment, before, or after) and whether the employee was operating under a contractual duty when making an invention of the relevant kind. Interestingly enough, whereas patent law is generally quite harmonized, ownership of employee inventions is a signal exception as the international conventions leave this to domestic law. The harmonization of EU trade secrets law by way of the EU Trade Secrets Directive has also left this question open for Member States to regulate. Domestic rules vary significantly between jurisdictions, so the whole area of employee entitlement to innovations, information and tacit knowledge post-termination has largely escaped the harmonization net. As well as patent law, labour law principles also play a part in resolving competing claims. Sometimes, these areas of law have divergent principles and policy goals, so that the law of trade secrets post-employment lives in a very complex environment.[36]

§1.07 COMPARATIVE TRADE SECRETS LAW

A traditional approach to comparative law is to divide jurisdictions along 'common law' and 'civil law' lines. There are of course risks in structuring any analysis in this manner because, first, there is no real uniformity within each family, and second, as it stands, the law generates considerable doctrinal unease and uncertainty everywhere.

The law of trade secrets historically believes the contention that a fundamental distinguishing feature is that in civil law jurisdictions, every strand of the law is

---

climb to $1million in larger stakes cases.' *Ibid.*, at 1451. Further she says that '[I]n addition, companies who sue for trade secret theft may have difficulty recruiting employees.' *Ibid.*, at 1452.

36. There is also a question whether more harmony is desirable between the rules that determine control over unpatented technical trade secrets (which are not necessarily un-patentable) and ownership control of inventions. In the common law world, taking Australia as an example, the latter is substantially (but not wholly) determined by ownership and property principles, whereas the former is a question of equity – the duty of good faith as expressed in the action for breach of confidence determines the outcome. Whether or not this in fact makes much difference to the outcome of any given dispute is perhaps moot. *See also University of Western Australia v. Gray* (2009) 179 FCR 346; *Wilson v. Hollywood Toys (Aust) Pty Ltd* (1996) 34 IPR 293. But why treat differently an invention (one of) the parties intends to patent from one that may be just as patentable, but neither party is interested in patenting? There are particular difficulties in relation to inchoate inventions, which may be too early-stage to patent but sufficiently promising and specific to deserve some legal protection as a trade secret In terms of innovation policy. The proper legal approach to these issues is a significant question. *See* Robert P. Merges, 'The Law and Economics of Employee Inventions' (1999) 13(1) *Harvard Journal of Law & Technology* 1.

codified, whereas in the common law tradition, much law is based on the cases. This is well illustrated by the situation in Germany and France before the adoption of the EU uniform trade secrets laws. Both jurisdictions shared an unfair competition-based approach to trade secrets law but with very different systemic features. In Germany, there were extensive statutory provisions,[37] whereas, in France, the law was effectively based on the cases, although nominally derived from the basic principles of tortious liability in Articles 1240 and 1241 of the *Code Civil* (also referred to as the *Code Napoleon*). In effect, the French system was very similar to the English common law model: in the latter, the courts develop case law concerning breach of confidence on the basis of broad notions of equity, in the former on the basis of equally flexible (and uncodified in any detail) notion of fair (i.e., commercially honest) competition. In any case, although the law is now based on almost identical statutory rules in all EU jurisdictions, the rules remain quite broadly expressed.[38] If not for the unifying effect of the ECJ's jurisdiction concerning novel legal issues, it would be interesting to see how widely these countries' courts would diverge in their jurisprudence over time. It should be noted that not everything is harmonized by the EU Trade Secrets Directive: in virtually all civilian jurisdictions, the criminal law does extend to certain abuses of trade secrets, in particular by employees, and the Directive does not deal with penal liability.[39] As mentioned above, the area of non-competes is also not addressed by the Directive.

The common law world is also marked by divergence in trade secrets law. First, there is the divide between the US, both federally and at the state level, with its statutory tortious misappropriation approach and the English tradition lying solely in equity. The latter has given rise to many scholarly controversies in the modern context. As equity purports to vindicate good faith in the relationship between parties who share sensitive information, it experiences some doctrinal difficulty in responding adequately to instances of industrial espionage (where the party obtaining the information is not in a relationship of trust with the party holding it) and third-party liability (where the third party who obtains information is not in a relationship with its original purveyor). There is also a divide between the realities of commercial life, where trade secrets are traded as property and the doctrinal view, which insists on equity and denies trade secrets any proprietary status. Further, whereas the action for breach of confidence has been extended in the UK to cover breaches of privacy,[40] in Australia, the courts have refused to take that step openly.[41] The English attempt to protect the

37. Although the more detailed prescriptions are only concerned with criminal liability, civil liability being based either on the broad prohibition of unfair competition in §3 of the *Act Against Unfair Competition* (Germany) ('UWG') or two sections of the *Civil Code* (Germany) i.e., §823, 826 ('BGB'). *See* further below Chapter 7.
38. *See* Chapter II of the European Trade Secrets Directive.
39. As is also the case in some common law countries, notably the US. *See* the *Economic Espionage Act of 1996*, Pub L No 104-148, 110 Stat 3488 18 USC §1831; Law Commission (England and Wales), *Legislating the Criminal Code: Misuse of Trade Secrets: Consultation Paper* (LCCP150 25 November 1997).
40. *See Campbell v. MGN Ltd* [2004] UKHL 22; *Douglas v. Hello! Ltd (No 2)* [2006] QB 125.
41. *See Australian Broadcasting Corp v. Lenah Game Meats Pty Ltd* (2001) 208 CLR 199.

privacy interest by means of the action for breach of confidence have also resulted in an unsettled and contested area of law.[42]

Although there are instructive traces of various traditions to be found in the trade secrets laws of different jurisdictions, in the result perhaps little more can be said then that there is a 'patchwork' of approaches around the world. This is inherently interesting because doctrinal differences interconnect with fundamental policy priorities, for instance, concerning how 'watertight' the law of trade secrets should optimally be and 'bigger picture' issues such as freedom of speech, the rights of whistleblowers and society's attitude to openness (as protected, for instance, by Freedom of Information laws) versus secrecy.[43] However, it also has practical repercussions, in no large measure, because it presents a challenge to any cross-border business, both in relation to its employees and in relation to the background law that informs contractual provisions.

§1.08 THE INTRINSIC SIGNIFICANCE OF TRADE SECRETS

Owing to the ubiquity and significance of trade secrets protection, the multi-faceted and uncertain state of the law is somewhat surprising. As indicated above, it lies at the heart of two major confrontations: between the opposing forces of openness, freedom of discourse and communication, and the forces of privacy, secrecy and limited circulation of information; and between freedom of competition by inquisitiveness, appropriation and imitation, and proprietary control over knowledge. Each of these policy positions has its advantages and disadvantages, and supporters and detractors of striking a balance at varying points. The Intellectual Commons movement promotes openness and open systems of innovation and knowledge diffusion and has garnered much support partly by its opposition to overbearing proprietary systems and, above all, patent law. But firms tend to see knowledge in terms of competitive advantage and adequate control. The self-interest in secrecy thus contrasts with the public interest in securing a certain degree of openness and free circulation of information in markets. We leave largely out of consideration here the equally significant question of openness versus secrecy in government, where a trend towards greater 'Freedom of Information' rights contrasts with a movement towards greater anti-espionage and state secrets protection.[44]

Importantly, for our purposes, this debate plays out against the background of two significant policy realities: on the one hand, the democratic nature of the jurisdictions here under consideration, and on the other hand, their free market

42. *See*, for instance, Thomas Bennett, 'Confidence, Privacy, and Incoherence' (2022) 14(2) *Journal of Media Law* 245 https://doi.org/10.1080/17577632.2022.2139571. In relation to breach of confidence involving MPI in cross-border circumstances, *see* Michael Douglas, 'Characterisation of Breach of Confidence as a Privacy Tort in Private International Law' (2018) 41(2) *UNSW Law Journal* 490 https://doi.org/10.53637/eakf6390.
43. As considered, for instance, in Australian Law Reform Commission, 'Secrecy Law and Open Government in Australia (Report 112)' *Australian Government* (online) 11 March 2010, https://www.alrc.gov.au/wp-content/uploads/2019/08/ALRC112.pdf.
44. *See* further below, Chapter 5.

systems. Freedoms of information and communication have both an inherent value in a democracy and an instrumental value in a market economy, so that in such countries, they attract a significant premium. Indeed, this should be the starting principle: that communication and competition are free and are only to be limited to the extent that there is an overwhelming case for a counter-interest to prevail. In fact, we shall see that the law commonly recognizes this.

The tensions mentioned arguably experience their most acute expression in the post-employment phase, where, unsurprisingly, much trade secrets litigation transpires.[45] The right of employees to transfer to new employment with their full panoply of knowledge clashes with the ambition of former employers to control knowledge and information acquired on the job. At the heart of this ambition lies a concern that they will face very direct competition from their former employees who rely on what they have learned during their employment. From one viewpoint, such use seems unfair; from another, it is the essence of competition in a free market and also based on a fundamental right first formally recognized during the early stages of the French Revolutionary period.[46] The employee cannot compete without her inherent knowledge and know-how, without her learning that cannot be separated from her 'self'. But if commercially significant secrets cannot be secured by the firm, there is an incentive to move away from investment, which is vulnerable to this kind of dilution or spillover, and from investing in the training and education of employees.

Markets operate by virtue of labour mobility, by freedom to imitate, by competitive and astute gathering of information, by open circulation of what needs to be known to compete, and trade secrets protection militates against all this. It, therefore, sits at the very eye of the competitive storm. Those who impose it must and do tread very carefully. Important congruencies of labour law principles and policies and IP law occur here. In that context, significant debate and disagreement are not surprising.

§1.09 THE ADEQUACY AND APPROPRIATENESS OF LEGAL PROTECTION

High-profile cases of ex-employees fleeing to the opposition with valuable knowledge in their heads or USB sticks have agitated the commentators.[47] Some say that firms are too vulnerable to the poaching of employees, as well as to such industrial espionage, but others highlight the anti-competitive effect of too much trade secrets protection or overly chilling penal provisions. As indicated above, there is an emerging trend in some jurisdictions for legislators or the executive to limit employers' ability to restrict the

45. During employment, different legal remedies apply in relation to contractual obligations of confidentiality and the wider duty of fidelity of the employee.
46. The 'Décret d'Allarde' which abolished the privileges of the guilds, which was passed by the Assemblée nationale on 2 March 1791 and became law on 17 March of the same year. Note also the 'Lois Le Chapelier' of 14 and 17 June 1791, that abolished the guilds of the 'Ancien Régime'.
47. *Seven Network (Operations) Ltd v. Warburton (No 2)* (2011) 206 IR 450.

mobility of knowledge by way of non-competes.[48] But this is not the only area of controversy. For instance, in England, providing privacy protection by extending breach of confidence has caused a stir.[49] In Germany, France and the US, large figures have been bandied about that quantify the damage caused by industrial espionage by foreign companies and even governments. In civilian jurisdictions, the fluidity of the unfair competition tort, the lack of uniformity within integrated economic areas, and a perceived lack of protection for commercial secrets in industrial circles have given rise to harmonizing statutory intervention.[50] The criminalization of employee trade secrets abuse and other trade secrets abuses (in particular cross-border commercial espionage) is or has recently been under review in multiple jurisdictions.[51] Some commentators even call for the extension of criminal liability to employees who deal unconscionably with information they were entitled to access during the course of their employment, as opposed to information they are not entitled to see but set out to discover with illegitimate intent.[52] However, there is concern about the harsh deterrent effect and forensic difficulties inherent in constituting trade secrets misuse as a criminal offence – this has come to the fore in relation to some instances of long jail sentences being handed down in China.[53] Within civil law countries, much of the debate centres on the extent and precise parameters of criminal liability, in particular for employee misuse, whereas in the English legal system, criminal liability has traditionally been virtually non-existent, although, within certain bounds, there is some interest in introducing penal provisions.[54]

---

48. Resulting in part from prominent work by scholars such as Matt Marx, Deborah Strumsky & Lee Fleming, 'Mobility, Skills, and the Michigan Non-Compete Experiment' (2009) 55(6) *Management Science* 875 https://doi.org/10.1287/mnsc.1080.0985; Matt Marx & Lee Fleming, 'Non-compete Agreements: Barriers to Entry ... and Exit?' in Josh Lerner & Scott Stern (eds), *Innovation Policy and the Economy* (University of Chicago Press, 2012) 39; Matt Marx, 'The Firm Strikes Back: Non-compete Agreements and the Mobility of Technical Professionals' (2011) 76(5) *American Sociological Review* 695. *See* further below, Chapter 8.
49. Tanya Aplin, 'The Future of Breach of Confidence and the Protection of Privacy' (2007) 7(2) *Oxford University Commonwealth Law Journal* 137 https://doi.org/10.1080/14729342.2007.11421481.
50. *See* further below Chapters 6 & 7. Also *see* from the period before the EU Trade Secrets Directive, Committee on Constitutional Law, Legislation and Administration, National Assembly of France, *Report of the Proposed Law (No 3985) of Bernard Carayon to Punish the Violation of Trade Secrets* (11 January 2012); *Civil Code* (Belgium*) (Juris, 1998); Council Directive 84/450/EEC of 11 May 2005 on Unfair Commercial Practices* [2005] OJ L 149/22; and now the EU Trade Secrets Directive and its national mirror legislations.
51. *See* Suzana Nashkova, 'Addressing Criminal Liability for Misuse of Trade Secrets Under Australian Law: Is the Current Legal Framework Adequate to Protect the Interests of Owners of Trade Secrets?' (2024) 55 *International Review of Intellectual Property and Competition Law* 1281 https://doi.org/10.1007/s40319-024-01490-4. In relation to Canada *see* Matt Malone, 'Criminal Enforcement of Trade Secret Theft: Strategic Considerations for Canadian SMEs' (2020) 10(11) *Technology Innovation Management Review* 40 https://doi.org/10.22215/timreview/1402.
52. This appears to be one of the main concerns in Sweden.
53. John Garnaut & Sanghee Liu, 'Stern Sentenced to 10 Years by Chinese Court' *The Age* (online), 29 March 2010, http://www.theage.com.au/business/stern-sentenced-to-10-years-by-chinese-court-20100329-r7x0.html. Further, the US Congress quite recently introduced criminal sanctions by way of the EEA. The various states in the US also commonly provide for criminal liability. *See* further below Chapter 5.
54. Non-existent in Australia, for instance.

In relation to the post-employment phase, the current debates are more concerned with whether the default law strikes an adequate balance between the parties concerned. Does it leave firms too vulnerable, or alternatively, ex-employees exposed to unknowable liability? Is it enough to say that firms can and should rely on contract to protect their secrets? And if they do so by entering into non-competes with their employees, how actively should the courts policy such provisions, as they stymie competition, self-development and freedom of communication? Do courts at present either too readily enforce them, stymieing employee mobility, or make enforcement too difficult, hence stymieing investment in employee knowledge development and firm innovation? These questions are further considered in Chapter 8, against the background of the already referenced trend towards restricting non-competes in multiple jurisdictions. The debate about criminalization is further considered in Chapter 2.

§1.10 THE PUBLIC DOMAIN AND DEVELOPMENT

On a final introductory note, the debate in IP circles concerning the public domain is also relevant to trade secrets law. The historic expansion of IPRs has been conceptualized by some as optimizing incentives to invest in knowledge creation by others as a threat to the public domain and knowledge sharing and diffusion. In an orthodox view, IPRs incentivize the creation of *new* knowledge which enters the public domain after a *limited* monopoly term.[55] This is to everybody's benefit if monopolistic rights are properly calibrated and applied to *new* rather than existing knowledge. There is a far more acute and direct relationship between the scope of protection and the size of the public domain when it comes to trade secrets law. What is protected as a trade secret does not and possibly *will never* enter the public domain; proprietary rights are contrastingly temporary. Therefore, if either the trade secrets regime itself or contiguous IP rights are structured so as to over-incentivize reliance on secrecy protections, this is a direct and immediate detriment to the public domain with uncertain potential future benefit. Of course, trade secrets law is also a means of encouraging the sharing of information, for instance, in a contractual or employment relationship. Trade secrets protection is also relatively brittle, since independent invention or public disclosure can undo it at any time.

Arguably, for that reason, the public domain advocate should consider the scope of trade secrets protection critically important. At an abstract level, knowledge diffusion decreases as legal protection for trade secrets increases. The pool of public domain knowledge that every firm and person can draw on is diminished. This may be negative in terms of the inherent value of openness and public access to information referred to below. It is why some scholars support the 'holy-ness' of trade secrets law – that protection is relative rather than absolute, as further discussed in Chapter 2.

55. *See* William van Caenegem 'The Public Domain: *Scientia Nullius*' (2002) 24(6) *European Intellectual Property Review* 324-330; Graham Greenleaf & Catherine Bond, 'Public Rights in Copyright: What Makes Up Australia's Public Domain?' (2013) 23 *Australian Intellectual Property Journal* 111-138; Graham Greenleaf, 'National and International Dimensions of Copyright's Public Domain (An Australian Case Study)' (2009) 6(2) *SCRIPTed* 259.

But it is important to translate this highly conceptual debate to the more concrete level of economic development in developing economies. If FDI and connected local employment are to have long-term economic benefits for the recipient country, then excessive restrictions on the transfer of employee knowledge and know-how, through the means of trade secrets law and concomitant non-competes, have obvious economic implications. In terms of economic development, therefore, trade secrets law is very significant to knowledge transfers that can increase educational and technological standards. Close scrutiny of both the default law and contractual provisions is important. Local laws require appropriate counter-balancing principles and public policy measures that permit effective review of trade secrets clauses. Where trade secrets law has escaped much supra-national scrutiny, this side of the equation has failed to attract the attention it deserves from the perspective of the development agenda in IP law.[56]

§1.11 THE FOLLOWING CHAPTERS

The next chapter considers some of the doctrinal and theoretical issues in trade secrets law, with a particular focus on the question of property rights. Then, in Chapter 3, the international underpinnings of the law are addressed, with the basics of the common law (Chapter 4, the English law system and Chapter 5, the US), the civil law of France (Chapter 6) and of Germany (Chapter 7) following. In Chapter 8, some aspects of trade secrets law in the (post-) employment phase are examined, and in Chapter 9, conclusions are drawn, including some comparative comments.

56. *See also* the TRIPS development work and also the World Intellectual Property Organization (WIPO) Development Agenda.

CHAPTER 2
Property, Propriety and Policy

§2.01 INTRODUCTION: POLICY AND DOCTRINE

Owing to its unsettled doctrinal foundations, policy debates about trade secrets law tend to crystallize around the optimal choice between various existing protection regimes, being: property, tort, equity, unfair competition, unjust enrichment or an established sui generis regime. Even if it is ultimately inconclusive, the debate about property in particular is a useful foil for addressing central issues of policy and principle in trade secrets law across jurisdictions. This debate is, of course, a subset of the broader debate concerning property rights in information and intellectual 'property'. In a doctrinal sense, the debate is particularly relevant to the US and other jurisdictions, where the statutory tort of 'misappropriation' of trade secrets has some property overtones. It is, furthermore, relevant to the English common law as the equitable obligation of good faith has to be overstretched to cope with common factual circumstances, such as industrial espionage. Property, as an apparently more consonant alternative, has therefore occasionally reared its head in both judgments and academic debate. Trade secrets are also often traded as if they were proprietary assets. Nonetheless, courts have almost universally rejected the property approach, and they will continue to do so. In civilian jurisdictions as well, where the relationship between IP and a universal tort of unfair competition is critically scrutinized, the more normative question of property rights in trade secrets is decidedly relevant. It also resonates in the debate about criminal liability for trade secrets misuse, and whether 'theft' of information is analogous to theft of physical property.

Does property really matter? The Scandinavian realists would have it that whether or not something is designated as property is irrelevant or even misleading; rather, it is sorting out the underlying relationships and individual instances of proprietorship that counts.[1] The difficulty with property in the context of incorporeal goods is that while the thing that contains information is subject to possession, the information itself is not and therefore we have property without possession. In other words, the object of rights is purely a creation of the law itself. Knowledge or information does not inherently have any separate and distinct existence, and it does not diminish through 'consumption'. Not only some US commentators[2] but also European scholars[3] stress the essential importance of property rights as a policy tool in IP law, but Hill warns against the arguably untoward inflationary dynamic inherent in the *rhetoric* of property:[4]

> The judicial tendency to classify trade secrets, and ideas generally, as property has its philosophical dangers. One such danger is that judges may be invoking the notion of 'value as property.' Critics including Felix Cohen have pointed out that the theoretical underpinning of many decisions is the following analysis: X has 'created a thing of value; a thing of value is property; X, the creator of property, is entitled to protection against third parties who seek to deprive him of his property.' Justice Oliver Wendell Holmes was apparently concerned about this equation of value with property. In *International News Service v. Associated Press*, the defendant was a news service that had copied the plaintiff's news stories from public sources, including early newspaper editions and bulletin boards. The Supreme Court found that the defendant had tried to 'reap where it had not sown.' The Court further ruled that the news was 'quasi-property' and enjoined the defendant from copying further news stories from the plaintiff. In his concurrence, Justice Holmes disagreed with this property conception by the Court, stating that '[p]roperty, a creation of law, does not arise from value, although exchangeable,' and that the existence of exchangeable value is 'a matter of fact,' rather than law. In other words, if a thing has value, that is a fact, but there is no automatic requirement that the law protect that thing as property. One problem with giving property status to everything of value is that it can lead to social paralysis. As Felix Cohen first

---

1. *See* Ulf Petrusson, 'Patents as Structural Capital: Towards Legal Constructionism' in Ove Granstrand (ed.) *Economics, Law and Intellectual Property* (Kluwer, 2003); Karl Olivecrona, 'Legal Language and Reality' in Ralph Newman (ed.), *Essays in Jurisprudence in Honor of Roscoe Pound* (The Bobbs-Merrill Co., 1962); Alf Ross, *On Law and Justice* (Berkeley University Press, 1958); Claes Martinson, 'The Scandinavian Approach to Property Law, Described Through Six Common Legal Concepts' (2014) 22 *Juridica International* 16 https://doi.org/10.12697/ji.2014.22.02. Alternatively, the distinction is expressed as one between a unitary (substantive) approach and a functional approach that does not recognize the transfer of ownership as a whole at a specific moment in time. *See* Astrid Millung-Christoffersen, 'The Scandinavian "Functional" Approach to Movable Property from a Danish View: Including the Question of "Tradition"' (2019) 8(1) *European Property Law Journal* 4 https://doi.org/10.1515/eplj-2019-0003.
2. For example, F. Scott Kieff, 'Property Rights and Property Rules for Commercializing Inventions' (2001) 85 *Minnesota Law Review* 697 https://doi.org/10.2139/ssrn.229981; F. Scott Kieff, 'Removing Property from Intellectual Property and (Intended?) Pernicious Impacts on Innovation and Competition' (2011) 19 *Supreme Court Economic Review* 25 https://doi.org/10.1086/664561; F. Scott Kieff, 'Coordination, Property & Intellectual Property: An Unconventional Approach to Anticompetitive Effects & Downstream Access' (2006) 56 *Emory Law Journal* 327 https://doi.org/10.2139/ssrn.910656.
3. *See* Griffiths, J. and McDonagh, L., 'Fundamental Rights and European IP Law: The Case of Art 17(2) of the EU Charter' in: Geiger, C (ed.), *Constructing European Intellectual Property Achievements and New Perspectives* (Edward Elgar Publishing, 2013) 75-93, ISBN 1781001642.
4. *See* James Hill, 'Trade Secrets, Unjust Enrichment, and the Classification of Obligations' 4 *Virginia Journal of Law and Technology* 2, 25-27.

> observed, another problem is that the 'property from value' approach can be circular: the approach 'purports to base legal protection upon economic value, when, as a matter of actual fact, the economic value of a sales device depends upon the extent to which it will be legally protected'.

Hill correctly points out that the value, at least in an economic sense, is created by legal rights: he contends that by its nature, an idea or a piece of information has no value since its exploitation cannot be monopolized. Trade secrets are a case in point: a trade secret must be exposed to some degree at least to be commercially exploited. Without legal rights and obligations, others would do what they will with the information – so the value is arguably created by the law, although it is also true that secrets can be described without necessarily disclosing them in detail. Nonetheless, there is a risk that without legal protection, the information would be kept hidden and not disclosed and would, therefore, not be optimally utilized – those who could exploit it efficiently would not learn it or would have to duplicate the effort of the possessor of the information to generate it. They might also not be able to estimate its value accurately if it is not fully disclosed. Where a trade secret can be exploited and kept secret (a secret manufacturing process hidden in a factory), again, it is the law – of contract and of equity which allows the secrecy to be maintained, since that is what binds employees.

[A] Property in Information?

In terms of actual trade secrets law, the question of property rights is certainly relevant in a number of jurisdictions. Divergent approaches can affect outcomes. For instance, in Australia, Latham CJ in *Federal Commissioner of Taxation v. United Aircraft Corp* said:

> I am unable to regard the communication of information as constituting a transfer of property. Upon such communication the transferor still has everything that he had before, and the transferee continues to hold what he received ... knowledge is valuable, but knowledge is neither real nor personal property.[5]

Contrast these words with the US Supreme Court's statement in *Ruckelshaus v. Monsanto Co:* 'Trade secrets have many of the characteristics of more tangible forms of property. A trade secret is assignable. A trade secret can form the *res* of a trust, and it passes to a trustee in bankruptcy.'[6] Trade secrets *could*, therefore, be property for the purpose of the 'takings' clause in the US Constitution.[7] In an analogous manner, the issue has arisen in the context of Article 1 of the First Protocol of the European Convention on Human Rights ('ECHR'). Under the title 'Protection of Property', this provision says that every person 'is entitled to the peaceful enjoyment of his possessions'. In *Veolia ES*, Rix LJ, with whom the other members of the Court agreed, said that commercially valuable confidential information *could* fall within the terms of

5. (1943-1944) 68 CLR 525, 534-535.
6. 467 US 986 (1984).
7. 467 US 986 (1984), 1001-1004.

Article 1. His Honour analogized not so much with tangible property but with other forms of immaterial property to which the concept of 'possession' was said to extend.[8]

Those different approaches vary not only in tendency but also in nature. On the one hand, in the US, trade secrets law has rules analogous to physical property law so, therefore, it is also concerned with property. Whereas, on the other hand, in Australia (and the English common law tradition), trade secrets themselves as a species of information do not exhibit the characteristics of physical property (articles or things) and, therefore, are not property. The highest Courts in the US and in Australia used two very distinct approaches, admittedly at different historical junctures, to resolve the same question in opposing ways. Rix LJ's approach occupies a middle ground as it relies on analogy with something that arguably lacks the inherent characteristics of property (and possession) but is an artifice generated by statute.

In the Australian case of *Smith Kline & French v. Secretary, Department of Community Services,*[9] Gummow J[10] had to consider the same question as in *Ruckelshaus,*[11] with regard to the analogous but not identical Australian provision, section 51 (xxxi) of the Australian Constitution[12] (acquisition of property on just terms). He compared this section with the takings clause in the US constitution.[13] Although other arguments disposed of the section 51 (xxxi) question in favour of the Commonwealth, Gummow J did deal with the question of whether the concept of property in the Constitution 'extends to information which is of sufficient substance to be the subject of an equitable obligation of confidence'.[14] He concluded that, given that a court in this constitutional context should lean towards a broader concept of property and look at substance rather than form, the data supplied to the Secretary 'plainly answer the description of "property" within the meaning of s 51 (xxxi) of the Constitution (Cth)'.[15] The approach in *Veolia ES* sits comfortably with Gummow J's views in *SKF*.

The 'form' element referred to in SKF was that the remedy for breach of confidence lies only in upholding a requirement of good faith in equity. However, the 'substance' was that the information in question has to be confidential; that trade secrets may devolve by operation of law, as, for instance, upon bankruptcy and by

8. *See Veolia ES Nottinghamshire Ltd v. Nottinghamshire County Council & Ors* [2010] EWCA Civ 1214; Tanya Aplin, 'Confidential Information as Property?' (2013) 24(2) *King's Law Journal* 172 https://doi.org/10.5235/09615768.24.2.172; Tanya F. Aplin, 'Right to Property and Trade Secrets (January 1, 2014)' in Christophe Geiger (ed.), *Research Handbook on Human Rights and Intellectual Property* (Edward Elgar, 2015), Chapter 22, 421-437.
9. (1990) 22 FCR 73, 112 ('SKF').
10. Sitting as a single judge of the Federal Court of Australia.
11. *Ruckelshaus v. Monsanto Co,* 467 US 986 (1984).
12. *Commonwealth of Australia Constitution Act 1900* (Imp).
13. While paying due regard to the High Court's previous warnings about applying the reasoning from US cases to the Commonwealth constitutional guarantee, Justice Gummow thought those warnings particularly apposite in relation to *Ruckelshaus* even though it had factual parallels to *SKF,* both relating to the disclosure of confidential information to government. Because of the relevant differences, the Judge said he did not 'derive any immediate profit from it' (i.e., from *Ruckelshaus v. Monsanto Co* 467 US 986 (1984)). *See also Smith Kline & French v. Secretary, Department of Community Services* (1990) 22 FCR 73, 116 at 119.
14. *Ibid.,* 119.
15. *Ibid.,* 122.

testamentary provision; and that a secret process may be held in trust in connection with a trust in a business and may be the 'subject of an equitable charge given to a creditor'. Finally, the obligation may be extended in some circumstances to third parties.[16] His Honour pointed out that:

> the degree of protection afforded by equitable doctrines and remedies to what equity considers confidential information makes it appropriate to describe it as having a proprietary character. This is not because property is the basis upon which that protection is given, but because of the effect of that protection.[17]

By inference, at least, his Honour also held that the right or interest in confidential information is 'definable, identifiable by third parties, [has] some degree of permanence or stability, and [is] capable in its nature of assumption by third parties':[18] characteristics which Lord Wilberforce in *National Provincial Bank Ltd v. Ainsworth* is said to have identified as essential to the category of property.[19]

This is illustrative of a doctrinal or formalistic approach (as taken in *Ruckelshaus*) which ignores the inherent character of the object of the rights, that is, that information is not amenable to possession, depletion or deprivation, instead to ascertain the presence of the typical legal characteristics of property – a reasoning by doctrinal analogy. The implications of the former approach, which takes the law away from its historical focus on unfair competition and commercial morality in the US and Europe and from the focus on good faith in equity in countries such as Australia and the UK, have significant implications. Kapczynski refers to this trend as a 'retheorizing' of trade secrets law as a form of 'intellectual property following prevailing neoliberal arguments about the economics of information'.[20] Kapczynski points out that this 'property' approach empowers corporations to resist disclosing information that in the public interest should be made publicly available on proprietary and constitutional grounds.

Also significant in this context is contract law. Parties often deal with trade secrets as if they are property. The language used, at least in the common law world, is often analogous, even if its practical effects are not: terms such as 'assignment', 'sale', 'asset transfer', or 'assumption by third parties' are used. By contrast, civilian jurisdictions, such as France, take a more radical stance and do not recognize that contracts relating to trade secrets can transfer property rights. Instead, the holder can in law only agree to disclose information to, and authorize use by, a particular party, potentially excluding all others, including the grantor of the authorization. The difficulty with this approach is that although it quite logically rejects assignment of something that is not property, it does not provide a legal justification for the exclusive right to license which the possessor enjoys. In common law jurisdictions, however,

16. *Ibid.*, 121.
17. *Ibid.*
18. *Ibid.*
19. [1965] AC 1175, 1247-1248.
20. Amy Kapczynski, 'The Public History of Trade Secrets' (2022) 55 *University of California Davis* 1367.

purported transfers of property rights in trade secrets are given effect in contract.[21] Again, the focus is on a self-reinforcing doctrinal approach rather than on observation of the factual characteristics of information. Contract also enters the debate in a different manner: if a relational as opposed to a property (*erga omnes*) approach is adopted as the fundament of trade secrets protection, then analogies with contract rather than property predominate. This way of thinking lies at the breach of confidence end of the spectrum: confidential information is governed by way of rules that vindicate personal obligations of good faith relating to exchanged information by means of equity and not by some analogy to property. Graves contrasts this 'relational conception' of trade secrets law with a 'property conception'. He says: 'There are important reasons to limit the relational, contract-based model of trade secrets law', which require further scholarly exploration, but he importantly argues that a property-based approach better protects employee mobility[22] than 'a relational conceptions that places too much emphasis on one-sided loyalty obligations and too little emphasis on defining the information at issues and comparing it to information in the public domain'.[23]

In any case, although courts in various jurisdictions have occasionally been sympathetic to a proprietary approach in specific contexts, none have consistently held that trade secrets law vindicates a right to property or ownership of information. Rather, relational (good faith) or commercial conduct (propriety, honest trading) rationales tend in reality to prevail in a manner central to the resolution of disputes by legal means. Nor have legislators where they have intervened in relation to civil liability expressly provided for property rights in trade secrets. The inherent difficulties with conceiving of trade secrets law as vindicating property in information are legion: absence of exclusive possession; inexhaustibility; impression in delineation; and the absence of any coherent theory of original acquisition, as Fishman and Varadarajan point out. They call for a limiting requirement that requires proof of some meaningful economic investment before trade secrets rights vest. This would prevent the extension of the cover of trade secrets law to areas they argue it should not go.[24] Graves and Katyal echo this concern about the expansion of trade secrets law in their argument from being a tool to protect IP from misappropriation to one that serves the goal of what they call seclusion, which means hiding information that should be openly available in the public interest.[25]

Interesting to consider in this context, however, are crimes and offences relating to trade secrets. Traditionally, at least in the common law world, the general criminal

21. *See Painaway Australia Pty Ltd v. JAKL Group Pty Ltd* (2011) 91 IPR 298; *Inline Logistics Ltd v. UCI Logistics Ltd* [2002] RPC 32; [2001] EWCA Civ 1613.
22. Something we argue below is crucial when considering the scope and extent of trade secrets remedies. *See* Chapter 8.
23. Charles Tait Graves, 'Trade Secrets as Property: Theory and Consequences' (2007) 15(1) *Journal of Intellectual Property Law* 39.
24. Joseph P. Fishman & Deepa Varadarajan, 'Earning Trade Secrets' (2024) 109 *Cornell Law Review* (Forthcoming).
25. Charles Tait Graves & Sonia K Katial, 'From Trade Secrecy to Seclusion' (2021) 109 *The Georgetown Law Journal* 1337 https://doi.org/10.2139/ssrn.3760123.

law tended not to recognize property rights in information, which can thus not be the subject of theft other than by express statutory provision (my trade secret is not just another one of my possessions in this context).[26] However, with criminalization of trade secrets misuse (as, for instance, in Germany or in the US with the *Economic Espionage Act* (EEA), and as proposed in France),[27] it could be argued that the concept of property in trade secrets gains credibility and then again, if the property view gains support among legislators, criminalization inevitably follows. This argument, however, can be nuanced for several reasons. First, the use of criminal law in trade secret protection often reflects motives beyond simply intensifying the state's protective measures for trade secrets themselves. For instance, criminal law may target behaviours such as breaches of trust between employees and employers[28] or unauthorized computer system intrusions. While criminalizing these actions can indeed bolster trade secret protection, the primary purpose of such laws is generally to penalize behaviours deemed socially harmful, potentially serving interests beyond trade secrets alone. Additionally, criminal penalties frequently apply to violations occurring in an international context. In these cases, states often adopt a protectionist stance, aiming to safeguard national industry competitiveness from foreign espionage.[29] Given that economic assets belonging to the foreign perpetrators are often out of reach of national law, criminal sanctions imposed on individuals within the state's jurisdiction may serve as the only effective deterrent. Lastly, it is worth noting that criminalization in IP law remains relatively uncommon. Typically, civil remedies are sufficient not only to compensate for losses but also to restore the initial exclusive rights of the IP holder. Criminal law may seem redundant in these areas. By contrast, the more frequent recourse to criminal sanctions in cases of trade secret infringement can be seen as compensating for the absence of an *erga omnes* exclusive right. In cases of trade secret disclosure, for example, civil remedies like damages may not fully restore the holder's original control over the information; once disclosed, the information ceases to be secret. Criminal law, therefore, acts as a preventive measure, discouraging the initial violation. The use of criminal law in this context can thus be viewed both as a way of reinforcing the exclusivity enjoyed by the holder of a trade secret, lending support to the proprietary interpretation of this right, and, conversely, as a tool deployed precisely to compensate for the absence of a firmly established property right over these assets.

Whether criminalization in this sphere is a positive policy development has, however, been doubted by scholars and commentators.

26. Brian Yeh, 'Intellectual Property Rights Violations: Federal Civil Remedies and Criminal Penalties Related to Copyrights, Trademarks and Patents' (Congress Research Report RL 34109, Congress Research Services, 13 December 2012).
27. *See* further below Chapters 5, 6 and 7.
28. *See*, for instance, Art. L. 1227-1 of the french labour code.
29. *See* in the US: 18 USC. §1831.

[B] IP, Crime, and Property

Criminal liability for certain misuses of trade secrets has long been an accepted part of the law in many jurisdictions, in particular those with civil law roots. The English common law tradition has largely rejected it, but in the US, it has been on the rise. But what is the basis for criminal liability: the unauthorized acquisition of others' 'property' in information, dispossession, or some behavioural wrong?

In this regard, Moohr usefully analyses the US federal *EEA*.[30] She points out that the Federal act introduced a very broad and flexible concept of what is a trade secret. It is the *mens rea* requirement that limits criminal liability.[31] Moohr argues that Congress took a property view of trade secrets, and although it is conduct that is criminalized, 'condemning conduct that involves some interest inevitably sweeps that interest into a protected category'.[32] Congress views 'trade secrets [...] much like any other property',[33] and thus, since the criminal provisions are constructed around absence of authorization to do what constitutes the object of the charge, owners have effectively been given complete control over trade secret information. Moohr points out that this approaches 'exclusive use', which she by implication considers characteristic of property rights – rights against 'erga omnes'. Moohr points out that Congress was influenced by evidence of the value of trade secrets, but as she also says, this is partly a circular argument, as it is only the recognition of legal rights that gives a trade secret its value. Also she contends much of the evidence was self-serving and called on unreliable estimates of value.

As to the analogy with *intellectual* property, Moohr is not in agreement with Lemley on this point:[34] IP is instrumental in nature, but trade secrets law does not achieve one of the fundamental instrumental goals of IP – it does not result in the wider availability of information and knowledge, quite the contrary. What is more, the exclusion of the public is not necessarily a temporary characteristic of IP law. Finally, she points out that much secret information would be produced even if the legal protection (default) were not available, so the rights do not perform the incentive function typical of IP.[35] However, this argument ignores the point we make higher up that trade secrets law can in fact encourage the sharing of information, for instance, in a contractual context, and that partial revelations are possible without threatening the requirement that information not be in the public domain.

The doctrinal debate about property and the question of criminal liability naturally fit within the broader debate about the policy basis for trade secrets law. A

30. *See* Geraldine Szott Moohr, 'The Problematic Role of Criminal Law in Regulating the Use of Information: The Case of the Economic Espionage Act' (2002) 80 *North Carolina Law Review* 853.
31. Requiring knowing interference or use; knowledge that the information was a trade secret; intent to convert the secret to the defendant's own economic benefit or that of another; and an intention to or knowledge that the owner would be injured by the conduct concerned. *See* Chapter 5.
32. Szott Moohr, above n 30, 898.
33. *Ibid.*
34. We comment on Lemley's article in this regard further below in this Chapter.
35. Above n 22, 899-903.

useful starting point here is Friedman, Landes and Posner's law and economics analysis of trade secrets law. Much of their account contrasts trade secrets law with a particular form of IP law: patents granted for inventions.

§2.02 SOME ECONOMICS OF TRADE SECRETS

Friedman, Landes and Posner ('Posner et al.') addressed the economics of trade secrets law in 1991, at which time they said there was little work in this area, with the exception of Kitch.[36] They focused on technical secrets without addressing commercial secrets and were therefore free to conceptualize trade secrets law as a supplement to the patent system.[37] They investigated the contrasting feature that permits reverse engineering and independent discovery in trade secrets but not in patent law.[38] In other words, as they put it, 'Why is trade secret protection limited?'[39] As Moohr puts it, it is lawful to extinguish a trade secret holder's rights by reverse engineering and independent discovery. Relevantly, she adds that holders of trade secrets also do not have an exclusive right because 'the holder's right to sue is triggered only when the secret is wrongfully used or taken. Thus, the interest in a trade secret is not protected against the world, but only against malefactors'.[40] This asserts the more traditional view of trade secrets, increasingly under pressure from the more property-centred approach considered above.

Posner et al.'s analysis is confined to the protection of *technical* secrets under US law, so it cannot substantiate the law's protection of commercial secrets. But they are also ambiguous as to whether there in fact exists a separate law of trade secrets, saying that there is 'in a sense no law of trade secrets',[41] because there is always some other wrong that can be identified as the real basis for liability. However, they modulate this proposition by pointing out that the granting of a remedy without some other common law wrong being established indicated 'the emergence of one [that is, a specific law of trade secrets]'.[42] Also, they say that once liability is established based on an 'independent common law wrong', courts take into account the value of trade secrets when

36. David D. Friedman, William M. Landes & Richard A. Posner, 'Some Economics of Trade Secret Law' (1991) 5(1) *Journal of Economic Perspectives* 61 https://doi.org/10.1257/jep.5.1.61; Edmund W. Kitch, 'The Law and Economics of Rights in Valuable Information' (1980) 9(4) *Journal of Legal Studies* 683 https://doi.org/10.1086/467661.
37. Friedman, Landes & Posner, above n 36, 64.
38. Note that reverse engineering is not entirely 'free' in every jurisdiction here considered. *See* further below Chapter 8 concerning German law.
39. There is some analogy here with the legal question why trade secrets are not property. The authors point out that a trade secret is 'not property in the usual sense ... because it is not something that the possessor has the exclusive right to use or enjoy'. For them, 'property in the usual sense' includes personal property and 'such areas of intellectual property law as copyrights'. Copyright is a somewhat surprising inclusion, since there are parallels between copyright and trade secrets law, both permitting independent creation. However, neither bestow a true monopoly right, in contrast with patents law. Above n 29, 61-62.
40. Above n 22, 867-868.
41. They echo Professor Bone, whose main argument is that there is no independent or separate wrong of trade secret misappropriation. Above n 29, 62.
42. Above n 29, 62.

determining the remedy.[43] Their rejection is thus tenuous and accords less with the *present-day* situation in the US, where the adoption of statutory trade secrets protection by the states (reflecting the *Uniform Trade Secrets Act* (UTSA)) has become widespread.

But Posner et al. do focus on the two fundamentally different legal approaches to trade secrets referenced above.[44] One focuses on the characteristics of the information itself and 'misappropriation', and the other on the alleged wrongdoer's improper method of obtaining or using the information. The first suggests a *property* approach, examining the characteristics of the information and then the relationship with the possessor of that information. The other invites a *liability* approach, which focuses on the wrongfulness or propriety of the method or practice of obtaining or using the information. This second approach places more emphasis on monitoring competitive practices and information-gathering methods, whereas the first approach associates trade secrets law more with IP, with its typical parcelling and incentive functions. The first approach is the more traditional one in the US, and civil law jurisdictions historically adopted it as well: the wrong lies in unfair, meaning commercially dishonest, competition using information within the rightful control of another party. English equity also primarily adopts the second approach, which entails measuring personal behaviour against a yardstick of honest and trustworthy conduct that is expected within a relationship.

This leads Landes and Posner to ask the question, 'Why does the law deny property-type rights to possessors of trade secrets?'[45] In response, they focus mostly on the beneficial impact of the less-than-absolute protection of trade secrets alluded to above. They emphasize the benefits of reciprocity, of being able to learn something about competitors' secrets, saying that any party that retains information desires two things: (1) to keep that information exclusively to them; and (2) to access the information that others control. The law then attempts to strike a balance between the two desires by giving some legal protection which will reduce the need to invest in the most expensive and absolute forms of physical security or protection of secrets. If the legal system goes too far in granting protection, 'the benefits of shared information are likely to exceed the net benefits of legal protection'.[46] Thus, allowing *some* access to secrets through reverse engineering enables competitors to improve their own products, which is a social benefit and also limits legal costs.[47] Additionally, trade secrets might also simply cease to exist over time, in particular when a secret ceases to be used: Hrdy and Lemley argue that trade secrets law, at least in the US, already incorporates

43. *Ibid.*
44. *See* above §2.01[A] Property in Information?.
45. Above n 29, 66.
46. *Ibid.*, 67.
47. *Ibid.* There are some further aspects to the authors' analysis, in particular concerning the economic characteristics of an approach that focuses on the method of obtaining the information from another rather than focusing on the economic character of the information itself. Here, the analysis is subtle, and I will not attempt to address it.

abandonment and that this principle properly applied has beneficial economic implications.[48]

One might add that legal protection for secrets actually encourages disclosure and information sharing between those who can use it most efficiently, in particular in collaborative environments such as within firms, organizations, prospective commercial collaborations, etc. At an aggregate level, it applies to a networked innovation economy with a mobile workforce as a whole.[49] This is vindicated in part by recent governmental initiatives to limit the use of non-competes in the US, UK and Australia.[50] A strong disincentive to disclose information to those whom it would be beneficial to share it with would be very detrimental to the cooperative ventures, which lie at the heart of economic activity and exchange. This point is reflected in the reasoning of the US Supreme Court in *Kewanee Oil* 'Trade secret law promotes the sharing of knowledge ...; it permits the individual inventor to reap the rewards of is labor by contracting with a company large enough to develop and exploit it.'[51]

Expanding the analytical framework of the authors to include commercial secrets is of further assistance here. It makes logical sense to include remedies for wrongs concerning such information in the realm of competitive - and more broadly - behavioural liability. Additionally, for technical information, the contrast with patents makes it sensible to avoid the property approach. Little would be gained from maintaining two property-based systems relating to inventions, with one (trade secrets) overbearing the other (patents). Thus, a relational or behavioural approach makes sense when both commercial and technical secrets are considered. Alternatively, property-style ('over') protection would engender very great policing and legal costs. If no marketed product could be reverse-engineered, then firms would invest much more than is socially valuable in finding out whether competing products were produced by reverse engineering. As Posner et al. note this would give rise to very high administrative and legal costs, which would be wholly counterproductive and greatly disrupt competitive processes. We have patents to do this anyway. Reverse engineering was not allowed to the same extent across all jurisdictions considered here. For instance, in Germany, before the implementation of the EU Trade Secrets Directive, it could amount to unfair competition if considerable effort and resources were invested in performing it. However, the new European regime requires reverse engineering to be permitted in all Member States.[52]

48. Camilla A. Hrdy & Mark A. Lemley, 'Abandoning Trade Secrets' (2021) 73 *Stanford Law Review* 1 https://doi.org/10.2139/ssrn.3534322.
49. *See* the sources considered in Chapter 8 and Laura Pedraza-Farina, 'Spill Your (Trade) Secrets: Knowledge Networks as Innovation Drivers' (2017) 92(4) *Notre Dame Law Review* 1561 https://doi.org/10.2139/ssrn.2944701.
50. *See* more below, Chapters 3, 4 and 5.
51. *Kewanee Oil Co v. Bicron Corp* 416 US 470 (1974), 493.
52. In fact, the EU Trade Secrets Directive Art. 3(1)(a) allows the acquisition of trade secrets through independent discovery and creation. Furthermore, Art. 3(1)(b) provides that reverse engineering is a lawful means of accessing a trade secret when it is obtained by 'observation, study, disassembly or testing of a product or object that has been made available to the public or that is lawfully in the possession of the acquirer of the information who is free from any legally valid duty to limit the acquisition of the trade secret'.

Another further point needs to be made drawing on the emphasis of the authors on 'the cooperative nature of information production' and 'reciprocity'.[53] The real underlying point is that there is some benefit in competitors being able to *know something* but not everything about its competitor.[54] In other words, it is useful that competitors should flag something to each other about what sort of inventive capacity and direction they have because this will reduce wasteful duplication of research investment and duplicative choices of research direction. In this sense, there is an analogy with rent-dissipation theory in patent law.[55] It will also provide some information that might help identify targets for cooperation or commercial exchange. There is an important element of this in the context of employee knowledge: too much protection of secret information would disenable prospective employees from finding out more about the internal resources of a firm and thus optimise their decision about where to work.

In summary, property rights are not really appropriate for trade secrets, in the authors' view, because it makes sense to have weak rights with many 'holes' and limitations. Trade secrets are like Swiss cheese, its attendant rights too porous to justify the 'property'-label. In other words, trade secrets law does not recognize the level of exclusivity traditionally associated with property. However, Posner et al.'s analysis needs to take better account of commercial as well as technical secrets and requires more emphasis on the encouragement of disclosure that trade secrets law enables, which generates collaboration in trust. Further, too high a level of protection is even more unworkable than the authors say, as well as making the internal workings of firms too invisible to competitors and potential employees alike.

[A] Lemley: Trade Secrets as IP in the US Context

However, all these arguments in favour of a porous system of rights do not deter Lemley from advocating trade secrets as a species of intellectual *property*.[56] He, like Posner et al., contrasts trade secret law with patent law. He agrees that trade secrets law 'actually encourages disclosure, not secrecy'.[57] He agrees with Posner et al. that without it, companies would invest too much in keeping secrets.[58] He sees as the main benefit of trade secrets law the fact that it imposes limits on the amount of investment required in secrecy measures, which would otherwise be wasteful; legal investments (mostly in litigation) are by contrast only required at a time when there is an actual

53. Above n 29, 66.
54. Comp. Luc Desaunettes-Barbaro, *Trade Secrets Legal Protection: From a Comparative Analysis of US and EU Law to a New Model of Understanding* (Springer, 1st ed., 2023) 291-311.
55. *See* Robert Merges, 'Rent Control in the Patent District: Observations on the Grady-Alexander Thesis' (1992) 78(1) *Virginia Law Review* 359 https://doi.org/10.2307/1073312.
56. *See* Mark A. Lemley, 'The Surprising Virtues of Treating Trade Secrets as IP Rights' (2008) 61 *Stanford Law Review* 311 https://doi.org/10.31235/osf.io/srz5t. Lemley, similar to Posner et al., seems largely ignorant of trade secrets protection in civil law jurisdictions, basing himself on the example of Japan. He does not address the unfair competition approach in Germany and France. *See* above n 29, 67.
57. Above n 42, 313.
58. *Ibid.*

misappropriation. Physical restrictions also interfere with useful flows of information that enable improvements and commercialization. Trade secrets law also serves as a solution to 'Arrow's Information Paradox'.[59] Disclosure for evaluation purposes is made possible by trade secrets law. Importantly, Lemley says:

> The fact that trade secret law reduces rather than increases an innovative firm's investment in secrecy answers many of the objections people have offered to trade secret law, in particular Bone's claim that legally-induced secrecy will interfere with rather than promote innovation.[60]

He favours a property view largely owing to the state of US trade secrets law, which focuses most intensely on the conduct alleged to amount to misappropriation.[61] Seeing trade secrets as part of IP 'limits business tort claims to circumstances in which there is really a trade secret to be protected, and therefore compensates for a lack of clear standards in what constitutes misappropriation'.[62] Phrased differently: to focus on the information standard - whether certain information is in the public domain or not - would give more clarity than the present focus on *behavioural* standards. According to Lemley, this would actually *limit* restrictions on information flows and vigorous information gathering in a competitive market economy. The present misappropriation-behaviour (propriety rather than property) focused approach means that 'Close cases abound in this area, not simply because of the creativity of competitors in rooting out information about their rivals' businesses and products but because

59. *Ibid.*, 336.
60. Referring to Robert Bone, 'A New Look at Trade Secret Law: Doctrine in Search of Justification' (1998) 86 *California Law Review* 241 https://doi.org/10.2307/3481134. To put it in Moohr's words 'The law tries to balance the need to protect business assets from certain interferences with the need to promote competition between businesses. The freedom to compete for business is a fundamental premise of the free enterprise system; competition creates incentives to offer quality products at reasonable prices and fosters the general welfare by promoting efficient allocation of resources. Notwithstanding the benefits of competition to the public, all businesses do not benefit from competition; competitors necessarily harm one another. The law of unfair competition thus imposes liability for competitive harms only when the particular method of competition is determined to be unfair. The concept of unfair competition echoes a theme that permeates misappropriation cases, the unfairness that results when someone who has not expended time or money profits from another person's efforts' above n 30, 891. There is an interesting parallel here with the French approach, and it also triggers, in my view, thinking about what is meant by unfair competition. Unfairness such as impropriety in the method used, or the simply unfairness of taking advantage of another's work without paying anything, even if indirectly. The latter seems to be the focus of French law rather than the former.
61. Nonetheless, he also acknowledges that in the present state of doctrinal confusion of trade secrets law in the United Sates, the property rationale has gained some ground. He quotes the Supreme Court in *Ruckelshaus* '[t]rade secrets have many of the characteristics of more tangible forms of property. A trade secret is assignably. A trade secret can form the rest of a trust, and it passes to a trustee in bankruptcy'. *Ruckelshaus v. Monsanto Co*, 467 US 986 (1984) 1001-1004. He goes on to say that 'many have argued that the *Uniform Trade Secrets Act* ushered in a property view of trade secrets as well'. Above n 42, 325; he cites one source for this being Lyyn C. Tyler, 'Trade Secrets in Indiana: Property vs Relationship' (1998) 31 *Indiana Law Review* 339 https://doi.org/10.18060/3291, it is probably correct that property has become more prominent since Posner et al. wrote this piece.
62. Above n 42, 314.

the concept of misappropriation is itself ill-defined.[63] Lemley's views are relevant to the pre-EU Trade Secrets Directive civilian approach, as the latter focused significantly on measuring alleged misuse in terms of fairness, that is, against the standard of the 'honest trader'. Traditionally, one reason the unfair competition tort has been rejected in the common law is precisely because of the supposed vagueness and idiosyncrasy of these 'fairness' standards of behaviour. Nonetheless, the English equity-based approach also attaches remedies to an evaluation of behavioural propriety. But to some degree, Lemley's view is inspired by the particular conditions prevalent in the US rather than a more profound theoretical insight.

Lemley's further reason for advocating trade secrets as IP, which encourages us to see the centrality of the secrecy requirement, is that the latter 'serves to channel inventors into the appropriate form of IP protection'.[64] According to Lemley, trade secret protection dissuades firms from over-investing in secrecy for inventions that cannot be reverse-engineered. However, trade secrets law denies protection where marketing a new product immediately reveals its secrets, that is, in relation to 'inventions that companies would not keep secret in the absence of patent protection'.[65] In terms of intermediate cases where reverse engineering is possible but difficult, the weakness of trade secrets law by virtue of the 'defences' of reverse engineering and independent invention means that it 'does not entice inventors to choose secrecy over patent protection'.[66] Therefore:

> [t]aken together, the secrecy requirement and the relative weakness of the trade secret law help ensure that the law protects those who would otherwise rely on secrecy without law, and encourages disclosure in those cases, while not displacing patent law as the means of protection for self-disclosing inventions. Put another way, the secrecy requirement channels particular inventors to the form of IP protection that best achieves the goals of society.[67]

Lemley argues that a property approach is good for the law since it places the secrecy requirement at the centre, avoids reliance on vague alternative torts such as unjust enrichment and unfair competition, and has various other positive effects. He addresses the concern that propertization will impact negatively on the 'freedom of others to use information to compete' and will also negatively affect 'employee mobility and robust competition, and perhaps even ... free speech'.[68] He emphasizes that it will have the opposite effect if the focus is on the core requirements and limits of trade secrets law rather than on 'standardless theories of unfair competition and unjust enrichment that seem the most obvious alternatives'.[69] Nonetheless, he seems to presume that a risk of an IP approach is criminalization, which others worry will

63. *Ibid.*, 317.
64. *Ibid.*, 340.
65. *Ibid.*
66. Above n 42, 340-341.
67. *Ibid.*, 341.
68. *Ibid.*, 351-352.
69. *Ibid.*, 352.

have a chilling effect.[70] More recently, the impact of the Defend Trade Secrets Act (DTSA) on the proper conceptualization of trade secrets law is also to be considered: Goldman argues that despite its extended reach, the Act is not an 'intellectual property' law.[71]

Lemley also refers to trade secrets as property-like because a trade secret owner 'is entitled to control certain information even once it has left the owner's possession'.[72] However, this is a somewhat questionable point: is possession the appropriate term to use where the owner *still* possesses the information and another obtains it even without permission? There is no deprivation of the owner in any factual sense, although he might lose exclusive legal rights. Is disclosure which destroys secrecy a form of dispossession and one where an owner is still 'entitled to control it?' And is it not the case that the owner's control once information leaves his possession is very tenuous? Its return cannot be forced, and if it is disclosed publicly, the original owner cannot 'get it back'.

Although Lemley does mention business information, his main focus, like Posner et al., is on the contrast between patents and trade secrets. From this perspective, he sees trade secrets law 'as providing an additional incentive to innovate beyond those provided in patent law'.[73] His theory recognizes trade secrets as a species of the minor regime of incentives to invent, compared to the major regime of patent law. This incentive function tends to classify trade secrets law as part of IP.

However, this tends to overestimate just how inventive something must be to qualify for patent protection. If trade secrets law is a minor incentive system for inventions, one would expect legal protection to be proffered where secrecy is most difficult to maintain and makes efficient use of information difficult, but in fact, it is where information is able to be kept secret that the law intervenes to support it. That is why reverse engineering is free. In Lemley's view, it should surely not be, as revealing your secrets through selling your product would seem to be the greatest disincentive for investing in the innovative development of that product.

In conclusion, Lemley's pro-property view is largely inspired by a scepticism that is reminiscent of common law mistrust of unfair competition torts: scepticism about the potential for consistent application of a more 'behavioural' approach to trade secrets law. He presumes it would result in a clearer delineation of what is protected and what is not, the focus being on meeting criteria properly identifying trade secrets. This is interesting from a civil law perspective, as in those countries, although no longer in the EU Member States, the focus is on the unfairness of the behaviour of the user of the information. But nonetheless, in all systems, this focus is balanced by the clear requirement of particularization of the secret information and of establishing whether it is in the public domain or not. Lemley's solution to the particular problems with the

70. In a footnote at this point, he refers to the article of Geraldine Szott Moohr that I commented upon above, relating to criminalization.
71. *See* Eric Goldman, 'The Defend Trade Secrets Act Isn't an "Intellectual Property" Law' (2017) 33(4) *Santa Clara High Technology Law Journal* 541.
72. Above n 42, 326.
73. *Ibid.*

application of the law in the US, which is to adopt a property approach, seems rather radical in the circumstances, although it draws useful attention to the centrality of particularization and rigorous standards concerning whether information is secret or not. Nonetheless, it sits uneasily with his support for reverse engineering and independent invention, which can at once destroy the legal status of any trade secret. A property approach also sits uncomfortably with Lemley's advocacy for the adoption of an abandonment doctrine in the law of trade secrets.[74] Despite his alleged analogy with trademark law, perhaps it can be argued that true property is not supposed to vanish when it is not used.

[B] The Property Rationale in English Law

Lemley's point about addressing uncertainty in trade secrets law by shifting attention from behaviour to delineation of the object of rights is significant. Certainly, in the English tradition, the courts have become more insistent on proper particularization of trade secrets and a similar trend seems to appear in the emerging jurisprudence in Europe following the adoption of the Trade Secrets Directive.[75] They reject ambit claims and abstract descriptors and require actual identification.[76] If proper particularization is required, unacceptable uncertainty might become essential flexibility: the law has broad standards, as it must be applied in very varied factual circumstances. Arguably, therefore, as suggested above, the analogy to property misses the point, as the action serves the purpose of granting a right of action even where the information concerned has not been as carefully documented and catalogued *a priori* as in patent law, for instance. But by requiring the litigant to clearly identify it at trial, prove that it is not in the public domain and establish that it was treated as a trade secret, the law arguably strikes a balance between certainty of object and flexibility of application.

US, English, Australian and other kindred courts have traditionally largely rejected the property rationale, despite some of the above-mentioned findings in relation to 'takings' or the right to compensation for compulsory acquisition of property[77] and other inconsistent decisions referred to below. The action for breach of confidence in England does not vindicate property in information but the obligation of good faith and conscience of the recipient. Megarry J in the leading authority *Coco v. Clark* [1969] 86 RPC 41 included the relational element. Nonetheless the relational foundations of the action, always shaky, have been further undermined by recent developments in England.[78] In industrial espionage cases,[79] the courts have accepted that a remedy can be granted even though the information was not 'imparted' in a

74. Above n 48.
75. *See* Chapter 6 'The European Trade Secrets Directive'.
76. *See* Robert Dean, *The Law of Trade Secrets and Personal Secrets* (Lawbook Co., 2nd ed, 2002). The information's confidentiality during proceedings can be guaranteed by appropriate orders of the court.
77. Above n 11.
78. *See* the *Campbell* and *Douglas* cases, as further commented upon below; but Australian cases have not adopted the English approach: *Douglas* was mentioned in *Lenah Game Meats* but not applied or found to be useful to the plaintiff; *Campbell* has been mentioned in several cases

manner that enlivens the recipient's conscience. Instead, they have held that the recipient's *knowledge* of the confidential or secret nature of the information alone can be sufficient.[80] In other words, the action has been extended and, in the process, has tended to divorce the award of a remedy from vindication of an underlying relationship of trust towards treating confidential information as property, a right *erga omnes*.

The Court of Appeal in *Douglas v. Hello!* expounded the new rationale as follows:

> Where an individual ('the owner') has at his disposal information which he has created or which is private or personal and to which he can properly deny access to third parties, and he reasonably intends to profit commercially by using or publishing that information, a third party who is, or ought to be aware of these matters and who has knowingly obtained the information without authority, will be in breach of duty if he uses or publishes the information to the detriment of the owner.[81]

As indicated above, it is the lack of consent or authority from the possessor which *ipso facto* constitutes the wrong – just as the lack of consent to use or obtain physical property constitutes a wrong in terms of personal property.[82]

But the *Douglas* court also insisted that even though they were often dealt with as if it were the case, there was in fact no property right in trade secrets.[83] The court fixed its denial on the requirement that the defendant must be aware that information was 'private or confidential. In fact, the right depends upon the effect on the third party's conscience'.[84] That requirement does not exist with personal or IP, since such rights can be 'exercised against a third party regardless of' that party's knowledge of its private or confidential character.[85]

Hull and Abbott point out that although the Court of Appeal expressly rejects a property approach to trade secrets, there are nonetheless a number of authoritative

(*Giller v. Procopets* [2008] VSCA 266, *John Fairfax v. Hitchcock* [2007] NSWCA 364 and *Dye v. Cth Securities Ltd* [2012] FCA 242) but also not applied or found to be of use to the parties.

79. As has been consistently done since *Franklin v. Giddins* [1978] Qd R 72 in Australia and *Attorney-General v. Guardian Newspapers Ltd (No 2)* [1990] 1 AC 109.
80. So where the traditional approach is one that insists on a relationship but accepts that the relationship can be founded in the circumstances of the exchange of information itself, and that the wrong lies in not complying with the obligations which flow from the context of the exchange, i.e., usually going beyond what is authorized, the more modern or alternatively the wider approach holds that notice of the fact that a person in possession of secret information intends to control it is sufficient to impose an obligation on the recipient not to obtain or use it outside the scope of authorization the possessor wants to give.
81. [2005] EWCA Civ 595, [118]. This statement can arguably not be taken as universally true since it would on one view outlaw reverse engineering.
82. Nonetheless, there is with trade secrets no *right* but only a *right in personam*. Further, it is England as in Australia the case that information cannot be the subject of a theft, as the 'owner' is not dispossessed of it if another acquires it without his approval.
83. The important consequence was that *Douglas*, which had secured substantial damages below, was now deprived of them, since there had been no breach of contract, and it had not been deprived of any property rights. *See* John Hull & Sarah Abbott, 'Property Rights in Secrets: *Douglas v. Hello!* in The Court of Appeal' (2005)27(10) *European Intellectual Property Review* 379, 383; Smriti Tripathi, 'Treating Trade Secrets as Property: A Jurisprudential Inquiry In Search of Coherency' (2016) 11(11) *Journal of Intellectual Property Law & Practice* 841.
84. *See* above n 63 at [126].
85. *Ibid.*

judgments that favour that approach. They list these cases,[86] however, some of them treat trade secrets as property not to construct trade secrets law as such but for external purposes, for example, taxation; as an asset and thus property of a trust; or as an asset of a partnership.[87] Further, the authors also point to the high Australian authority of Latham CJ's judgment in *Federal Commissioner of Taxation v. United Aircraft Corp,*[88] as referred to above, and the high Canadian authority of *R v. Stewart*[89] both constitute significant and unequivocal rejections of property rights in trade secrets.[90]

It is nonetheless true, perhaps surprisingly so, that the traditional English approach had more property-like overtones than the US law. It vindicates control by the 'owner' of the information to a greater extent because the wrong consists of the use of information contrary to the purpose of the communication;[91] in other words, contrary to the *authorization* of the confidor. Although this is a more property-like approach, it only goes so far, as English law of course also allows reverse engineering and independent discovery.[92]

[C] Risch: The Centrality of Cost Reduction

Risch undertakes a more comprehensive review of trade secrets theory than Posner and Lemley, maintaining that the 'current law of trade secrets grew out of a need to hold third parties liable for misuse of information despite a lack of privity with the owner'.[93] He points out that the law in the US has shifted from property to unfair competition and substantially back to property, with tortious elements in the UTSA.

Like Lemley, Risch attempts to give some doctrinal consistency and purpose to trade secrets law, recognizing that it has an existence separate from other causes of action but no clear normative basis. He advances various economic justifications without considering them mutually exclusive: incentive to spend less on secrecy protections, Lockean labour value theory, and means 'for the public to enforce populist norms about "commercial ethics"'.[94] He points out that 'it is up to the jury to determine improper means',[95] which directly introduces a community standard of commercial

86. *See* above n 65 at 382-383.
87. Which reminds us of the particular purpose for which Trade secrets were treated as property in *Ruckelshaus, see* above n 61.
88. At (1943-44) 68 CLR 525. *See* above n 65.
89. [1988] 50 DLR (4h) 1.
90. As the authors also point out, in their view the rejection of the property approach is mitigated by the rejection of 'the limiting constraint of an initial relationship of confidence ...: "Now the law imposes a 'duty of confidence' whenever a person receives information he knows or ought to know is fairly and reasonably to be regarded as confidential"' (at 383, quoting *Campbell v. MGN Ltd* [2004] UKHL 22 [14] (Lord Nicholls)).
91. Although the confidor's purpose is not universally determinative. *See, e.g., Smith Kline & French v. Secretary, Department of Community Services* (1990) 22 FCR 73.
92. *See Mars UK Ltd v. Teknowledge Ltd* [1999] All ER (D) 600.
93. Michael Risch, 'Why Do We Have Trade Secrets' (2007) 11(1) *Marquette Intellectual Property Law Review,* 4.
94. *Ibid.* However, it is not clear whether the latter is an economic justification.
95. *Ibid.*, 6.

morality and fair or reasonable conduct.[96] This is an interesting point of comparison with civilian jurisdictions, where juries are unknown in civil cases (as in England and Australia these days), but sometimes commercial or labour courts or tribunals sit with a number of lay members.[97]

In Risch's view, trade secrets policy contrasts with other areas of IP for a number of reasons: it *discourages* - allegedly - information sharing, and it provides 'little or no marginal incentive to innovate because the owner obtains protection of the information by keeping it secret even in the absence of the law'.[98] Further, unlike other IP, trade secrets need not have any *inherent* qualities at all. He analyses trade secrets law by reference to three property theories: exclusivity, integrated theory, and bundle theory. The exclusivity theory does not properly apply as trade secrets are not exclusive: reverse engineering is allowed, and rights do not extend to independent inventors. Integrated theory draws inferences from 'how the asset is acquired, used and disposed'[99] and seems mostly aimed at refuting that exclusivity is a basic requirement of property.

Risch refers to the 'bundle of rights' property theory but rightly points out that it really makes the concept of property redundant.[100] If property is no more than a bundle of rights, does it matter if trade secrets are property or not? According to Risch, it may matter because of potential collateral effects, i.e., 'a statutory or constitutional right is triggered by "property"', something we have referred to above.[101] But he rightly says that the fact that trade secrets are treated as property in some collateral areas does not shed much light on 'why we have trade secrets'.[102] In any case, if exclusivity is the critical characteristic of 'property',[103] then a 'bundle of rights' approach simply misses the point. Further, even the core forms of property do not have an unlimited right of exclusion but are subject to many limitations and restrictions, so this aspect of trade secrets law cannot logically be conclusive either way.[104]

Leaving characterization as property aside, Risch usefully lists the bundle of rights that makes up trade secrets law,[105] including the right to 'transfer, devise or

96. Rather than this being applied by judges who are not usually representative members of a commercial community, or differently put, are only one possibly idiosyncratic member. The standard of fairness and equity in English law and of honest commercial practice in civilian jurisdictions is applied by judges.
97. As is for instance the case in Norway and in Germany.
98. Above n 75, 6.
99. *Ibid.*, 9.
100. *Ibid.*
101. *Ibid.*; as in *Ruckelshaus, see* above n 61. Further, he uses the concept of 'substantive property' in the sense that whether trade secrets 'are normatively justified as "substantive property" will depend on whether the bundle of rights itself is normatively justified'. Above n 76, 10.
102. Above n 75, 11.
103. The fact that trade secrets law does not provide for exclusivity is thus problematical. And in any case, in fact, the law has fluctuated between a property and non-property substantive analysis: thus Risch points out that the California Supreme Court refused to answer the question whether trade secrets under the UTSA were property 'and argued that substantive trade secret rights do not fall exclusively under either the property view or the liability view' (*see* above n 75 at 10); referring to *Cadence Design Sys, Inc v. Avant! Corp.*, 57 P.3d 647, 649-50 (Cal 2002).
104. Above n 75, 12.
105. *Ibid.*

otherwise make exclusive grants of certain information'. As long as we adhere to this list of rights and duties, there is only a limited risk of over-protection, whether we use the rhetoric of property or not.

Risch goes on to argue that the Lockean labour theory view is not particularly applicable to trade secrets. It is inconsistent with the porous nature of trade secrets protection which does not allow for remedies once information has become public. More generally it is lacking in underlying justification: why should '*the state of nature result in a world where people own what they create*?'[106] Hobbes' conclusions were the opposite: that everybody should be free to take what they want or defend what they have until a contrary rule is agreed upon. Risch accurately points out that if transaction costs are low, it does not matter to whom rights are initially allocated.[107] In terms of contractarian theory, Risch points out that the veil of ignorance (Rawls)[108] does not establish what the founders would decide about trade secrets law or whether it would include such things as allowing reverse engineering.

Nonetheless, even if the 'current set of rules cannot be predicted', he points out that it is still useful to consider them from a normative perspective:

> For example, if one assumes that people value that which they create more than others do, but at the same time that people want to build on the work of others, it is well within the bounds of reason that some form of limited protection for trade secrets would be the outcome of a negotiation under the veil of ignorance.[109]

Risch also analyses what he refers to as 'populist' justifications of trade secrets law, i.e., that it is enough that the majority want it. This justification may derive some force from the apparent tendency of legislatures to adopt trade secrets legislation, as is, for instance, the case in most states of the US and federally, and was also proposed in France before the EU Trade Secrets Directive and obviously brought about in many jurisdictions by that same Directive. But the difficulties with this approach are too obvious to require much further comment. It is perhaps a realist explanation, but it does not explain the emergence of trade secrets law in the courts rather than by parliamentary fiat (i.e., rather than representing a putative majority will). In many and diverse jurisdictions, trade secrets law is more a creature of the courts than of statute, at least in its specific detail, for example, in France, England, Australia, the US, Canada and New Zealand. It is in itself an interesting point that trade secrets protection developed independently but with different doctrinal foundations and policy justifications in many jurisdictions around the world.

Calculating the marginal costs of trade secrets law lies at the heart of Risch's own analysis. He sees it as a subsidiary regime to contract or torts theory.[110] In terms of theoretical utility, his cost-benefit analysis applies to US trade secrets law and is therefore not necessarily of universal application because some requirements are specific to the US. For instance, information that has economic value derived from its

106. Above n 75, 14.
107. *Ibid.*, 15.
108. John Rawls, *A Theory of Justice* (Oxford University Press, revised ed., 1999).
109. Above n 75, 6.
110. And remedies not offered by the common law. Above n 75, 17.

secrecy is essential in US law but not in English common law, nor, for instance, in German law. But the *relative* nature of trade secret requirements is both an essential and universal attribute: the law requires no more than *reasonable efforts* to maintain secrets: 'The fact that trade secrets may be protected without requiring more than reasonable efforts is a primary economic justification for having trade secret law.'[111] Whether a more proprietary, tortious or equitable approach is adopted, this essential requirement remains the same and gives credence to the cost-mitigation analysis because of its universality across jurisdictions.

In other words, trade secrets law universally prevents over-investment in protective measures – a signalling function is all that it has to perform so other parties can infer what their obligation is from the visible measures the trade secret owner has taken or his behaviour. That is a plausible key to requiring some evidence of protective measures, *additional* to it being required that the information is not actually public. In German law, the equivalent requirement before the adoption of the EU Trade Secrets Directive's provisions was that the trade secret owner demonstrate the will and intent to maintain the secret, although this is easily established. Risch points out that fewer resources will thus be expended by those *trying to obtain* secrets as well as by those trying to protect them.[112] He also stresses that where there is a low risk of divulgation, for instance, because the recipient is also subject to other obligations, a low standard of reasonable precautions makes even more sense. Importantly, this applies to employees, who are subject to the duties inherent in the contract of employment and, in some cases, to professional levels of duty (of a fiduciary kind).[113]

Risch asks what the additional value is of the improper means test, which is central to US law. This is relevant as well to the traditional civilian unfair competition approach, where the standard against which unfairness is measured is commercial honesty. It is perhaps less relevant to equity in the English tradition, which focuses primarily on the unauthorized nature of the use of information but nonetheless also uses an unconscionability or impropriety standard in cases of industrial espionage and the like. He usefully points out that one effect of this test is to extend liability to third parties, 'either due to a lack of wrongdoing or lack of intentional tort'.[114] Wasteful over-protection would occur if third parties were not held liable.[115]

This draws attention to the fact that third-party liability is a very important aspect of general trade secrets law, since the primary parties will most often already be bound by contract or some other tortious or fiduciary obligation. Third-party use of information was central to the European unfair competition approach, particularly in France, where the focus was more on those who actually exploited the information in competition with its 'owner'. They may well be initial recipients, but more often than

111. Above n 75, 20.
112. Trade secrets law also limits costs in this manner by not requiring absolute secrecy. Above n 75, 20.
113. Risch uses as an interesting example the greater measures that are required in China than in the US, the former having no effective legal protection.
114. Above n 75, 23.
115. *Ibid.*

not, it is an entity to which the information has been divulged, such as the new employer, that makes an actionable, unfair, competitive use of the information.[116]

Risch's key point thus amounts to a cost reduction argument, being that the trade secrets law provides an incentive to invest *less*, both in protection of one's own and in the obtaining of another's secrets. Bone and Lichtman stress that the extent of this benefit is indeterminate, but arguably, this type of criticism can apply to *any* economic analysis that focuses on cost reduction: it is very difficult to test empirically, which compels us to take a guarded approach to it. Risch accepts that even in the presence of trade secrets law, economic actors will still invest amounts in litigation and protection and we cannot know by how much this is reduced by the existence of trade secrets law,[117] but stresses that the latter is quite modulated. There are legitimacy exceptions, such as reverse engineering and independent development, which will constrain and interrupt the arms race. In any case, he thinks that if cost is reduced in some cases, at least, that is justification enough.

Nonetheless, Risch's analysis suffers from a weakness inherent in the economic analysis of law: the involved actors' calculations depend on their utility on perfect information. They presume the *ex ante* knowability of the status of a legal claim, whereas parties in the real world do not possess the perfect knowledge about alternatives that would necessarily result in efficient decision-making. They might not know or understand or incorrectly estimate the law or facts that are in the exclusive possession of the other party. This is particularly problematic in an area where many of the facts relevant to the resolution of a claim are by definition hidden from public view. For instance, a litigant against a party accused of misusing a technical secret might have no knowledge about that party's own research efforts, which have led to independent invention and thus an effective defence because that party will naturally keep such research efforts secret from the world.

In any case, there are many reasons parties may litigate, the state of the law being but one of them. Risch acknowledges this where he says that 'we do not know how much trade secret misappropriation has been deterred, how many cases are frivolous or meritorious, or how often the misappropriation attempt was efficient given the costs of alternatives and likelihood of detection'.[118]

Risch concludes, sensibly but perhaps rather lamely, that the 'question remains whether the need for more empirical information is sufficient to render trade secret law void of support'.[119] He thereby accepts the speculative nature of his theorizing, which accords with Fisher's scepticism concerning theory in IP.[120] Although Risch's thorough analysis of costs and benefits of various settings of the law is useful, it is perhaps both over-ambitious and inconclusive and focuses on the details of the law in the US rather

116. Risch points out that 'improper means' are also a signal for the value of the trade secret and the reasonable efforts of the trade secrets owner. This seems to be based on the improper means being more expensive. Above n 75, 24.
117. Above n 75, 28.
118. *Ibid.*, 29.
119. *Ibid.*
120. *See* William W. Fisher, 'Theories of Intellectual Property' in Stephen Munzer (ed.), *New Essays in the Legal and Political Theory of Property* (Cambridge University Press, 2001).

than the universal principles in a broad outline. In any case, if the present specific settings of US law were all economically optimal, this would mean that every jurisdiction with different settings is sub-optimal. This seems unlikely. There is also a question in relation to changes in the law over time. While it may be rational to analyse the broad or fundamental aspects of trade secrets law that are consistently required over time, it is perhaps less persuasive to do so in relation to the specifics that fluctuate with changing circumstances.

Further, economic theory skirts around the simple fact that there may be a much more fundamental value in respecting confidence: societal intercourse going beyond economic relationships. In a sense, this norm has been recognized by English courts which in protecting confidence do not distinguish between commercially valuable and personal information outside the public domain. Risch's present approach does not suit an English protection regime which also covers personal secrets. On a final note, Risch and others seem to largely ignore Moohr's ominous warning:

> in the long run, protecting interests against competitors often allows the protected party to charge a higher price for the product. When viewed from this perspective the law of trade secrets may be seen to inhibit competition and economic efficiency by creating a monopoly producer. Creating a monopoly is not usually considered a constructive way to support competition.[121]

Desaunettes-Barbero has recently argued that the justifications proffered for trade secrets protection 'rely either on an inadequate approach or are [incapable of offering] an encompassing justification for the whole system'. He points out that the impossibility of finding a justification for trade secrets law as a single homogenous body of law is resolved by recognizing that there are in fact two subject matters: the undertaking's secret sphere and secret pieces of information.[122] The significance of the insight lies in the former more than the latter: in policy terms, protecting the 'secret sphere' is important as 'it describes an area in which information must freely circulate without outside interference for undertakings to play their entrepreneurial role within markets'. This accords with what we say above about the important function that trade secrets law serves as it promotes the 'safe' exchange of information, for instance, in a pre- or non-contractual situation. It also points to the importance of mobility between organizations and the economic importance of the firm as a space within which information can be freely shared on non-exchange, non-contract-based foundation.

§2.03 A BEHAVIOURAL AND SOCIO-LEGAL APPROACH

Feldman advances a radically different approach, less concerned with economic theory than with people's perceptions of the importance of trade secrets law, with attitudes to

121. *See* above n 22, 890.
122. Luc Desaunettes-Barbaro, *Trade Secrets Legal Protection: From a Comparative Analysis of US and EU Law to a New Model of Understanding* (Springer, 1st ed., 2023) 263-265.

observing confidentiality.[123] His principle testing ground is confidentiality in the employment context, which in any case is the most important area of trade secrets law. From participants' attitudes and perceptions, he draws certain useful inferences, which are relevant because he argues that it is better if the law aligns more closely with people's attitudes to what is right or wrong. Legitimacy and credibility are crucial to the law's survival.

Feldman indirectly and implicitly says something about the property rationale by pointing out that the law does not or only weakly distinguishes between self-developed and learned information in employee trade secrets cases. His analysis is focused on US law, although this distinction is consequential in other jurisdictions as well, without necessarily being decisive. The failure to distinguish is in his view *inconsistent* with a property rationale: in all other areas of IP (except for trademarks), property results from authorship. Feldman finds that in terms of perception, 'employees placed greater importance on the fact that the information was downloaded and not learned (memorized) than on the fact that the information was developed by the employee and not learned'.[124] Tangibility was thus considered more important than authorship in terms of employees' decisions concerning use of trade secrets when changing employment. This is reminiscent of the 'rule of thumb' sometimes applied in the cases that any natural recollection is fine, but deliberate recording of information is questionable.[125]

Feldman's observations are interesting because they tend to focus more on the *propriety* (behavioural) standard than on the *property* norm – what seems to count for employees is the *method* of the taking. Going beyond what is naturally learned to deliberate actions was more important than the inherent characteristics of the information.[126] Feldman draws some contrasting conclusions from the importance of tangibility for employee attitudes: one, if the law does or would make a distinction based on tangibility, it would increase legitimacy and enforceability: 'aligning the law with people's intuition ... may make it easier for people to accept the law of trade secrets in general'.[127] The alternative view is that there are strong social norms controlling use of downloaded information, but not of memorized information, and therefore, the law should be more focused on such information as law is the only way of dealing with it – given the lack of social norms. Feldman prefers the first approach as he sees legitimacy and credibility as crucial to social support and thus to the long-term functionality of the law.

123. Yuval Feldman, 'The Behavioural Foundations of Trade Secrets: Tangibility, Authorship and Legality' (2006) 3(2) *Journal of Empirical Legal Studies* 197 https://doi.org/10.1111/j.1740-1461.2006.00068.x. His approach has overtones of the 'populist' explanation referred to by Risch. Above n 75, 17.
124. Feldman, above n 123, 224.
125. *See also Robb v. Green* [1895] 2QB 315.
126. In my view, once the taking of trade secrets is in a physical record, it may be associated with the taking of physical property and thus attract more opprobrium. Interestingly, Feldman found that the attitude of the current employer and co-workers (i.e., at the new place of employment) was the most important factor working on the employee. Above n 104, 230.
127. This is a kind of natural law theory approach, but according to Feldman, it is also adopted by some law and economics scholars. Above n 104, 231.

Feldman's findings also tend to show that employees understand the ideas, etc., that they produce in the course of their employment to be legitimately within the scope of the employer's claims. This accords with common sense, as it is difficult to distinguish between proprietary information and know-how where they are both in the mind and much easier and more acceptable to distinguish between what is in the mind and what is recorded. It is not possible to unlearn, and it is not possible to formulate a legal order or regime that reliably divides between free know-how and indentured knowledge.

It may be that Feldman's analysis adds to what Hill refers to as the 'expressive function' of trade secrets law.[128] Feldman makes an important point when he draws attention to the actual behaviour of actors rather than to abstract rules of law. Alternatively, it may be that there is indeed little to be gained from law, which is at odds with what most actors would perceive as right or wrong; therefore, the normative underpinnings of the law may lie simply in what actors see as a fair division of rights over IP. Feldman's approach accords nicely with the traditional civilian unfair competition and equity's approach to trade secrets, and also with the requirement of impropriety as employed in US law. Although Feldman's approach is important, it should be noted that he himself expresses quite extensive reservations about some of his research findings, drawing attention to the limitations of his study.[129]

Saunders also employs a more behavioural method and is, therefore, relevant in the context of Feldman's work.[130] Saunders points out that trade secrets law is different from other areas of IP as it does not penalize mere unauthorized use 'rather the defendant must have improperly used, acquired or disclosed the trade secret as a result of some wrongful or unethical conduct, such as by theft, fraud or breach of confidential duty'.[131] He describers maintaining standards of commercial ethics as a main policy aim of trade secrets law,[132] which amounts to an unfair competition rationale. Most importantly, drawing on Landes and Posner's 'The Economic Structure of Intellectual Property Law',[133] he stresses that '[o]verall social welfare is enhanced when individuals are encouraged to acquire knowledge and practice useful skills where they are in demand'.[134] Inversely, one could say that a regime that too greatly discourages or prohibits individuals from using their useful knowledge also discourages them from

128. *See* James Hill, 'Trade Secrets, Unjust Enrichment, and the Classification of Obligations' 4 *Virginia Journal of Law and Technology* 2, [25].
129. *See* above n 104, 225. Feldman also points out that employees do not expect to own the trade secrets they produce, excluding the employer, but 'did not feel that they ought to feel guilty had they been willing to disclose trade secrets'. Above n 104, 229.
130. Kurt M. Saunders, 'The Law and Ethics of Trade Secrets: A Case Study' (2006) 42 *California Western Law Review* 209.
131. *Ibid.*, 210.
132. Above n 111, 209.
133. William M. Landes & Richard A. Posner, *The Economic Structure of Intellectual Property Law* (Harvard University Press, 2003) 364.
134. Above n 111, 212.

acquiring it (from learning) in the first place.[135] Again, the porousness of trade secrets law emerges as a critical characteristic from a legal and policy perspective.[136]

If the core of trade secrets law is the standard of conduct that it enforces – of commercial honesty, good faith in relationships or ethical behaviour more generally – then Saunders provides a good framework for thinking about these standards. Various theoretical approaches are possible: justice theory, in particular, derived from Rawls, focuses on fairness.[137] But utilitarianism, rights theory and formalism are also advanced as theoretical frameworks that can inform actions or their ethical analysis. Nonetheless, Saunders's approach, although instructive, suffers from the same indeterminacy and inconclusiveness which Fisher accurately identifies as endemic in IP theory.[138]

§2.04 A DOCTRINAL APPROACH

[A] Focus on the Nature of Remedies

Therefore, rather than taking a law and economics or, more broadly, theoretical approach, Hill suggests that we should start our examination of rationales with the remedies that courts *actually* award.[139] As Hill puts it:

> Legal remedies can reflect their underlying rationales, and thus the choice of the measure of recovery in a given case can in fact be normative. [...] Furthermore, rather than courts always moving from rights to remedies, courts sometimes appear first to determine what level of intervention and protection is appropriate and then derive from their conclusion the nature of the plaintiff's 'right.'[140]

135. Saunders also points out that where industries are subject to very high rates of obsolescence, employers will be highly motivated to lure employees from competitors. Saunders, above n 130.
136. The US law is firmly in the camp of policing improper conduct: it is the use of improper means that the UTSA fixes upon to impugn certain abuses, which according to Saunders 'improper means ... involve a breach of contract of confidential relationship or other wrongful or commercially unethical conduct'. Therefore, there is a knowledge element, in that the person must know or have reason to know the information was acquired by improper means. So, in US law, the focus is either on some improper way of obtaining information or on a breach of duty. As Saunders unsurprisingly points out 'The boundary between proper and improper means of acquiring competitive intelligence is the focus of most trade secret litigation and ethical dilemmas.' Above n 111, 220-221. A duty of confidence may arise where information is disclosed for business purposes, as well as within certain relationships.
137. Above n 111, 234.
138. *See* Fisher, 'Theories of Intellectual Property', as referred to above at n 120.
139. In 'Trade Secrets, Unjust Enrichment, and the Classification of Obligations' above n 128. In fact, in the trade secrets cases, the courts are mostly intent on fashioning a tailored remedy rather than rigidly adhering to principle. That is certainly the case in the English breach of confidence tradition – a quintessentially equitable search for a flexible remedy. Often the merits and feasibility of some practical solution come first, the adapted rationale to follow. Further, often trade secrets cases are de facto determined by an interim decision, the focus at that stage being on the strength of the case (an approximation being sufficient) and most importantly the balance of convenience, i.e., the practical implications of (not) granting the remedy.
140. Above n 109, 45.

This may be particularly apt in trade secrets cases, whether in equity, misappropriation or unfair competition, where considerations of principle often seem to take second place to practical determination of possible remedies in the light of all the facts. It is also particularly significant taking into account that many trade secrets cases are finally determined with some intermediate or interlocutory decision of a court, rather than being fully ventilated at a later trial.

Hill employs the well-known Calabresi/Melamed model of distinguishing between property and liability-based remedies.[141] He asserts that property vindicates control, whereas liability vindicates well-being or utility.[142] Control is more highly valued and, therefore, more likely to result in the award of some *restitutionary* remedy, whereas loss of utility is remedied by a *compensatory* remedy accounting for harm. Liability rules are weaker than property rules since they focus on a more objective measure of real market value.[143]

According to Dagan, on whom Hill draws, property lies at the heart of a distributive scheme, which explains why we choose either property rules or liability rules.[144] The core of what Hill derives from Dagan in terms of the choice between property and liability is to be found in the underlying values that society prefers in each case:

> From this, one can see the correspondence between rationales and social goods (or goals): Control reflects the goal of individual liberty, well being reflects a person's security in her wealth, and sharing reflects the responsibility of other members of society for a person's fate.[145]

Hill goes on to say that:

> The goals of control and sharing are in conflict ... For example, sharing infringes upon another's control of the resources she possesses and, thus, undermines individual liberty. On the other hand, granting a resource-holder control over a resource necessarily curtails other persons' claims to share the resource. Each point along this control-sharing continuum is a societal choice, involving the sacrifice of some values for others.[146]

Protection of 'personhood' or self lies at the core, according to Dagan, and our interests diminish centrifugally:

> From this framework, one can see that the control individuals are accorded by the doctrinal rules in our paradigm exists along a continuum of diminishing interests: from core interests (protected against almost any kind of invasion or infringement) through less protected interests to least protected interests. More precisely, one

141. Guido Calabresi & A. Douglas Melamed, 'Property Rules, Liability Rules and Inalienability Rules: One View from the Cathedral' (1972) 85 *Harvard Law Review* 1089.
142. *Ibid.*
143. As well as profits or even returns, which do not account for the infringer's contribution to the gain made.
144. *See* Hanoch Dagan, *Unjust Enrichment: A Study of Private Law and Public Values* (Cambridge University Press, 1997) 5, as relied on and explained by Hill, above.
145. Above n 109, 75.
146. *Ibid.*, 76.

> can imagine that our doctrine draws concentric circles of diminishing control (and attachment) around the self.[147]

The Hill/Dagan approach posits something close to moral neutrality about the interests protected by liability rules – the law in a sense allows you to invade another person's rights as long as you pay compensation afterwards. In other words, where liability rather than property rules apply, the law does not as greatly value negotiation and consent, nor the independent setting of conditions of acquisition. However, it still values it enough to bestow rights and enable a remedy and it does not ascribe *no* value; otherwise, there would be no rights.[148]

In applying his scheme to trade secrets, Hill then focuses on the remedies that the UTSA bestows and concludes from them that US trade secrets law provides for greater remedies than what would typically be associated with a mere 'liability regime'. He criticizes Dagan for stepping outside his framework when it comes to trade secrets and classifying trade secrets law as having a '[p]ropriety of means' rationale.[149] Hill insists that Dagan's broader scheme can be applied to trade secrets:

> While it is certainly true that one may legally acquire a trade secret only through proper means, Professor Dagan appears to make an unfounded empirical assumption in claiming that, relative to (other) 'intellectual properties,' a trade secret is 'the least connected to its holder's identity.' In doing so, he mistakenly discards the consistency of his model by denying the existence of well-being and hypothetical-consent rationales in trade-secret remedies.[150]

Hill points out that if only propriety of means was intended to be vindicated by the UTSA, compensatory measures alone would have been allowed. In fact, disgorgement of profits is also provided for: 'A proportional-profits remedy even goes beyond vindicating the plaintiff's well being; it also gives her the benefit of the bargain she never had the opportunity to make with the defendant. That is, the remedy vindicates her hypothetical consent.'[151]

Hill goes on to say that there is no basis for Dagan's approach, which puts trade secrets lower on the scale of 'personhood' than copyrights, trademarks or patents; in fact, 'There is no empirical reason to suspect that any less labor, creativity, or innovation might go into the production of a trade secret than the creation of a copyrighted work.'[152] He also points out that patents and trade secrets are often connected and similar, and also that in fact the remedies for trade secrets infringement go beyond those for patents, suggesting that society values the former more highly than the latter. He says:

---

147. Above n 125, 79.
148. In terms of critique, one could say that taking into account the fact that it is not the case no value is bestowed where only liability rules apply, we are back to a sliding scale: where is the clearly justifiable break-line or demarcation between property and liability rules?.
149. Above n 109, 83.
150. *Ibid.*, 84.
151. *Ibid.*, 86.
152. *Ibid.*, 88.

> Finally, there is reason to conclude that trade-secret law not only affirms the rationales of wellbeing and hypothetical consent, but also the rationales of control and condemnation. That is, trade-secret remedies can vindicate both a trade-secret owner's control over her resource and society's condemnation of the misappropriator's behaviour.[153]

The 'control' of which Hill speaks is in his view vindicated by the award of injunctions.

Hill's analysis seems to lead to a conclusion which is not all that striking, i.e., that trade secrets law is a rather sui generis regime that has both property and liability traits; it not only aims to vindicate property-style control but also condemns improper behaviour. It is also not clear that Hill's model is robust enough or that his inverse reasoning is warranted – i.e., from remedies to value. It may be that certain remedies are compelled by practical concerns; for instance, an injunction is essential to maintain the existence of the secret, let alone vindicate some underlying value to the plaintiff. But Hill does make a significant point in that the remedies for trade secrets infringements are quite extensive and suggest a high value attached to them by society.[154] This accords with a sentiment sometimes expressed in English cases that to respect confidence is an obligation of trust and good faith, which sustains societal intercourse at a most fundamental level. It is difficult to imagine a well-ordered society and commerce without some such legal duty.

[B] Bone's Radical Take: No Law of Trade Secrets

Whereas most writing on trade secrets law tends to justify its existence and to find some rational explanation for its features, Bone famously rejects the notion of a separate law of trade secrets.[155] His paper is frequently cited not only because of its well-reasoned and thorough analysis but also because of its startling suggestion that there is no trade secrets law and no comprehensive and distinct theoretical basis for it. He sees only a grab-bag of other wrongs and remedies associated with it. His analysis is interesting in light of the fact that trade secrets law has in many cases emerged quite recently. Certainly, in English law, it only clearly emerged in the mid-twentieth century, where it is in any case part of the broader law of equity, which extends not just to commercially valuable but also personal information. The same can be said for French law, where before the imposition of EU Trade Secrets Directive standards, it had only quite recently achieved a separate doctrinal status, outside contract and outside other wrongs often associated with trade secrets misuses, such as trespass, theft,

153. *Ibid.*, 92.
154. If trade secrets are appreciated in their intellectual property context, then that accords with the greater importance – both in terms of legal remedies and in terms of asset valuation – society attached to intellectual or knowledge goods today. To some degree both in the United States and England, this area of law is nonetheless a historical novelty, suggesting that trade secrets have become more highly valued in more recent times.
155. In his controversial but seminal article entitled 'A New Look at Trade Secrets Law: Doctrine in Search of Justification' (1998) 86(2) *California Law Review* 241 https://doi.org/10.2307/3481134.

inducement of breach of contract or invasion of privacy.[156] Arguably, in the civilian tradition, there is in any case no really separate trade secrets law, since it was seen as a species of unfair competition or else of civil liability in delict (prior to the EU Trade Secrets Directive's passage).

Bone stresses that trade secrets law is different from other IPRs because appropriation of information is not actionable per se; rather, there must be acquisition, disclosure or use in a 'wrongful manner'.[157] Its liability rules have a 'relational focus' unlike IP law, although the law does not impose duties in contractual relationships alone. In this, his analysis accords well with the traditional English approach, which also stresses that trade secrets remedies vindicate good faith in relationships, and the traditional civilian approach, which attaches liability to unfair or dishonest methods of using or acquiring information in competition.

His main point is that 'trade secrets law is ... parasitic: it depends on a host theory for normative support'.[158] Therefore:

> I propose that we stop seeking a functional justification for trade secret law and recognize this body of law for what it really is – a collection of other legal wrongs. With this insight much of trade secret law becomes comprehensible, especially its parasitic quality. At the same time, however, much of its doctrinal structure becomes difficult to justify.[159]

Bone argues that the property theory was rejected in *Dupont v. Masland*[160] and that at that moment 'trade secret law lost its justifying theory and its source of normative independence from other fields of law'.[161] He successively rejects various underlying theories that have been advanced by others: first of all, the incentive theory, strongly advanced by Posner et al., because it does not sufficiently address and inculcate the costs associated with protecting trade secrets: 'it is not clear that trade secret law promotes creation incentives to the extent necessary to justify its additional costs. Indeed trade secret law runs the risk of undermining the socially beneficial incentives of the patent system'.[162]

As pointed out above, this argument has merit because sustaining two similarly targeted property-style regimes really makes little sense, certainly not where one regime (trade secrets) has an adverse impact on the other as it undermines patents' incentive function. It also accords with the broader point that commercial secrets (or personal ones in England) are not explained by an innovation-based theory and that much of this protection could in any case be achieved by contract. The latter is particularly true in relation to the argument that trade secrets law makes it unnecessary to seek a patent at every stage of ongoing research rather than just at the endpoint.[163]

---

156. *See* Chapter 4 concerning English law and Chapter 6 concerning French law for support for this assertion.
157. Above n 46, 244.
158. *Ibid.*, 245.
159. *Ibid.*, 246.
160. *E.I. Du Pont de Nemours Powder Co. v. Masland*, 244 US100 (1917).
161. Above n 46, 260.
162. *Ibid.*, 270.
163. *Ibid.*, 271.

In fact, there is a cogent argument that trade secrets law may be useful not as some alternative scheme to encourage technical inventions or as a useful supplement to patents but exactly where the information concerned is commercial and *cannot* be patented.[164] In reality, its value might lie in protecting the kind of strategic and competition-oriented information that a firm can keep secret. Perhaps this ability is central to its competitive potential and thus to sustaining a competitive dynamic in the marketplace. As Bone rightly points out, in that sphere, there is 'no risk of interfering with patent goals'.[165]

But he readily dismisses the argument: first, there is no lack of incentive to make business plans, have complete financial data, etc. – businesses cannot live without them. He also says:

> Conceivably, a firm might invest more if it knew it could protect the results through trade secrets law, but it is not evident [check] that the additional investment would enhance competition or product quality enough to justify the social costs.[166]

One might reiterate the point here that in any case much of this information can be secured through employment contracts and the like or through non-disclosure agreements (NDAs). Bone points out that contract can do the job in particular where the theoretical case is strongest, i.e., for ex-employee start-ups.[167]

However, the argument that this is the kind of information that a firm has no choice but to develop does not establish that some form of special legal protection might not improve efficiency. If there were no legal consequences for acquiring a firm's plans and data by whatever means, no matter what efforts it had taken to protect them, competition would function under considerable stress and scarce resources might be diverted to a wasteful protective arms race, as was suggested above.

But Bone tackles this 'over-investment in security in the absence of trade secrets law' argument. Not only protecting secrets but also *stealing* secrets would absorb too many resources. The two balance each other out. Licensing, which can only occur in the presence of legal rights in the object of the licence, is, however, said to be a less expensive form of ordering as it limits transaction costs. Bone accepts that the market is considered to be a less costly transfer mechanism than theft, but, he says, this 'ignores enforcement costs and underestimates the transaction costs of licensing, both of which are likely to be especially high when secret information is involved'.[168] Bone points out that trade secrets theft is in any case still a serious problem and litigation is frequent even though we have trade secrets law. Therefore, trade secrets law does not

164. For further consideration of the patents-trade secrets relationship *see* Lionel Bently & Tanya Aplin, 'Patents and Trade Secrets' (2022) *SSRN Electronic Journal* https://doi.org/10.2139/ssrn.4134558; Tanya Aplin & Johnathon Liddicoat, 'Discussion Paper on the Interplay between Patents and Trade Secrets in Medical Technologies' (2023) *SSRN Electronic Journal* https://doi.org/10.2139/ssrn.4606923; Neil Wilkof, Shamnad Basheer, & Irene Calboli (eds), *Overlapping Intellectual Property Rights* (Oxford University Press, 2nd ed., 2023) Chapter 3.
165. Above n 46, 272.
166. *Ibid.*
167. Above n 46, 282.
168. *Ibid.*, 273.

have the desired effect of reducing transaction costs in the real world,[169] 'it seems unrealistic to assume that with trade secret law we have achieved the happy state of infrequent theft and few lawsuits'.[170]

Bone makes the significant point that unlike tangible property, information theft is actually expensive and difficult to detect, since there is no obvious deprivation when we are dealing with intellectual assets. Since reverse engineering and independent invention are legitimate, no necessary inference can be drawn just from the fact that a competitor has the information.[171] Litigation is costly because it has many open-ended standards and 'vague balancing criteria' which create incentives for parties to seek to gain from litigating. Further, transaction costs are also high because of Arrow's paradox and the risk of foreclosure of a potential licensee and because the vague state of trade secrets law and its exceptions make valuation difficult.[172] Patent licensing is therefore less costly than licensing trade secrets, according to Bone.[173] This account obviously is not relevant to non-technical trade secrets.

However, Rowe asserts that trade secrets litigation is not more uncertain than any other IP litigation.[174] Although uncertainty does leave defendants at a disadvantage, she considers this a universal problem:

> Thus the sentiment that 'something must be done' to restrain runaway plaintiffs is understandable. But whether the articulated concern is free speech or otherwise, and whether the field is trade secret law or any other civil area, it is important to recognize the larger inter-connected complexities involved, and resist the temptation to 'fix' isolated pieces such as changing the substantive law, or restricting plaintiff's rights to file actions.[175]

Problems are often more systemic and should be tackled, if at all, in a holistic manner. Rowe's proviso is important, but it tends to ignore Bone's point that the factual and forensic difficulties inherent in trade secrets litigation, coupled with vague standards, further *exacerbate* systemic problems of uncertainty. For Bone, this supports his argument that trade secrets law is superfluous; for Rowe, the difficulties with trade secrets reinforce her call for more systemic reform.

Bone does not ignore arguments from rights and fairness rather than economics. He dismisses privacy rights for obvious reasons when it comes to the commercial secrets of corporations. He also debunks the contractarian arguments, in particular as constructed by Scheppele.[176] In a manner similar to Lemley, he strikes at the whole contractarian approach itself:

---

169. *Ibid.*, 274.
170. *Ibid.*, 275.
171. *Ibid.*, 279.
172. *Ibid.*, 280.
173. *Ibid.*
174. About which she gives various examples in her article, Elizabeth A. Rowe, 'Trade Secrets Litigation and Free Speech: Is It Time to Restrain the Plaintiffs?' (2009) 50(5) *Boston College Law Review* 1425.
175. Rowe, above n 174, at 1441.
176. In Kim Lane Scheppele, *Legal Secrets: Equality and Efficiency in the Common Law* (University of Chicago Press, 1988).

> Why should persons in the real world heed the results of a bargaining process that does not reflect their actual preferences? Consider firm A, with no valuable secrets and little inventive ability. Firm A would like to use all possible methods to steal its competitors' secrets. Why should firm A comply with even the relatively limited constraints Scheppele proposes? When told that it would have agreed to those constraints if it knew nothing about itself, Firm A would protest that it did not in fact agree and that some hypothetical agent cannot possibly represent its interests.[177]

He points out that Scheppele's argument ultimately falls back on morality (an impartial and non-self-interested way of organizing society) and that trade secrets law is not about moral norms but about competition constrained by rules of legality. In effect, Bone contends that the contractarian approach is no more than an appeal to morality to organize market behaviour, but there is no reason for doing this since the legal rules are already there to do this job.[178] This is indeed an interesting point, but the English approach, with no distinction between commercial and other secrets and an emphasis on acting in good faith, approximates Schepelle's approach more than his. The traditional civilian unfair competition approach is also more in line with applying standards of morality of a particular kind to commercial conduct.

However, Bone doubts the theory that trade secret law is a mechanism for enforcing standards of commercial ethics and honesty. He points out that in competitive and unstable markets, it might be difficult to identify an industry norm. This goes to the general objection that it is impossible to predict what might be found 'fair' or 'unfair', which has deterred courts in English common law jurisdictions from adopting a tort of unfair competition. Judges even recently have pointed out that one person's 'unfair' is another person's shrewd competition:

> What one man calls 'unfair', another calls 'fair'. The market involves the interests of traders, their competitors and consumers. They all have different perspectives. [...] So I think there are real difficulties in formulating a clear and rational line between that which is fair and that which is not, once one goes outside the requirement of no deception.[179]

Bone also points out that norms will vary a great deal depending on contextual factors.[180] These arguments are particularly significant where one wants to encourage dynamic competition and the disruption of markets by innovation, etc. To add a further question to Bone's: what is the point of regulating honest practices by the oblique method of trade secrets law rather than simply regulating it directly as an element of a broader tortious or statutory action for unfair competition or in equity?

Bone's focus is naturally on US trade secrets law, where liability only follows from acquisition, disclosure or use in a 'wrongful manner'. He thus equates wrongfulness with the breach of some norm other than the simple norm: 'you shall not disclose information that you have received in confidence'. In that US law seems to differ from

177. Above n 46, 293.
178. *Ibid.*
179. *L'Oreal SA v. Bellure NV*, [2007] EWCA Civ 968; [2008] RPC 9 at [139]-[140].
180. Above n 46, 296.

the English tradition, as the critical question in an action for breach of confidence is whether the information has been used in a manner contrary to the purpose or authorization of the confidor. According to Bone, US law fixes on an external rather than an inherent norm.[181] He gives two examples of 'wrongfulness': 'a person is liable if he uses or discloses trade secret information in violation of a duty of confidence or acquiring the information by theft or fraud'.[182] This suggests that the duty of confidence is based on a particular pre-existing relationship between the parties rather than, as in English law, deriving directly from the circumstances of the disclosure itself. In other words, English law holds that any disclosure for a limited purpose, or that a reasonable man would recognize as confidential, gives rise to an obligation not to use or disclose it in certain ways. The standard there is internal to the action for breach of a trade secret or breach of confidence.

To put it differently, Bone says that one of the situations in which trade secrets law offers a remedy is 'when and independent legal norm has been violated': he does not seem to include 'violation of a confidential relationship' in this category but in the other category of impropriety without breach of a legal norm. From the standpoint of English law, this is a highly artificial approach. In any case, the Restatement of Unfair Competition imposes a duty of confidence in paragraph 40 if:

> (b) the trade secret was disclosed to the person under circumstances in which the relationship between the parties to the disclosure or the other facts surrounding the disclosure justify the conclusion that, at the time of the disclosure:
> (1) the person knew or had reason to know that the disclosure was intended to be in confidence, and
> (2) the other party to the disclosure was reasonable in inferring that the person consented to an obligation of confidentiality.

In the circumstances, it would seem strained to argue that breach of this so-created duty of confidence is somehow breaching an *extraneous* norm. Bone himself notes that when the property view of trade secrets was rejected, Justice Holmes did so in terms that '[t]he property may be denied, but the confidence cannot be. Therefore, the starting point for the present matter is not property or due process of law, but that the defendant stood in confidential relations with the plaintiffs'.[183] In the circumstances, it seems that Bone's argument that US trade secrets law is somehow bereft of any inherent or internal norm of conduct and thus latches onto external norms of conduct already policed by other legal actions is somewhat artificial.

Finally, in relation to the property question, Bone nicely explains a more traditional view of property:

> At common law, property rights depended on possession. Possession was a prerequisite to ownership, and ownership was necessary for common law rights.

181. Thus, he argues US trade secrets law is different from IPRs: a breach of copyright does not depend on the question whether you have breached any norm other than that prescribed by the copyright act itself: you shall not copy without authorization of the copyright owner.
182. Above n 46, 244.
183. *See* Bone, quoting from *EI du Pont de Nemours Powder Co v. Masland*, 244 US 100, 102 (1917). Above n 46, 259-260.

> Moreover possession required clear acts manifesting an intent to bring the thing under exclusive control and to appropriate it to individual use. A person obtained exclusive property rights by exercising actual control over things in the world.[184]

There were and are many difficulties with trade secrets as property, as Bone points out, as information is not subject to physical control, nor does another person obtaining it means that the initial holder loses possession – possession of information is not inherently exclusive. Also, it is impossible to unlearn information and thus somehow dispose of it absolutely or return it.

Thus, Bone concludes that there neither is nor need be a separate regime of trade secrets law. It is certainly the case that in the majority of cases, some other action will 'do the job'. The relevant actions are not few and include contract (e.g., employment), physical property-related torts or offences (theft, trespass to land or to chattels), breach of fiduciary duties (e.g., in a professional relationship), misuse of communications equipment, copyright, breach of privacy. Further, in relation to some of these actions, the remedies or penalties can reflect the collateral fact that a breach of secrecy is involved; for instance, the punishment for the theft of a memory device might reflect the fact that the devices contained valuable commercial information, or copyright infringement by reproducing a document containing such information might be met by additional (aggravated) damages. Nonetheless, there appear to be situations that fall outside all other actions, at least in the common law world, but which arguably merit some legal consequences. Very important is the situation where confidential information is disclosed in the pre-contractual phase and without a formal NDA being agreed upon. But perhaps of even greater significance is the situation of the post-termination employee who is no longer bound by any provision of the contract of employment. In the common law world, there would be no remedy against an employee who profits from a secret learned on the job in the absence of an action for breach of confidence or trade secrets. However, in civilian jurisdictions, this is less clear: in Germany, for instance, an employee may in some cases be in breach of residual post-contractual obligations if relying on a trade secret to compete with an ex-employer.

§2.05 THE PRIVACY RATIONALE

English law (unlike in the US and the civilian jurisdictions) knows no separate action or tort of breach of privacy. With certain limitations, the action for breach of confidence may provide relief, as it applies equally to commercial secrets and personal or family information. One of the earliest manifestations of the action related to such information: in the case of *Prince Albert v. Strange* concerning Queen Victoria's own artworks not intended for publication.[185] But it is not the privacy interests of personal integrity and autonomy that are thus vindicated but rather the obligations of honesty and good faith that attach to somebody who receives information in confidence.

184. Above n 46.
185. (1849) 64 ER 293.

Trade secrets law in the US concerns only information which derives commercial value from being secret. Where personal information is at stake, the action for invasion of privacy comes into play, counterbalanced by the constitutional right of free speech and freedom of the press. In that country as in England, privacy interests are not central to trade secrets/breach of confidence. However, Rowe suggests that we should make more of privacy. She refers to the importance of 'commercial privacy' and quotes from the 1974 Supreme Court decision in *Kewanee Oil*: '[a] most fundamental human right, that of privacy, is threatened when industrial espionage is condoned or is made profitable; the state interest in denying profit to such illegal ventures is unchallengeable'[186] and 'the basic decency of society is threatened when companies steal from one another'.[187] She points out that this commercial privacy approach has received little attention in subsequent cases or scholarly writings.[188] However, the passages she quotes refer to illegality – so it is not clear what the advantage is of making much of the additional privacy breaches, where remedies would in any case attach to the associated illegality (e.g., theft or trespass).[189]

The issues canvassed above invite consideration of the divide between the black letter law and the perceptions of the law. Two points are particularly apposite here. First, how the law actually does or does not influence the actions of the relevant actors is crucial rather than what the law in the books says. The latter is only part of the picture concerning policy effects: also important is how the law is perceived and influences actions in the real world. Further, partly because the law of trade secrets is advanced as being very uncertain, parties are encouraged to engage in contractual bargains that promise (if not always deliver) greater certainty. Arguably, therefore, the

186. *Kewanee Oil v. Bicron Corp*, 416 US 474 (1974), 487.

187. Quoted at Rowe, above n 174, at 1434-1435.

188. *Ibid.*; *see* however also as to the notion of commercial or corporate privacy: 'A Right of Privacy for Corporations?' in Paul Torremans (ed.), *Intellectual Property & Human Rights* (Kluwer, 2008), 475-505. Note however that in *FCC v. AT&T*,582F 3d 490 (3rd Cir, 2011) the *Supreme Court* of the US ruled that corporations do not have a personal privacy interest although the court did earlier rule that they have a free speech interest, in the case that decided that companies could not be restrained from spending on political ads. *Citizens United v. Federal Election Commission*, 558 US 310 (2010). *See also* Pamela Samuelson, 'Principles for Resolving Conflicts Between Trade Secrets and the First Amendment' (Research Paper No 925056, UC Berkeley Public Law Research Paper, 9 August 2006).

189. Rowe does point out that the free speech – and I would add competition – interest is sometimes vindicated by the court's decision about costs in an unwarranted prosecution of a matter. She cites as an example *Contact Materials Processing Inc v. Kataleuna GmbH Catalysts*, 222 F Supp 2d 733 734 (d. Md, 2002), where the court held the action had been brought in bad faith because the plaintiff had failed to keep its information confidential: 'This "bad faith" approach respects a trade secret owner's right to "petition" by filing an action when it believes its trade secret has been misappropriated, while also ameliorating free speech concerns by deterring the plaintiff from filing a baseless action because it knows that it may be liable for the defendant's attorney's fees' (Rowe, above n 174 at 1439-1440). This is reminiscent of the finding in *GlaxoSmithKline Australia Pty Ltd v. Ritchie & Anor* [2008] VSC 164 in Australia, where the court awarded indemnity costs against a plaintiff who had pursued a lengthy action against an ex employee which was ultimately found to have very little merit. However, the court there expressed itself more concerned about interference with legitimate competition than with freedom of speech. In other post-termination cases the courts have also pointed to the potential *in terrorem* effect the uncertain trade secrets law and law concerning non-competes may have.

state of the general law has quite limited impact: more often than not contract provides the relevant legal mechanism and solution for a dispute: for instance, non-competes in employment contracts, which are justifiable if they protect company secrets, and NDA's in pre-contractual negotiations.

A further point that emerges from the survey of theoretical and conceptual uncertainties above is that the relevant law is constantly evolving. This is either by express measures such as legislative reforms and harmonization efforts or because certain actors tend to push the boundaries of protection. Graves and Katyal thus draw attention to and critique what they call an 'alarming extension of trade secrets arguments in a host of different areas of law'.[190] They point to the negative impact of the ever-extending cover of trade secrets law in terms of openness in the functioning of society, an openness that does not always suit commercial actors. Examples they consider are the position of journalists and whistleblowers and employers' attempts to control employee attributes such a diversity data and workplace harms.[191] On a final note, as has also emerged from the text above and is a focus of this book, trade secrets law is very varied across jurisdictions, which makes both doctrinal and theoretical treatment of the topic challenging. Variety exists not only between nations but also within federal states such as the US and to some degree Australia. All this results in calls for and some efforts at harmonization at the national and international levels[192] obviously heeded in the EU with the introduction of the EU Trade Secrets Directive, which is considered in Chapter 6. Some significant areas of trade secrets law, such as post-employment secrecy obligations and intricately related non-compete agreements, remain outside some of these reform efforts or are addressed obliquely, but measures such as the executive prohibition on all labour non-competes advanced in the US (*see* further Chapter 5).

§2.06 CONCLUSIONS

Nonetheless, some aspects of trade secrets law seem universal across jurisdictions: the requirement to identify precisely the information claimed to be a trade secret; the requirement to establish that the information is not in the public domain, and some evidence of measures to limit its circulation; the requirement of some wrongful (illegal, inequitable, improper, dishonest or unfair) aspect in the taking or use of the information; and the fact that reverse engineering (with some reservation in the case of some civilian jurisdictions) and independent discovery are permitted.

Much of the analysis of trade secrets policy and theory considered above focuses on the law in the US and either expressly or by implication on *technical* information. Nonetheless all jurisdictions recognize that commercial secrets are also covered by the

190. Above n 25, 1337.
191. *See also* Jamillah Bowman Williams, 'Diversity as a Trade Secret' (2019) 107(6) *The Georgetown Law Journal* 1685.
192. In relation to the US, *see* Suzana Nashkova, 'Defining Trade Secrets in the United States: Past and Present Challenges – A Way Forward?' (2023) 54(5) *International Review of Intellectual Property and Competition Law* 634 https://doi.org/10.1007/s40319-023-01310-1.

law, and the civilian jurisdictions traditionally consider trade secrets specifically from a competition perspective. A theory or policy explanation that covers both commercial and technical secrets should be preferred. That point of departure tends to undermine arguments that trade secrets law performs an incentive function much as other areas of IP law do. It generally points away from an IP rationale: secret information would be produced even if the general legal protection were not available, so the rights do not perform the incentive function typical of IP.[193] Protection is also not only available for information to which the possessor has made some original or creative contribution but also for any information that is secret and has some commercial value. Further, trade secrets law does not achieve one of the fundamental instrumental goals of IP – it does not result in the wider availability of information and knowledge. The applicable law in fact discourages detailed and specific (as opposed to inchoate) information sharing, and the exclusion of the public is not necessarily of limited duration, which is a characteristic of IP law. Additionally, there is no logic in the incentive theory because there would be little point in bestowing or not the incentive on the basis of a totally aleatory distinguisher: whether or not the new knowledge can be kept secret while being commercially exploited. Why would the law provide an incentive in relation to a manufacturing process which can lie hidden in a factory but not in relation to a product which will reveal its secrets when sold? Both arguably have equal advantages to society. Why also allow reverse engineering if incentive is the key?

There are also difficulties in treating trade secrets as property *simpliciter*. According to Landes and Posner, possession and exclusivity are central to property, as the possessor must have the exclusive right to possess and enjoy. Bone also emphasizes that at common law, property rights depended on possession. Possession was a prerequisite to ownership, and ownership was necessary for common law rights. Moreover, possession required clear acts manifesting an intent to bring the thing under exclusive control and to appropriate it for individual use. A person obtained exclusive property rights by exercising actual control over things in the world.[194] There are thus many difficulties with this, as Bone points out, as information is not subject to physical control, nor does another person obtaining it means that the initial holder loses possession – possession of information is not inherently exclusive. Also, it is impossible to unlearn information and thus somehow dispose of it absolutely or return it to its author. Conversely, typical for property are alienability and exclusion: both of these are questionable in the trade secrets context. The reverse engineering and independent invention limitations are also not consistent with possession and exclusivity.

Further, property rights are typically rights against the entire world, exclusive rights. They are *rights in rem* rather than *in personam*. *Rights in rem* are typically property rights, whereas rights in personam are not. As Balganesh explains, '[p]roperty rights are in rem interests because the set of individuals against whom they operate remains indefinite at all times, unlike in personam rights that operate against a definite

193. *See* Moohr, above n 30, 899-903.
194. *See* above n 46.

set of individuals'.[195] In arguing that property rights are not appropriate for news, Balganesh says that 'structurally though, such individual exclusion rights make the most sense only when the intangible is individually produced by, and therefore in some sense unique to, the right holder'.[196] Feldman makes a related point about the property rationale, if only indirectly and implicitly: as we saw above, he points out that the law does not or only weakly distinguishes between self-developed and learned information in employee trade secrets cases. This would tend to be inconsistent with a property rationale, since then there would be a distinction drawn on that basis – after all, to look at the IP parallel, the property is intimately connected to authorship in all cases except trademarks. Moohr makes a related point: 'Property rights flow from a natural right that goes to the first person to discover or to occupy some object, or to those who use their labor, be it physical or intellectual, to create an object, whether tangible or intangible.'[197] For Locke, property rights are justified by labour; as Merges says, according to Locke, true property rights 'are held by individuals who work on things so as to justify removal from the primordial commons'.[198]

The primordial state is when everything is held in common, before individual property rights and before the State. The removal from the commons is legitimate even though it is unilateral, i.e., does not depend on or require the consent of all other members of the society, because 'he explains that it would be infeasible for each individual who wanted to claim something to get the permission of all existing co-owners of that thing – for example, from all humanity, who again initially hold the earth and its contents in common'.[199] Merges says that this is in truth a transaction cost argument. As Risch points out, the Lockean view will tend towards over-protection, and it is generally inconsistent with the nature of trade secrets law, which does not allow for remedies once information has become public.

As indicated, the porousness of trade secrets law also appears inconsistent with a property rationale. Posner et al. point to the real difficulties if there were no reverse engineering allowed and also emphasize the importance of information sharing and, therefore, the lack of absolute control in trade secrets law. Moohr also emphasizes the need for freedom of competition and the right to reverse engineer and use independently discovered information which are clearly competition-enhancing facets of trade secrets law.

195. Shyamkrishna Balganesh, '"Hot News": The Enduring Myth of Property in News' (2011) 111(3) *Columbia Law Review* 419, 435. *See also* Shyamkrishna Balganesh, 'The Role of Unfair Competition in the Common Law' in Shyamkrishna Balganesh & Gideon Parchomovsky (eds), *Intellectual Property and the Common Law* (2012).

196. Balganesh also says that since 'an individual property right granted to each news collector might deter free riding, but could potentially affect the nature of cooperation in the market'. He suggests that 'deterring such free riding ... by focusing, as a normative matter, on the unfair gain to the defendant rather than on the loss to the plaintiffs, offers a more tailored, equally effective, and less problematic solution than a property mechanism'. Above n 172, 426-427.

197. Above n 22, 892.

198. *See* Robert P. Merges, 'Locke for the Masses: Property Rights and the Products of Collective Creativity' (2008) 36(4) *Hofstra Law Review* 1179, 1185 https://doi.org/10.2139/ssrn.1323408.

199. This is Merges's explanation of Locke, *see* above n 198.

However, Lemley refers to trade secrets as property-like because a trade secret owner 'is entitled to control certain information even once it has left the owner's possession'.[200] I question this above.[201] He addresses the concern that propertization will impact negatively on the 'freedom of other to use information to compete' and will also negatively affect 'employee mobility and robust competition, and perhaps even ... free speech'.[202] He emphasizes that it will have the opposite effect by focusing on the core requirements and limits of trade secrets law rather than on 'standardless theories of unfair competition and unjust enrichment that seem the most obvious alternatives'.[203] With Graves and Katyal, one could add that it will also negatively affect broader societal interests.[204]

It is true that, as in *Ruckelshaus*, courts often point out that trade secrets have (some of) the juridical characteristics of property: they can be traded, be the object of a trust, pass to a trustee in bankruptcy. However, they are thus treated as property for the purpose of other legal regimes, while at the same time, courts tend to say that they are not property for the purpose of the action for trade secrets infringement itself. The English Appeal Court in *Douglas* insisted that there was no property right in trade secrets, even though they were often dealt with as if that were the case. As pointed out earlier, the court fixes the requirement that the defendant must be aware that information was 'private or confidential. In fact, the right depends upon the effect on the third party's conscience'.[205] Hull and Abbott point to the fact that although the Court of Appeal firmly rejects a property approach, a number of authoritative judgments favour that approach. But most of these cases again treat trade secrets as property for particular contingent purposes only, for example, taxation, as an asset of property of a trust, or as an asset of a partnership. Courts in some ways sit on the fence. Risch points out that the California Supreme Court refused to answer the question of whether trade secrets under the UTSA were property 'and argued that substantive trade secret rights do not fall exclusively under either the property view or the liability view'.[206] In *Ruckelshaus*, the Supreme Court 'both affirmed that trade secrets could be property and left the issue up to the states'.[207] In my view, nobody really appropriates a trade secret; they merely share in it or destroy it. Is it not the essence of property that it can be restored to a plaintiff when it is established that it was wrongly taken? In trade secrets cases, this is impossible in some cases (where the misuse takes the form of

200. Above n 42, 326.
201. *See* above commentary.
202. Both at above n 42, 351-352.
203. Above n 42, 352.
204. Above n 25.
205. Above n 63 at [126].
206. Above n 76, 11. Referring to *Cadence Design Sys, Inc v. Avant! Corp.*, 127 Cal Rptr 2d 196 (200).
207. Above n 76, 10. In this case, Monsanto challenged the EPA of Missouri's statutory right to disclose its trade secret data to the public as a 'Fifth Amendment taking': 'The Court determined that under Missouri law, which followed the Restatement (first) of Torts at the time, trade secrets were property, and thus could be subject to a taking. In doing so, the Court relied in part on a Missouri case decided in 1917, which makes sense because the shift from "property" to "unfair competition" around the time of *Masland* had not yet become widespread.'

publication) but may be possible in others (where the misuse takes the form of unauthorized non-public use), but only in a limited way, since information acquired can never really be unlearned and thus 'restored' completely to its rightful owner.

In terms of the US, Moohr also refers to the fact that the *EEA* revolves around the notion of breaching authorization and argues that it means that the act construes rights akin to property. If this is correct, then the same could be said of the traditional approach in England and like jurisdictions, which focused on use contrary to authorization. She says Congress took a property view of trade secrets.[208] As pointed out above, although it is conduct that is criminalized, 'condemning conduct that involves some interest inevitably sweeps that interest into a protected category'.[209] She points out, however, that in the view of Congress, 'trade secrets are much like any other property'.[210] Since the criminal provisions are constructed around absence of authorization to do what constitutes the object of the charge, owners have effectively been given complete control over trade secret information.

Perhaps the most persuasive view of the rationale of trade secrets is Risch's key point, also made by others, that the trade secrets law provides an incentive to invest less in protecting one's own and obtaining another's secrets.[211] It thus aims to reinforce certain standards of conduct by imposing legal sanctions on those who deviate from a norm of behaviour. A legally sanctioned norm limits the need for practical measures to achieve and maintain secrecy. It is here that we come to the essence of trade secrets law: the required value does not lie in the information, but in a negative fact, that no other potentially competing party has the information. In trade secrets law, the plaintiff must prove, at least in the US, EU, French and German law, that she derives a competitive advantage from her unique possession of the information rather than from its inherent value. The latter is also of no real significance in the English law, but the former lies at its core. This is also what distinguishes trade secrets from patents.

But most importantly, since this is the apparent rationale for trade secrets protection both in the criminal and civil law in the civilian jurisdictions, it explains why the TRIPS and previous German and French approaches centred on unfair competition law might be an appropriate framework as the misuse of a trade secret amounts to the unfair destruction of a rival's competitive advantage. The unfairness lies in the failure to observe some standard of good conduct: a breach of a duty of trust or good faith assumed in favour of another party in equity; recourse to an illegal or improper act; or engaging in conduct that is against recognizable commercial mores. In the final analysis, applying some measure of appropriate conduct lies at the heart of the judgments made in trade secrets law, whether honest commercial conduct in the unfair competition countries, or faithful conduct in the English jurisdiction, or propriety in the US. In the traditional civilian and US approach, the law centres on policing commercial conduct, whereas in the English approach, a more general standard of honesty and good faith applies to all societal intercourse. In all jurisdictions, difficulties will be

208. *See* above n 22, 898.
209. *Ibid.*
210. *See* above n 22, 899.
211. But he also tackles criticisms of this point notably by Bone & Lichtman.

experienced in defining, consistently applying and evolving these standards, but there seems little doubt that there is a need for such a process if commerce and human intercourse are to function properly. It may be, however, that it is impossible to generate a 'unifying theory of trade secrets law' and that we have to accept, as Desaunettes-Barbero has suggested, that there are at least two very distinct spheres of protection and justification.

CHAPTER 3
International Standards

§3.01 INTRODUCTION

As mentioned before, trade secrets law is the least harmonized regime traditionally included in IP law.[1] It was not expressly dealt with in the Paris Convention on Industrial Property (Paris Convention), misuse of a trade secret being seen to fall under the general obligation of Article 10*bis(2)* to provide remedies for unfair competition. However, although Article 10*bis(3)* non-exhaustively lists specific instances of unfair competition, none of these are concerned with misuse of trade secrets.[2] Remedies for unfair competition per se were well established in civilian jurisdictions but have been largely rejected in common law countries. Rather the common law recognizes more specific wrongs such as passing off and breach of confidence (the latter in equity), and the US has a now well-established separate misappropriation regime for trade secrets. TRIPS, however, expressly requires protection for 'undisclosed information' but nonetheless harks back to the unfair competition provision in the Paris Convention.[3] It does not mandate that approach, however.

This Chapter first examines the international treaty provisions, then sketches the principal approaches in the common law and civilian (continental) law in relation to trade secrets protection. The law of a number of specific jurisdictions is dealt with in more detail in the following chapters. In a comparative sense, this book focuses on the common law of England, including Australia, New Zealand and Canada as well (Chapter 4). The EU Trade Secrets Directive has now impacted the law in England but obviously not in those other jurisdictions. The book gives a separate account of the law

1. *See* above Chapter 2.
2. *Paris Convention for the Protection of Industrial Property*, signed 20 March 1883, Art. 10*bis*: (1) the countries of the Union are bound to assure to nationals of such countries effective protection against unfair competition, (2) any act of competition contrary to honest practices in industrial or commercial matters constitutes an act of unfair competition.
3. *See* WTO/TRIPS Art. 39.

in the US (Chapter 5). It then also examines the law in France (Chapter 7) and Germany (Chapter 8). Until the advent of the EU Trade Secrets Directive, these two jurisdictions were divergent examples of an unfair competition approach to the law, Germany based on explicit statutory provision and France on judicial interpretation of the broad standard of tortious or 'delictual' liability for fault. However, these two jurisdictions have now implemented the EU Trade Secrets Directive. They are dealt with in [Chapter].

§3.02 FROM PARIS TO TRIPS

[A] The Paris Convention: First Step Towards an International Standard

The first international norm relevant to the protection of trade secrets is the prohibition of unfair competition mandated by the Paris Convention, signed in 1883.

Article 10*bis(2)* stipulates that 'any act of competition contrary to honest practices in industrial or commercial matters constitutes an act of unfair competition', and by virtue of Article 10*bis(1)*, all member countries are bound to assure protection for their nationals against unfair competition. By virtue of subsection (3), various false, misleading, confusing and disruptive acts, indications or allegations are 'in particular' prohibited. Although misuse of trade secrets is not expressly mentioned and does not fall under the particular prohibitions, if, in a particular instance, it is considered to be contrary to honest practices in industry or commerce, it must be deemed unfair competition.

[B] Article 39 TRIPS: First Explicit International Obligation to Provide Legal Protection of Undisclosed Information

The first explicit treaty reference to trade secrets – albeit under the broader term *undisclosed information* – appears in section 7 of the TRIPS Agreement, which consists solely of Article 39. Hence this provision is the first in a multilateral agreement to require Member States to protect trade secrets and to provide a formal definition of the concept.[4] In this sense, Article 39 of TRIPS is often regarded as one of the 'most significant innovations brought about' by the agreement.[5] Accordingly:

> In the course of ensuring effective protection against unfair competition as provided in Article 10bis of the Paris Convention (1967), Members shall protect undisclosed information in accordance with paragraph 2 and data submitted to governments or governmental agencies in accordance with paragraph 3.

4. Daniel Gervais, *The TRIPS Agreement: Drafting History and Analysis* (Sweet & Maxwell, 2008) §2.335; Sharon Sandeen, 'The Limits of Trade Secret Law: Article 39 of the TRIPS Agreement and the Uniform Trade Secrets Act on which it is Based' in Rochelle Dreyfuss & Katherine Strandburg (eds), *The Law and Theory of Trade Secrecy* (Edward Elgar Publishing, 2011) 539, noting that trade secrets were first included in a bilateral agreement in the NAFTA in 1994.
5. Carlos M. Correa, *Trade-Related Aspects of Intellectual Property Rights: A Commentary on the TRIPS Agreement* (Oxford University Press, 1st ed., 2007) 366.

2. Natural and legal persons shall have the possibility of preventing information lawfully within their control from being disclosed to, acquired by, or used by others without their consent in a manner contrary to honest commercial practices (10) so long as such information:
   (a) is secret in the sense that it is not, as a body or in the precise configuration and assembly of its components, generally known among or readily accessible to persons within the circles that normally deal with the kind of information in question;
   (b) has commercial value because it is secret; and
   (c) has been subject to reasonable steps under the circumstances, by the person lawfully in control of the information, to keep it secret.
3. Members, when requiring, as a condition of approving the marketing of pharmaceutical or of agricultural chemical products which utilize new chemical entities, the submission of undisclosed test or other data, the origination of which involves a considerable effort, shall protect such data against unfair commercial use. In addition, Members shall protect such data against disclosure, except where necessary to protect the public, or unless steps are taken to ensure that the data are protected against unfair commercial use.

The detailed provisions of Article 39(3) which deal with data submitted to government for administrative or regulatory purposes are left aside here; the focus below is on the general protection provision of Article 39(1) and the more specific Article 39(2).

[C] TRIPS Negotiations: Tensions Concerning the Nature and Inclusion of Trade Secret Protection

The inclusion of trade secrets within the TRIPS Agreement was, from the outset of negotiations,[6] an explicit objective of the United States;[7] later supported by the European Communities.[8] However, developing countries initially opposed this inclusion, which is not surprising given that universal mandatory standards for trade secret protection did not align with their immediate national interests.

An analysis of the documents from the Negotiating Group in charge of negotiating the treaty reveals that discussions regarding trade secrets initially concentrated less on the substantive provisions and more on the upstream question of whether trade secrets should be part of the TRIPS negotiations at all.[9] There was a significant debate over whether trade secret protection qualified as an IP issue suitable for inclusion in TRIPS.

6. For a detailed investigation of this negotiation process, *see* Desaunettes-Barbero, *Trade Secrets Legal Protection* (Springer 2023), 72-84.
7. *See*, for instance, *Suggestion by the United States for Achieving the Negotiating Objective*, 20 October 1987, MTN.GNG/NG11/W/14, 8.
8. *Guidelines and Objectives Proposed by the European Community for the Negotiations on Trade-Related Aspects of Substantive Standards of Intellectual Property Rights*, 7 July1988, MTN.GNG/NG11/W/26, 10.
9. For a very informative description of the negotiations, *see* Peter Drahos & John Braithwaite, *Information Feudalism: Who Owns the Knowledge Economy?* (New York New Press, 2007), Chapters 7-9.

The negotiating mandate, as outlined in the 1986 Punta del Este Ministerial Declaration, referred only to the trade-related aspects of *IP* as part of the agenda.[10] Some developing nations opposed the inclusion, arguing that contracts, rather than IP laws, provided the appropriate protection framework for trade secrets. According to Pires de Carvalho, developing countries opposed the inclusion of trade secrets because they believed that their secretive nature conflicted with the objectives of IP law, which are to disseminate rather than conceal information. Proponents of inclusion countered this argument by highlighting Article 10bis of the Paris Convention, which, despite being part of an international agreement dedicated to IP, explicitly included provisions for effective protection against unfair competition.[11]

The late acceptance of trade secrets into the TRIPS Agreement by the developing countries – achieved as part of broader concessions in other WTO negotiation areas – had a paradoxical effect: it limited the influence of the latter over the substantive provisions of the agreement. Their sustained refusal to engage in detailed negotiations on trade secret standards left developed countries to dominate these discussions.[12]

As a result, the standards set by developed nations found their way into TRIPS almost uncontested. Among these, a draft proposal named the *Basic Framework*, prepared by representatives of industry groups from developed countries, heavily influenced the final text.[13] The proposal relied on the US model of trade secret protection as synthesized in the UTSA. The UTSA's broad and flexible definition of trade secrets gained traction because it accommodated a range of legal systems. Hence, according to negotiation reports, most delegations did not raise significant objections to the US proposal. Many even acknowledged that, while their laws lacked explicit trade secret definitions, the substance of US law aligned with existing protections in their jurisdictions.[14] This broad acceptance facilitated the adoption of the UTSA's standards into TRIPS.

[D] TRIPS Approach to Trade Secret Protection

The tension during the TRIPS negotiations regarding the nature of trade secret protection is evident in the final text of the Agreement. On the one hand, the title of the Agreement refers exclusively to *IPRs*, and section 7, addressing the protection of

10. *Ministerial Declaration on the Uruguay Round*, 20 September1986, MIN.DEC.
11. *See*, for instance, the US position reported in *Meeting of Negotiating Group of 30 October-2 November 1989 – Note by the Secretariat*, 4 December 1989, MTN.GNG/NG11/16, §61.
12. Speaking from 'strategic mistake', *see* Nuno Pires de Carvalho, *The TRIPS Regime of Antitrust and Undisclosed Information* (Kluwer Law International, 2008) 221-224.
13. Basic Framework of GATT Provisions on Intellectual Property – Statement of Views of the European, Japanese and United States Business Communities, 1988 in Friedrich-Karl Beier et al. (eds), 'GATT or WIPO?: New Ways in the International Protection of Intellectual Property' (1989) 11 *International Protection of Intellectual Property* 333, 394-6 https://doi.org/10.1016/0267-3649(91)90147-n.
14. *Note on Informal Meeting on Intellectual Property Standards*, n°9783527279449, 17-11 March 1988, in Friedrich-Karl Beier et al. (eds), 'GATT or WIPO?: New Ways in the International Protection of Intellectual Property' (1989) 11 *International Protection of Intellectual Property* 333, 346 https://doi.org/10.1016/0267-3649(91)90147-n.

undisclosed information, is situated within Part II, which is dedicated to 'standards concerning the availability, scope, and use of Intellectual Property Rights'. Furthermore, the preamble of the Agreement explicitly acknowledges 'that intellectual property rights are private rights'. This placement and language seem to underscore an intent to align trade secrets with IP. Yet the text of Article 39 links directly to the Paris Convention and thus unfair competition: members shall protect undisclosed information 'in the course of ensuring effective protection against unfair competition as provided for in Article 10*bis* of the Paris Convention (1967)'.[15] As indicated above, Article 10*bis(2)* of the Paris Convention defines unfair competition as '[a]ny act of competition contrary to honest practices in industrial or commercial matters'.[16] It is likely that this approach is in fact favoured by TRIPS, even if the latter is ultimately very open about the form that the protection should take on the national level.

Regarding the unfair competition standard outlined in the Paris Convention, to which Article 39 of TRIPS refers, Pires de Carvalho argues that this standard involves bad faith or fraudulent intent rather than mere negligence. He notes: '*It is important to note that a majority of delegations at The Hague were adamant that only bad faith could make an act become contrary to honest practices in commerce.*'[17] Pires de Carvalho thus asserts that member countries are free to implement or not measures against *unlawful* competition, whereas they are *compelled* to provide measures against *unfair* (i.e., intentionally dishonest) competition.[18]

Be that as it may, Article 10*bis(3)* then goes on to list some acts of unfair competition which 'in particular shall be prohibited', i.e., a non-exhaustive or exemplary list which does not include misuse of trade secrets.[19] Pires de Carvalho maintains that whatever uncertainty may have resulted from the absence in the list in Article 10*bis(3)* of any reference to trade secrets misuse concerning whether the Paris Convention required domestic protection of trade secrets, 'Union Members were obliged to protect trade secrets whenever their (mis)appropriation by others would

15. The reference is to the 1967 revision of the *Paris Convention*, Stockholm, 14 July 1967.
16. According to Pires de Carvalho, this formulation ignored a 'subtle distinction', 'long well established in European doctrine' between unlawful and unfair competition. Above n 4, [39.1.16, 39.1.18]. The former judges the act of competition by reference to a standard of carelessness or negligence, whereas the latter requires an element of intention: the aim at diverting 'others' clientele with the recourse to fraudulent means.' Above n 4, [19.1.16).
17. Above n 4, [39.1.35]. Pires de Carvalho recounts that the German delegation at the Hague Conference (Hague revision of the *Paris Convention*, 1925) proposed that countries should also undertake to adopt criminal measures in cases of fraudulent practices. Such measures would be potentially relevant to unfair competition but not to unlawful competition which lacks the necessary element of 'fraudulent intent'. *See also* above n 4, [39.1.15].
18. Pires de Carvalho makes a distinction between parasitisme, which he says does not necessarily [involve] dishonesty, and unfair commercial practices which do. Parasitisme for him means taking advantage of the investments of another party, but not necessarily dishonestly. *See* above n 4, [39.1.33].
19. Pires de Carvalho suggests that the notion of trade secrets was 'implied' by this proposal of the French Delegation at the 1925 Conference. Above n 4, [39.1.34]. In fact, Pires de Carvalho points out that there is only one express reference to be found in the records of six Diplomatic Conferences following the 1880 Paris Conference, and one indirect reference, which interestingly concerned inducement of breach of contract by an employee being characterized as an act of unfair competition.

involve dishonest acts.'[20] Enforcement was left open so that member countries could choose civil or criminal measures or both.[21]

The crux of the matter is that Article 39.1 eliminated whatever uncertainty there might have been about the reach of Article 10bis of the Paris Convention in relation to misuse of trade secrets.[22] Importantly, Article 39.1 also established that protection of undisclosed information was not something new introduced for the first time in TRIPS.[23] The explicit reference to 'honest practices in commercial and industrial matters' provided a more uniform standard and consequently scope. However, this is somewhat problematic as what is considered the prevailing standard of commercial honesty may vary considerably between jurisdictions. Ladas suggests the standard is objective: the honest practices within a certain community at a certain time can be forensically ascertained.[24] Local variations will, therefore, make it difficult to attempt to formulate a uniform international standard establishing what 'honest practice' is.[25] In this regard, the example of the European framework is particularly instructive. Despite the fact that all EU Member States claimed their legal systems were compliant with Article 39 of TRIPS, the significant divergences among them were so pronounced that they prompted the European legislator to intervene, leading to the enactment of the EU Trade Secrets Directive.

There was concern in TRIPS to accommodate the fact that member jurisdictions had well-established but varied ways of dealing with trade secrets. Thus, the EC proposed the term 'undisclosed information' instead of 'trade secret', although seemingly a small difference was, in fact, important 'because some participants believed that a mere reference to the term "trade secrets" might imply the acknowledgement of proprietary or exclusive rights, which are not generally accepted in civil law countries'.[26] Another reason advanced for the reliance on this terminology was to distance the TRIPS agreement from the US system. And such a distancing may have been considered necessary because of the proposed definition of a trade secret in paragraph 2, which is directly inspired by the UTSA. The intention was not to prejudge 'the type of protection to be afforded, nor the type of legal instrument'.[27] This desire not to impose any particular approach is also reflected in the very loose language of the article, which refers to Members giving 'the possibility of preventing information

20. *See* above n 4, [39.1.43].
21. Pires de Carvalho points out that in many countries 'acts of industrial espionage and of bribery of competitors' employees' are sanctioned by criminal law. Above n 4, [39.1.51].
22. In this sense, he considers that 'the first sentence of Article 39.1 establishes *[sic]* an operative and declaratory interpretation of Article 10bis that is binding for WTO members'. Above n 4, [39.1.43].
23. Pires de Carvalho says that the purpose of Art. 39.1 is to make clear that TRIPS is not new and additional to the Paris Convention. In this way, Art. 39.1 goes beyond Art. 2.1. Above n 4, [39.1.50].
24. *See* the reference in Chapter 1 to this being a so-called jury question.
25. *See* S. Ladas, *Patents, Trademarks, and Related Rights. National and International Protection*, Vol. III (Cambridge 1975), 1685-1686, 1689, as quoted in UNCTAD, Resource Book on TRIPS and Development, at p. 528, available at https://unctad.org/system/files/official-document/ictsd2005d1_en.pdf.
26. Above n 4, [39.2.22].
27. EC clarification of the proposal, quoted by Pires de Carvalho. Above n 4, [39.2.22].

lawfully within their control from being disclosed', so that both statutory and case law-based approaches would meet the requirement. No new legislation would thus be required unless perhaps in countries where there was no pre-existing law that could be applied to trade secrets.[28] The decision to use the term 'undisclosed information' was primarily a political compromise due to its neutral connotation rather than a result of debates on the term's precision. As Daniel Gervais points out, this terminology could be considered misleading, as 'if no one has disclosed it to anyone, it could not be used at all'.[29]

Pires de Carvalho points out that the TRIPS language is very broad also in the sense that the term 'information' is used with little restriction other than that 'rights in trade secrets must be enforced in an economic environment'.[30] The information, although it must have value derived from its limited circulation, can but need not be the result of study and investment – it can result from chance discovery or be an isolated fact or piece of data. Although some value must result, the context need not be one of trade.[31] He also points to the use of the word 'control' rather than any reference to property or proprietary rights in the text, which emphasizes possession, and 'it follows that the idea of control is closely associated with the notion of measures taken to keep the information secret'.[32] Because the rights are listed according to the normal chronological order of events, as Pires de Carvalho says, being against disclosure, acquisition and use, the injunction is the key legal measure, whereas value is reduced when another uses the trade secret without authorization; it is destroyed if it is publicly disclosed.[33]

The 'honest commercial practices' of Article 39(2) are further explained in footnote 10 of the Article.[34] The footnote clarifies this as:

> at least practices such as breach of contract, breach of confidence and inducement to breach, and includes the acquisition of undisclosed information by third parties who knew, or were grossly negligent in failing to know, that such practices were involved in the acquisition.

Acquisition is perhaps best understood here in terms of turning the information to one's own account or advantage; in English law, if the information was communicated between parties for a specific purpose and the recipient uses it for a different (unauthorized) purpose, there is *ipso facto* infringement. Strictly speaking, there is no wrong in the acquisition but only in the use of the information in such a case. If the information is secret but is obtained by a third party to whom it was not *deliberately imparted* for any purpose, then only if either illegal or unconscionable means are used to obtain it will liability follow. Perhaps the difference is not great because, in the US,

28. Above n 4, [39.2.35].
29. *Ibid.*
30. Above n 4, [39.2.37].
31. For example, it might be, as Pires de Carvalho points out, in the context of gathering donations for a cause. Above n 4, [39.2.37].
32. Above n 4, [39.2.38].
33. *Ibid.*, [39.2.40].
34. But the first requirement is absence of consent.

communication in breach of an obligation of confidence is seen as one category of wrong that potentially gives rise to liability.

Pires de Carvalho sees the three options of breach of contract, of confidence, and inducement to breach as breaches of an obligation of trust.[35] He stresses that the defendant must know that an obligation exists before duties can be imposed.[36]

Although Germany proposed the current text referring to acts contrary to honest commercial practices,[37] Article 39(2)(a-c) heavily relies on the US framework, reflecting the preparatory work undertaken by industry representatives in the *basic framework* previously mentioned. Accordingly, the relevant subsections provide that information is protected as long as such information:

(a) is secret in the sense that it is not, as a body or in the precise configuration and assembly of its components, generally known among or readily accessible to persons within the circles that normally deal with the kind of information in question;
(b) has commercial value because it is secret; and
(c) has been subject to reasonable steps under the circumstances, by the person lawfully in control of the information, to keep it secret.

Article 39 closely mirrors US law in these aspects, with only minor variations. First, regarding the requirement for the piece of information to be secret, the definition provided in Article 39 adopts the relative standard that previously existed in US law. The relative nature of the secrecy standard is today obviously a fairly universal standard: it is well established in domestic laws considered in this book, and it also appears in the definition in TRIPS: absolute secrecy is not a requirement. The standard is quite different from the patent standard of novelty: any publication anywhere, whether or not it is actually or would be accessed by the relevant circles within the country of consideration, is sufficient to constitute anticipation there. In other words, the fact that nobody or only the most exceptionally inquisitive person would find the publication is of no consequence for patent law: that publication constitutes anticipation in the patent law sense. In relation to trade secrets, only publications that the relevant circles in industry within the relevant jurisdiction could normally be expected to ascertain or know about can mean that information is in the public domain.

Regarding the divergences between the TRIPS and the UTSA definition, the major deviation lies in the condition of the secret's 'economic value'. Three key changes can be observed in the evolution from the UTSA to TRIPS: first, the adoption of a three-step requirement structure, formally separating the commercial value from the secrecy requirement; second, the substitution of the term 'economic' with 'commercial' to describe the value; and third, the removal of the specification that the value could also

35. The focus seems to be on dishonesty in the means of obtaining the confidential information rather than just their use. Pires de Carvalho says that in terms of Art. 39, it is for this reason that reverse engineering is acceptable: *see* [39.1.49]. He says the focus is not on the information but on the means and gives as examples: 'Stealing, espionage, inducing disclosure by persons bound to secrecy etc.' (*Ibid.*).
36. *See* Pires de Carvalho, above n 12, [39.2.45].
37. *Ibid.*, [39.1.12].

be 'potential'.[38] First, the 'commercial value' is presented as the second requirement, which is distinct and, at least formally, autonomous from the secrecy requirement, thus ostensibly necessitating an independent assessment. However, the potential implications of this structural separation are immediately diluted. The text specifies that the information 'has commercial value because it is secret', thereby re-establishing the causal link between the first and second requirements. Second, replacing the adjective 'economic' with 'commercial' could suggest a narrower scope, as it may imply that information only has 'commercial' value if it is actively used in commerce. Similarly, removing the reference to 'potential' value appears to limit protection to information that currently possesses actual value. However, there is little documentation regarding the debates within the negotiating group on these changes, making it difficult to construct a robust historical narrative about this evolution. Interestingly, this definition – despite the uncertainty surrounding it – has been highly influential. It was later incorporated into the provisions of the EU Trade Secrets Directive and subsequently into the trade secret laws of the EU Member States.

Article 39 expressly extends liability to third parties who knew or were grossly negligent as to the fact that unfair practices were involved in the acquisition of the trade secrets.[39] This may be one of the most important facets of the international regime and is more or less reflected in domestic laws. Third-party liability would not lie under contract because of privity; therefore, this is one situation in which the general law of trade secrets has a real role to play.

[E] Treaty Standards, Domestic Implementation and Transborder Trade

Pires de Carvalho's statement that the intent of TRIPS was not to displace existing protection regimes is manifest in its provisions. They accommodate the American UTSA and English common law positions, as well as the inclusion of trade secrets protection within unfair competition, which is so typical of the civilian approach. They do not mandate a property or misappropriation approach, thus assuaging the concerns of some developing countries referred to above.[40] However, some aspects are not found in domestic laws. For instance, in English law, the action for breach of confidence does not require that the information have commercial value, since it also accommodates private and personal secrets. This is not problematical as the English tradition in many ways goes *further* in its protection, setting a lower threshold: in English law, there is also no requirement of impropriety, since use of a trade secret in a manner not in accordance with the authority of the confidor can suffice to vest liability. Nor is it necessary to establish fraudulent intent or even a knowing breach *simpliciter*: in the English common law, a person may be liable for unintentional and subconscious

38. For a detailed analysis of the negotiation process and the potential implication from an interpretation perspective, *see* above n 6, 77.
39. The text of Art. 39.2 is replicated above.
40. As already indicated, the same cannot be said in relation to Art. 39(3), the special provisions concerning confidential regulatory data supplied to governments. There a more quasi-property regime is created.

misuse of a trade secret.[41] The suspicion that English (and thus Australian and other related) laws do not meet the requirements of TRIPS appears to be without foundation.[42] German law before EU Trade Secrets Directive implementation also did not require that the plaintiff establish that the information concerned has commercial value, although it had to be relevant to competition, and the owner had to have the intent to and an interest in maintaining secrecy.

The TRIPS provisions, although controversial in the eyes of some developing nations, therefore, did not intend to harmonize the details of the law or increase levels of protection already found in industrialized nations. In any case, the lack of harmony they reflect exists also within the civilian and common law families of law, as is illustrated below. However, within significant regional trade blocks (EU, United States-Mexico-Canada Agreement (USMCA), Comprehensive and Progressive Agreement for Trans-Pacific Partnership (CPTPP)), harmonization of trade secrets law is now further advanced. Most striking is that European institutions decided to turn their attention towards trade secrets law as a potential target for harmonization of equal significance with other areas of IP.[43]

This in fact recognizes that trade secrets protection is one of the most significant issues in transborder trade, multinational investment and collaboration.[44] It is particularly relevant to corporate dealings with personnel and movement of the latter between countries. It appears that commercial actors have mostly dealt with matters of confidentiality and trade secrets through contract. In the employment context, this included non-compete agreements, and in the general commercial context, it includes NDAs.[45] It is striking that for a long time, there were more frequent calls for the reform of domestic trade secrets law than for greater harmonization efforts at the international level. Partly, this was due to the very disparate nature of the legal approaches to trade secrets across the globe. However, the recent international efforts described above seem to coalesce around mostly American approaches to trade secrets protection. Be that as it may, the next part of this work gives an initial overview of some of the traditional differences in approach to trade secrets law, which are then further detailed in the subsequent chapters.

---

41. *See* William R. Cornish, 'Confidence in Ideas' (1990) 1 *Australian Intellectual Property Journal* 3.
42. John E. Giust, 'Noncompliance with TRIPS by Developed and Developing Countries: Is TRIPS Working?' (1997) 8 *Indiana International Law and Comparative Law Review* 69 https://doi.org/10.18060/17805. Answers by member countries to TRIPS questionnaires confirm this picture.
43. *See* Hogan Lovells International LLP, 13 January 2012 'Report on Trade Secrets for the European Commission' (Study on Trade Secrets and Parasitic Copying (Look-alikes)). http://ec.europa.eu/internal_market/iprenforcement/docs/trade/Study_Trade_Secrets_en.pdf. This link is no longer active but the authors hold a copy of the document concerned.
44. Lydia Lundstedt, *Cross-Border Trade Secret Disputes in the European Union: Jurisdiction and Applicable Law Elgar Monographs in Private International Law* (Edward Elgar Publishing, 1st ed., 2023).
45. Such agreements may be aimed more at protecting personal or private data than commercial information.

§3.03 OTHER INTERNATIONAL PROVISIONS INCLUDING THE EU TRADE SECRETS DIRECTIVE

[A] Free Trade Agreements Incorporating an Obligation to Protect Trade Secrets

Other than TRIPS and the Paris Convention, there are few international provisions regulating trade secrets law in terms that travel beyond the requirements of TRIPS. North America Free Trade Agreement (NAFTA) had a provision that is almost identical to TRIPS Article 39, although it allowed for potential as well as actual commercial value and prohibited certain impediments on licensing trade secrets.[46] However, the United States, Mexico, and Canada reached an agreement to 'modernize' the NAFTA with a new USMCA, which entered into force on 1 July 2020 and in fact supplanted the NAFTA. The USMCA contains more detailed provisions concerning trade secrets than before. It similarly requires parties to ensure that persons within their jurisdictions have the legal means to prevent trade secrets lawfully in their control from being disclosed to, acquired by, or used by others (including state-owned enterprises) without their consent in a manner contrary to honest commercial practices but additionally provides that state parties must provide for judicial redress for misappropriations. As did NAFTA, the USMCA prohibits state parties from limiting the duration of trade secrets protection when conditions for the latter remain present. These conditions are the standard ones found in US law, as is the prescribed meaning of the term 'misappropriation', which is defined in USMCA but was not in NAFTA.

The USMCA treaty text also contains additional express provisions relating to criminal liability for trade secret theft, including by state-owned enterprises. It is expressly provided that reverse engineering and independent invention of a technical trade secret must be allowed.[47] The USMCA also provides that in civil, criminal, and regulatory proceedings in which trade secrets may be submitted to a court or government entity, each state party must prohibit the unauthorized disclosure of a trade secret by a government official at the central level of government outside the scope of that person's official duties, in relation to which the state party must provide for deterrent penalties.[48]

The CPTPP: negotiations for which were initiated by the US in the form of the Trans-Pacific Partnership, but to which the US did not become a signatory)[49] also contains provisions concerning criminal liability relating to trade secrets. The criminal

46. *North American Free Trade Agreement*, Art. 1711 'Trade Secrets'.
47. *See* USMCA Art. 20.69-20.77.
48. *See* USMCA Art. 20.77.
49. *See* Australian Government, 'Comprehensive and Progressive Agreement for Trans-Pacific Partnership (CPTPP)' *Department of Foreign Affairs and Trade* (online) https://www.dfat.gov.au/trade/agreements/in-force/cptpp/comprehensive-and-progressive-agreement-for-trans-pacific-partnership. Note that despite its name, CPTPP membership is not restricted to pacific nations: on 16 July 2023, Ministers responsible for trade from CPTPP Parties and the UK signed the UK's Accession Protocol to enable the UK to join the CPTPP. The United States is not a Member State of the CPTPP.

liability obligations in the CPTPP are limited to providing criminal sanctions for wilful or fraudulent access, misappropriation or disclosure of trade secrets, and Member States can limit liability to certain categories of cases. This includes acts that are for the purposes of commercial advantage or financial gain; acts related to a product or service in national or international commerce; acts that are intended to injure the owner of such trade secret; acts that are directed by or for the benefit of or in association with a foreign economic entity; or acts that are detrimental to a Party's economic interests, international relations, or national defence or national security.[50] Generally speaking, therefore, these two treaties have strengthened the requirements for trade secrets protection imposed on their Member States; these states are Canada, the US and Mexico for the USMCA; and Australia, Brunei, Canada, Chile, Japan, Malaysia, Mexico, New Zealand, Peru, Singapore, and Vietnam for the CPTPP. As mentioned above, the UK will join the agreement when it has been ratified by all parties or after 15 months from 16 July 2023 if the UK and a majority of CPTPP parties have ratified it. Altogether this amounts to a very substantial number of countries that are obliged to provide criminal liability for trade secrets theft. By contrast, the EU Trade Secrets Directive does not address criminal liability, which remains a matter for Member States.

Mercosur has not adopted any common standards, and customarily bilateral and Free Trade Agreements (FTAs) tend to reiterate the TRIPS obligations and additionally refer to the particular rules applying to regulatory data, without more detail about trade secrets protection generally; this is, for instance, the case in the US-Australia FTA.[51]

[B] The European Trade Secret Directive

For a long time, despite all the international concern and activity about IP and development, little attention was devoted to undisclosed information. In part, this is because developing countries regarded trade secrets with suspicion as an additional barrier to the transfer of useful knowledge and information. The only sphere of international action related to test and regulatory data confidentiality, a matter we do not further address here. Nonetheless, trade secrets protection is one of the most significant impediments to the transfer of knowledge and know-how and thus to international trade and integration. More recently, this has led the EU to take action to harmonize trade secrets law, at least in relation to civil liability.[52] The classification of this directive as a text of international law is undoubtedly open to debate. Indeed, any European lawyer would likely reject such a classification – and rightly so – due to the

50. Article 18.78 of the CPTPP.
51. Regulatory data protection is dealt with in Art. 39.3 of TRIPS. In the AUSFTA, *see* Art. 17.10. *See also e.g.*, CAFTA Art. 15.10; United States-Jordan FTA Art. 4(22); United States-Bahrain FTA Art. 14.9.
52. European Commission, Report, European Commission Conference of 29 June 2013, 'Trade Secrets: Supporting Innovation, Protecting Know-How' 2, 15; Directive (EU) 2016/943 of the European Parliament and of the Council of 8 June 2016 on the Protection of Undisclosed Know-how and Business Information (Trade Secrets) Against Their Unlawful Acquisition, Use and Disclosure [2016] OJ L 157/1.

unique nature of European law. However, it remains that this legislation is a 'supra-national' instrument designed to harmonize national laws. From this perspective, the directive, which will be examined in depth in Chapter 6 of this book, is noteworthy for several reasons.

First, its necessity in the European context highlights the ultimately limited impact of TRIPS in terms of unifying the law. Second, it is striking that the definition of trade secrets in Article 39 - despite its imperfections and its roots in numerous compromises whose details are particularly difficult to unravel - was fully adopted in the European text. Thus, while Article 39 itself had limited direct influence on legal harmonization within the EU, the European legislator chose to grant it unexpected significance. Today, almost all EU Member States have enacted legislation effectively mirroring the TRIPS definition. Furthermore, we will establish that this definition's origins in US law led European legislator to adopt several solutions inspired by American legal principles.

§3.04 SYSTEMIC DIFFERENCES

[A] Remaining Relevance of Common Law Versus Civil Law Distinctions?

Although the potential impact was perhaps significant in developing countries, in jurisdictions with an established domestic law of trade secrets, TRIPS was not intended to have much effect.[53] The core law of trade secrets, diverse before TRIPS, remained so after its adoption. This is true not only in relation to the central principles of trade secrets law but also in relation to important contiguous areas of law, such as the complex rules that apply in the immediate post-termination phase of an employment relationship. Labour law, contract law, including the law relating to the validity of non-compete clauses ('non-competes'), and general civil liability played a role in determining the competing rights and obligations of employees and employers at that time.

Some of the differences between domestic laws of WTO member countries are doctrinal and, hence, systemic. By this we mean that the doctrinal characteristics of trade secrets law are in part inherent but in part also the consequence of the broader 'system' of wrongs and remedies in a given jurisdiction. Historically, trade secrets law fell within the equitable jurisdiction in the English system, whereas in the civilian tradition, it was an actionable wrong, attracting liability for fault either generally, as unfair competition or as a statutory tort. The civilian tradition is one of codification and entrenched basic rights, whereas the common law tradition is not. We dwell on some of these issues below, but in large part, they emerge from our treatment of the law in various jurisdictions in the following chapters.

The importance of the civilian versus common law distinction might be diminishing, and it is also the case that the substantive tests developed in jurisdictions that

53. This is leaving aside the provisions relating to regulatory data.

fall within different families are remarkably similar, but nonetheless, many jurisdictions retain characteristics typical of one or the other approach, apart from those considered in more detail in subsequent chapters, in China, for instance [more detail, unfair competition approach] and in India [more detail, equitable doctrine].

Immediately below, we focus on some of the more significant contextual or systemic differences.

[B] Fundamental Rights

An important contextual difference between the English common law tradition and others lies in the structure of fundamental rights. Historically, and in England and some Commonwealth jurisdictions to this day, no entrenched constitutional protection for basic civil and political rights exists.[54] As a result, the right to free speech and press freedom to report, rights that are significant in the present context, do not trump ordinary law, whether statute or case-derived, including the law of trade secrets (breach of confidence). England has no single constitutional enactment and no Bill of Rights in the modern sense. In Australia at Federation, the Constitution of the Commonwealth did not include a Bill of Rights or systematic enumeration of basic rights and freedoms against which ordinary laws were to be measured. Subsequently, the High Court of Australia has found an implicit freedom of political discussion, but no generalized freedom of speech or of the Press has as yet been held to be constitutionally guaranteed. In England, the constitutional structure has only changed with the adoption of the ECHR and the jurisprudence of the European Court of Human Rights. In some jurisdictions with an English legal heritage, fundamental rights protection has now been entrenched, for instance, by way of the Bill of Rights in Canada, but in others, such as Australia and New Zealand, the situation remains that human rights are still only protected by unentrenched legislation. The civilian jurisdictions considered here have well-established and entrenched constitutional protection of basic rights, as well as the applicable ECHR standards.

Freedom of expression and of the press, or of 'information' in particular, is relevant to trade secrets law because it impacts the structure and inherent equilibrium of that law. In particular, freedom of the press to report certain information, although it is confidential or secret, may counterbalance the desire of its possessor to keep it from prying eyes even though the public interest would be served by exposure. In most jurisdictions, this balance is partly addressed by limiting remedies to information that has commercial value or where the alleged misuse occurs with a commercial or competitive intent. Where information is of a personal, private or purely public interest nature, the civil law of trade secrets does then not come to the possessor's aid. This is naturally the case in jurisdictions where the civil remedy lies in unfair competition law: only if the third party unfairly uses information in competition with the legitimate

54. At least until recently, however, the ECHR now has a considerable impact; *see also*: Charter of Fundamental Rights' *BCC News* (online), 16 July 2007 http://news.bbc.co.uk/2/hi/europe/6225580.stm.

possessor will a remedy normally lie.[55] It is also the case where trade secret claims are governed by statute, now including in all EU Member States. Naturally, there may be issues as to where the private finishes and the commercial starts.[56]

In the US as well, a distinct regime of protection against misappropriation of *commercial* secrets has a similar limiting effect. By contrast, the English tradition is characteristically unitary - both commercial and personal information are protected by the same action for breach of confidence lying in equity. This means that exceptions to the right of the possessor of a secret to keep it so by resort to the law of confidence must come from within that law itself - in particular from the application of the test itself (would a reasonable person in receipt of the information in the particular circumstances of the case consider himself duty bound not to reveal the information) and from the application of the so-called iniquity or broader public interest defence.[57] The latter gives the recipient of hitherto secret information concerning iniquity (e.g., criminal activity, activity endangering life and limb) the right to disclose it and others the right to publicize it in certain circumstances and in certain ways. In the US and other jurisdictions, additionally to any defence forming part of trade secrets itself, the general right to freedom of speech, of information or of the press may be called in aid by a defendant in certain cases.

Another important fundamental right comes into play in this context: the right to privacy and the concomitant tortious action for invasion of privacy. In the English tradition, this right is not recognized at the fundamental constitutional or human rights level - as no rights are - and its invasion is also traditionally not recognized as a tort. This is again in contrast with the European and American traditions, the former finding expression at the constitutional level in the European Convention's privacy protection,[58] but also nationally. This means that in the English tradition, the clash between the rights of the individual to control dispersion of information about private life and the right of the press to report on matters[59] is mediated through the elements of the action for breach of confidence. By contrast, in the US and continental civilian tradition, it might rather be mediated through the right to privacy or tort for invasion

55. *See* below Chapter 6concerning French law where it will become apparent that a tort of *agissements parasitaires* may be established even where no direct commercial rivalry exists between the parties concerned.
56. This was, for instance, an important issue in the *Douglas* case - was the couple's interest commercial (an exclusive deal with a magazine to cover the wedding) or private (their right to conduct their wedding in private if they so wished).
57. *See* Denning LJ in *Initial Services Ltd v. Putterill* [1968] 1 QB 396 - where the public interest defence was said to extend to 'crimes, frauds, and misdeeds'. *See also Fraser v. Evans* [1969] 1 QB 349, where there was no breach of confidence since the report was of such public concern; *Hubbard v. Vosper* [1972] 2 QB 84 (a public interest defence); *Woodward v. Hutchins* [1977] 2 All ER 751; and *Gartside v. Outram* (1856) 26 LJ Ch 113 ('there is no confidence in iniquity').
58. The *European Convention on Human Rights and Fundamental Freedoms* (ECHR), opened for signature 4 November 1950, 213 UNTS 221 (entered into force 3 September 1953), as amended by *Protocol No 15 to the Convention for the Protection of Human Rights and Fundamental Freedoms*, opened for signature 24 June 2013, CETS No 005 (not yet in force), Art. 8. *See also Axel Springer v. Germany* [2012] ECHR 227; *Von Hannover v. Germany (No 2)* [2012] ECHR 228; *Mosley v. News Group Newspapers* [2008] ECHR 177; *Civil Code (France)* Art. 9.
59. *See, e.g., Mosley v. News Group Newspapers* [2008] EWHC 1777 (QB).

of privacy on the one hand and the constitutional rights of a free press or freedom of speech on the other. At any rate, in civilian jurisdictions and the US, private information is subject to a separate legal regime, whereas that is not the case in the English law tradition.

This is a significant structural difference. However, the law regarding privacy in England is evolving (arguably more than it is in countries such as Australia). In particular, not only the *Douglas* and *Campbell* cases but also more recent decisions[60] have seen a relaxation of the traditional strictures imposed on the action for breach of confidence to accommodate the privacy interest. The law has evolved so as to relax and find circumstances that give rise to a relationship of good faith or conscience before any remedy in equity can be granted. By contrast, in Australia, the High Court has insisted on the law of confidence being restricted to the four corners of its recognized elements.[61] In New Zealand, the courts have newly recognized the existence of a tort of invasion of privacy.[62] These matters are examined further below in Chapter 4 on the common law jurisdictions.

A final point about the constitutional rights context relates specifically to the post-employment situation. At that moment, the rights of the employees to use legitimately acquired knowledge to advance themselves clash with the rights of the employer to protect critical assets of a business. This clash is in the English tradition determined by way of the imposition on public policy grounds of restrictions on the freedom of contract and on a fine distinction between real trade secrets of the employer and the employee's know-how which is free. However, in civilian jurisdictions, fundamental rights that are constitutionally guaranteed come into play: the right to self-advancement, the freedom to work, the right to carry on a business, the freedom of enterprise, etc., which are reflected in constitutional clauses to varying degrees. The courts are required to weigh up these fundamental constitutional rights and guarantees. These matters are further explored in the following chapters.

[C] Law and Equity

As well as the fundamentally different constitutional background, a further important distinction lies in the dividing line between equity and law in the English common law tradition. In many ways, that distinction has become less significant in practice, with the abolition of separate courts applying law and equity; the greatly increased flexibility concerning remedies;[63] and the development of theories with a more unifying tendency such as unjust enrichment.[64] Nonetheless, it remains significant that

60. *See* Tanya Aplin, 'The Future of Breach of Confidence and the Protection of Privacy' (2007) 7(2) *Oxford University Commonwealth Law Journal* 137 https://doi.org/10.1080/14729342.2007.11421481.
61. *Australian Broadcasting Corp v. Lenah Game Meats Pty Ltd* (2001) 208 CLR 199, 230 [55].
62. *See* Katrine Evans, 'Hosking v Runting Balancing Rights in a Privacy Tort' (2004) 11(2) *Privacy Law and Policy Reporter* 34.
63. In particular, pecuniary remedies such as equitable damages becoming available in equity.
64. *See* Peter Birks, 'The English Recognition of Unjust Enrichment' (1991) *Lloyds Maritime and Commercial Law Quarterly* 473.

equitable remedies are discretionary in nature and not granted as of right as they are at law when a wrong has been established. This is particularly significant in relation to breach of confidence, as the primary remedy in equity, the injunction, is also the most critical in the *ad interim* stage of litigation in trade secrets matters. Once the secret has entered the public domain, it is utterly destroyed in a legal sense, and compensation will by definition almost always be partial. Anything that affects the applicant's right to the remedy, either at the interlocutory or the trial stage, is thus of considerable significance.

Whereas the court in a country with an equity jurisdiction, such as England, Australia or New Zealand, may take into account the established discretionary factors such as laches and delay, unclean hands, and the applicant's own actions and position, a court granting a statutory or tortious remedy may have less freedom of decision-making. The remedy may be available 'as of right': to what extent that is in reality the case forms an interesting topic of comparative study that cannot be undertaken here. However, in most jurisdictions, applications concerning trade secrets are heard at the interim or interlocutory stage, so that the tests tend to revolve around appreciation of the strength of the applicant's case and the balance of convenience - i.e., the practical implications and potential harm associated with granting or denying a restraint on the use of communication of information before trial. Therefore, from a comparative perspective, the factors taken into account and the conditions imposed on interim injunctions may be as significant in practice as the substantive elements of the various actions relating to trade secrets.

[D] Cases, Statutes and the Role of the Courts

A further contextual difference that is trite in terms of traditional comparative law but nonetheless relevant in this particular context is between case law and statute as sources of the relevant law. The civilian tradition is that all law is ultimately based on statutory provisions - on Acts of Parliament. In the common law, at least some law is exclusively based on the jurisprudence of the courts. In relation to trade secrets, this relevantly includes equity in the English tradition; in the US, the law of trade secrets was, until quite recently, also based exclusively on the cases. However, now it is mostly based on state statutes modelled on the UTSA; although in the American way, there is of course a mass of not necessarily consistent case law as well. Any lawyer must contend with differences between the law in different states, and thus with conflict of law and contract issues. At the Federal level, the US now also has a statutory basis for trade secrets protection, the *Economic Espionage Act* 18 USC §1831 (1996).

In the civilian tradition, there is no law without a statutory basis - or so it seems. In Germany, the law until recently was based on a statute dealing with unfair competition, which in a typical civilian way contains reasonably detailed provisions concerning trade secrets. However, the civil liability rules relating to trade secrets were elaborated by the courts on the basis of a few very general provisions in the *Law on*

Unfair Competition (UWG) and the *Civil Code* (BGB).[65] In France, although the relevant law is based on two short provisions of the *Civil Code*, in reality, it was almost exclusively derived from the courts' jurisprudence to the extent that the courts sometimes omit to mention the theoretical statutory basis in the Civil *Code*. This was relatively problematical, but the scholarly writings come to the aid of the person wanting to understand and predict the law through so-called *chroniques* and the like.[66] However, France also has one narrow penal provision concerning *secrets de fabrique*.[67] This provision still exists post-EU Trade Secrets Directive because that Directive left the criminal law untouched.

Thus, where traditionally, the civil law jurisdictions are said to be codified and statute-based, and the common law countries case-based, the reality is that much of the trade secrets law in the civilian jurisdictions we consider here was also based on the cases. It remains to be seen what the effect of the almost uniform legislation now introduced in Germany and France (as instructive exemplars) will be. The provisions in the relevant statutes are relatively broad, so the role of the courts will be considerable. Will the courts derive much guidance from the pre-existing law and what will the ECJ's position be? These matters are further discussed in [Chapter 6] below. There seems little doubt that the influence of the courts will remain very significant, perhaps even more so than under some previous enactments. This will be the case as well in the UK, where the piecemeal resolution of compliance with the EU Trade Secrets Directive has left many questions to be answered, as is discussed in Chapter 6].

It is also important to keep in mind that some of the relevant law might in the civilian tradition be found in other heavily regulated areas of law, such as labour law in particular. There, the rules tend to be more extensively prescribed by the legislator or the executive, in France as in Germany, as they assuredly are in other civil law jurisdictions. In the common law jurisdictions, however, labour and employment law tends to be found more in the cases and is not universally codified as it is in the civil law countries. In other words, although there may be specific relevant enactments, there is no universal code of labour law in England, Australia, the US or like jurisdictions, whereas that is generally the case in civil law countries.

§3.05 GLOBAL DOCTRINAL DIFFERENCES

The matters considered above are broadly contextual and of background relevance to any comparative review. Below, the main doctrinal differences in the treatment of trade secrets are introduced, the principal matters addressed being whether a special regime in equity, tort or statute applies uniquely to trade secrets; unfair competition, misappropriation and equitable approaches; and the relevance of the criminal law. These matters are dealt with in more detail in subsequent jurisdiction-specific chapters.

65. The Law on Unfair Competition: UWG – Gesetz gegen den unlauteren Wettbewerb; Civil Code: BGB – Buergerliches Gesetzbuch. *See* further below, Chapter 7.
66. Examples of *Chroniques* can be found below in Chapter 6 concerning French law.
67. *See* further below Chapter 6 concerning France.

[A] Equity Versus Tort

As already intimated, a major difference between the English common law and other regimes[68] is that the former does not have a separate protection regime concerning only commercial or technical secrets. The action for breach of confidence, equitable in nature and originating in the Court of Chancery in the UK, extends to both confidential information that has value in trade and commerce and information that is private, personal or family-related. It is apparent, therefore, that the rationale underlying the protection of trade secrets as a species of confidential information in the English common law must differ radically from that in others. For the English common law, it cannot lie in prevention of unfair competition, or protection of commercial values resting on unique possession, or of technical or practical knowledge that the possessor has invested in and devised. The rationale must be able to encompass private and intimate interests as well and lies in the nature of the relationship within which confidences pass between parties.

In most other jurisdictions, the term 'trade secret' is a legal term of art; in other words, it is a sub-class of information to which particular legal rights and obligations attach. In the English common law, it is not a term of art but simply one species of 'confidential information': in law, nothing turns on whether such information is commercial (i.e., a trade secret) or private and personal in nature.[69] A significant consequence is that the requirement that information must be of commercial value, which generally applies elsewhere, is not a core element of the action for breach of confidence in England (before the EU Trade Secrets Directive), Australia and other Commonwealth jurisdictions. Rather, it may be relevant to determining other factors, such as the correct particularization of the information concerned, whether its description is too vague or inchoate to merit protection or to help identify whether information is in the public domain or not. Commercial value may result from those requirements being met, but it is traditionally not a requirement per se.

Particularly important is the fact that at the heart of breach of confidence lie the obligations of good faith that arise in parties who share confidential information. These are personal obligations of trust rather than obligations not to compete unfairly with the information they have gleaned or treat particular pieces of information in prescribed ways. The standard is that of the reasonable person placed in the same position as the receiver and is the same whether personal or commercial information is at stake. Where the measure of liability lies in unfair competition, however, it is determined by reference to the objective standard of the expectations of the 'honest trader' in the relevant market.

68. Here, 'common law regimes' refers to those jurisdictions that have followed the UK model not including the US, also referred to as 'the English law system'.
69. Except in some specific and narrow ways, e.g., where a distinction is drawn between a trade secret and mere know-how in the possession of an employee post-termination.

[B] The Different Levels of Statutory Intervention

It is true to say that in the English law systems, statutory intervention in trade secrets law, both on the civil and criminal fronts, has been minimal. That is not the case in the US nor was it the case in Germany, but up until the adoption of trade secrets legislation, it was effectively also the situation in France. Legislation that 'strengthened protection' against misuse and misappropriation of trade secrets has done so in a piecemeal, indirect or tangential manner. For instance, statutes relating to: the misuse of telecommunications equipment;[70] phone tapping and the use of surveillance equipment; interference with computers and the like; directors' duties; the supply of test data to government; misuse of government information (such as the Official Secrets Act in the UK),[71] etc. These measures all have the indirect effect of strengthening protection against invasion of secret information or the secret sphere of organizations. All in all, various pieces of tangential legislation taken together have a quite significant impact, but the central private action for breach of confidence has not been translated into statute, whether by way of codification or reform. This only happened in the UK (just prior to Brexit) by way of the implementation of the EU Trade Secrets Protection and not because of some internal impetus. The matter did not attract much debate by legislators or policy makers in England, nor in countries with derivative systems (not including the US). Nonetheless, some piecemeal measures strengthening criminal enforcement and protecting against foreign (state) misappropriation were adopted, for instance, in Canada and New Zealand.[72]

One explanation is the common law's traditional reluctance to apply the criminal law of theft to information, but another possible explanation for this lack of intervention is the flexibility, perhaps typical of equity, with which the courts have felt able to approach breach of confidence cases. The traditional rationale and policy goals of breach of confidence have not stood in the way of adaptation to contemporary conditions and concerns. The courts have tended to sweep them aside: examples are the way the law has dealt with cases of industrial espionage, with third-party liability, and more recently in the UK, with accommodating the privacy interest as mandated by the ECHR.

By contrast, the US is marked by extensive statutory intervention. In that country, the *UTSA* has been a remarkable success and has been adopted with little variation by

70. *Telecommunications (Interception and Access) Act 1979* (Cth); *Regulation of Investigatory Powers Act 2000* (UK) c 23. *See also* Simon Bronitt & James Stellios, 'Regulating Telecommunications Interception and Access in the Twenty-First Century: Technological Evolution or Legal Revolution?' (2006) 24(4) *Prometheus* 413 https://doi.org/10.1080/08109020601030001; David Ormerod & Simon McKay, 'Telephone Intercepts and Their Admissibility' (2004) *Criminal Law Review* 15.
71. *Official Secrets Act 1989* (UK) c 6, s. 5.
72. *See* Peter Taylor, 'The New Zealand Crimes Amendment Act: A Legal White Elephant?' (2003) *Computers & Law September, inter alia,* considering the introduction of a new offence of 'theft of trade secrets'; Noel Courage, 'The Past and Future of Canada's Criminalization of Trade Secret Theft: Part I' *Lexology* (online) 2 March 2020 https://www.lexology.com/library/detail.aspx?g=a7db362e-6c01-4ea0-849d-d21baa68d398 referring to amendments criminalizing trade secrets theft resulting from CUSMA (USCMA).

the large majority of state legislatures. Nonetheless, some states have retained the common law, and there is some variation in the statutes based on the UTSA as enacted – so that the law is by no means uniform. In the civilian jurisdictions here considered, there were few calls for statutory change in recent times in Germany, but there were influential calls for wholesale intervention by parliament in France, for instance, by way of the Loi Carayon, which proposed adopting provisions based on the *EEA* in the US. The motivation was similar: apparent threats from abroad to significant technical secrets developed in France and frighteningly large figures said to be losses to French industry from industrial espionage more generally. These matters are further considered in the chapter on French law (below).

All EU civilian jurisdictions have now adopted sui generis legislation, i.e., statutes that deal specifically with trade secrets, not as a subspecies of unfair competition. However, this approach was not unknown before the adoption of the EU Trade Secrets Directive, perhaps the most well-known example within Europe being Sweden, where criminal and civil liabilities were prescribed in a separate trade secrets statute.[73] However, many civilian jurisdictions regulate trade secrets law within the confines of statutes dealing with unfair competition: this is, for instance, the case with China.[74]

[C] The Unequal Application of the Criminal Law

The Law Commission of England and Wales recommended in 1997 that criminal sanctions for certain misuses of trade secrets should be introduced, but until recently, no government in England had implemented this.[75] A fundamental difficulty with criminal liability in the common law tradition, but more broadly too, is that information per se is not a species of property, and therefore, general property offences such as theft are not applicable to the unauthorized taking of trade secrets. Thus, specific offences must be created in relation to trade secrets; with the National Security Act 2023 (the Act), which received royal assent on 11 July 2023, the legislator in the UK created a very specific offence of trade secret misappropriation in the context of industrial espionage by a foreign government. The Act makes the unauthorized conduct of obtaining, copying, recording or retaining a trade secret or disclosing or providing access to a trade secret, under certain circumstances, a criminal offence. The

73. *Protection of Trade Secrets Act* (Sweden) No 1990:409 [Ministry of Justice (Sweden) trans, *Act on the Protection of Trade Secrets (1990:409)* (1990)]; the Directive has since been translated into Swedish law: the Trade Secrets Act, lagen (2018:558) om företagshemligheter. This Act came into force on 1 July 2018 and consists of 28 sections that set out the related criminal offences, the damages for violating trade secrets and how to pursue injunctions and preliminary injunctions. There have been some changes, in particular in relation to the requirement that 'reasonable measures' must have been taken to secure a trade secret.
74. *See* Chapter 2. Also *see* Law Against Unfair Competition of the People's Republic of China (People's Republic of China) National People's Congress, 1993, Art. 10; and *see* further Chapter 9.
75. England & Wales Law Commission, *Legislating the Criminal Code: Misuse of Trade Secrets Consultation Paper*, No LCCP150 (25 November 1997). New Zealand dealt with the matter in the *Crimes Act 1961* (NZ), s. 230, *see*, http://www.legislation.govt.nz/act/public/1961/0043/latest/DLM330238.html.

conduct is only an offence under this provision if it is carried out on behalf of a foreign government and the alleged offender had actual or constructive knowledge of that fact.[76] Other jurisdictions, such as France, are said to be less reluctant in this regard, with jurisprudence recognizing that theft can apply to information.[77] In the US, misappropriation of trade secrets is now well established as a criminal offence if certain conditions are met: *see* further Chapter 5.

Other than by creating specific offences relating to the misuse of trade secrets *as such*, reliance may also be had on tangential areas of the criminal law, some of which were enumerated above. As indicated, the UK has chosen not to go down the first path, partly because of a sense that the second path, multifarious as it is, provides sufficient deterrence. Apart from specific technology-related offences, mostly abuse of the internet, computers or telecommunications systems-related, there are two broad areas of criminal liability that can come into play indirectly: theft and other property offences applying to the carrier or record containing the secret information and fraud.[78] The problem with the former is of course that the value of the carrier is commonly far less than the value of the enclosed secrets, and therefore, the penalties do not have much of a deterrent effect, or to put it differently, do not fit the crime. The possible application of theft and fraud to trade secrets is further considered below in the relevant chapters.

In statute-based jurisdictions, by contrast, criminal liability for misuse of trade secrets is commonly expressly instigated, although perhaps not frequently prosecuted.[79] In some jurisdictions, criminal liability is specifically extended to abuse of trade secrets by employees;[80] in others, it applies to certain kinds of secrets only[81] or to the use of certain methods of industrial espionage, as is the case in Germany or where such espionage is carried out on behalf of foreign governments or corporations. In the US, certain forms of industrial espionage give rise to both civil and criminal liability – as is provided in the federal EEA and also in certain state laws.[82] In France, express and specific criminal liability extends to *secrets de fabrique*, as is further discussed in the chapter relating to that country.

Specific criminal liability does extend to state secrets related to national security and espionage in most countries. This type of legislation does not properly belong in a discussion of trade secrets law, where the secret information is of a commercial rather than a government nature, so no further analysis is undertaken here. Nonetheless, in

76. The statutory definition of 'trade secret' under this Act differs from that given in the Trade Secrets (Enforcement, etc.) Regulations 2018 which implement the EU Trade Secrets Directive in the UK. *See* Inga-Marlene Pietsch, 'Trade Secrets Misappropriation: A New Criminal Offence in the UK', *Covington & Burling* (online), 12 September 2023 https://www.globalpolicywatch.com/2023/09/trade-secrets-misappropriation-a-new-criminal-offence-in-the-uk/.
77. *See* Art. 311-1 to 311-16 of the French Criminal Code, and case law holding that information misappropriation may qualify as theft (Cass. Crim., 28 June 2017 n°16-81.113). The party receiving the information may also be charged with fencing (Art. 321-1 French Criminal Code).
78. The applicability of fraud offences to trade secrets law is dealt with below in Chapters 4 and 5.
79. Although apparently prosecutions are not rare in Germany: as indicated by Richard Schloetter in conversation.
80. As in Sweden and Germany.
81. Theft of a *secret de fabrique* in France, for instance, which only concerns technical secrets.
82. United States state laws also provide for criminal liability.

light of recent experience,[83] and as the UK legislation mentioned above illustrates, it is worth noting that the distinction between private commercial secrets and espionage is gradually evaporating and also that commercial secrets are not always easily distinguished from state secrets. If a state-owned enterprise owns commercial secrets concerning a strategically significant mineral resource, for instance, does this turn them into secrets of state?

On a final note, criminal liability and civil liability have quite different scopes. The standard of proof is of course generally higher in criminal cases. But in other ways as well the operation of the criminal law is restricted to a narrower category of case. The principal requirement that narrows criminal liability is the applicable standard of *mens rea* or level of intent or intentionality (an intention to harm the commercial interests of the possessor being commonly required); often, such liability also applies only to certain kinds of more narrowly circumscribed secrets, such as the *secrets de fabrique* (technical or industrial secrets of a business) of French law, and the technical and commercial secrets of German law.[84] Civil liability is much wider and less targeted in scope.

§3.06 DOCTRINAL SIMILARITIES

[A] Property Rights in Trade Secrets Not Recognized

There are thus quite a number of conceptual and theoretical distinctions between the jurisdictions here considered, and they do not necessarily run along civil law versus common law lines. No doubt there are others than those mentioned above, and they are explored in more detail in the following chapters. But there are also common factors, both in terms of ratio and theory, and in terms of practical issues that arise in the application of the law.

One apparent matter of consensus is that secret information is not regarded doctrinally as property, even if sometimes it has the appearance of it or is treated as such for contiguous purposes.[85] Thus, trade secrets law does not perform the function of vindicating property rights in information. As was discussed in Chapter 1, the American system and commentators have perhaps the closest affinity with a property approach. Certainly, during the late nineteenth century and the first part of the twentieth century, courts were sympathetic to property thinking there, but that came to

83. *See, e.g.*, the Stern Hu case. John Garnaut & Sanghee Liu, 'Stern Sentenced to 10 years by Chinese Court', *The Age* (online), 29 March 2010 http://www.theage.com.au/business/stern-sentenced-to-10-years-by-chinese-court-20100329-r7x0.html.
84. German law refers to *Betriebsgeheimnisse* and *Geshäftsgeheimnisse* in the UWG, terms that are not further defined. Nothing turns on the difference between the two, the first relating to technical and the second to commercial secrets. Note also the German *Criminal Code*, s. 203(1) and (2).
85. In relation to intellectual property, the nearest and most relevant regime is perhaps patents, although that is of course only the case where the confidential information is of a technical or practical kind.

an end with the *Masland* case[86] and it cannot now be said that courts or statutes recognize property in trade secrets, as is further discussed in the relevant chapter.[87] In civilian jurisdictions, unfair competition thinking tended to predominate, and the EU Trade Secrets Directive has not introduced a property right in secret information. In the English common law approach, obligations of trust and good faith have dominated in the form of equitable action for breach of confidence.

During the US 'property-period', the cases focused primarily on the measures taken by a plaintiff to secure the trade secrets in question. The 'owner' had to manifest possession, a critical element of property, by putting in evidence the measures taken to secure their secrets from competitors. However, after Holmes J's rejection of the property approach in *Masland*, the focus shifted to unfair competition or unfair (mis-)appropriation. Examination of the behaviour of the alleged abuser of trade secrets and whether it fell below some standard, or was illegal or in breach of the obligations inherent in a confidential relationship became unavoidable. The First Restatement of Torts of 1939 placed trade secrets law in the unfair competition frame, the focus being on the defendant's use of 'improper means'. The 'wrongful conduct' approach gradually squeezed out references to a property approach until the advent of the 1980 Uniform Trade Secrets law, later followed by the Third Restatement of the Law of Unfair Competition in 1995. Most states adopted the UTSA, an act that reflects the fluctuating history of trade secrets law in the US, in particular, section 1(4(ii)) in its insistence on the plaintiff establishing that it has made 'efforts that are reasonable under the circumstances to maintain its secrecy'. This requirement must be met separately from the requirement of actual secrecy, which must be the source of economic value. Various commentators point out that the courts in the US have tended to vacillate between a more property-style approach, focusing on the requirements of secrecy and reasonable precautions, and a more impropriety-style approach, focusing on honest commercial conduct.[88] Nonetheless, in terms of the property approach in the current American context, the UTSA does not mandate it. One can safely adhere to the words of Bone who says it is fundamentally different from IP regimes: 'It does not impose liability for mere appropriation. Rather, the appropriator must have acquired, disclosed, or used the information in a wrongful manner.'[89] Or, as Lemley puts it, '[j]ust because a person's information is valuable does not make it wrong for another to use it or disclose it'.[90] Thus, the rejection of a property rationale can safely be said to be universal among the jurisdictions here considered, although it cannot be said that the law does not have a tinge of property about it. In commercial dealings and

86. *EI Du Pont De Nemours Powder Co v. Masland* (1917) 244 US 100, 102.
87. Note, however, what Moohr has said about the *Economic Espionage Act* – as referred to in Chapter 1.
88. In the famous *Christopher* case, for instance, it seems that disapproval of the trickery involved in obtaining the information drove the court to find in favour of DuPont. *EI duPont deNemours & Co v. Christopher*, 431 F.2d 1012 (1970).
89. *See* Chapter 1; Robert G. Bone, 'A New Look at Trade Secrets Law: Doctrine in Search of Justification' (1998) 86(2) *California Law Review* 241-244 https://doi.org/10.2307/3481134.
90. *See* Chapter 2; Mark A. Lemley, 'The Surprising Virtues of Treating Trade Secrets as IP Rights' (2008) 61 *Stanford Law Review* 311, 317 https://doi.org/10.31235/osf.io/srz5t.

contractually the topic of trade secrets is often dealt with as if property rights subsist in secret information.

[B] The Level of Secrecy Required Is Not Absolute

A universal feature of trade secrets law is that the standard of secrecy imposed is not absolute. The standard is far lower than it applies in patent law, where any publication can destroy novelty. Thus, trade secrets can be compilations of material that take time and effort to achieve, even though individual items contained within can each be accessed from public sources. The fact that a technical solution can be achieved with publicly available information does not mean it is not sufficiently secret, if effort and investment are required to actually reproduce it. Information can circulate within an organization or firm or be shared between people as long as an element of control exists, or the individuals concerned know they are under an obligation of secrecy or confidence. Sometimes, industry standards will determine whether information passed on in certain circumstances is to be treated as still confidential or not. It is important, however, that information be sufficiently particularized, concretely described and confined - otherwise, it will be impossible to determine whether it is in the public domain or not and also, as required in some jurisdictions, whether it has some commercial value or competitive advantage. It may also be required so that the claimant can establish that the information was deliberately kept secret, i.e., can point to measures put in place to limit its circulation or contain it within specific confines.

[C] Trade Secrets Law Is Default Law

Another general feature is that trade secrets law stands free from contract and largely operates as a default regime when contractual terms are absent. Some commentators argue that it is in fact sufficient for parties to be able to rely on contract to protect their secrets. As discussed in Chapter 1, Bone argued there was either no actual trade secrets law, or alternatively no need for it, partly because the contract can do what is required,[91] and as we have seen above, some of the developing countries in TRIPS also advanced the view that contractual provisions and remedies were sufficient and no broad default liability for trade secrets misuse was therefore required.

Obligations of confidence or secrecy are indeed often associated with contract or are based on the implied or express terms of agreements. Some contracts have as their main purpose the maintenance of secrecy (so-called NDAs). But, as indicated above, contract does not reach into pre-contractual disclosures, and securing those from untoward use is arguably crucial to commercial intercourse. Second, contract commonly does not apply in the post-employment faze, where the contract of employment has been terminated. During the currency of the employment contract, the implied contractual duty of good faith governs the use of information by employees, but this is more a matter of labour law.

91. *See* Chapter 1.

Further, contractual obligations do not extend to certain parties that are not privy to an agreement who use illegal or disreputable measures to obtain information, so-called (industrial) espionage-type cases, and to those who have obtained information from a party who is privy to a contract with the original confidor - so-called third-party liability.

In many ways, therefore, autonomous trade secrets law precisely fills some significant voids left by contract. Of course, contract law most often prevails over the law of trade secrets, where express or implied terms govern the use of confidential information between the parties. Nonetheless, the default law plays a significant shadow role in the context of contract, as parties cannot make trade secrets by contractual means, i.e., by providing in a contract that certain information is a trade secret, where it is in fact in the public domain.[92]

Accounts of English law often stress that the action for breach of confidence freed itself from contract during the twentieth century. The regimes in civil law countries are either originally based on unfair competition - i.e., regulating relationships between strangers in competition - or sui generis statutory regimes. If contracts were the real basis of all liability for trade secrets misuse, then obviously, no special statutory regime would be required. As Lemley points out, contract is also not compatible with the imposition of criminal penalties, which are a traditional facet of trade secrets law in civil law (including France and Germany) and now also of US federal law, if not of English law.

[D] Complexity and Uncertainty Is Best Resolved by Contract

In reality, the majority of trade secrets cases in all jurisdictions considered here relate to the post-employment situation. But here, the law is at its most complex and unpredictable, as important principles and policies collide at that time. Employees have the right to work and also the right to compete with their former employers. For those purposes, they should be able to draw on the knowledge acquired during employment. Nonetheless, the employer has the right to protect significant assets of the business, and perhaps to a certain standard of fair competition. These two competing interests must be resolved in an environment often of urgency and where the relevant proof is difficult to come by. Commentators in every jurisdiction remark on the difficulty of predicting the outcome of such cases. Unsurprisingly, employers revert to contractual means to address this uncertainty and improve their forensic and tactical position.

That is why the restraint of trade or non-compete clauses figure so widely in all jurisdictions and are a significant topic in the law of trade secrets. Until recently, the law has allowed them almost everywhere if they genuinely serve the purpose of protecting trade secrets, but they are subject to intense judicial scrutiny. However, there is a significant difference in the level of regulation of their impact and extent, with the civilian jurisdictions more inclined to adopt prescriptive rules. Now the US has introduced a federal prohibition on non-competes, however, which mirrors the existing

92. *Maggbury Pty Ltd v. Hafele Australia Pty Ltd* (2001) 210 CLR 181.

situation in California; it remains to be seen how the measure survives legal and political headwinds. These matters are considered further in the following chapters, and in particular in Chapter 8 on Employment.

§3.07 CONCLUDING COMMENTS

In other respects, there are some surprising differences in principle between jurisdictions, where similarity may have been expected or presumed. Perhaps the most striking are the limitations on the freedom to reverse engineer that are imposed in German law and also the principle in that country that employees are free to use all information and knowledge acquired on the job, including trade secrets, in their subsequent employment or (competitive) pursuit. In other jurisdictions, freedom to reverse engineer, if no IPRs are breached, is seen as axiomatic. It seems self-evident that a departed employee should not be able to use trade secrets belonging to a previous employer, but nonetheless, German law insists that this is allowed. However, the reality is that the cases have imposed limits on this freedom by applying general standards of unfair competition and civil liability, as further explained in the chapter on Germany. Finally, it is striking that the debate about unfair competition cuts through this area of the law. The common law traditionally treats this approach with scepticism, and it has barely a foothold in most such countries. In the civilian jurisdictions, however, it is well established, and courts apply standards of fairness daily – they have arguably developed consistent factors to apply, as will be seen below. In any case, the uncertainty inherent in unfair competition is not far removed from the uncertainty attending the application of principles of equity, to which breach of confidence belongs.

CHAPTER 4

The Common Law Approach: The English Law System

§4.01 INTRODUCTION TO THE ENGLISH APPROACH

Until recently, trade secrets fell exclusively under the broad umbrella of the equitable action for breach of confidence in England and Wales. That action not only concerned technical and commercial secrets, i.e., trade secrets properly so-called, but also private, personal or family information that is not in the public domain. However, two relatively recent developments have clouded the picture. First is the passage of the EU Trade Secrets Directive, which came just before the UK's exit from the EU. As Aplin and Arnold point out: 'Member States were obliged to implement the Directive by 9 June 2018, and despite the UK having given formal notification of its withdrawal from the EU on 29 March 2017, with "Brexit" expected to occur on 29 March 2019 (eventually delayed to 31 January 2020), the UK chose to implement its extant obligations by the deadline. This was done in the form of the Trade Secrets (Enforcement, etc) Regulations 2018 ("Regulations"), in reliance on section 2 of the European Communities Act 1972.'[1] Second, in recent times, the category of personal and private information is now also protected by the newly forged tortious action for misuse of private information ('MPI').[2]

These two actions have, however, not replaced equitable remedies in this field, although whether vindicating privacy interests is now the exclusive province of the tortious action for MPI or can still also be brought in equity for breach of confidence is not entirely clear. Before these infusions of statute law and tort, the equitable action for

1. *See* Tanya Aplin & Richard Arnold, 'UK Implementation of the Trade Secrets Directive' in Jens Schovsbo, Timo Minssen, & Thomas Riis (eds), *The Harmonization and Protection of Trade Secrets in the EU: An Appraisal of the EU Directive* (Edward Elgar Publishing, 2020) 64.
2. For a recent account of the controversial emergence and status of the MPI action, *see* Thomas D.C. Bennett, 'Confidence, Privacy, and Incoherence' (2022) 14(2) *Journal of Media Law* 245 https://doi.org/10.1080/17577632.2022.2139571.

breach of confidence stood entirely apart from its tortious equivalents both in the US and in civilian jurisdictions. In those jurisdictions, a distinct legal regime applies to valuable *commercial secrets*, and a conceptually and doctrinally entirely separate regime to private personal information. There, the appropriate action relating to misuse or unauthorized publication of private personal information falls within the sphere of an action for invasion or breach of privacy, whether based on a fundamental constitutionally sanctioned right to privacy (as in France),[3] ordinary statutory provisions or jurisprudential development of a specific tort. In some common law jurisdictions, such as Australia, privacy is only protected by way of a regulatory approach,[4] whereas in others, such as New Zealand, courts have brought a new and entirely separate tortious action for invasion of privacy into life.

Historically, the English approach granting remedies for breach of confidence in equity was adopted in many countries which received the common law, such as Australia, Canada and New Zealand. The law has developed along similar but not uniform lines in those jurisdictions. In typical fashion, the case law of each jurisdiction has persuasive force in the other, with some significant English cases also lying at the heart of modern breach of confidence law in other countries.

Then, in very recent times, English law took a radical turn. In a series of cases beginning with *Spycatcher*[5] and developing further in *Campbell v. MGNl*,[6] *Douglas v. Hello*,[7] and *Tchenguiz v. Imerman*,[8] the equitable action for breach of confidence was held capable of performing the role of a tort of invasion of privacy. According to some, it simply morphed from an equitable into a tortious remedy for MPI. This development, advanced in England in part because of the ECHR, has not been followed in like jurisdictions. Instead, there has been parliamentary consideration of the introduction of a statutory tort of invasion of privacy in Australia. In that country, that is in part due to the fact that the obstacles at the highest level of judicial development appear quite immutable at present.[9] The High Court authority of *Victoria Park Racing*, which holds that the common law in Australia knows no action for invasion of privacy, thus stands, as reiterated more recently in *Lenah*.[10] Relevantly in relation to trade secrets, the High Court's rejection in the same case of a tort of unfair competition also stands in Australia as it does traditionally in England. In New Zealand, however, the courts were more

3. *See* the decision of the French Constitutional Court of 2010 to this effect: at http://www.conseil-constitutionnel.fr/conseil-constitutionnel/francais/les-decisions/acces-par-date/decisions-depuis-1959/2010/2010-604-dc/decision-n-2010-604-dc-du-25-fevrier-2010.47970.html.
4. Imposing certain standards of personal information management on corporations, organizations and government. *See Privacy Act 1988* (Cth).
5. *AG v. Observer* [1990] 1 AC 109.
6. *Campbell v. MGN Ltd* [2004] UKHL 22; *Douglas v. Hello! Ltd (No 2)* [2006] QB 125; *Mosley v. News Group Newspapers* [2008] EWHC 1777.
7. *Douglas v. Hello! Ltd* [2006] QB 125.
8. [2010] EWCA Civ 908; [2010] 2 FLR 814.
9. Australian Law Reform Commission, *For Your Information: Australian Privacy Law and Practice*, Report No 108 (2008); *Grosse v. Purvis* (2003) Aust Torts Reports 8, 706; *Doe v. Australian Broadcasting Corporation* [2007] VCC 281.
10. *Victoria Park Racing and Recreation Grounds Co Ltd v. Taylor* (1937) 58 CLR 479. Also *see Australian Broadcasting Corp v. Lenah Game Meats Pty Ltd* [2001] HCA 63, [186].

receptive concerning the development of a new tort of invasion of privacy, and in *Hosking v. Runting* simply created a new freestanding tort.[11]

In the English system, courts of equity have a broad power to grant remedies in cases where no remedy exists at law, i.e., for a tort or breach of contract. Equity acts as a court of conscience and intervenes to repress unconscionable conduct, and in the area of trade secrets, it has always done this with considerable flexibility. Whereas in jurisdictions such as Australia, this flexibility has been tempered by judicial affirmations of the principle that the action for breach of confidence should remain 'within the four corners' of its traditional elements, this has not been the case in England. In *Spycatcher*, the requirement of a pre-existing relationship of good faith was effectively abandoned in cases where it would be obvious that information was secret and that opened the doors wide for both industrial espionage and invasion of privacy cases to be accommodated within breach of confidence, as is further discussed below.

It should be noted that equity is particularly apt in trade secrets cases because the court's primary equitable remedy was and remains an injunction. This particularly suits trade secrets actions, since it is rare that compensatory remedies can properly compensate for the destruction of a trade secret by unauthorized publication.

Historically, the court in its equitable jurisdiction was said to award an injunction only to protect an existing legal right.[12] In other words, as in the US, the courts in England were traditionally concerned with identifying a right that the grant of the injunction would vindicate or uphold. Where various forms of information are concerned, the bases were multifarious and varied over time: property, contract, patents and the law of 'master and servant'. However, from the early days, there were instances of the grant of an injunction which could either not be explained by reference to any such rights or relied on a very broad interpretation of their existence and contours. Hence, while the early cases are marked by the search for a property interest

11. *Hosking v. Runting and Pacific Magazines NZ Ltd* [2004] CA 101-03. *See also* Katrine Evans, 'Hosking v. Runting Balancing Rights in a Privacy Tort' (2004) 11(2) *Privacy Law and Policy Reporter* 34.
12. In *Lenah, see* above n 10, at HCA [175] Kirby J approved of the following statement to that effect made by Young J in the New South Wales Equity Court:

> [t]his Court still continues both in private and commercial disputes to function as a court of conscience. What is unconscionable will depend to a great degree on the court's view as to what is acceptable to the community as decent and fair at the time and in the place where the decision is made. ... [O]pinions may differ as to where the line of unconscionability is to be drawn, but that does not remove from this Court its responsibility to make a decision as to whether conduct is unconscionable in new commercial situations.

But Gummow and Hayne JJ in *Lenah* said that 'the notion of unconscionable behaviour does not operate wholly at large as Lenah would appear to have it.' (at HCA [98]). In the action for breach of confidence in England and related jurisdictions we have an exact example of the tension represented by these statement: on the one hand, an action which has repeatedly been held to vindicate an obligation of conscience, good faith, trust, confidence deposed, but on the other hand a hardening of the broad obligation to act in good faith in relations with others in an action with defined elements. The High Court rejected the existence of a power 'at large' of the courts to grant an injunction in any case of unconscionability, requiring instead that some legal or equitable right of the plaintiff be at stake.

in an information asset, later courts emphasized that an *autonomous* basis for granting injunctions relating to confidences existed. Thus, Lord Cottenham, in the leading case of *Prince Albert v. Strange*, where there was nonetheless an arguable (copyright-style) property right in unpublished works (etchings) at stake, stated that the case did not depend 'solely upon the question of property; for a breach of trust, confidence or contract itself would entitle the Plaintiff to the injunction'[13] (emphasis added). It was the surreptitious and improper obtaining or use of the etchings in the context of a relationship, at the very least of trust or confidence (if not of contract), that provided a potential autonomous basis for the grant of the injunction. Upholding trust or good faith obligations between parties was after all an essential role of the equity jurisdiction. Thus, the difficulty of holding there was property in informational goods outside the statutory rights was gradually overcome by granting injunctions solely on the basis of an abuse of trust relating to information shared. In that way, the concern that the courts not usurp the role of the legislator in creating property rights in forms of information (such as copyrights or patents) was addressed.

Sir George Turner V-C in *Morrison v. Moat* made a famous judicial statement acknowledging that the basis for the grant of an injunction was not or not *solely* a right in property or contract:

> In some cases it has been referred to property, in others to contract, and in others, again, it has been treated as founded upon trust or confidence, meaning, as I conceive, that the Court fastens the obligation on the conscience of the party, and enforces it against him in the same manner as it enforces against a party to whom a benefit is given the obligation of performing a promise on the faith of which the benefit has been conferred; but, upon whatever grounds the jurisdiction is founded, the authorities leave no doubt as to the exercise of it.[14]

One of the difficulties inherent in restraining a breach of trust only on the basis of other rights, in particular contractual ones, is *privity*, which prevented liability extending to a third-party recipient or user of information initially imparted under contract. The independent action based on trust and confidence per se as recognized in *Prince Albert* and *Morrison* overcame this difficulty and meant that third-party recipients with actual or constructive knowledge could be injuncted if certain conditions were fulfilled.

Morrison confirmed that an injunction could be granted on the simple basis of a breach of trust or confidence alone, but it took a long time before the conditions that would have to be satisfied in a given case were further elaborated. Other areas of law continued to provide an alternative legal basis for restraining orders. The law did not (and still does not) have to fix upon the conscience of the party where it could fix upon an implied or expressed contractual term, for instance. This could occur in cases where confidentiality was not just an implied term of another contract but the central object of the contract itself. Wherever persons received information in confidential circumstances, an implied contract could be found to exist whose whole terms were that the

13. *Prince Albert v. Strange* (1849) 47 ER 1302, 1311 (Lord Cottenham).
14. *Morrison v. Moat* (1851) 68 ER 492, 498.

recipient would not use the information concerned to harm the interests of the confidor. If, however, another contract, for instance, for the sale of a personal business, existed between the parties, the court could readily imply a term that obliged the parties to observe confidentiality.[15]

The situations in which contract could be found to do the job of protecting confidences became so multifarious that Lord Greene MR in *Vokes Ltd v. Heather* was able to say that 'the introduction of equitable principles, apart from contract, into relationships of this kind is a thing which I think should be, in general, repudiated'.[16] The contract being in existence, whether or not the parties were held to an obligation of confidence could simply be deduced by implication from the express terms. Thus, courts granted injunctive relief on the basis of a breach of a contractual term and in the absence of any proprietary interest, this difficulty being simply ignored. Any problems of *privity* could be dealt with either by recourse to the *Morrison* principle or by reference to the developing tort of inducement of breach of contract, the latter from the decision of 1835 in *Lumley v. Gye* onwards.[17] Naturally, the most common cases concerned post-employment obligations. Wrongfully, wilfully or knowingly inducing an employee to breach terms of his employment contract by hiring them, where damage to the previous employer could be established, became actionable.[18] The action was extended beyond only employees and could thus form the basis for the grant of an injunction against any party who approached another who was under a contractual obligation of confidence.

Apart from the employment cases, which contained the earliest references to an obligation of confidence in the English courts, during a later period, the law of copyright in unpublished works was also called upon to do much of the work to protect confidential material. Before the *Copyright Act 1911*, Geo 5, c 46, the law granting rights in unpublished copyright works extended so far that a virtual common law copyright regime was created.[19] Importantly for our topic, the works concerned often contained information that could be described as confidential.[20] But although the real motivation for an action might lie more in privacy or an abuse of trust, such as where unauthorized publication of unpublished letters was at stake, the action based on common law rights in unpublished works was very attractive. The authors of the second edition of *Gurry on Breach of Confidence* said the following about copyright:

> Moreover, with the common law property right [i.e. common law copyright] there was no need for an obligation of confidence, nor even for damage. Infringement of

15. Trade secrets being a legitimate interest to protect, even as against former employees and not just in the sale of a business, such clauses were an acceptable exception to the policy of holding restraints of trade invalid in the public interest.
16. *Vokes Ltd v. Heather* (1945) 62 RPC 135, 142.
17. (1853) 118 ER 749.
18. *Temperton v. Russell* [1893] 1 QB 715 extended the action beyond employment contracts.
19. Tanya Aplin, Lionel Bently, Phillip Johnson & Simon Malynicz, *Gurry on Breach of Confidence: The Protection of Confidential Information* (Oxford University Press, 2nd ed., 2012) 58, [2.108].
20. In fact, the connection between copyright and confidentiality was of course also apparent in *Prince Albert v. Strange* (1849) 47 ER 1302, which concerned drawings made by Queen Victoria in the family circle.

the common law right came to be viewed as a matter of strict liability, and applied not just to duplication of the words or expressive form. There were few exceptions to this phenomenally restrictive right. Importantly too, the rights were transferable, could survive death, and may even have been enforceable by licensees.

All things that for an action based solely on an obligation of confidence would have been problematic, to say the least.[21] This history of association between confidence and copyright has led Professor Cornish 'to characterize the duty of confidence developed after 1911 as the "modern derivative" of the common law action for copyright in unpublished works'.[22]

§4.02 ELEMENTS OF THE MODERN ACTION

Be that as it may, there were very few cases based on the *Morrison* principle until the late 1940s. The critical new impetus then came from *Saltman Engineering Co Ltd v. Campbell Engineering Co.*[23] For reasons that may or may not have been justified on the facts, the matter was not dealt with on the basis of a contractual relationship between the parties. The court stressed that the absence of a contractual basis for a remedy was no bar to a finding that there was a legal obligation to respect confidences. Lord Greene MR approved of a statement of the law which held that a defendant who used information obtained from the plaintiff without the latter's express or implied consent would be guilty of an infringement of the plaintiff's rights.[24] Interestingly enough, Lord Green felt it unnecessary to refer in any great detail to the cases from which this principle was derived. In the later case of *Coco v. Clark,* the elements of the action were summed up as follows:

> First, the information itself ... must 'have the necessary quality of confidence about it'. Secondly, that information must have been imparted in circumstances importing an obligation of confidence. Third, there must be an unauthorized use of that information to the detriment of the party communicating it.[25]

Thus, in a short time, the action had morphed from a near-death experience to a fully fledged independent action. Although the elements were settled, they were rather broad and vague and the doctrinal basis remained somewhat uncertain. Justice Deane of the High Court of Australia pointed out in *Moorgate Tobacco* that:

> it is unnecessary ... to attempt to define the precise scope of the equitable jurisdiction to grant relief against an actual or threatened abuse of confidential

21. The authors provide case citations in their footnotes. These are to the following cases: *Prince Albert v. Strange* (1849) 47 ER 1302; *Kenrick v. Danube Collieries and Minerals Co Ltd* (1891) 39 WR 473; *Philip v. Pennell* [1907] 2 Ch 577; *Labouchere v. Hess* (1898) 77 LT 559. Above n 19, 56 [2.105] p. 322.
22. *Gurry* referring to Cornish et al., *Oxford History of the Laws of England* (Oxford University Press, first published 2010) vol. 13, 897. *See* above n 19, 58 [2.109] n 339.
23. *Saltman Engineering Ltd v. Campbell Engineering Co* (1948) 65 RPC 203 (*Saltman*).
24. This is a rewording of the statement of the law approved by Lord Greene MR at *Saltman Engineering Ltd v. Campbell Engineering Co* (1948) 65 RPC 203, 13; [1963] 3 All ER 413.
25. *Coco v. AN Clark (Engineers) Ltd* [1969] RPC 41, 47 (*Coco*). The quoted part is from Lord Green MR's reasons in *Saltman*.

> information not involving any tort or any breach of some express or implied contractual provision, some wider fiduciary duty or some copyright or trade mark right. A general equitable jurisdiction to grant such relief has long been asserted and should, in my view, now be accepted (see The Commonwealth v. John Fairfax & Sons Ltd [1980] HCA 44; (1980) 147 CLR 39, at pp 50-52). Like most heads of exclusive equitable jurisdiction, its rational basis does not lie in proprietary right. It lies in the notion of an obligation of conscience arising from the circumstances in or through which the information was communicated or obtained.[26]

Saltman concerned information that could rightly be described as a trade secret, but that rights and obligations could arise irrespective of the commercial value of the information concerned was soon established.[27] In a famous case concerning the marital affairs of the Duke and Duchess of Argyll,[28] the latter wished to prevent the publication of information about her private life and conduct by her former spouse. Justice Ungoed-Thomas categorically stated that an obligation of confidence could arise outside contract or property and that it could be enforced in equity 'independently of any right at law'.[29] The underlying policy goal was simply the protection of confidential communications, as between husband and wife in this case, and therefore, there was no reason to confine the obligation to commercial communications alone.

Thus, the action for breach of confidence in England is not concerned with protection of commercial values or with suppression of unfair competition, unjust enrichment and parasitic behaviour. Rather, it in essence derives from a central moral tenet of societal intercourse and communications or as Lord Denning MR said in the significant case of *Seager v. Copydex*, having pointed out the law did not depend on implied contract 'it depends on the broad principle of equity that he who has received information in confidence shall not take unfair advantage of it. He must not make use of it to the prejudice of him who gave it without obtaining his consent'.[30]

Of course, the information must be confidential enough, but in English law, as elsewhere, this is a relative concept falling far short of the patent standard. Lord Green MR in *Saltman* put it as follows:

> The information, to be confidential must, I apprehend, apart from contract, have the necessary quality of confidence about it, namely, it must not be something which is public property and public knowledge. On the other hand, it is perfectly possible to have a confidential document, be it a formula, a plan, a sketch, or something of that kind, which is the result of work done by the maker upon materials which may be available for the use of anybody; but what makes it

26. *Moorgate Tobacco Co Ltd v. Philip Morris Ltd (No 2)* (1984)156 CLR 414; [1984] HCA 73, [28], 438.
27. That there is no need for commercial value was confirmed in *Moorgate Tobacco* (*see* above n 26): 'Relief under the jurisdiction is not available, however, unless it appears that the information in question has "the necessary quality of confidence about it" *Saltman*, 215(Lord Greene MR) and that it is significant, not necessarily in the sense of commercially valuable (*see Argyle v Argyle* (1967) Ch 302, 329) but in the sense that the preservation of its confidentiality or secrecy is of substantial concern to the plaintiff.' *Moorgate Tobacco Co Ltd v. Philip Morris Ltd (No 2)* (1984)156 CLR 414; [1984] HCA 73 [28].
28. *Duchess of Argyll v. Duke of Argyll* [1967] Ch 302.
29. [1967] Ch 302, 322.
30. *Seager v. Copydex Ltd* [1967] 1 WLR 923, 931.

> confidential is the fact that the maker of the document has used his brain and thus produced a result which can only be produced by somebody who goes through the same process.[31]

In the later but equally significant case of *Coco v. AN Clark (Engineers) Limited* (1969) RPC 41, 47, Megarry V-C followed suit:

> First, the information must be of a confidential nature. As Lord Greene said in the Saltman case at page 215, 'something which is public property and public knowledge' cannot per se provide any foundation for proceedings for breach of confidence. However confidential the circumstances of communication, there can be no breach of confidence in revealing to others something which is already common knowledge. But this must not be taken too far. Something that has been constructed solely from materials in the public domain may possess the necessary quality of confidentiality: for something new and confidential may have been brought into being by the application of the skill and ingenuity of the human brain. Novelty depends on the thing itself, and not upon the quality of its constituent parts. Indeed, often the more striking the novelty, the more commonplace its components. Mr Mowbray demurs to the concept that some degree of originality is requisite. But whether it is described as originality or novelty or ingenuity or otherwise, I think there must be some product of the human brain which suffices to confer a confidential nature upon the information.

Where the action is concerned with trade secrets only, the questions of commercial value on the one hand and actual damage on the other are significant. But given its policy basis, the requirement of detriment is all but absent from the English law. The authors of *Gurry* devote very little space to it, and in the leading case of *Coco*, Megarry V-C pours cold water on it, pointing out that some cases are for and others against recognizing detriment as a separate requirement.[32] More recently, in *Weiss Technik UK Ltd*,[33] it was confirmed that there is no need to prove loss or damage in order to make out an equitable breach of confidence claim. It may be that an intention to disclose confidential information without the authorization to do so makes the action complete, as was said in *Tchenguiz*.[34]

In other words, in English law, there is injury enough in the fact itself of acting contrary to the owner's authorization or consent. This focus on authorization is consistent with a property-like approach, one that vindicates the power of control. But it is also consistent with the putative basis in equity of the action, the upholding of an obligation of honest and 'loyal' conduct. Given the centrality of an injunction as a remedy and the fact that usually, an injunction is sought at a time when disclosure is threatened but not yet effected, it is also not surprising. Although some issues that are in truth related to damage or detriment are in fact dealt with as questions of standing, the reality of the English law is that establishing breach or anticipated breach itself is almost always sufficient. Naturally, although the action in England has property-like

31. *Saltman*, above n 23 at 215.
32. *Coco*, above n 25, at 48.
33. *Weiss Technik UK Ltd and other companies v. Davies and others* [2022] EWHC 2773 (Ch).
34. *See* above n 8.

characteristics, the courts do, however, categorically reject the notion that confidential information *is* property, as discussed in Chapter 1.

The principal legal determinant in the English action for breach of confidence is whether the surrounding circumstances of the communication are such as to give rise to an obligation of confidence. Once that has been determined, the nature and extent of the obligations is then a matter of fact: what were the limits of the authorized use? So is the remaining question of whether the actions of the defendant breach those obligations.[35] The extent of the complainant's rights is not tempered by any additional requirements in English law but simply depends on whether what was done was authorized. In this respect, English law differs from the US, where we shall see that it is the improper, dishonest or unfair manner of obtaining or using the information that is central to liability. We address below how these compare to the Regulations that implement the EU Trade Secrets Directive in the UK.

However, it is immediately apparent that communication in the context of a pre-existing relationship and consent as controlling factors cause difficulties where the alleged misuser is a third party - in other words, a person to whom the information has not been 'communicated', with whom no communication has taken place and, thus, not relationship exists, and who has not consented expressly or implicitly to abide by a particular obligation.[36] As pointed out by Duncan Stewart, '[s]uch a specific communication between the parties is absent when trade secret acquisition is surreptitious, even though information is transferred'.[37] A doctrinal difficulty in English law, therefore, was whether and how an unrelated third party (a putative spy) can be fixed with a particular obligation. Various theories have been advanced to resolve this, *inter alia*, by Gurry, who suggested (in the first edition of his work) that the surreptitious acquisition itself created a confidential relationship.[38] Others have suggested that all participants in a market owe each other a duty of good faith, trust or honesty - this is similar to the French and German approach that stresses fair competition is in the public interest - or have implied a contractual duty from the simple fact of acquisition. Finally, recent cases in England have suggested that the basis for a spy's liability in relation to secret information lies simply in the *knowledge* of the fact that its possessor intends to keep it so. This far-reaching development, which accelerated with the decision in the *Spycatcher* case, is further examined below.

By contrast, two other difficulties resulting from the English relational or communications approach - extending liability to third parties and recognizing the transferability of trade secrets - are more readily dealt with. As indicated above, the

35. Finally, in some cases, the defendant will be able to raise a 'public interest' defence. This is not a matter further examined in this context: for an account of the iniquity or public interest defence. *See* Jason Pizer, 'The Public Interest Exception to the Breach of Confidence Action; Are the Lights about to Change?' (1994) 20(1) *Monash University Law Review* 67; Trent Glover, 'Scope of Public Interest Defence in Actions for Breach of Confidence' (1999) 6 *James Cook University Law Review* 109.
36. There is then no communication from which an obligation can or cannot be inferred.
37. *See* Duncan Stewart, *Trade Secrets Law in New Zealand* (Doctoral Thesis, Massey University, 1996), 3.05.
38. *See* Francis Gurry, *Gurry on Breach of Confidence: The Protection of Confidential Information* (Oxford University Press, 1984) 164.

action in its earlier forms was viewed as specifically serving the purpose of overcoming the limitations of privity of contract. In any case, there can be little objection in logic to extending the scope of an ethical obligation of good faith to a recipient who knows of the supplier's breach. Perhaps more difficult is the position of the person who neither knew nor ought to have known that the information was passed on in breach of duty at the time: a 'third party acquisition for value without notice'. The English law has persistently held that such a person has no absolute defence, and it will depend on the equities of each case whether an injunction is granted against the third party who has received notice of breach from the original confidor.[39]

In terms of transferability, it is true that confidential information is not property and, therefore, in theory, not assignable. However, there is no doubt that in the relevant jurisdictions, trade secrets or know-how are regularly and validly transferred, for instance, as an asset in the sale of a business. As indicated in Chapter 1, some judges have accepted the US approach that trade secrets can be property for the purpose of the 'takings clause' or its equivalent – for instance, in Australia in the *Smith Kline French* case.[40] Trade secrets are also dealt with elsewhere in ways analogous to property rights, such as for taxation purposes. In any case, even if trade secrets are not property – and there is even less support in England and other common law jurisdictions than in America for the proposition that they are – there is really no great practical problem of transferability. The party possessing the trade secret can agree with another party to disclose the information and also not to use it any longer itself, nor to disclose it to any other party. The main question then is what the position of the transferee is vis-à-vis others to whom the transferor already disclosed the information. But the law finds different ways of dealing with this, and it is not inherently a property-related problem or one that can only be resolved by recourse to property concepts.[41]

Therefore, the English action for breach of confidence has a somewhat split personality: on the one hand, the breadth of the action, its basis in violation of consent or authorization, the absence of any need to establish commercial value, the absence of any strict requirement to establish damage or detriment resulting from alleged misuse, all characterize it as more proprietary in nature. On the other hand, in theory, it is relational and communication basis is far narrower than a property right, not operating *erga omnes*. It is a *right in personam* and not *in rem*, but as discussed below, nonetheless, the courts have ignored doctrinal difficulties and substantially extended liability to unrelated third parties in industrial espionage-type matters in a manner reminiscent of US law. In one other aspect, the English legal scene is less accepting of property in information, and that is in relation to criminal liability. Although criminal offences exist that indirectly impact the safeguarding of trade secrets, as indicated previously England and other jurisdictions such as Australia had no criminal regime

39. Even if notice is by solicitor's letter, for instance. *See Wheatley v. Bell* [1982] 2 NSWLR 544. *See also Earl Nationwide News Pty Ltd* [2013] NSWCA 839; *Ingersoll-Rand (Australia) Ltd v. Industrial Rollformers Pty Ltd* [2000] NSWCA 712; *AG Australian Holdings Ltd v. Burton & Ors* (2002) 58 IPR 268.
40. *Smith Kline & French v. Secretary, Department of Community Services* (1990) 22 FCR 73. Also *see* Chapter 2.
41. This matter is dealt with in *Gurry*. Above n 38, 340, [8.93].

applying expressly to trade secrets as such.[42] In recent times, this has changed but only in a very specific manner: the National Security Act 2023 (the Act) concerns trade secret misappropriation in the context of industrial espionage by a foreign government. Obtaining, copying, recording or retaining a trade secret, or disclosing or providing access to a trade secret, under certain circumstances, has become a criminal offence, with a penalty of a maximum of fourteen years imprisonment and/or a fine.[43] This is a measure that aims to address threats to national security and not misappropriation of trade secrets in general.

§4.03 IMPLEMENTATION OF THE EU TRADE SECRETS DIRECTIVE IN THE UK: TRADE SECRETS (ENFORCEMENT, ETC.) REGULATIONS 2018

[A] Introduction

As indicated above, the action for breach of confidence has been impacted by two significant recent developments: the emergence of the tortious action for MPI, crafted by the courts; and the implementation of the EU Trade Secrets Directive.[44] The former development does not have to concern us here, as it does not concern trade secrets but private personal information that in most other jurisdictions is covered by a statutory or tortious action for breaches or invasions of privacy. The 2018 Regulations are, however, significant, although they do not replace the action for breach of confidence. The two actions, one based in statute and the other in equity, now coexist and it is for a claimant to decide which to pursue or whether to rely on both. Many of the Directive's provisions were not translated into provisions in the Regulations because the government determined that the action for breach of confidence was already compliant with the Directive's requirements. The Regulations do explicitly incorporate elements of the enforcement and remedies aspects of the Directive.

As Aplin and Arnold point out: 'However, what counts as "unlawful" acquisition, use or disclosure remains defined according to the existing UK law on breach of confidence and there has been no attempt explicitly to incorporate the provisions on lawful acquisition, use or disclosure.'[45] Arguably, the odd effect of the Regulations is that a definition of trade secrets has been introduced that is in many ways narrower than what is required to obtain a remedy in equity. 'Trade secret' is defined in the same terms as in the Directive, which requires commercial value and proof of reasonable steps to keep information secret. These are not necessary to establish liability for breach of confidence. Further, the definition in the Regulations does tie secrecy to knowledge or accessibility by persons within circles that normally deal with the kind of information in question (as per the Directive's terms), whereas the requirement in breach of confidence actions is broader requiring restrictions to accessibility to the

42. Except now for New Zealand – *see* further below.
43. Ascent was received on 11 July 2023. *See* s. 2 of the Act.
44. *See* above §4.01, first paragraph.
45. *See* above n 1.

wider public. The Regulations in their final form provide that the 'acquisition, use or disclosure of a trade secret is unlawful where the acquisition, use or disclosure constitutes a breach of confidence in confidential information'.[46] Thus, it seems that the definition in terms of English law is quite circular and also arguably fails to comply with the Directive as it ties infringement back to the limitations of the action of breach of confidence and does not explicitly make unauthorized acquisition without any underlying relationship of good faith an infringement. Aplin and Arnold put it as follows: 'On the face of it, this provision is not consistent with Article 4, which specifies various circumstances in which the acquisition, use or disclosure of a trade secret shall be considered unlawful. For example, according to Article 4(2), unlawful acquisition occurs when there is: Unauthorized access to, appropriation of, or copying of any documents, objects, materials, substances or electronic files, lawfully under the control of the trade secret holder, containing the trade secret or from which the trade secret can be deduced; Any other conduct which, under the circumstances, is considered contrary tohonest commercial practices. According to the Court of Appeal decision in Tchenguiz v Imerman, it is a breach of confidence "for a defendant, without the authority of the claimant, to examine, or to make, retain, or supply copies to a third party of, a document whose contents are, and were (or ought to have been) appreciated by the defendant to be, confidential to the claimant." While this common law principle implements aspects of Article 4(2), it does not explicitly refer to access to objects, materials or substances or, more significantly, to "other conduct which ... is considered contrary to honest commercial practices." Also, the Imerman principle requires that the defendant intentionally acquires the confidential information knowing that it is confidential, which is not a requirement of Article 4(2). Indeed, the element of intention, which was present in the draft Directive, was omitted following a suggestion from the Council. Thus, to maintain a requirement of intention when it comes to unlawful acquisition would appear inconsistent with Article 4(2).'[47]

Aspects that were not translated into the Regulations because they were considered already part of the law of breach of confidence are the provision permitting reverse engineering; and the provision concerning acquisition, use or disclosure of a trade secret for the purposes of exercising the right to freedom of expression and for revealing misconduct, wrongdoing or illegal activity for protecting the general public interest, respectively, as instances where enforcement of trade secret protection should not occur. Aplin and Arnold critique these two deliberate omissions, arguing that the law of breach of confidence is not in fact absolutely congruent with the terms of the Directive.[48] The Regulations also provide that a trade secret holder may apply for, and a court may grant 'measures, procedures and remedies' available in an action for breach of confidence which provide 'wider protection' to the trade secret holder than that available under the Regulations, provided that they 'comply with the safeguards referred to in' Article 1 of the Directive. Thus, the intention is clear to ensure that the

46. Regulations 3 & 1.
47. *See* above n 1, 74-75.
48. *Ibid.*, 77-78.

action for breach of confidence in its arguably broader reach remains available to claimants, with the noted reservation.

[B] Recent Developments and Decisions Concerning the Regulations

Although, in some respects, imposing more stringent substantive requirements, bringing an action (either exclusively or cumulatively or; *see, e.g., Corrigan v. OneE*) under the Regulations has some procedural advantages. Although equity already catered for trade secrets to be kept out of the public eye during and after trial, the Regulations establish an arguably clearer framework for departing from the normal standard of public justice: *see* In *ASA v. Mitchell*;[49] *Bamford Excavators v. Manitou.*[50] In *Salt Ship v. Prysmian Powerlink*,[51] a claim under breach of confidence was at issue, but the Regulation was relied on to obtain a publicity order, requiring that certain elements of a judgment be withheld from publication. The Regulations also allow for an order that the losing side publish the relevant outcome in an appropriate format, such as on a website.

The Regulations expressly allow for reverse engineering, and this is one area where it will be interesting to observe how the regulatory position accords with the relevant principles in breach of confidence. Traditionally, the fact that information can, in theory, be obtained by a process of reverse engineering does not necessarily mean it is in the public domain and therefore not protected in equity. In *Kerry Ingredients v. Bakkavor*, the Court held that there had been misuse of confidential information relating to the method of production of edible infused oils. That information could, in fact, be obtained by a process of reverse engineering or trial and error. However, since this required considerable work and could not be considered to be second nature to a developer, it was sufficiently secret. The information had imparted confidence in the sense of a specific purpose: safety and regulatory compliance. A springboard injunction was granted.[52] The Regulations also make it explicit that a court where it finds that there has been an unlawful acquisition, use or disclosure of a trade secret, the court may, on application by the trade secret holder, order recall of the infringing goods from the market; depriving the infringing goods of their infringing quality (i.e., modifications to the goods); and destruction of the infringing goods or their withdrawal from the market, provided that the withdrawal does not undermine the protection of the trade secret in question.[53] The Regulations mirror the Trade Secrets Directive in other specific procedural ways, such as in relation to interim injunctions, corrective measures, safeguards, and proportionality factors relevant to the granting of interim relief.

49. *Advertising Standards Authority Limited v. Robert Neil Whyte Mitchell* [2019] EWHC 1469 (QB).
50. *JC Bamford Excavators Limited v. Manitou UK Limited & Anor* [2023] EWCA Civ 840; this matter proceeded in multiple jurisdictions and was ultimately settled. *See* Amy Sandys, 'JCB and Manitou Settle Litigation Over Telehandler Patents' *Juve Patent* (online) 15 December 2023, https://www.juve-patent.com/cases/manitou-jcb-settle-european-litigation-telehandler-patents/.
51. *Salt Ship Design AS v. Prysmian Powerlink* SRL [2021] EWHC 2633 (Comm).
52. *See* Art. 3 (1)(b) of the regulations; *see also* the pre-Regulations case of *Mars v. Teknowledge.*
53. Regulations Arts 2(4) and 4(5).

§4.04 INDUSTRIAL ESPIONAGE IN ENGLISH LAW

English legal doctrine means a person who has been supplied information in circumstances that imply a duty to use it for particular purposes is tied to its supplier by an obligation of good faith not to use or communicate it for other purposes. An unrelated third party has not received information in such circumstances, so it has no such obligations to the original confidor. In theory, therefore, the possessor of a trade secret has no recourse against a spy or surreptitious acquirer who is not in a relationship that generates good faith obligations. This is a curious position, and in an article published in 1998, Hull rightly pointed out that:

> it would be extraordinary if a defendant, who acquired by eavesdropping or other improper covert means the secrets of the plaintiff because he would not have been able to get them by consensual arrangement, could defend proceedings by the plaintiffs on the ground that no obligation of confidence could arise without communication of the information by the defendant.[54]

But there were some obstacles in the way of progress in the logical direction the author suggests. At that time, the author points out, no *English* case had actually held a surreptitious acquirer liable. However, with the *Spycatcher* decision in England,[55] obligations not to deal with secret information in certain ways started to be separated from the search for an underling relationship between information sharers.

But perhaps a useful starting point is to consider what third parties *are* legally entitled to do in relation to others' secrets. In terms of industrial espionage, it is clear that a third party is entitled under English law, as under US law, to reverse engineer any product that has been supplied or put onto the market for the purpose of finding out what is hidden within.[56] This reflects the fact that freedom of trade, of work and of competition is highly valued in English law, whether it be post-employment, in relation to restraints of trade, or with regard to broad confidentiality clauses. That is the case on the basis of the well-recognized principle that restraints of trade are 'against public policy' rather than on the basis of constitutional guarantees of freedom of work and of industry that have a long pedigree in jurisdictions such as France. Arguably, in English law, there is not even a legal 'fair competition' requirement, since there is no action for unfair competition, nor a requirement to respect privacy as there is no tort that stands in the way of prying eyes – or at least not until recently. Vigorous competition and the associated information gathering are therefore the norm.

---

54. *See* John Hull, 'Stealing Secrets: A Review of the Law Commission Consultation Paper on the Misuse of Trade Secrets' (1998) 4 *Intellectual Property Quarterly* 422, 426-427.
55. *Attorney-Gaeralfor the United Kingdom v. Heinemann Publishers Australia Pty Ltd [NO 21]* (1988) 62 ALJR 344. In Australia, *see Attorney-General for the United Kingdom v. Heinemann Publishers Australia Pty Ltd* (1987) 8 NSWLR 341. For consideration of the latter, *see* Matthew Howard, 'Spycatcher Downunder: AG for the UK v Heinemann Publishers Australia' (1989) 19(1) *University of Western Australia Law Review* 158.
56. *See Mars UK Ltd v. Teknowledge Ltd* [1999] All ER 600.

In other words, a third party hungry for information is under fewer general legal restraints in England than in many other countries.[57] No criminal liability for industrial espionage existed in England until recently, when the National Security Act 2023 was passed, albeit without generally criminalizing trade secrets theft.[58] There is also no general principle of civil (or '*delictual*') liability for fault as exists in France, and that in reality applies in equity as much as at law, wrongs such as unconscionability or unjust enrichment providing a cohesive rationale concerning remedies for *existing* actions rather than a generalized basis for obligations or remedies per se.[59] However, there are of course numerous specific actions that will operate on the acquisitive competitor or curious investigator, both criminal and civil. For instance, in terms of criminal liability: misuse of communications equipment or computers, interfering with mail and telephone conversations, general theft relating to information carriers, fraud and the like.[60] In terms of civil wrongs: trespass, conversion, detinue, and inducing a breach of contract, among others. But all these, and most acutely theft and fraud, tend to depend on some physical possession and taking or interference.

Is it then otherwise open to a person to use any trick, deceit, sharp practice or improper and surreptitious method to obtain hidden information in England? Unsurprisingly, even though the country is well-known for a vigorous and unrestrained tabloid press, the answer these days is no. As far as the action for breach of confidence is concerned, this has come about because of relatively recent developments, first, in relation to the requirement of a pre-existing relationship or an act of communication to a confidee who is thereby fixed with an obligation of confidence. In the 1978 Australian (Queensland) case of *Franklin v. Giddins,*[61] a common starting point of any account of this legal question, the defendants were guilty of trespass (onto the land of the plaintiff) and theft of some budwood containing confidential genetic information. The defendants were aware of the value of the confidential information and the plaintiffs intended to keep it to themselves. According to the court, the defendant was in effect in the same position as a third party who knowingly received trade secrets from a person who was not entitled to pass them on. Nonetheless, it is fair to say that the doctrinal difficulties inherent in extending a legal obligation to a party with whom the budwood owner had no particular relationship or communications were simply brushed aside.[62] The emphasis was on the reprehensible nature of the conduct, the

57. Perhaps also until recently because of the vigour and power of the tabloid press, even where there are specific legal regimes (such as against phone hacking), there appears to be a culture of unrestrained information gathering.
58. National Security Act 2023, available at https://www.legislation.gov.uk/ukpga/2023/32/contents.
59. *See*, however, the Canadian cases where an action for unjust enrichment as such has attracted more support: *Cadbury Schweppes Inc. v. FBI Foods Ltd* [1999] 15 SCR 142; *Free-Trade Network Inc. v. BC Travel Insurance Co.* (2005) 29 CCLI (4th) 244 (Ontario Supreme Court of Justice).
60. *Theft Act 1968* (UK), c 60, ss 1, 4; *Criminal Justice Act 1987* (UK), c 38, s. 3; *Computer Misuse Act 1990* (UK), c 18, s. 1.
61. [1978] Qd R 72 ('*Franklin*').
62. In US law, where there were manifest *indicia* of the plaintiff's intent to keep the genetic information to himself, and improper, to wit illegal methods used to acquire the information, there would be little doubt about the outcome.

court considering the thief who steals a trade secret to use it in competition with his target no 'less unconscionable than a traitorous servant'.[63] In fact, although the case is commonly cited as the first to extend the obligation of confidence to unrelated third parties, some have argued that the court sidestepped the issue and instead decided the matter on a wider basis of unconscionability.[64]

Perhaps the court's willingness to extend liability was understandable where the defendant's conduct was so calculated, deliberate and illegal. But in a famous and influential *dictum* in the *Spycatcher* case, Lord Goff took an even more expansive approach, extending the obligation to accidental discoverers as well, in circumstances where the information was 'obviously confidential'.[65] Either this means simply that a third party is beholden just because of their knowledge or that the impropriety or dishonesty of making use of information that is 'obviously confidential' justifies the imposition of a remedy. Whatever the case may be, *Spycatcher* (UK) stands for the proposition that there might be a remedy in some circumstances, even where there is no underlying relationship of good faith between the supplier and the abuser of the information.

In cases after *Franklin*, the illegality of the conduct concerned was less clear, but in each case, there were sufficient signals on display for the surreptitious acquirer to know that the plaintiff intended to keep information confidential. This was, for instance, the case in *Shelley Films v. Rex Features Ltd*[66] and *Creation Records Ltd v. News Group Newspapers Ltd.*[67] However, both reported decisions only concerned interlocutory applications, so that no more than an arguable case in breach of confidence was necessary. They concerned stealthily obtained photographs of scenes hitherto kept hidden from the public, and arguably, there was a trespass and breach of contract involved (in relation to implied conditions of entry). Nonetheless, from the bold step taken in *Franklin*, courts have regularly accepted that on some basis or another, a third party who uses either illegal, tortious, improper or surreptitious means to obtain information they know to be confidential can be held liable in breach of confidence. Alternatively, some have gone so far as to suggest that it is wrong per se for a person who knows information is confidential and/or where it is 'obviously confidential' to use it in an unintended manner. With the latter view, there are considerable difficulties, not the least is how the recipient or obtainer is to know what the 'owner' of the information intended to be done with it or what is 'obvious'; this

63. *See Franklin*, above n 61 at 80.

64. *See* Duncan Stewart, *Trade Secrets in New Zealand* (PhD Thesis, Massey University, 1996). The author says 'Dunn J decided the case on the broad principle of unconscionability', and also points out that Gurry in the first edition of his book, *Breach of Confidence* (Clarendon Press, 1984) 165 criticized this approach as being too broad and open-ended a principle that would make it impossible to distinguish between illegitimate espionage and legitimate competition or surveillance. *See* 3.07-3.08 Thesis available at https://www.managingip.com/article/2bhoso75 2z5oo1dlne2o0/sponsored-content/enforcement-strategy-litigation-vs-administrative-actions#:~:text=For%20example%2C%20the%20civil%20litigation,manufacturers%20or%20original%20equipment%20manufacturers.

65. *Attorney General v. Guardian Newspapers Ltd (No 2)* [1990] 1 AC 109, (HL), 281-282.

66. [1994] EMLR 134.

67. [1997] EMLR 444.

matter is further discussed below and has developed in particular in cases relating to personal private information. In the UK, the bases for remedies for unauthorized obtaining and misuse of such information have metamorphosed in surprising ways.

After *Franklin*, it took a while before a *Christopher*-type case,[68] where there was neither civil nor criminal illegality associated with obtaining the information, but merely surreptitious or improper means arose clearly before a court. *Bernstein v. Skyviews* has analogies,[69] but the action against a company that took aerial photographs of the plaintiff's property without permission was not framed in breach of confidence. Both nuisance - if the flying over were a persistent interference with enjoyment of land - and trespass - depending on how high the property rights extended - were at issue, as well as a putative invasion of privacy. If the action *had* been framed in breach of confidence, there were probably arguable instances of illegality (in the civil sense) which could attract liability.[70] The more difficult problem of mere impropriety as a basis for attaching liability to a third party presented itself in *Malone v. Metropolitan Police Commissioner* in the form of telephone tapping.[71] Megarry V-C's judgment illustrates the difficulties inherent in applying a standard such as impropriety because whereas some might say that tapping a person's phone without their knowledge is improper, if not downright dishonest,[72] Megarry V-C treated the risk of such eavesdropping on the phone as systemic and therefore not to be complained of. In a famous passage, he posited that late workers overhearing office cleaners, indiscreet users of an office intercom, the unseen neighbour in the toolshed, or nearby passengers with acute hearing should not be exposed to liability:

> I do not see why someone who has overheard some secret in such a way should be exposed to legal proceedings if he uses or divulges what he has heard. No doubt an honourable man would give some warning when he realizes that what he is hearing is not intended for his ears; but I have to concern myself with the law, not with moral standards. There are of course many moral precepts which are not legally enforceable.[73]

One view of Megarry V-C's approach is that it reflects a risk-assumption policy radically different from Lord Goff's position in *Spycatcher*. The latter gives the example of a passer-by finding an obviously confidential letter that has been blown out of an office window by a fan or a diary accidentally dropped in a public place, as ones where the obligation arises in the finder. Perhaps Megarry V-C's view would be that the owners should have been more careful and that the risk somebody would read the documents was theirs to prevent. Nonetheless, it became passably clear that actual

68. *EI DuPont de Nemours & Co Inc v. Christopher*, 431 Fd 2d 1012 (5th Cir,1970); *see* further below in the discussion of US law in Chapter 5 - this case concerned overflying a property to take photos.
69. [1978] QB 479.
70. Although then there would be a question whether the property owner had taken such measures as would indicate that he intended to keep things within the property boundaries private from prying eyes.
71. [1979] 2 All ER 620; *(No 2)* [1979] Ch 344.
72. Leaving aside any statutory authority in the case of the Police. *See Gurry*, above n 38, 563 [13].
73. *Malone v. Metropolitan Police Commissioner (No 2)* [1979] Ch 344, 376.

illegality is not required, and mere impropriety is enough to vest liability; and in England, in some circumstances, even showing impropriety may no longer be required, in particular where personal private information is concerned, as is further explored below.

[A] Impropriety or No Impropriety, What Is Impropriety?

As indicated above, in the English context, personal and commercial secrets fall within the remit of the one action for breach of confidence. The question of whether surreptitious or improper taking of confidential information amounts to an actionable wrong arises in both contexts, but perhaps, in truth, calls for different approaches because arguably very different interests are at stake in each. An obvious way to develop a distinct approach in relation to personal information is to accept invasion of privacy as a separate actionable wrong or tort. In one view, that has now become the English way. However, this is an area of development still attended by some uncertainty, as we reflected upon above. *See* [Introduction to the English approach]. However, where it comes to trade secrets as opposed to private personal information (where not privacy interest is at stake), it still falls to judges to assess a third party's acts against some standard of propriety, good conscience or 'honest commercial trading' within the framework of the action for breach of confidence. Alternatively, trade secrets misuse can be pleaded in terms of the Regulations. In that context, Regulation 3 paragraph 1 provides that the 'acquisition, use or disclosure of a trade secret is unlawful where the acquisition, use or disclosure constitutes a breach of confidence in confidential information'. As we noted above, arguably, this provision does not fully implement Article 4 of the Directive, which says that trade secret holders are entitled to prevent or obtain redress for unlawful acquisition, use or disclosure of their trade secret. It also defines the circumstances that constitute unlawful acquisition, use or disclosure, including by third parties and in the case of infringing goods. According to Article 4(2), this includes any conduct that is considered contrary to honest commercial practices. Had the latter phrase been adopted in the UK Regulations, looping back to breach of confidence would have been rendered unnecessary, and it would have been abundantly clear that a third party using means considered dishonest in commerce to obtain or deal with trade secrets was open to liability, whether or not that constituted a breach of an obligation of good faith to some other party.

The difficulty lies in predictably and factually determining (in the absence of a jury these days) what, in the context of breach of confidence, the standard of conduct is against which actions are to be assessed. At present, this is vaguer and broader than nonconformity with standards of honest commercial conduct, something about which objective evidence can be supplied. The problem is perhaps best solved by creating a new category of wrongs specifically surrounding the private sphere, as the courts have now effectively done, either in the form of a new tort of misuse of[74] or by a transmogrified breach of confidence action (*see* above 4.01 Introduction to the English Approach. In a modern society where all sorts of surveillance and tracking are becoming ubiquitous, that is perhaps not an unwarranted step; additionally, it reflects a legitimate expectation based on a fundamental and recognized (in the ECHR) right to privacy. That an invasion of privacy itself, irrespective of any use or communication of what is learned by it, is actionable may be a useful deterrent. In the UK, but not in Australia or other common law jurisdictions because of the UK's adherence to the ECHR, that is arguably what has occurred, in one way or another. The advantage of recognizing a separate tort is that if a court determines that information was obtained by way of a tortious invasion of privacy, then there is a clear legal wrong which can justify a remedy against further uses of that information. For instance, the photographer who points a telephoto lens from a public road to take a photo of a person in a bathroom or of a patient in a hospital foyer can be enjoined from publishing that photo in a magazine. The public interest or the freedom of the press can be evaluated to determine whether the invasion of privacy can be excused so no wrong has in fact been committed; standards of proportionality come into play in a well-established fashion. Of course, this depends on the circumstances being such as would indicate to a reasonable person that the plaintiff intended to keep actions or information private or had a reasonable expectation of privacy.

In the absence of such a tort of invasion of privacy, which can be an independent vehicle for elaborating a legal standard of acceptable conduct over time, the law is left, as in Australia (but no longer in the UK), with a vague standard of 'impropriety' or 'surreptitiousness' applied in all sorts of breach of confidence actions. Perhaps that is not satisfactory: whereas in privacy cases, the freedom of the press is commonly at stake, in trade secrets cases, what is at stake is free, vigorous and competitive information gathering. In other words, the optimal functioning of markets. To sacrifice that on the altar of impropriety is problematical because of the vagueness and unpredictability of the standard.

Whereas the problem has now been solved by developing a separate tort of breach of privacy in relation to *personal* information in the UK, this does not help in commercial cases because the privacy interest of corporations is barely recognized or accepted. This is relevant in two ways: first, in the manner discussed above because there is no legal wrong or illegality to which liability for breach of confidence can be attached, and second, because, in the absence of a right to privacy, the information concerned may not be confidential or a trade secret at all. If there is no legal privacy standard, measures indicative of the fact of and intention to maintain information secrecy are required; the plaintiff cannot simply say information or events occurred or were contained on private premises, *and that is enough*. However, where there is a right to privacy, it may *indeed* be enough. This was effectively the problem in *Lenah Game Meats*, where it was held that the possum meat processing was not simply

74. Also *see* Michael Douglas, 'Characterisation of Breach of Confidence as A Privacy Tort in Private International Law' (2018) 41(2) *UNSW Law Journal Volume* 390 https://doi.org/10.53637/eakf6390.

confidential because it happened on private premises alone.[75] In terms of the Regulations, what is required is that the claimant can point to some reasonable measures taken to secure the secrecy of the information concerned.

In this context, the *Douglas* case in the UK is interesting because it concerned a mix of commercial and privacy interests.[76] The couple had surrounded their wedding with security measures, but this was at least in part for the sake of securing their exclusive publicity deal with the magazine *OK!* – so not just to protect themselves against unwanted intrusions per se. The fact that photographs of the wedding were to be published in a large circulation magazine made it rather artificial, at least in terms of the publication of images, to complain about the effect on their privacy of the intruder's photographs appearing in the rival *Hello!* magazine. What was really at stake was the right of the celebrity couple to control the commercial exploitation of their confidential information.

Nonetheless, Lindsay J at first instance pointed to the plaintiff's intention to keep their wedding confidential, the extensive measures taken to keep it so, and the fact the sneaky photographer knew or ought to have known that an obligation of confidence was attached to him. His causing the photos to be published then constituted a breach.[77] It seems, therefore, that the extended action for breach of confidence, requiring only that the information be confidential, that measures have been taken to keep it so, that the defendant knew of these measures, and that he nonetheless obtained and/or published the information without authorization, might in fact apply both in cases where there is a personal privacy interest at stake and in cases that are more concerned with trade secrets, i.e., commercial interests. The judgment of Lord Hoffmann in the House of Lords lends further credence to the statement that now the law of trade secrets more generally has to some extent changed character in England. It has moved closer to an *action in rem* than an action in personam. George Wei points out that 'the fact that information is confidential, in the sense that it is not known to the general public, does not by itself generate any rights against the world at large'.[78] He also points out that:

> if it is right that confidential information does not create proprietary rights, then the mere fact of a taking cannot be a ground for liability. If it did, the action would have taken on the characteristics of in rem liability. The issue is to determine the control factors necessary to support equity's intervention in the case of surreptitious takings. These control factors must be developed in a manner that is consistent with the fundamental notion of liability based on concept [sic] of good faith and conscience.[79]

75. Nonetheless, the High Court in that case did envisage that the liability for breach of confidence was not restricted to information passed between two parties, Gleeson CJ saying that 'equity may impose obligations of confidentiality even though there is no imparting of information in circumstances of trust and confidence'. *See Australian Broadcasting Corp. v. Lenah Game Meats Pty Ltd* (2001) 208 CLR 199, [34].
76. *Douglas v. Hello! (No 5)* [2003] EWHC 786 (Ch).
77. *Ibid.*
78. *See* above n 56, 303.
79. *Ibid.*, 305.

In *Sullivan v. Sclanders*, a nice statement of the approach which charges equity with the policing of conscientious conduct is to be found:

> A person who has confidential information belonging to another may be restrained from using it without the owner's consent, by injunction. Equity acts in regard to the unconscionable circumstances in which the confidential documents were obtained and disseminated. Equity may grant relief from the consequences of reprehensible conduct. To be effective, this relief may bind third parties who may have come into possession of the information and can protect the defendants from oral or written dissemination or other use.[80]

In reality, breach of confidence has become a very far-reaching action, and perhaps by extension, so have the rights under the Regulations, since they refer back to this action in the determination of what constitutes actionable misuse. Its already rather proprietary character in relation to unauthorized *communications* of confidences is extended to grant the possessor rights *erga omnes* in England. In the older cases and in other common law jurisdictions, the emphasis was and is on the illegal, surreptitious and improper nature of the obtaining of the information – the use of espionage in the pejorative sense of the word. The cases that impose liability on third-party spies are mostly ones where such actions involved illegality or a civil wrong, such as trespass, nuisance or conversion of goods. Conversion can arise where a person keeps a document long enough to take copies or note down information. It seems, therefore, that there are almost always legal wrongs that can be pointed to and that there is arguably no need, in light of the interests of maintaining freedom of competition, imitation, speech and labour, to go so far as to say that disclosing another's secret knowledge is wrong simply because the acquirer knows the possessor intends to keep it secret. But that is effectively what has happened in the UK.

In this context, it is interesting to consider the situation in other common law jurisdictions. In New Zealand, the courts simply and clearly 'created' a right of action totally separate from breach of confidence and intended to vindicate the privacy interests of individuals. The statement of Gault P in *Hosking v. Runting* is explicit as to the elements of the action and the fact that it does not fit well with protection of privacy:

> The elements of the breach of confidence action are well established in New Zealand, and our courts have adopted the formulation in Coco v Clark in areas such as employment, trade secrets and information about a plaintiff's private life; [he cites a number of New Zealand cases]. As the law currently stands, a successful action requires information that is confidential, communication of that information to another in circumstances importing an obligation of confidence and unauthorized use or disclosure. Many privacy cases simply do not fit within this analysis, yet undoubtedly justify legal remedies.[81]

Interestingly enough, the Court of Appeal in the same case accepted this recognition of a tort of invasion of privacy, although only by a majority of three to

80. *Sullivan v. Sclanders & Goldwell International Pty Ltd* [2000] SASC 273, [31] (Gray J).
81. *Hosking v. Runting* [2005] 1 NZLR 1, [46].

two.[82] Australia does not know a privacy tort, and it has not adopted the approach of the recent UK cases; it relies on a corporate regulatory approach to protect privacy rights.

In conclusion, the English equity tradition grew from a desire to hold persons to their obligation to act with good faith and '*loyauté*' in the context of communications between them. But it now well and truly changed in England itself, where with the justified ambition of protecting the privacy of the individual, the courts have, perhaps surprisingly, moved further towards a proprietary approach for confidential information as a whole. In the American jurisprudence, by way of contrast, the courts have, under the influence of the *UTSA*, embraced the quest for impropriety as a significant control factor in determining liability, as is addressed below. In that sense, US courts are closer to the traditional equitable view and closer to the law of breach of confidence as it now stands in jurisdictions such as Australia and New Zealand. The latter has fortunately (in terms of doctrinal coherence at least) seen the emergence of a separate tort of invasion of privacy, which is a preferable way to progress things compared to the artificial expansion of breach of confidence, as suggested above. In Australia, the introduction of a statutory tort of invasion of privacy has been under active consideration, but it remains a controversial topic.[83] The comparison between England and Australia is most apt because in neither country does the criminal law come directly to the aid of the possessor of trade secrets as it does in the US and, for instance, also in New Zealand, although now in a narrow manner relating to state-sponsored espionage, this has changed in the UK. The role of the criminal law is further considered below.

A final point relates to the liability of third-party recipients of secret information: it is difficult to insist that an action for breach of confidence only lies against a person to whom information was communicated and not against a spy. Gareth Jones points out that it would be inequitable that a person who is an innocent acquirer of value who has been put on notice concerning a breach of confidence by his supplier should be worse off than a spy who obtains information by reprehensible means. It is after all the position in English law that an innocent acquirer for value once on notice is liable under an obligation of confidence.[84]

---

82. *See* Andrew Geddis, '*Hosking v Runting*: A Privacy Tort for New Zealand' (2005) 13 *Tort Law Review* 5; Russell Brown, 'Rethinking Privacy: Exclusivity, Private Relation and Tort Law' (2005-2006) 43 *Alberta Law Review* 589, 609. *See also Bradley v. Wingnut Films* [1993] 1 NZLR 425; *P v. D* [2000] 2 NZLR 591; Sirko Harder, 'Gain-Based Relief for the Invasion of Privacy' (2011) 1 *DICTUM* 62 https://doi.org/10.2139/ssrn.2142288.
83. *See* Australian Law Reform Commission, *For Your Information: Australian Privacy Law and Practice*, Report No 108 (2008). *See also* Des Butler, 'Torty of Invasion of Privacy in Australia' (2005) 29 *Melbourne University Law Review* 339; Dan Meagher, 'Freedom of Political Communications, Public Officials and the Emerging Right to Personal Privacy in Australia' (2008) 19(11) *Adelaide Law Review* 175 https://doi.org/10.1126/science.175.4021.498; Dan J.B. Svantesson, 'Privacy Law: Australia: Conflict of Laws Issues Associated with an Action for Interference with Privacy' (2007) 23(6) *Computer Law and Security Report*, 523-528.
84. *See* Gareth Jones, 'Restitution of Benefits Obtained in Breach of Confidence' (1970) 86 *Law Quarterly Review* 463, 482-483.

§4.05 THE ROLE OF STATUTE AND CRIMINAL LAW IN ENGLAND AND SIMILAR JURISDICTIONS

In the common law 'breach of confidence' countries, statutes, whether civil or criminal traditionally, played a very minor role. There was long a sense that the law of equity is flexible enough to develop in a manner consistent with new conditions and community expectations. The developments around private information in England are an example of such flexibility, although much of the impetus there did come from statute in the form of ECHR privacy protection. In New Zealand, the Torts and General Law Reform Committee stated that it saw little advantage in 'a statutory restatement of the existing rules' because the courts were willing to 'develop the equitable principles relating to breach of confidence in order to cover new types of situations'.[85] In Canada, a Uniform Trade Secrets law was developed but not adopted by the relevant legislators.[86] In the UK, the Law Commission's recommendation was not taken up, but of course, not due to some sense of a need for statutory intervention but because of EU obligations, the Regulations were introduced: not to codify the law of trade secrets, but to tinker with it in the most minimal way possible for the sake of conformity with the EU Trade Secrets Directive.

Nonetheless, with little fanfare, the New Zealand parliament, by an amendment to the *Crimes Act 1961* (NZ) in 2003, created a new offence of taking, obtaining or copying trade secrets (*see* section 230).[87] It is now a criminal offence to dishonestly and without claim of right, take, obtain or copy documents, models or other depictions, or copies thereof containing or embodying any trade secrets, knowing that it does so (contain or embody trade secrets). The required *mens rea* is the intent to obtain any pecuniary advantage or to cause loss to any other person. As commentators have pointed out, due to *the Crimes Act 1961* definition of the term 'obtain',[88] the section applies where a trade secret is *retained* as well as obtained, so that it would extend to an employee who keeps a trade secret after termination, as well as to one who copies and passes on secret documents to a competitor.[89] It is perhaps unclear whether the section applies to a person who deliberately memorizes trade secrets, as this might not constitute a taking. A trade secret under the Act is defined to mean any information that is (or could be) used industrially or commercially, is not generally available, has potential economic value, and is the subject of 'all reasonable efforts' to preserve its secrecy. The definition is based on the common law and is quite wide in scope, but obviously, a specific regime applying only to trade secrets is created by this reform. The

85. *See* New Zealand Torts and General Law Reform Committee, *Report on the Protection of Trade Secrets* (December 1973), Conclusion; *see* Brown & Grant, *Intellectual Property Law in New Zealand* (1989), 642.
86. A *Uniform Trade Secrets Act* was drafted in 1989, however, it was not adopted in any province.
87. *Crimes Amendment Act 2003* (NZ). The amending Act also introduced a number of computer-related specific offences, which attracted more attention in the period prior to enactment.
88. *Crimes Act 1961* (NZ) s. 217.
89. *See* Bell Gully, *Trade Secrets Theft Becomes a Criminal Offence* (July 2004) *Intellectual Property*, previously available at http://www.bellgully.com/newsletters/Intellectual_Property/tradeSecret.asp.

mental elements of the offence, however, are quite stringent, and as the same commentators indicate prosecutions will probably remain rare, as has proven to be the case in other jurisdictions.[90] For litigants, the commentators identify some considerable advantages, however: avoiding costly breach of confidence litigation; avoiding the cost of executing an Anton Piller order because the public authorities can execute a search warrant;[91] and the possibility for complainants under the Act and the *Proceeds of Crime Act 1991* (NZ) to receive 'the equivalent of civil remedies'.[92] In a recent case (2019), an architect was convicted under section 230 (to community detention, although a prison sentence is possible) because he had downloaded thousands of files before transferring to new employment.[93] In terms of the application of the general law of theft, in Canada, the Supreme Court held that the taking of confidential information could not constitute theft because there is no property in information, and that represents the traditional and global view. In the absence of a physical taking, there could be no offence of theft in Canada. In 1986, the Federal Working Party recommended the introduction of a statutory regime for civil liability in relation to trade secrets and also the creation of federal criminal provisions. The weakness of the existing civil and criminal regimes and the cost of civil actions were cited in favour of the intended reform, the increased cost to the public purse, the dearth of prosecutions in the US and the problem of identifying exactly what behaviour should attract a criminal penalty and thus prosecution were cited against. Canada did not then follow in the footsteps of its southern neighbour. However, Canada has now followed New Zealand by way of an amendment to the Crimes Act (section 391). The amendment came about because, on 1 July 2020, the Canada-United States-Mexico Agreement (CUSMA) came into force, requiring this change (as discussed above in Chapter 3). This section now provides that everyone commits an offence who, 'by deceit, falsehood or other fraudulent means, knowingly obtains a trade secret or communicates or makes available a trade secret'. It also establishes related offence for any third-party who obtains, communicates, or makes available a trade secret obtained in the above-mentioned manner.[94] This provision has not been tested in the courts at the time of publication of this edition. Criminal law is a federal matter in Canada, so there are no provincial trade secrets offences. In Australia, criminal law is a state matter, but IP (although not expressly trade secrets) is a federal (Commonwealth) matter.[95] The

90. *Ibid.*
91. An Anton Piller order is a private search warrant permitting seizure of evidence, named after the case of *Anton Piller KG v. Manufacturing Processes Ltd* [1976] Ch 55.
92. *Ibid.*
93. Sam Hurley, 'Trade Secrets Theft: Architect Convicted, Sentenced to Community Detention' *New Zealand Herald* (online), 6 September 2019 https://www.nzherald.co.nz/nz/trade-secrets-theft-architect-convicted-sentenced-to-community-detention/TP2QM6HUSVZ4EWWXMVJGYXZS5E/#:~:text=He%20instead%20convicted%20Davies%20and,the%20architecture%20firm%20Design%20Partners.
94. *See* Matt Malone, 'Consequences of the Criminalization of Trade Secret Theft in Canada' (2021) 54(3) *UBC Law Review* 889.
95. Under the *Commonwealth of Australia Constitution Act 1900* (Imp) s. 51 (xviii) – Copyrights, patents of inventions, designs, and trademarks.

well-known problem applies to theft generally in terms of its application to information. In terms of fraud, which requires defrauding of 'any property, money or valuable security or any service', confidential information not falling within any of those categories[96] There is also some suggestion that if the possessor of a trade secret is deprived of the right to profit from the secret, this may be sufficient to constitute the offence. But this argument proceeds by analogy with decisions that have found fraud in relation to copyright, where unauthorized copies were made and turned to account, although the copyright owner was not strictly deprived of ownership. The difficulty is that trade secrets might not 'get to first base' as they are not property to start with.[97]

In England, the Law Commission in 1997 provisionally concluded that unauthorized use or disclosure of a trade secret should under certain conditions be a criminal offence.[98] Steele and Trenton referred to 'the anomaly of there being no criminal legislation specifically targeting the theft of "boardroom secrets"'.[99] The Law Commission had regard to the Alberta and Federal Working Party report in Canada (*see* above) and the American Law Institute's Restatement of the Law of Torts and the US *UTSA*. The *Economic Espionage Act 1996* (US) introduced criminal liability at the federal level in the US, but it already existed in various states (*see* further below). However, the US examples were not in fact then followed in Canada, either in terms of the adoption of a Uniform Trade Secrets law or in terms of criminal liability for trade secrets theft (as stated just above, a general offence was introduced more recently). This is despite the Law Commission itself making the point at the time that it was inconsistent not to impose criminal sanctions in relation to trade secrets.[100] In the UK, the situation remains the same as in Australia: no general offence of misuse of a trade secret; the only recent change is the introduction of an offence relating to transborder industrial espionage. However, as noted above, the inspiration therefore lies not in the sphere of better protection for trade secrets but in the sphere of national security.

§4.06 CONCLUSIONS

The countries that have adopted and adhered to the English equity approach live under a flexible regime of trade secrets protection, where civil liability predominates. Many

96. However, some commentators have maintained that the Supreme Court in *R v. Stewart* gave some obiter support for the notion that deprivation of a valuable trade secret that the victim had intended to exploit could amount to fraud: *see* above n 79, at [47] (SCC) per Lamer JA. That the court left the possibility of fraud open, *see*: John T. Cross, 'Protecting Confidential Information under the Criminal Law of Theft and Fraud' (1991) 11(2) *Oxford Journal of Legal Studies* 264, 267-268 https://doi.org/10.1093/ojls/11.2.264.
97. *See* Brenda L. Nightingale, *The Law of Fraud and Related Offences* (Carswell, 1996) 4-19.
98. England & Wales Law Commission, *Misuse of Trade Secrets*, Consultation Paper (No. LCCP 150 (1997). In 1981, the Law Commission produced a Report on Breach of Confidence which considered civil law aspects. England and Wales Law Commission, Breach of Confidence, Report No 110 (1981).
99. Carl Steele & Anthony Trenton, 'Trade Secrets: The Need for Criminal Liability' (1998) 20(5) *European Intellectual Property Review* 188 (Comments).
100. England & Wales Law Commission, *Misuse of Trade Secrets*, Consultation Paper, above n 98, [3.41].

matters are resolved on the basis of the typical steps in civil litigation in such countries, in particular at the stage of an application for a preliminary injunction. Thus, in terms of the operation of the law, the standards applied to the grant of such injunctions are often of critical importance. An applicant who does not receive satisfaction from the court at the preliminary stage is not likely to go to trial, and *a contrario* the respondent who is on the receiving end of such an injunction is likely to settle. Since litigation in common law countries tends to be expensive, there are strong reasons to settle, and this happens in most cases, in particular in the post-employment context where usually undertakings of one kind or another are obtained from respondents.

Nonetheless, the law of confidence is of central importance to commercial life, as its flexible application in many circumstances (e.g., in pre-contractual negotiations) provides parties with a level of comfort in disclosing otherwise secret information for a useful purpose. In terms of extension into industrial espionage and third-party liability, the law has arguably proven to be flexible enough so as to move with the times - without many doctrinal hang-ups. In that sense, this is an area that appears typical of what we expect from the common law: flexible evolution over time without too much concern about doctrinal obstacles. Nonetheless, that has generated some uncertainty and arguably some doctrinal inconsistencies, but perhaps more in the sphere of private personal information than commercial secrets. In the latter sphere in the UK now has been added to the action for breach of confidence, as extended in some relevant ways in recent times, the action based on the Regulations. It will take some time to work out with precision how the relationship between these two instruments will settle. But it does seem that there is an ample supply of remedies and avenues open to a claimant, whatever their precise doctrinal and conceptual relationship may be.

CHAPTER 5

The Common Law Approach: The United States

§5.01 INTRODUCTION

Although English law arrived in the US with early settlers, the law of trade secrets has ultimately followed a very different path there. The relevant law in both jurisdictions was originally founded on the cases, but the developments in equity that gave the action for breach of confidence a clear and separate status in English law occurred after American law diverged from its imperial roots. In more recent times, US trade secrets law has become mainly statute-based, which is not the case in England and like jurisdictions. The *UTSA* has now been adopted in most US states, unlike in Canada, where a similar codification effort has not yet borne fruit. Both at the State and the federal levels, criminal law has played a more direct role in the US than in English common law jurisdictions, although only since the 1960s.

In the US, a separate right of action concerning commercial and technical secrets developed – a genuine trade secrets law rather than a common action covering confidences of all sorts. At the same time, a separate tort of invasion of privacy has also developed from the cases, which covers personal confidences. Naturally, the law in the US has progressed against the backdrop of the Bill of Rights amendments to the Constitution, which protect freedom of speech and with which the law of trade secrets can thus come into conflict. Further, US law is marked by greater acceptance of the notion of a common law tort of unfair competition, although its fortunes, with the various Restatements, have ebbed and flowed over time.[1] Similarly, actions related to trade secrets have been viewed as protecting changing perspectives over time, from a misappropriation approach to an unfair competition focus via a more general intent to repress 'impropriety' in commercial conduct.

1. *See* further below in this Chapter: *'Unfair Competition and Other Actions'*.

As elsewhere, the emergence of a separate law of trade secrets has been controversial to some degree, at least in academic discourse: we have already referred to Professor Bone's argument that there really is none in the US – or alternatively that there is no need for one as other rights and actions do more than enough.[2] Whatever the merits of those arguments might be, it is clear that with the adoption of state statutes modelled on the UTSA and express criminal provisions both at the federal and the state levels, a separate body of trade secrets law emerged during the second half of the twentieth century. There is also a well-developed body of law concerning contractual protection of trade secrets, in particular 'non-competes' or restraints of trade imposed on former employees.[3] That too is a controversial subject matter in the US. Some have long advocated for the wider adoption of the Californian approach (the statutory invalidity rule) for other States, whereas others favoured non-competes. Recently, the balance seems to have tipped in favour of the former, with the Federal Trade Commission's intervention, further discussed in Chapter 9. In this context and also in relation to trade secrets law more generally, conflicts of laws issues between the US state jurisdictions (and with the federal law and courts) have become a significant factor in disputes or litigation about trade secrets. Often it is such issues, as well as the questions that are ventilated at the interlocutory stage, that determine success in any action for trade secrets breaches.[4] As elsewhere, a majority of cases concern ex-employees. Examples of industrial espionage by third parties and criminal prosecutions for such actions are by comparison relatively rare, although arguably on the rise.

[A] The Emergence of Trade Secrets Law in the US

In fact, know-how and trade secrets played a significant role in the process of industrialization in the US. The transition from agricultural polity to industrial powerhouse hampered the UK's attempts to maintain its industrial and commercial pre-eminence by preventing the export of UK know-how. To counteract this, the US sought to attract skilled craftsmen to settle and establish manufacturing industries with introduced technology, as the UK had in fact done (and other nations tried to prevent) in earlier times.[5] However, the mid-1800s saw the repeal of legislation in the UK that had made it illegal for skilled craftsmen to emigrate, and in 1854, the ban on exporting machines, plans and models was lifted.[6] Fetterley maintains that the earlier demise of mercantilism, the rise of '*laissez-faire*' policies during the industrial revolution and the

2. *See* Chapter 1.
3. *See* further below in Chapter 9: *Trade Secrets and Employment*.
4. *See, e.g.*, Gillian Lester & Elizabeth Ryan, 'Choice of Law and Employee Restrictive Covenants: An American Perspective' (2010) 31(2) *Comparative Labor Law & Policy Journal* 389.
5. *See* generally, John R. Harris, *Industrial Espionage and Technology Transfer: Britain and France in the Eighteenth Century* (Ashgate, 1998).
6. *See also* Daniel D. Fetterley, 'Historical Perspectives on Criminal Laws Relating to the Theft of Trade Secrets' (1970) 25(4) *The Business Lawyer* 1535, 1543. As an example of repressive laws Fetterley refers to the '*Act to Prevent the Inconvenience Arising from Seducing Artificers in the Manufactures of Great Britain into Foreign Parts*' of 1719 (5 Geo. I, c 27). He refers to five laws passed in quick succession between 1773 and 1786 to prevent export of 'machinery, models, drawings and specifications': at 1542.

removal of criminal sanctions for technology export from Britain provided the environment for the emergence of an American law of trade secrets.[7] Indigenous industrial development saw the further growth of a civil common law-based action concerning trade secrets, and during the mid-1960s, criminal protection emerged at the state (and only later at the federal) level in the face of growing international technological competition and perceptions of industrial espionage favouring foreign rivals.[8]

US courts in the later years of the nineteenth century and the beginning of the twentieth regularly cited English cases such as *Morrison v. Moat*,[9] *Lamb v. Evans*[10] and *Merryweather v. Moore*.[11] Nonetheless, the doctrinal basis for those English decisions was then not really clear, nor was what exactly amounted to a trade secret.[12] In that uncertain context, a distinct American approach developed in the second half of the nineteenth century, with a particular focus on technical trade secrets. The most influential but not the first of the early cases was the matter of *Peabody v. Norfolk*, heard before the Massachusetts Supreme Court.[13] Bone asserts that the court in this case 'seized the opportunity to generalize' in relation to the action in a manner that no earlier court had attempted.[14] That is because pre-1860s cases were more focused on addressing specific issues, such as whether agreements not to use or disclose trade secrets amounted to an illegal restraint of trade.[15] Further, the courts, concerned with identifying a basis for the intervention of equity, debated whether there was, but did recognize, a property right in a trade secret for that purpose. Recognition of this type of property right was also held not to be in restraint of trade. However, Bone points out that Justice Gray did state 'it is the policy of the law, for the advantage of the public, to encourage and protect invention and commercial enterprise'.[16] But although the inventor or discoverer of some new technique had a 'property in it', it was not the kind of property that amounted to an exclusive right against the public or against good faith acquirers; rather, he had a property 'which a court of chancery will protect against one who in violation of contract and breach of confidence undertakes to apply it to his own use, or to disclose it to third persons'.[17] Property, as well as permitting the grant of an equitable remedy and ensuring that a transfer contract is not in restraint of trade, also meant that third parties could be restrained even though they were not in a contractual relationship with the plaintiff.[18] Risch puts it more strongly, where he says that 'the current law of trade secrecy grew out of a need to hold third parties liable for misuse of

7. *Ibid.*, 1543.
8. *Ibid.*, 1537.
9. 68 ER 492, 501.
10. 3 Ch LR 462 (1892).
11. 2 Ch LR 518 (1892).
12. *See* Melvin F. Jager, *Trade Secrets Law* (Thompson Reuters, at April 2013) Part A - Chapter 2 - The Historical Development of Trade Secret Concepts.
13. 98 Mass 452 (1868). The first was, according to Jager, *Vickery v. Welch*, 36 Mass 523, 19 Pick. 23, 1837 WL 2540 (1837).
14. *See* Robert G. Bone, 'A New Look at Trade Secrets Law: Doctrine in Search of Justification' (1998) 86(2) *California Law Review* 241, 252 https://doi.org/10.2307/3481134.
15. *See Taylor v. Blanchard*, 95 Mass 370 (1866).
16. *Jet Spray Cooler, Inc. v. Crampton*, 377 Mass 159, 166 (1979).
17. *Peabody*, 458. As cited by Bone, *see* above n 14, 253.
18. *See* above n 14, 254.

information despite a lack of privity with the owner. This led to an early definition of trade secrets as property'.[19] The terminology of property, thus, had an instrumental purpose.

Jager points out that in the second half of the nineteenth century, courts also dismissed earlier concerns that an injunction concerning use of a trade secret was not workable;[20] it was an appropriate equitable remedy where 'injury *would be irreparable* and the remedy at law inadequate' (emphasis added).[21] As the Supreme Court of Pennsylvania put it in *McGowin v. Remington*:[22]

> there is property in the design, in the idea, and in the mental conception, as well as in the piece of paper on which it is expressed ... His property rights will be protected in such cases against a breach of trust, confidence or contract, and especially will be protected against a breach of confidence existing between an employer and an employee.[23]

In *Cincinnati Bell Foundry Co v. Dodds*, an Ohio Supreme Court decision, Judge Taft (later Chief Justice of the Supreme Court), explained the nature of the property nicely as follows: 'The property in a secret process is the power to make use of it to the exclusion of the world. *If the world knows of the process, then the property disappears.* There can be no property in a process, and no right of protection if knowledge of it is common to the world' (emphasis added).[24] Thus, Bone points out that IP and trade secrets law were neatly complementary:

> to late nineteenth century courts and commentators ... The common law protected information so long as it remained secret. Once published, however, the information became 'public property' and all common law rights ended. The public, which then owned the information, decided through legislation what exclusive rights, if any, to give to individuals. Thus rights in published information were statutory, conferred by the Patent and Copyright Acts.[25]

As well as recognizing a (rather instrumental in terms of equity's intervention) form of property in trade secrets, these early courts also accepted some other tenets of trade secrets law that remain fundamental today. For one, they regarded the level of secrecy required as not absolute – information might circulate within a factory and be shared between workers but remain sufficiently secret. This obviously had and continues to have significant practical implications because sharing a trade secret does not destroy legal protection if certain requirements are observed; in some views, this is the essential benefit provided by trade secrets law. In a similar vein, the Pennsylvania court in *Pressed Steel Car Co v. Standard Steel Car Co* also recognized that a trade secret may remain protected (sufficiently secret) by law if it could be reverse-engineered only

---

19. *See* Michael Risch, 'Why Do We Have Trade Secrets?' (2007) 11 *Marquette Intellectual Property Law Review* 1, 5.
20. Above n 12, [2.3].
21. *See* above n 13.
22. 12 Pa 56, 51 Am Dec 584 (1849).
23. *Ibid.* 57.
24. *Cincinnati Bell Foundry Co v. Dodds*, 10 Ohio Dec 154 (1887).
25. Above n 14, 255.

with investment and effort.[26] The *right* to reverse engineer, however, was recognized implicitly in *Hazelton Boiler Co v. Hazelton Tripod Boiler Co.*[27] Bone sees a certain logic in the emergence of the reverse engineering exception because the only way to invade what he refers to as common law property rights in secret information is by 'invading his secrecy. Thus, trade secret liability depended entirely on whether the defendant used unfair means to acquire the information'.[28] This meant independent discovery and reverse engineering were lawful because 'they did not cross the boundaries of the owner's secret and violate his factual exclusivity'.[29]

Nonetheless, the courts continued to express reservations concerning the granting of injunctions for a variety of reasons: the proper role of patents, the practical difficulties of enforcement, and the difficulty of keeping information secret during a trial.[30] However, in *Tabor v. Hoffman,* the court relied on *Morrison* and on *Peabody* to confirm that an author or inventor has, by virtue of the common law, exclusive property in inventions or compositions 'until by publication it becomes the property of the general public'.[31] In *Eastman Co v. Reichenbach,* further central elements of US trade secrets law emerged, in particular the novelty of technical trade secrets that is required to take them outside the public domain and the importance attached to the measures taken by the plaintiff to protect secrecy.[32] The novelty referred to was confirmed in the New Jersey case of *Stone v. Goss* not to be the equivalent of patent novelty but merely the kind of improvements 'that a good mechanic could make'.[33] In this case and the earlier decision of *Salomon v. Hartz,* liability was also extended to third parties 'in the know'.[34]

Thus, by the end of the nineteenth century, a distinct law of trade secrets had emerged, focused on technical information, employing property concepts, but mostly for the sake of explaining the intervention of equity, and in truth, according to Jager, 'focused on the relationship of the parties more than on the nature of the property being misappropriated'. Most cases had to do with the consequences of communication of technical secrets under the cloak of confidence in employment. Courts had expressed reservations about business or commercial secrets being covered by the law,[35] in part influenced by the restraint of trade doctrine, and in any case, the developing rationale did not really fit such information. That, of course, would come to change in later times. A list-based definition of a trade secret that would later be expanded and find its way, in approximately the same terms, into state trade secrets provisions[36] emerged in

26. *See* above n 12, [2.3].
27. 30 NE 339 (Ill Sup Ct 1892).
28. Above n 14, at 257.
29. *Ibid.*
30. As discussed by Jager, with particular reference to a number of New York cases, including *Deming v. Chapman,* 11 How 382 (1854) and *Bristol v. Equitable Life Assurance Society of US,* 132 NY 264, (1892). *See* above n 12, [2.3].
31. *Tabor v. Hoffman,* 118 NY 30, (1889), 12.
32. 79 Hun 183, 29 NYS 1143 (1892).
33. *Stone v. Goss,* 65 NJ Eq 756, 55 A 736 (1903).
34. *Salomon v. Hartz,* 4 NJ Eq 400, 2 A 379 (1886).
35. *See, e.g., Salomon v. Hartz,* 4 NJ Eq 400, 2 A 379 (1886).
36. In particular Michigan & Wyoming.

National Tube Co v. Eastman Tube Co:[37] 'a plan, process or mechanism known only to its owner and those of his employ to whom it is necessary to confide it in order to apply it to the use intended'. Tools and compounds were added in the *Victor Chemical Works v. Iliff* case.[38]

Because the development of the common law of trade secrets in the US mostly occurred in state courts, there is little federal Supreme Court authority on the matter. The most oft-quoted early decision is *EI du Pont de Nemours Powder Co v. Masland*, which contains the famous passage in Justice Holmes' reasons already referred to in Chapter 1, puts the concept of property in its place in trade secrets law:

> 'it is an unanalyzed expression of certain secondary consequences of the primary fact that the law makes some rudimentary requirements of good faith. ... The property may be denied, but the confidence cannot be'. The starting point for the matter at hand was not property or due process, but 'that the defendant stood in confidential relations with the plaintiffs'.[39]

This confirms that the concept of property in these early trade secrets cases was instrumental and flexible in nature. It stemmed from juridical or doctrinal concerns rather than from the inherent nature of the object of property rights and the relationship of the possessor to it. It also confirms that the property rationale was on the wane by the early twentieth century.

Bone emphasizes that the property approach, although it had important doctrinal benefits in relation to the availability of equitable relief and the like, also had drawbacks because it was clear that although 'property', related rights in reality did not operate *against the world*. Trade secrets protection was critically dependent on visible measures of protection, and reverse engineering and independent invention were permissible, thus distinguishing trade secrets from patents. That left the difficulty of distinguishing between proper and improper or actionable ways of obtaining a trade secret: the assertion alone that the trade secret was the property of the plaintiff and that he had not authorized its particular use, acquisition, or disclosure could not be enough, since independent invention or reverse engineering might lie at its source. By contrast, in England, the communication of a confidence for a particular purpose gives rise to an obligation of conscience not to use it for other purposes, and hence a right to a remedy in equity if the recipient acts in bad faith and uses it for a different purpose. Lord Goff of Chieveley in the *Spycatcher* case said that 'in the vast majority of cases [...] the duty of confidence will arise from a transaction or relationship between the parties'.[40] The authors of *Gurry* treat the action as sui generis and based on public policy: people ought to be able to disclose information to others with whom they enter into confidences without risk of wider publication.[41]

37. 23 Ohio 468, 470, 3 Ohio C C (ns) 459 (1902) aff'd, 69 Ohio St 560, 70 NE 1127 (1903).
38. 299 Ill 532, 32 NE 806 (1921).
39. *See E.I. du Pont de Nemours Powder Co. v. Masland*, 244 US 100 (1917), 102. (*Masland*).
40. *Attorney-General v. Guardian Newspapers Ltd (No 2)* [1990] 1 AC 109, 281 (*Spycatcher*).
41. *See* Tanya Aplin, Lionel Bently, Phillip Johnson & Simon Malynicz, *Gurry on Breach of Confidence: The Protection of Confidential Information* (Oxford University Press, 2nd ed., 2012).

In the US, however, there had to be a standard of wrongfulness or impropriety to distinguish actionable from acceptable ways of obtaining and/or using a trade secret. Wrongfulness became a critical issue; as Bone says, 'some courts and commentators glossed over the property theory and focused instead on the wrongfulness of the defendant's conduct as the true basis of liability, despite the strength of the common law property theory'.[42] This is the issue discussed above in relation to the English law – but the American law has taken a rather more consistent course in this regard.

[B] The Impact of the US Constitutional System on the Development of Trade Secret Law

A final element of context must be mentioned in this introduction, namely the importance that the constitutional system of the United States has had in relation to the development of trade secrets protection. In contrast to exclusive federal competence for patents and copyrights (*see* Article I, section 8, Clause 8), the US Constitution does not foresee an explicit – and even less exclusive – federal competence for trade secrets. It was not until the 1990s that federal regulations were finally adopted, namely the EEA and the DTSA, based on Article I, section 8, Clause 3. This clause permits the enactment of federal legislation for the regulation of trade with foreign nations and between the several states.

The authority to regulate trade secrets was hence originally vested in the individual states. Consequently, trade secret law emerged within the context of each state's common law, which could have resulted in the development of fifty distinct legal frameworks with little or even no convergence. However, in contrast to the disparate legal frameworks that persisted in Europe until recently,[43] this fragmentation was avoided in the US. This was accomplished through two pivotal initiatives undertaken by two autonomous organizations. The first was the publication of the Restatements, which are treatises established by the American Law Institute with the aim of clarifying and synthesizing common law principles. The process of amalgamation and centralization of the case law as evidenced in the First Restatement of Tort (1939) for trade secrets permitted the avoidance of an erratic development of the decisions across the federated states, despite the absence of a federal common law. The second instrument was the UTSA, a legislative proposal prepared in 1979 by the Uniform Law Commission. Intended as a model law for adoption by the states, the UTSA was highly successful, with 48 states adopting it and the remaining states implementing similar, convergent legislation.

While the development of the common law regime for the protection of trade secrets at the state level has not led to fragmentation, it has nonetheless been influential. As detailed further in section 5.03[A], the empirical, incremental evolution of this legal regime -shaped by judicial decisions – directly influenced the definition of

42. *See* above n 14, 259.
43. *See* the devoted chapter in this book.

trade secrets. Initially, courts identified certain 'factors' that determined what constituted a trade secret; over time, these were formalized into 'legal requirements' in the UTSA. This crystallization process resulted in a statutory definition that, while widely adopted by individual states in legislation mirroring the UTSA, retains a significant degree of interpretive uncertainty.[44]

The US constitutional system has also played a significant role in the development of the legal framework governing reverse engineering in trade secret law. Although early common law decisions generally accepted reverse engineering as a legitimate means of acquiring a trade secret and thus did not constitute a breach of good faith,[45] this position was later 'constitutionalized' by the Supreme Court in the Kewanee and Bonito Boats decisions. These rulings were informed by the constitutional division of powers between the federal government and the states. In order to prevent a conflict with federal patent policy, which is a domain of exclusive federal authority, the protection afforded by trade secrets had to be limited. For the Supreme Court, the absence of protection in instances of reverse engineering was a pivotal element in establishing that state trade secret legislation did not contravene the federal patent policy. In Bonito Boats, the Court emphasized:

> [F]ederal patent law has embodied a careful balance between the need to promote innovation and the recognition that imitation and refinement though imitation are both necessary to invention itself and the very lifeblood of a competitive economy [...]. [T]rade secret law provides far weaker protection in many respects than patent law. [...] The public at large remained free to discover and exploit the trade secret through reverse engineering of protects in the public domain or by independent creation. Thus, the possibility that trade secret protection would divert inventors from the creative effort necessary to satisfy the rigorous demands of patent protection was remote indeed.[46]

Following these decisions, it was natural for the UTSA to also consider reverse engineering as a legitimate practice, not constituting misappropriation of a trade secret.[47]

The interplay between federal and state powers had a further influence on the framework adopted at the federal level. In this instance, the rationale was reversed. The Commerce Clause of the US Constitution (Article I, section 8, clause 3) vests the federal government with the authority to regulate foreign and interstate commerce. However, matters pertaining to intrastate affairs remain within the purview of state law. Consequently, the federal regulations established under the DTSA are solely intended to govern disputes with an interstate element. This distribution of powers necessitated that the federal legislature aligns the DTSA with existing state legislation in order to avoid inconsistencies. Consequently, reverse engineering is also deemed permissible under federal law (*see* 18 USC §1839 (6)(B)).

---

44. *See* §5.03[B], [C] and [D] of this chapter.
45. American Law Institute, *Restatement (Third) of Unfair Competition* (1995) 4.
46. *Bonito Boats v. Thunder Craft Boats*, 489 US 141, 146, 155.
47. Uniform Law Commission, *Uniform Trade Secrets Act*, 5.

It is noteworthy that the legality of reverse engineering in US law does not appear to have been the result of a conscious decision to optimize trade secret legislation. Rather, it appears as the outcome of constitutional considerations. Nevertheless, the US approach has exerted an influence on other jurisdictions, including the EU, where as a result reverse engineering is similarly regarded as lawful in the context of trade secret protection. Further, in some of the theoretical considerations we addressed in [Chapter 2], a lot is made of reverse engineering; for instance, to deny a trade secret the character of 'property' as protection does not really operate *erga omnes*, and to identify the incomplete nature of trade secrets protection as a policy benefit.[48] It is then striking that such an apparently central and universal tenet of trade secrets law arguably came about for wholly contingent reasons.

§5.02 UNFAIR COMPETITION AND OTHER ACTIONS

[A] Unfair Competition

As just indicated, by the early twentieth century, support was draining away from common law property theory because perceptions of the nature of property shifted. This is clearly visible in Holmes J's famous dictum in *Masland* cited above. The 'exclusivity (as the trade secret owner enjoyed) implies property; property implies particular rights' – syllogism no longer held; rather, property rights became seen as something rationally bestowed by organized society with functionalist and instrumental goals.[49] In other words, the approach shifted from doctrinal to realist and socio-political. At the same time, the common law tort of unfair competition received a boost in the Supreme Court *INS v. AP* decision, which recognized misappropriation of trade values as a form of unfair competition, even in the absence of a misuse of trade secrets or of a deception of the consumer (the case related to unauthorized *republication* of news stories).[50] Alternatively, it laid the groundwork for an entirely separate 'tort of misappropriation'.

In the period before the UTSA and the *Restatement (First) of Torts 1939*, the tort of unfair competition provided an alternative to a common law tort of misappropriation of trade secrets. Unfair competition divides opinion in the common law world, but while it has been firmly rejected in England and Australia, in the US, it has been better tolerated, whether by way of statute in the various states (*see* further below) or by way of judicial recognition of a tort of unfair competition. Deutch contends that US law's acceptance of a *general* tort of unfair competition is based on recognition that it is not possible to compile a definitive list of *specific* forms of unfair competition.[51] In effect,

48. *See* above Chapter 2 for more detail.
49. *Ibid.*
50. *International News Service v. Associated Press*, 248 US 215 (1918). Alternatively, it recognized a separate tort of misappropriation.
51. Miguel Deutch, 'Unfair Competition and the "Misappropriation Doctrine": A Renewed Analysis' (2004) 48(2) *Saint Louis University Law Journal* 503, 507 https://doi.org/10.1017/cbo9780511495229.006.

in America, particular instances of unfair business practices are commonly grouped under the heading of the tort of unfair competition: passing off or 'palming off' is the most common. Recognition of the broad action leaves scope for facts that do not fit into any expressed category still to be held to be unfair competition; in this, it parts ways with the traditional English approach, which holds that if a specific action such as passing off or breach of confidence within its confining elements does not lie, no remedy is available: there is no general unfair competition fallback. It is more analogous to the German Law on Unfair Competition with its general clause and more specific clauses recognizing certain actions as particular instances of unfair competition.

Many US states have legislation covering unfair competition, and these statutes extend its remit to improper business practices not related to trademarks and reputation, including also at times theft of proprietary information.[52] A number of states have 'Little FTC Acts' modelled on 15 USC paragraph 45, which declares unlawful 'unfair methods of competition in or affecting commerce' or 'unfair and deceptive trade practices'.[53] Such statutes may extend to prohibit 'a practice that is unethical, oppressive, unscrupulous, or substantially injurious'[54] and frequently define 'unfair' or 'deceptive' conduct broadly.[55] Courts applying such statutes 'appear to zealously guard against allowing managers, employees, and persons in a special position of trust to profit from their wrongdoing'.[56] Other states have statutes with a similar reach but not based on the FTC Act. The *Restatement of Unfair Competition* also has proper status, although, in some ways, it is at present overtaken by other actions. Therefore, in theory, there is much greater scope in the United States to rely on an unfair competition tort in trade secrets cases than is possible in England. In this sense, the US approach is closer to the approach in France and Germany prior to the adoption of EU Trade Secrets Directive legislation.

However, the popularity of the *Restatement of Unfair Competition* of the tort and of unfair competition was affected by a number of developments: first, although the Supreme Court decision in *INS v. AP* gave support to the notion of a general tort of unfair competition and/or misappropriation, in fact the trend in later decisions has been to wind back its field of application to confine it to the particular facts of the case – therefore the tort has been pared down to one of 'Hot News Misappropriation.' Further, the popularity of the *Restatement (First) of Torts*, which codified the principles of the common law tort of trade secret misappropriation, and later of the UTSA has taken the wind out of the sails of the tort of unfair competition in trade secrets cases. By the time the better-regarded *Restatement (Third) of Unfair Competition* came along in 1995, much of the space for trade secrets law had been filled by the adoption of the

---

52. *See* David W. Quinto & Stuart H. Singer, *Trade Secrets: Law and Practice* (Oxford University Press, 2009) 66.
53. *Ibid.* At this point, they list all relevant state legislations. *See also* Henry Butler & Joshua Wright, 'Are State Consumer Protection Acts Really Little-FTC Acts?' (2011) 63(1) *Florida Law Review* 163.
54. *Reingold v. Swiftships Inc*, 126 F 3d 645, 653 (5th Cir, No 96-30173, 16 October 1997).
55. Above n 46, 64.
56. *See Reingold v. Swiftships, Inc.*, above n 54.

UTSA or its variants (in forty-nine states as of 2024, the exception remaining the state of New York).[57]

However, despite the success of the UTSA, variations in state law are still considerable; thus, Massachusetts' state law is not modelled on the UTSA; the statute of North Carolina is only loosely based on the 1979 version of the UTSA; and the important jurisdiction of New York has no civil trade secrets statute at all.[58] Most importantly, any claim in unfair competition or misappropriation may now be pre-empted by the patent and copyright laws and, more significantly, for present purposes, the UTSA.[59]

[B] The Other Relevant Causes of Action

Before examining some aspects of the UTSA more closely, it is as well, with Professor Bone's contention in mind, to point out that apart from the UTSA, unfair competition and common law trade secrets misappropriation, and leaving aside the criminal law (*see* further below), there are quite a number of other causes of action available depending on the particular facts of a case. Quinto and Singer list some potential advantages of pleading alternatives to UTSA misappropriation:[60]

- avoiding the requirements of reasonable particularity before commencing discovery;
- more advantageous remedies;
- increasing the number of venues where suit may be brought against an interstate employee; and
- in cases of government disclosure, avoiding the immunity claim in torts suits.

Naturally, there is both relevant state and federal law in the US, so that there is often a preliminary question as to proper forum and applicable law in any given dispute. Further, most often, disputes are concerned with former employees, in which case a contractual obligation will frequently pre-empt the need to rely on a default statutory or common law tort. In particular, where post-employment non-compete clauses are concerned, there is a very developed case law, both concerning validity and in relation to conflicts between state laws, which have rather variable policies in relation to restraints of trade. A recent Presidential initiative has resulted in an FTC Final Rule prohibiting non-competes throughout the federation. It takes effect on 4 September 2024: '[U]nder the FTC's new rule, existing noncompetes for the vast

57. There have been legislative proposals in New York State in relation to trade secrets law. At the time of writing, Assembly Bill A2701, which 'creates the Uniform Trade Secrets Act', is being considered by legislators.
58. In terms of a broader misappropriation tort, however, INS-type misappropriation as applicable to information placed into the public domain may be pre-empted by the Supreme Court's decision in *Bonito Boats v. Thunder Craft Boats Inc*, 489 US 11 (1989) which prevents state laws from being used to protect information placed in the public domain.
59. *See Accuimage Diagnostics Corp v. Terarecon Inc*, 260 F Supp 2d 941, 955 (ND Cal, 2003), which held that Californian common law misappropriation claims were pre-empted under the UTSA.
60. Above n 46, 50-54.

majority of workers will no longer be enforceable after the rule's effective date'.[61] If the Rule withstands various challenges, the different policies and rules in the various states concerning non-compete agreements will disappear.[62]

Whatever may transpire in this regard, US trade secrets cases often require the resolution of collateral issues before the applicable law is identified and the facts held up to the relevant legal standards and requirements. That does not detract from the fact that contract will be determinative in many cases.

Further, in some states, an implied duty of confidence can be pleaded *as such* in relation to confidential information. This action is quasi-contractual in nature. California and New York are said to be most supportive of breach of confidence.[63] The *Restatement (Third) of Unfair Competition* limits the duty of confidence to information that qualifies as a 'trade secret'.[64] However, policies that limit trade secrets protection also apply in breach of confidence cases.[65] The duty can come about not only because of an express prior undertaking, a contractual obligation, or an existing confidential relationship but also because other facts surrounding the disclosure 'justify the conclusion that, at the time of the disclosure', the recipient knew or had reason to know the disclosure was intended to be confidential and the provider was reasonable to infer that the receiver consented to an obligation of confidentiality. Many courts apply less restrictive standards, for example in California, the District of Columbia and Tennessee.[66] It is sometimes said that a claim for breach of confidence can even extend to information that falls short of being a trade secret if it is disclosed in confidence and used in breach of the obligation.[67] The duty of confidence does not only arise in a fiduciary relationship but may exist where parties are at arms' length, such as buyers and sellers. It can be created by an express or implied-in-fact promise, and because it is quasi-contractual in nature, a party cannot recover both for breach of contract and breach of confidence.[68]

In other cases, where a fiduciary relationship exists rather than a mere implied duty of confidence, the action can be framed as a breach of fiduciary duty. As elsewhere, the status and nature of the fiduciary duty is somewhat unsettled in the US, with some courts holding that all company officers and managerial employees owe a fiduciary duty going beyond a mere duty of loyalty and relating to all information rather

61. *See* Federal Trade Commission, 'FTC Announces Rule Banning Noncompetes' *Federal Register* (online) 23 April 2024, https://www.ftc.gov/news-events/news/press-releases/2024/04/ftc-announces-rule-banning-noncompetes.
62. The US Chamber of Commerce is challenging the non-compete ban. *See* US Chamber of Commerce, 'Ryan LLC v. FTC: Intervention in Challenge to FTC Noncompete Rule Banning Noncompete Agreements Nationwide' *US Chamber of Commerce* (online) 20 August 2024, https://www.uschamber.com/cases/antitrust-and-competition-law/ryan-llc-v.-ftc.
63. *See* above n 46, 59.
64. *See* above n 45, 41.
65. *See Jons-Manville Corp v. Guardian Industries Corp*, 586 F Supp 1034 (ED Mich, 1983).
66. In California, *see Entertainment Research Group Inc v. Genesis Creative Group Inc*, 122 F 3d 1211, 1227 (9th Cir, Nos 95-17123, 96-16689, 18 August 1997); in DC *see Doe v. Medlantic Health Care Group Inc*, 814 A 2d 939, 950 (DC, 2003); in Tennessee, *see Givens v. Mullikin ex rel Estate of McEwaney*, 75 SW 3d 383, 410 (Tenn, 2002).
67. *Lehman v. Dow Jones & Co*, 783 F 2d 285, 299 (2d Cir, No 40, 30 January 1986).
68. *See* above n 46, 60.

than just trade secrets. Such a duty persists after the termination of employment.[69] Other courts see the duty of loyalty and the fiduciary duty as coextensive, so that the duty terminates with the end of the employment contract.[70] Naturally, the duty of loyalty of all employees may be the basis for an action, but that normally applies only during the term of employment and is an implied contractual duty.

Apart from the common law tort of misappropriation, touched upon above, conversion is another tort that may be pleaded in some circumstances. Whereas that tort used to be confined to an intentional exercise of dominion over another's *tangible* personal property, nowadays, most jurisdictions have abandoned rigid adherence to this requirement, as noted by Kozinski J in *Kremen II*: 'Many courts ignore or expressly reject it.'[71] The majority of states have now recognized that intangible property can be converted where it is merged with tangible property, such as where information appears in a document. A New York court recently held that electronic records can be converted. According to Quinto et al., the law is evolving to eliminate the merger requirement.[72] Nonetheless, they point out that few states have so far expressly held that trade secrets as such can be converted.[73]

In terms of third-party liability, the option of pleading the tort of intentional interference with contractual relations is significant. Under section 766 of the *Restatement (Second) of Torts*, intentional interference with contractual relations can be asserted when the conduct of a defendant interferes with economic relationships without being legally justified. In *Bushnell*, the court allowed claims based on allegations of improper interference with prospective business relations by using misappropriated trade secrets to proceed.[74] Also relevant to third parties is a claim alleging civil conspiracy, which is not ordinarily a tort in and of itself but is a claim that parties conspired to effect another tort, such as misappropriation of a trade secret. The tort may be useful to extend liability to a party who can pay where a misappropriation has not yet been completed by a new employer, but a former employee is caught misappropriating a trade secret.[75] Parties must each have agreed to do something to further the conspiracy, so that the new employer might be deemed to have adopted the tort and become jointly and severally liable.

Both at state level and federally, a civil claim may also lie in relation to unauthorized use or access to computers. Some of the states provide for civil rights of action for violation of criminal law prohibiting unauthorized access to computers,

69. *Ibid.*, 61.
70. *See, e.g., Hilb, Rogal and Hamilton Co v. DePew*, 440 SE 2d 918, 923 (Va, 1994).
71. *See Kremen v. Cohen*, 337 F 3d 1024, 1030 (9th Cir, No 01-15899, 25 July 2003).
72. *See* above n 46, 65.
73. *Ibid. See* Robert Milligan, 'Conversion Claim for Theft of Confidential Information Not Pre-empted By Trade Secrets Act' *Seyfarth Shaw LLP* (online) 4 August 2013, https://www.tradesecretslaw.com/2013/08/articles/trade-secrets/conversion-claim-for-theft-of-confidential-information-not-preempted-by-trade-secret-act/; Jason Culotta, 'Fifth Circuit Rules Louisiana Trade Secret Claim Does Not Preempt Claim For Conversion Of Confidential Info' *Jones Walker LLP* (online) 6 December 2018, https://www.tradesecretsinsider.com/fifth-circuit-rules-louisiana-trade-secret-claim-does-not-preempt-claim-for-conversion-of-confidential-info/.
74. *Bushnell Corp v. ITT Corp* 973 F Supp 1276 (D Kan, 1997).
75. *See* above n 46, 67.

computer systems and data.[76] At the federal level, the *Computer Fraud and Abuse Act* (CFAA) may apply, which also provides for compensatory damages as well as injunctive or equitable relief. A person who intentionally accesses without authorization and thereby obtains information from a protected computer may be liable if the conduct involves interstate or foreign trade. Thus, a website operator was able to obtain relief against a competitor who obtained unauthorized access to its website and obtained trade secrets – both under the *Idaho Trade Secrets Act* and the *CFAA*.[77] Also relevant in some cases may be the *Electronic Privacy Act* (1986).[78] In theory, at the federal level, a *RICO* claim may also be levelled, such as was included in the *Volkswagen* case and said to have encouraged parties to settle because of its powerful deterrent effect.[79] In other matters, it might be appropriate to lodge a complaint with the US *International Trade Commission* (ITC), which can launch an investigation when misappropriation of a trade secret has resulted in the importation of goods with design or manufacturing methods that incorporate misused trade secrets and cause damage to a competitor in the US. The ITC can act rapidly and the result of an investigation may be the total prohibition of the targeted import goods. Quinto and Singer identify some advantages and disadvantages of such ITC involvement, but that does not take away from the ITC's considerable power to eliminate unfair acts and unfair methods of competition that tend to injure an industry in the US, including by misappropriation of trade secrets.[80]

No doubt there are other legal avenues available in the US, but the above suffices to illustrate the multiplicity of options open to the possessor of trade secrets without even having to rely on the UTSA. These actions can be pleaded cumulatively, although there are always issues of 'pre-emption' in US law. Nonetheless, the core action is the state law of misappropriation of trade secrets, based on the UTSA as adopted by state legislatures. The states have either adopted the UTSA or substantially done so, as drafted in 1979 or as drafted in 1985. By 2024, forty-nine states, as well as the District of Columbia, the US Virgin Islands, and Puerto Rico had adopted the UTSA,[81] but as pointed out above, the state of New York is still considering uniform trade secrets law introduction at the time of writing.

76. *See, e.g.*, the *Economic Espionage Act* 18 USC §1030 (1996) – *Fraud and Related Activity in Connection with Computers*.
77. *See Creative Computing v. Getloaded.com LLC*, 386 F 3d 930, 933 (9th Cir, No 02-35856, 15 October 2004).
78. 18 USC §2701 (1996).
79. *Racketeering Influenced and Corrupt Organisations Act* 18 USC (2000), [1961]-[1968] (RICO); *General Motors Corp v. Ignacio Lopez de Ariortua*, 98 F Supp 656 (ED, Mich, 1996). Volkswagen settled a trade secrets claim in this case.
80. *See* above n 46, 77. The ITC relies on s. 337 of the *Antidumping Act of 1921*, USC §1337.
81. According to some sources, 48 states have adopted it. *See* Legal Information Institute, 'Trade Secret' *Legal Information Institute* (online), https://www.law.cornell.edu/wex/trade_secret. The state laws may be based on or derived from a uniform restatement of trade secrets law but are not therefore uniform between states, as the latter are not compelled to adopt the UTSA in the exact form proposed by Uniform Law Commission.

[C] Misappropriation and INS

A tort of misappropriation can apply to secret as well as to public information – the latter as in *INS*. Therefore, trade secrets misuse can fall under a general 'tort of misappropriation', not conceived of as a subspecies of unfair competition (misappropriation of business or trade values, as referred to above). After all, the elements of actionable misappropriation in *INS* were: substantial investment of time, skill or money by the plaintiff; the defendant appropriated the 'property' of the plaintiff at little or no cost to itself, and that without authorization of consent; and the plaintiff has been injured by the defendant's conduct. More recently, in *LinkCo Inc v. Fujitsu Ltd,* it was said about the tort of misappropriation by the federal court that 'it is normally invoked in an effort to protect something of value not otherwise covered by patent or copyright law, trade secrets law, breach of confidential relationship, or some other form of unfair competition'.[82] The action is not limited to secret information, but any information that has been developed with effort and investment, and the circumstances of its use by the defendant determine whether or not there is an actionable wrong: there must be an act of free-riding. The action is of course less firmly rooted than an action for trade secrets misuse, whether based in the common law or on statute, but a misappropriation of a trade secret can just as well fall within its remit. The state of New York is one of those that have continued to recognize the tort. In 2006, in *Confold Pacific Inc. v. Polaris Industries Inc.,* Posner J noted that although *INS* had now been discredited, some states continue to recognize it. In that case, the Second Circuit court, interpreting New York law, summed up the elements as: the plaintiff generates information or collects it at some cost or expense; the value of the information is highly time-sensitive; the defendant's use constitutes free-riding and is in direct competition; and the ability to free ride would so reduce the incentive to produce the information that its existence or quality would be substantially under threat.[83] That obviously represents a very narrow ratio as it is limited to 'hot news'.

Thus, the developments in the US have remarkable similarities with the situation in France, but the situation until recently has been quite different in England. There, the tort of unfair competition was always firmly rejected, and a tort of misappropriation was not even considered; nonetheless, principles of actionable unjust enrichment per se (as more widely relied on in Canadian law) may to some extent play that role in that jurisdiction. Only in very recent times has a general theory of misappropriation emerged in the recent *Campbell* and *Douglas* cases because a wrong was possibly identified there in the appropriation of others' trade secrets in the knowledge that they intended to keep them so. The wrong would be recognized even in the absence of unfair competition with the trade secrets so obtained, or irrespective of the impropriety or otherwise of the means of obtaining the information. That comes very close to a misappropriation approach along the lines set out above in INS. In France, misappropriation finds expression either in the tort of parasitic competition, or of parasitic

82. *LinkCo Inc v. Fujitsu Ltd,* 230 F Supp 2d 492, 501-502 (SDNY, 2002).
83. *Confold Pacific Inc v. Polaris Industries Inc,* 433 F 3d 952, 960 (7th Cir, No 05-1285, 10 January 2006).

actions ('*agissements parasitaires*'), as is discussed in the relevant chapter. This latter tort coexists with the action for unfair competition (*concurrence deloyale*), one instance of which is the misuse of another's trade secrets.

§5.03 CIVIL LAW PROTECTION

[A] Background of the UTSA

As previously outlined in the introductory section of this chapter,[84] the UTSA, a legislative proposal drafted in 1979 by the Uniform Law Commission, has been instrumental in fostering harmonization of trade secret law across the various states.

The proposal exclusively addresses civil liability. While the UTSA claims to codify 'the principles of common law trade secret protection', it extends beyond this task in several instances, particularly, as will be explained more in detail in the next section, in its approach to defining trade secrets. For the rest, a comparison with the Restatement of Torts reveals a number of discrepancies. The UTSA refers to information deriving 'actual or potential value' from not being known, whereas the Restatement does not mention 'potential' value; the Restatement requires continuous use of the information concerned in the plaintiff's business, and there is less emphasis on efforts to maintain secrecy in the Restatement than in the UTSA.[85] Further, the Restatement requires disclosure or use of the information, whereas under the UTSA, wrongful acquisition per se can constitute misappropriation.

The states can adopt the UTSA as is or with variations of their own, and as a result, the law is in fact not entirely uniform across the US.[86] Any discussion of the UTSA itself has, therefore, to take into account that there may be differences between that Uniform Law and the particular laws of any given state. However, the UTSA remains a fundamental work in the field of trade secret law, exerting influence that extends beyond the boundaries of US state law. Indeed, it has influenced the US federal legislator in the drafting of the DTSA and, perhaps more surprisingly, has also influenced EU lawmakers in the formulation of the European Directive.[87]

Protection only extends to a trade secret as circumscribed by the Act; that the information concerned derives economic value from its secrecy; that the plaintiff has made efforts that are reasonable under the circumstances to maintain its secrecy; and that the defendant has engaged in an act of misappropriation as defined. Protection is automatic in the sense that no registration or formality is required, but it is a significant aspect of US trade secrets law that the law will not extend to information unless the plaintiff can demonstrate measures (efforts) to protect what is claimed to be a trade

84. *See* §5.01[B] of this chapter.
85. *See* above n 19, 8.
86. At present, only New York State has not adopted a specific statute-based on the UTSA. However, a proposal is currently under consideration. *See* Assembly Bill A2701 (January 26, 2023) amending the general business law and the civil practice law and rules in relation to the Uniform Trade Secrets Act.
87. *See* further above, Chapter 4.

secret.[88] What amounts to misappropriation is defined generally as involving some impropriety in the acquisition, disclosure or use of a trade secret, the emphasis being more on the 'mis-' than on the 'appropriation'.

[B] Origins of UTSA Trade Secrets' Definition

Section 1(4) UTSA defines trade secrets as follows:

> 'Trade Secret' means information, including a formula, pattern, compilation, program, device, method, technique, or process, that:
>
> (i) derives independent economic value, actual or potential from not being generally known to, and not being readily ascertainable by proper means by, other persons who can obtain economic value from its disclosure or use, and
> (ii) is the subject of efforts that are reasonable under the circumstances to maintain its secrecy.

In developing the UTSA, the drafters explicitly drew upon the Restatement but chose to go beyond merely codifying the common law, particularly in their approach to defining trade secrets. Their contribution, as they put it, was 'the substitution of unitary definitions of trade secret'. This was in contrast to the First Restatement of Torts, which had asserted that 'an exact definition of a trade secret is not possible'. Consequently, the Restatement drafters identified a non-exclusive list of six factors that courts generally consider when determining whether a piece of information merits protection:

> Some factors to be considered in determining whether given information is one's trade secret are:
>
> the extent to which the information is known outside of his business;
> the extent to which it is known by employees and others involved in his business;
> the extent of the measures taken by him to guard the secrecy of the information;
> the value of the information to him and to his competitors;
> the amount of effort or money expended by him in developing the information;
> the ease or difficulty with which the information could be properly acquired or duplicated by others.[89]

The UTSA drafters proposed a unitary definition with the intention of shifting the approach from a flexible list of criteria that could be weighed against each other to a set of mandatory conditions that must be cumulatively met. Nevertheless, the way the UTSA drafters constructed section 1(4) is open to question. As Sandeen observes,[90] the definition they proposed effectively crystallized five of the six factors from the

88. It is a requirement in most states that the possessor must take some reasonable measures to protect the trade secret.
89. American Law Institute, *Restatement (First) of Torts* (1939), 6.
90. Sharon Sandeen, 'The Evolution of Trade Secret Law and Why Courts Commit Error When They Do Not Follow the Uniform Trade Secrets Act' (2010) 33(3) *Hamline Law Review* 493, 521.

Restatement into legally binding requirements:

UTSA Requirements	*Restatements Factors*
(i) derives independent economic value, actual or potential,	4. the value of the information to him and to his competitors
from not being generally known to,	1. the extent to which the information is known outside of his business
and not being readily ascertainable by proper means by other persons who can obtain economic value from its disclosure or use, and	6. the ease or difficulty with which the information could be properly acquired or duplicated by others
(ii) is the subject of efforts that are reasonable under the circumstances to maintain its secrecy.	3. the extent of the measures taken by him to guard the secrecy of the information; 2. the extent to which it is known by employees and others involved in his business.[91]

The result is not entirely satisfactory and contributes to the significant uncertainty surrounding the interpretation and rationale of each condition. The use of vague terminology was not a significant issue under the Restatement because the factors could be considered overlapping and there was no need to identify the exact rationale for each one. However, as formal requirements, each condition must now possess a clear and precise meaning that allows for *straightforward* verification of its fulfilment, and each should provide independent normative value justified by a specific rationale. This is not fully achieved, as illustrated by the ambiguity surrounding the 'reasonable effort' condition.

[C] Conditions Pertaining to Confidentiality and Value of Information

The first element of the UTSA definition requires that a trade secret be 'information, including a formula, pattern, compilation, program, device, method, technique or process'. The tendency of this definition is obviously towards technical information, with which most cases are indeed concerned. However, it is not limited to that as the list of specifics is not exhaustive and in any case contains 'compilations'. In fact, any information that derives economic value from being secret – provides a competitive advantage – can be a trade secret. Thus, as well as applying to the famous Coca Cola formula,[92] customer lists, business methods and plans, and marketing research ideas have all been considered to be trade secrets.[93] Patentable or non-patentable techniques

91. *See* Luc Desaunettes-Barbaro, *Trade Secrets Legal Protection: From a Comparative Analysis of US and EU Law to a New Model of Understanding* (Springer, 1st ed., 2023) 40.
92. *See Coca-Cola Bottling Co of Shreveport, Inc v. Coca Cola Co*, 227 USPQ 18 (D Del 1985).
93. As listed by Bone. *See* above n 14, 250.

can be protected, and the standard of originality and novelty is not so high: the key requirement is that competitive advantage can be derived from the exclusive possession of the information.

While the standard of secrecy is not absolute, so that it is permissible for information to circulate in a limited manner, the requirement that actual efforts to keep it confidential must be made and put in evidence is significant. It may indeed be that information circulates only among a small group, but if there is no indication that this was by design, it will be difficult to establish that the requisite standard has been met. The standard of secrecy is also relative in the sense that even if a product is released into the public sphere, if reverse engineering requires considerable effort, it will still be considered sufficiently secret.[94] Further, what is relevant is knowledge within the circle of a firm's competitors: theoretical availability at some source that such people would not normally access does not necessarily undermine secrecy.

The requirement of continuous business use has recently been relaxed or ignored,[95] and the recent Third *Restatement of Unfair Competition Law* also does not require it. There appears to be a significant difference as well in relation to third parties on notice: under the UTSA, once a recipient is placed on notice, he or she may be liable for infringing use or disclosure, whereas a good faith acquirer for value or with reliance on a belief, resulting in a change of position, that no misappropriation has occurred has a defence under the Restatement.[96] It should be kept in mind that the legal protection for trade secrets is not pre-empted by the patent law, as the requirement of secrecy takes it outside that sphere, and that pre-emption by a host of other torts is a contentious matter, in relation to which courts have been split. In many instances in US litigation, the facts are pleaded in relation to a multitude of actions where the wrongs contended for are quite similar. The application of rules of pre-emption, a staple of US pleading and determination of cases, then becomes a key determinant of what claims are left standing.[97] Graves and Tippett say: 'These cases [where UTSA claims are not considered to preempt other tortious claims] arise in courts that follow the minority position on UTSA preemption, a position under which courts rule that the UTSA does not preempt tort claims that are said to be based upon information that does not qualify for trade secret protection, but that is nonetheless protectable in some ill-defined fashion.'[98]

In all these aspects, the US law is very similar to the English tradition, although with some reservations: one such is that in English law, it is not necessary to establish that some commercial value or advantage derives from secrecy. English law looks for value derived from the fact itself that the information is secret and thus has a practical exclusivity, apart from whatever inherent utility or commercial value the information

94. *See* above n 14, 249.
95. *Ibid.*, 250.
96. *See* above n 47, [2(b)] and [3(a)]; *See* above n 89, [758].
97. For an example *see Pelfrey v. Mahaffy, Schmidt and Exquadrum, Inc.*, Case No 17-cv-80920, 2018 WL 3110797 (S.D. Fla Feb 07, 2018). *See also* Charles Tait Graves & Elizabeth Tippett, 'UTSA Preemption and the Public Domain: How Courts Have Overlooked Patent Preemption of State Law Claims Alleging Employee Wrongdoing' (2012) 65(1) *Rutgers Law Review* 59.
98. *Ibid.*, 61.

might have. Partly, that is because the action for breach of confidence does not only cover commercially sensitive information but also personal and private communications. Nonetheless, in English law, where a trade secret is at stake, the plaintiff might have to establish a number of things that have a similar tendency as the commercial value or competitive advantage requirement: first, particularization of the trade secret(s) concerned, i.e., precise and concrete identification; second, that the information is not so vague as to be impossible to identify with precision, and impossible to place in the public domain or not; and lastly, equity will not intervene to protect information that is old, stale or trite. In terms of reasonable measures, the English law does not advance this so much as a separate requirement but more as a factor in determining two things: whether certain information amounts to a trade secret and whether the circumstances of its communication impose an obligation of confidence on its recipient. Naturally, whereas a right of action against third parties who improperly obtain information by industrial espionage or other surreptitious means is a central part of US trade secrets law, it is a relatively novel aspect of breach of confidence. If protection against improper appropriation by others is central to the legal regime, then it is rational to require that the possessor should be able to put in evidence measures or precautions that were taken that would flag the secret nature of the information concerned.

[D] Evidence of Measures to Protect Secrecy

The express and distinct requirement of Reasonable Secrecy Precautions (RSPs) under the UTSA, therefore, sets the US law, at least where the UTSA is concerned, apart from English law and also civilian law (prior to the EU Trade Secrets Directive in EU member countries) to some extent. Bone criticizes the requirement of RSPs, fearing that their effect is to encourage an over-investment in self-help. Without this requirement, a trade secret owner 'will use self-help up to the point where the marginal private benefits just exceed the marginal costs, and then rely on litigation after that point'.[99] The main problem in policy terms is that over-investment in security measures has the effect of shielding too much information from the public domain: self-help 'restricts public access more effectively than litigation'.[100] However, Bone also notes the countervailing arguments: that RSPs provide notice to the world that information is intended to be kept secret and that secrecy precautions 'provide circumstantial evidence of actual secrecy, value, and improper appropriation ...'[101] However, the latter is not relevant, as he points out, where there is enough *other* evidence available. In other words, litigation is more porous than self-help, so that 'substituting self-help

99. *See* Robert G. Bone, 'Trade Secrecy, Innovation, and the Requirement of Reasonable Secrecy Precautions' (September 3, 2009), in Rochelle C. Dreyfuss, Katherine J. Strandberg (eds), *The Law and Theory of Trade Secrecy: A Handbook Of Contemporary Research* (Edward Elgar Press, 2010), Boston Univ. School of Law Working Paper No. 09-40, Available at SSRN: https://ssrn.com/abstract=1467723.
100. *Ibid.*, 3.
101. *Ibid.*

for litigation at the margin is likely to reduce information access and impede further innovation'.[102]

In origin, RSP is symptomatic of possession and thus accords with a property view, as predominated in America until the 1920s or so. Bone argues that failing to take RSPs meant failing to exercise dominion or control.[103] However, the rise of the unfair competition approach 'left the precautions requirement without a clear foundation', he argues,[104] because this approach focused not on possession and control but on evaluation of the conduct of an appropriator. Bone contends that the drafters nonetheless maintained the requirement because of precedent but relegated it to lesser importance by incorporating it in a list of six factors indicating secrecy. From 1940 to 1980, the courts were, because of the predominance of unfairness thinking, more focused on:

> the wrongful nature of the defendant's conduct. Some courts insisted on strict secrecy requirements. Others skimmed over potential secrecy problems in an obvious effort to provide relief for egregious breaches of trust. And the more liberal courts tended to treat secrecy in a relatively cursory way.[105]

But with the adoption of the UTSA, the importance of the reasonable precautions requirement took centre stage again, since it is an essential requirement by virtue of section 1(4). The requirement also appears in the federal DTSA of 2016 and now has international resonance as it was adopted in the EU Trade Secrets Directive.[106]

The crucial point, and most interesting from a comparative perspective given what was said about the English situation above, is that the courts have interpreted section 1(4) as creating 'two distinct requirements for information to qualify as a trade secret - actual secrecy and reasonable precautions - and each requirement must be satisfied separately'.[107] This, Bone points out, sets the UTSA apart from the *First Restatement of Torts* and the *Third Restatement of the Unfair Competition Law*, which treat precautions as only one factor in determining secrecy, or as 'mere evidence of secrecy, value, and improper appropriation'.[108] The UTSA does not prescribe specific precautions and it is effectively left up to the court to decide whether in any given case the steps taken are 'reasonable in the circumstances'.

Bone contends that neither the courts nor the trade secrets scholars have been able to develop a convincing rationale for a separate RSP requirement. He maintains that it is not necessary to maintain RSPs as a separate requirement. Although not all information that is not generally known is a trade secret, it is enough to require that it be secret, and in some cases, but crucially not all, this will require establishing that measures were taken to protect the secret; this position approximates the English view.

---

102. Above n 79, 4.
103. *Ibid.*, 7.
104. *Ibid.*, 10.
105. *Ibid.*, 11-12 and cases cited there in support.
106. *See* Bianca Fox, 'Tripping Over the EU Trade Secret Directive: "Reasonable Steps" to Get Back on Track' (2020) 19(1) *Chicago-Kent Journal of Intellectual Property* 68.
107. *See* above n 79, 13.
108. *Ibid.*, 14.

As indicated above, Bone's view is that for no good purpose, the separate requirement encourages protective measures that are too extensive. However, another view might be that it makes trade secrets protection cases in some instances more difficult to win, which could have the broad policy advantage of making the litigation more porous. Finally, if the critical requirement in most cases is that there be contractual undertakings of confidence with employees and the like, this is perhaps a not unreasonable or overly onerous requirement. Almeling et al., in their studies of trade secrets litigation, conclude that '[t]he data show that two measures – confidentiality agreements with employees and confidentiality agreement with third parties – were significantly associated with a finding that this element was satisfied'.[109] Evidence of physical security measures, limited circulation and the marking of documents as 'secret' or 'confidential' are also of significant relevance.[110]

[E] Impropriety

The gravamen of the misappropriation provision (section 1(2) definition) requires identification of some form of impropriety at the source of the defendant's possession of the trade secret, as opposed to legitimate means (such as reverse engineering or independent invention) it may have used to acquire it. Also, the plaintiff must establish that the defendant knew or had reason to know of the wrongful disclosure, so that new employers, for instance, may be fixed with liability not only if they knew but also if they failed to make reasonable enquiries of an employee who brings secret information into the firm, or had studiously ignored the issue.[111]

US law differs from English common law systems in that liability can arise from an improper acquisition by a third party, i.e., without any offence against a relationship of good faith and trust. Impropriety must always be established under the UTSA, and generally, it falls into one of three broad categories: breach of a duty of confidentiality arising in a contractual or another confidential relationship; a civil or criminal wrong committed by the defendant; or appropriation by actions that are not illegal but breach norms of honest commercial or competitive conduct. So, a remedy might lie in circumstances where the defendant's conduct is perfectly legal yet 'improper'. In other words, as said in the UTSA Minneapolis Comments (1985),[112] improper means could

109. *See* David S. Almeling, Darin W. Snyder, Michael Sapoznikow, Whitney E. McCollum & Jill Weader, 'A Statistical Analysis of Trade Secret Litigation in Federal Courts' (2009-2010) 45(2) *Gonzaga Law Review* 292, 294.

110. For a typical example, *see Rockwell Graphic Sys. Inc. v. DEV Indus., Inc.*, 925 F2d 174 (7th Cir 1991). For a useful recent guide to trade secrets actions in the US, *see also* Peter Menell et al., *Trade Secret Case Management Judicial Guide* (Federal Judicial Centre, 2023).

111. *See Rohm & Haas Co v. Adco Chemical Co*, 89 F 2d 424, 431 (3d Cir, 1982); *Data General Corp v. Grumman System Support Corp*, 825 F Supp 340, 360 (D Mass, 1993).

112. *Uniform Trade Secrets Act with 1985 Amendments*, drafted by the National Conference of Commissioners on Uniform State Laws and by it approved and recommended for enactment in all the states at its annual conference meeting in its 94th year in Minneapolis, Minnesota, 2-9 August 1985 with Prefatory note and Comments; at p. 6.

include otherwise legal use that is improper in the circumstances.[113] 'Improper means' is defined in the UTSA as including 'theft, bribery, misrepresentation, breach or inducement of a breach of a duty to maintain secrecy, or espionage through electronic or other means'. But this is only an inclusive list so that 'trade secrets law is potentially capable of reaching any conduct that strikes a judge as unethical'.[114] Nonetheless, attaching consequences to improper yet legal acts makes sense if trade secrets law is about 'the maintenance of standards of commercial ethics'.[115]

Obviously, in most cases, the improper behaviour will in fact be civilly or criminally wrong, but not in all. The word improper itself is very broad and ill-defined, but one way of limiting its possible scope is by contradistinction with what is clearly *proper*. Identified as proper by the Uniform State Law Commissioners are: independent invention; reverse engineering; discovery under a licence from the trade secret owner; observation of the item in public or on public display; or obtaining the secret from the published literature.[116] An important characteristic of US law is that the problem of distinguishing proper from improper behaviour, intelligence gathering from industrial espionage, the commercially ethical from the dishonest is a question for a jury, and not a single (and potentially idiosyncratic) judge to resolve. The most famous but controversial example of a court finding actionable impropriety without illegality is *EI Du Pont de Nemours & Co v. Christopher*, where deliberately taking aerial photographs of a factory under construction fell on the wrong side of the line.[117] It is also significant that the impropriety standard may provide the distinguisher where memory is involved: casual recollection may be fine,[118] but where information is deliberately memorized, the line may be crossed.[119] Rummaging through a competitor's rubbish has been held to constitute impropriety despite the fact that ready means are available to shred documents as a preventive measure.[120]

While the first two forms of impropriety mentioned above are concerned with use or disclosure of information, the third is concerned with the manner in which information is obtained. In other words, third parties may be found liable for using illegal or dishonest means to obtain secret information. Third parties not in privity with the confidor can thus be liable, which Risch identifies as a critical benefit of trade secrets law, as noted above.[121] Third parties can also be held liable where they knowingly or negligently obtained information from a party who acquired or disclosed it unlawfully. By characterizing a breach of confidence as simply one among other

113. There is obviously a close connection with the subsistence requirement because the economic value can be derived by the information concerned 'not being readily ascertainable by proper means' by other persons (*see* the definition of 'trade secret' in the UTSA).
114. *See* above n 14, 250.
115. *See Kewanee Oil Co v. Bicron Corp*, 416 US 470 (1974).
116. Annual Conference Meeting Report, *Uniform Trade Secrets Act with 1985 Amendments* (August 1985), 5.
117. 431 F 2d 1012 (5th Cir, No 28-258, 20 July 1970).
118. *See, e.g., Tactica International Inc v. Atlantic Horizon International Inc.*, 154 F Supp 2d 586, (SDNY, 2001).
119. *See Sperry Rand Corp v. Rothlein*, 241 F Supp 549 (D Conn, 1964).
120. *See, e.g., Tennant Co v. Advance Machinery Co*, 355 NW 2d 720 (Minn App 1984).
121. *See* above n 19, 5.

relevant wrongs, the US law at once overcomes some of the theoretical difficulties English law experiences in extending liability to third parties with whom no confidential relationship exists, as discussed below. The focus of US law is, therefore, not solely on a breach of trust but on fixing with liability parties who have engaged in one of a number of possible wrongs to obtain information, use it or disclose it. The action is thus inherently more flexible than the English breach of confidence, although, as discussed, the courts in England have generally extended liability to third parties in similar circumstances without concerning themselves too much with doctrinal problems.

As indicated above, unintentional acquisition can still result in liability, as constructive knowledge (the party ought to have known) can be sufficient, as in the case where industry custom should have suggested unauthorized disclosure or use to a recipient.[122] Even inadvertent or unexpected acquisition can be sufficient, such as during job interviews or subsequent employment, and it is not necessary that the whole trade secret be revealed – the key question is what recipients subsequently do with the information, where they ought to have realized that it was a trade secret wrongfully disclosed. Use will occur even if the acquirer has further developed the information or expended resources on it, as much as where it is used as a springboard to avoid research expenses or deliver results more quickly.[123] A common instance of improper use is where a party goes beyond the constraints of a contractual agreement, such as a joint venture or research collaboration, to use shared information for its own purposes.[124]

What is known as third-party liability in England (the liability of a knowing participant in the breach of confidence) is in fact a form of primary liability in the United States. Thus, Bone points out that 'the principal trade secret doctrine imposing liability on third parties is in fact based on a form of primary rather than secondary liability'.[125] The UTSA makes a party liable who uses or discloses a trade secret, having acquired it from another with actual or constructive knowledge that it was wrongfully acquired or disclosed.[126] In other words, in the US, primary liability casts a wide net, catching those who pass on information; those who receive the information and use it or pass it on; those who encourage another to disclose the information for their own benefit, or to acquire it for that purpose, if the necessary elements of knowledge and impropriety are present. Third parties do not participate in another's breach in those cases but actually break the law themselves because of the way the UTSA is drafted and the central role impropriety plays in it. Most importantly, this means that new employers can be held liable on the basis of primary rather than secondary or contributory liability. New employers are of course a more attractive target for a

122. *See, e.g., Computer Associations International v. Altai Inc.*, 982 F 2d 693 (2nd Cir, Nos 91-1893, 91-7935, January 1992).
123. *See, e.g., Telex Corp v. IBM Corp*, 510 F 2d 894 (10th Cir, No 73-1874, 24 January 1975).
124. *See Morton v. Rank Am Inc*, 812 F Supp 1062 (CD Cal, 1993).
125. Robert Bone, 'Secondary Liability for Trade Secret Misappropriation: A Comment' (2006) 22 *Santa Clara Computer and High Tech Law Journal* 529, at 536.
126. *See* above n 47, 1(2) and (11) – Definition of Misappropriation.

compensatory remedy than a recently departed employee because they tend to be companies with more assets.[127]

[F] Inevitable Disclosure

Thus, on the whole, trade secrets law in the United States is fairly well developed and has a relatively consistent statutory basis around the country. Additional to the uniform trade secrets laws of almost all the states is now the DTSA of 2016, a federal statute which we comment on below.

As well there is a substantial number of other remedies available to any aggrieved party, as listed above. However, in the US, as in other jurisdictions, a number of difficult hurdles remain to be overcome in a given trade secrets case. In particular, in post-employment cases, the law is also protective of the free circulation of employees and of know-how. The former employer will have to particularize the information that is a trade secret, as distinct from mere know-how that the employee is free to take. It is obviously difficult to circumscribe personal know-how with provable security measures. Further, although the law accepts that misappropriation can lie in the deliberate memorizing of secret information, it will be difficult to prove that the individual employee has engaged in this practice, since by definition no physical evidence will be available. In any case, where inchoate ideas are concerned, potentially valuable as they may be, and arguably the 'property' of an employer, the law does not really assist the ex-employer, as Merges has explained.[128] Courts do not want to restrain the use of contiguous know-how by the grant of wide injunctions with uncertain targets, nor do they wish, in the US as elsewhere, to embarrass defendants by imposing obligations that are difficult to observe precisely. Therefore, the use of confidentiality clauses, and in particular non-competes, remains a significant tool for employers to safeguard trade secrets. An important body of law has grown around them, as is discussed elsewhere, and traditionally, they lie at the real and practical core of trade secrets law. However, that may come to change with the FTC measure that outlaws non-competes, commented upon elsewhere (*see* Chapter 9 Trade Secrets and Employees).

Another difficulty the employer has is to actually acquire and tender effective proof of the wrongful imparting of a trade secret by a former employee. In common law jurisdictions, the tendency of the law is to require real proof of actual disclosure or at least of imminent disclosure. Courts in England and like jurisdictions will not accept an argument that either it is inevitable that an ex-employee hired in a particular capacity will impart or rely on trade secrets learned previously or that where a new employer has the same products or similar information, this must inevitably come from a breach of confidence of the former employee, where there is actually only inferential and no

127. Note that injunctive relief as well as damages is available, with some jurisdictions providing for punitive damages and attorney's costs. In the US, the requirement of damage either actual or feared is implicit in the substantive requirements of the action.
128. Robert P. Merges, 'The Law and Economics of Employee Inventions' (1999) 13(1) *Harvard Journal of Law & Technology* 1.

direct evidence of such breach. This is exactly the kind of difficulty the non-compete is intended to alleviate. But in such cases in the US, there has been greater acceptance of the so-called inevitable disclosure doctrine.' Basically, in cases where there is insufficient evidence of actual or threatened disclosure by an ex-employee, courts will nonetheless accept that an employee would inevitably disclose trade secrets during their new employment. The employee may, therefore, be enjoined from working for the new employer. Alternatively, as Heer puts it, inevitable disclosure cases are those:

> [w]here a disclosure is a trade secret but is inseparable from the employee such that an injunction against disclosure would not suffice. ... an injunction against disclosure will not work because the disclosure is extremely likely even in the absence of bad faith. Thus a court order preventing an employee from working in some defined section of their field for a certain period of time is the only feasible pre-emptive remedy.[129]

The effect of the inevitable disclosure doctrine is that employees will be unemployable in the precise field in which they are most specialized and valuable, and, therefore, warnings and reservations about applying the theory abound. In effect, an order based on the theory imposes a non-compete the employee never agreed to. Although, in some cases, the courts seem to mix up cases where there is evidence of potential bad faith intention to misuse a trade secret (as in the *PepsiCo* case);[130] in other instances, courts have very clearly understood that the inevitable disclosure doctrine has nothing to do with suspected bad faith. Thus, in *Lumex Inc. v. Highsmith*, the court granted an injunction because it held that '[e]ven assuming the best of good faith, it is doubtful whether the defendant could completely divorce his knowledge of the trade secrets from any ... work he might engage in with a new employer'.[131] In 2009, Quinto and Singer pointed out that the theory had been rejected in six states, accepted in thirteen, and attracted mixed reactions in the others.[132] A more recent state by state account is given by Wiesner.[133] The controversy continues in the context of the DTSA at the federal level (*see* below).

Those that have accepted the doctrine have gone farther than the English law, which tends to be unsympathetic in these circumstances, for a number of reasons: first, the employer has the opportunity to protect itself by agreeing to a non-compete or restraint of trade clause in the employment contract – if it does not do this, it cannot complain of suffering the adverse consequences. Second, if trade secrets and personal know-how are inextricably linked, then public policy and the public interest in freedom to learn and work should prevail. The inevitable disclosure doctrine also seems to work

129. *See* Christoper Heer, 'Employees and Trade Secrets: How the Concept of Inevitable Disclosure May Fit into Canadian Law' (2006) 19 *Intellectual Property Journal* 323, 328-329.
130. *PepsiCo v. Redmond*, 56 F 3d 29 (7th Cir, No 94-3942, 20 January 1995). *See also* Jennifer L. Saulino, 'Locating Inevitable Disclosure's Place in Trade Secret Analysis' (2002) 100 *Michigan Law Review* 1184 https://doi.org/10.2307/1290506.
131. *Lumex Inc v. Highsmith*, 919 F Supp 624, 633 (EDNY, 1996).
132. Above n 46, 91-101.
133. Ryan M. Wiesner, 'A State-By-State Analysis of Inevitable Disclosure: A Need for Uniformity and a Workable Standard' (2012) 16(1) *Marquette Intellectual Property Law Review* 211.

particularly unfairly because the employee enjoys neither express nor implicit consideration for remaining out of work for the period of any injunction granted on the basis of it. Fortunately, perhaps, the doctrine is said to be in decline, although not entirely dead; although, as indicated, the issue has been revived under the DTSA.[134]

[G] The Defend Trade Secrets Act

Until the adoption of the DTSA in 2016, there was no federal civil trade secrets law.[135] As Rowe points out, 'The DTSA largely mirrors the UTSA, with a nearly identical definition of "trade secret," an identical definition of "misappropriation," and other similarities.'[136] The DTSA does not displace or pre-empt the state trade secrets laws, and therefore, claimants can bring a trade secrets action either in a state or in the federal courts. Congress considered one of the principal benefits of the DTSA to be that it would provide a 'single, national standard' for trade secret misappropriation with 'clear rules' and 'predictability for everyone involved'.[137] Rowe also pointed out (in 2019) that 'Since the DTSA is largely based upon the UTSA, and is likely to be interpreted in accordance with the UTSA; the existence of two separate trade secret laws is not likely to result in significant divergence of state and federal trade secret principles, for most of the country.'[138] However, as we point out above and as Rowe herself acknowledges, there are in fact considerable variations between trade secrets laws of the different states. This is due to some statutory differences and also to the fact that state courts developed separate bodies of law for each state act. The 'Uniform' trade secrets law is thus in reality not so uniform between the states, and to claim the federal law as consistent with the state laws is perhaps only correct at the level of general principle: Rowe puts it as follows: 'Nevertheless, the fundamental principles of trade secrecy have become relatively well grounded, so much so that the introduction of a federal law is unlikely to cause tremendous upheaval in its continuing doctrinal development.'[139] Duszczyszyn and Roland, also in 2019, maintained that: 'it cannot be disputed that many meaningful differences exist, including whether the owner must show that the trade secret is not "readily ascertainable by proper means," whether the owner has any rights against a party that innocently acquires a trade secret, and what is necessary to satisfy the requirement that the owner employ "reasonable measures" to maintain secrecy of the information. Sometimes, such as when a state has rejected the "inevitable disclosure" doctrine, the differences can be case dispositive'.[140] Despite

134. *See, e.g.*, *Bimbo Bakeries USA Inc v. Chris Botticella*, No 10-0194 (ED Pa 9 February 2010).
135. *Defend Trade Secrets Act* of 2016 (codified as amended at 18 USC. §§1832-1836). The Act went into effect on 11 May 2016.
136. Elizabeth A. Rowe, 'A Snapshot of Trade Secrets Developments' (2019) 60(45) *William & Mary Law Review* 45.
137. *See* H.R. Rep No 114-529, at 6; S. Rep. No 114-220, at 14-15; 162 Cong. Rec. H2032 (Rep Conyers).
138. *Ibid.*, 49.
139. *See* above n 121, 50.
140. Danielle Duszczyszyn & Daniel Roland 'Three Years Later: How the Defend Trade Secrets Act Complicated the Law Instead of Making It More Uniform' *Finnegan* (online) July/August 2019,

the differences, federal courts have unsurprisingly looked to judicial decisions about state trade secrets law for guidance, but since those laws are not quite as uniform as perhaps intended, this inevitably leads to resultant divergences in federal jurisprudence.[141] In some respects, federal courts have also left their own imprint on trade secrets law, as Hrdy points out while stressing the significance of the requirement of 'independent economic value': 'In recent years, some federal courts have grown skeptical of the type and quality of information asserted to be trade secrets and have begun to reference independent economic value as a limiting principle.'[142] Suffice it to say that the introduction of the DTSA and its coexistence with the various state iterations of the UTSA is grist for the US lawyers' mill.

[H] Some Characteristics of Litigation in the US

Although from the perspective of evaluating the importance of criminal law, Almeling et al., in 2009-2010, collected and analysed interesting data concerning trade secrets litigation in the US. They tend in some respects to reflect what we also suspect about litigation in other countries, first and foremost that 'in over 85% of cases, the alleged misappropriator was someone the trade secret owner knew – either an employee or a business partner'.[143] Nonetheless, 78% of their state cases involved employee misappropriations, whereas only 53% of federal cases did. They also found that internal business secrets were litigated in 70% of state cases and technical secrets in 36% (46% and 56% respectively in federal cases). Further, although '[f]or over 40 years after its publication in 1939, the *Restatement (First) of Torts* was almost always cited in state courts, whereas in their 1995-2009 study period it was only cited in 5% of cases.[144] In 30% of cases the laws of Illinois, California or New York were applied.[145] They also found that although federal litigation was increasing exponentially, state cases were also increasing but "in a linear pattern at a modest pace"'.[146] Now of course the availability of the DTSA has greatly impacted the relevant figures, with 890 cases 'with DTSA or with DTSA and state trade secret claims [...] terminated in 2023'. In the same year, 247 cases with state trade secret misappropriation claims but no DTSA claims were terminated.[147]

---

https://www.finnegan.com/en/insights/articles/three-years-later-how-the-defend-trade-secrets-act-complicated-the-law-instead-of-making-it-more-uniform.html.

141. *See* Suzana Nashkova, 'Defining Trade Secrets in the United States: Past and Present Challenges: A Way Forward?' (2023) 54(5) *International Review of Intellectual Property and Competition Law* 634 https://doi.org/10.1007/s40319-023-01310-1.
142. Camilla A. Hrdy, 'The Value In Secrecy' (2022) 91(2) *Fordham Law Review* 557, 561 https://doi.org/10.2139/ssrn.3897949.
143. Above n 94, 294.
144. *See* David S. Almeling, Darin W. Snyder, Micahel Sapozniko, Whitney E. McCollum & Jull Weader, 'A Statistical Analysis of Trade Secrets Litigation in State Courts' (2010-2011) 46(1) *Gonzaga Law Review* 57, 59-61.
145. *See* above n 88, 294.
146. *See also* above n 114, 61.
147. *See* Lexis Nexis, 'Trend Report: Trade Secret Cases Terminated in 2023' *Lexis Nexis* (online) 6 June 2024, https://www.lexisnexis.com/community/insights/legal/lex-machina/b/lex-mach

Of abiding significance are the findings that most cases concern either employees or business partners, and of those, the most concern employees (78% of state cases). In any case, these concerned cases where the wrong was most likely a breach of confidence in the context of a broader existing or previous contractual relationship. Cases of industrial espionage were in the minority. Also of interest is the steady growth in trade secrets cases. The authors offer no real explanation for this growth other than to say that '[T]rade secrets now constitute a core part of many companies' business strategies and IP portfolios'.[148] It is difficult to assess whether this growth is simply analogous to other areas of IP or whether trade secrets really have become relatively more important. It is also difficult to determine how justifiable it is to infer from the increased litigation that companies find trade secrets more important aspects of their IP portfolios. It might simply be that companies have become more litigious across the board. Whatever the case may be, Jones Day, the major US law firm, in its 2023 Trade Secrets 'white Paper' concludes that 'All signs indicate that 2024 will present more non-compete legislation, greater reliance on trade secrets as a preferred form of intellectual property protection, and an increasing number of trade secret disputes.'[149] The trend thus seems certain to continue.

Finally, it is as well to remember that the reality of the law in the United States (as perhaps to a lesser extent elsewhere) is that the outcomes of cases are often determined by collateral questions, such as choice of law, pre-emption or the factors courts assess to determine preliminary injunctions, for which the strength of the case is only one factor. Many of the decisions involve juries and their awards are often the subject of appeals, adding further layers of complexity and cost.

[I] Extraterritoriality of US Law

The principle of territoriality establishes that a state typically exercises jurisdiction only over actions occurring within its borders or committed by its nationals. This principle is firmly established in US law, as recognized by the Supreme Court, which imposes a presumption against the application of US statutes beyond its borders: 'It is a "longstanding principle of American law" that legislation of Congress, unless a contrary intent appears, is meant to apply only within the territorial jurisdiction of the United States.'[150] Nevertheless, this presumption may be overturned in two instances: first, if Congress explicitly intends a statute to have extraterritorial effect, or second, if such an effect can be inferred from the statute's purpose.[151]

ina/posts/trend-report-trade-secret-cases-terminated-in-2023#: ~ :text = Claimants % 20prevai led % 20over % 20claim % 20defendants,1 % 20and % 20December % 2031 % 2C % 202023.

148. *See* above n 88, 326.
149. Alexandra N. Fries, Alyssa M. Orellana, & Ariana S. Wilner, '2023 Annual Review: Key US Trade Secret Developments' *Jones Day* (online) January 2024, https://www.jonesday.com/en/insights/2024/01/key-us-trade-secret-developments-2023-annual-review.
150. *Ibid.*, 255.
151. *See* Elizabeth A. Rowe & Giulia Farrior, 'Revisiting Trade Secret Extraterritoriality' (2019) 25(2) *Boston University Journal of Science and Technology Law* 101.

With regard to trade secrets, a strict application of the principle of territoriality could result in significant gaps in protection. To illustrate, an act that constitutes trade secret misappropriation under US law may occur in a country where such actions are not prohibited. Although the violation may occur abroad, its impact may still reach the United States. This may occur, for example, through the importation of goods that benefit from the misappropriated trade secret or because the disclosing of the information (even abroad) would have resulted in annihilating the trade secrets status of the information at stake.

As Rowe and Mahfood observe, prior to the enactment of the DTSA, case law exhibited a disparate range of approaches.[152] Some decisions, in accordance with the Supreme Court's rigorous territoriality test, declined to extend the application of US law to instances of trade secret misappropriation occurring abroad. This was exemplified by the Third Circuit Court of Appeals' decision in *BP Chemicals Ltd. v. Formosa Chemical & Fibre Corp*,[153] wherein the court declined to apply US law to a misappropriation claim involving the alleged theft of trade secrets in Taiwan and the subsequent importation of goods derived from those secrets into the United States.

> In this case FCFC's alleged misappropriation and improper use of BP's trade secrets have occurred and continue to occur in Taiwan. The primary alleged injury to BP has occurred and continues to occur in Great Britain. See Horne v. Adolph Coors Co., 684 F.2d 255, 259-60 (3d Cir. 1982) (holding that in a trade secret case, the injury occurs to the owner of the trade secret wherever he resides). Thus, the primary tortious conduct giving rise to BP's claim against FCFC and to the injury caused thereby is unrelated to the United States.[154]

The Court's reasoning acquires further normative significance when applied to the US-based manufacturers of the equipment in question. Similarly, the Court declined to apply US law, underscoring the necessity to respect Taiwan's sovereign prerogative in formulating its own trade secret policies. This approach demonstrates a commitment to the principle of comity, reflecting a restraint in extending US trade secret law to actions that originate in foreign jurisdictions:

> [W]e conclude based on the current record that Taiwan had the more substantial interest in having its law applied and that a New Jersey court would apply that law in a case like this.
>
> We believe Taiwan has the greater interest in setting the standards regarding whether information that has been licensed by a British company to a Taiwanese company has been sufficiently safeguarded to warrant legal protection or whether it has entered the Taiwanese public domain. This issue implicates policy judgments regarding the appropriate balance between protecting trade secrets, thereby encouraging both the development of new technology and the willingness of foreign companies to share their technology with Taiwanese businesses, and free interchange and access to information, which also has profound implications for the health of the Taiwanese economy. New Jersey's interest, on the other hand,

152. *Ibid*. Elizabeth A. Rowe & Daniel M. Mahfood, 'Trade Secrets, Trade, and Extraterritoriality' (2014) 66 *Alabama Law Review* 63 https://doi.org/10.2139/ssrn.2418407.
153. *BP Chemicals Ltd. v. Formosa Chemical & Fibre Corp.*, 229 F.3d 254 (3d Cir. 2000).
154. *Ibid*. 261.

> would appear to be virtually nil. As we have previously pointed out, BP, the purported owner of the trade secret, is not a resident of New Jersey and, while it may suffer some marginal injury there, New Jersey is assuredly not the principal situs of either the direct or the indirect injury inflicted. Moreover, we are doubtful that a New Jersey court would apply New Jersey law even if BP were a New Jersey corporation. A state's interest in protecting its citizens from injury by protecting intellectual property which they choose to license to foreign companies cannot outweigh the interests of the foreign sovereign in setting the standards for the protection of intellectual property within its own borders.[155]

However, other courts approached the extraterritoriality argument with less rigour or stringency. For example, in a case involving the misappropriation of software source code, a Texas District Court chose to dismiss the extraterritoriality argument, reasoning that:

> Here, neither side has made any effort to prove Chinese law. 'In the absence of sufficient proof to establish with reasonable certainty the substance of the foreign principles of law, the modern view is that the law of the forum should be applied.' [...] Therefore, for purposes of assessing the request for a preliminary injunction, the court will analyze the trade secret questions with reference to Texas law.[156]

The court's decision not to address the extraterritorial nature of the situation was thus due to an insufficiently developed argument by the parties involved. A more strategic approach for a trade secret owner wishing to apply US standards – without relying on the opposing party's lack of effort in presenting an extraterritoriality argument – would be to seek an exclusion order from the ITC under section 337 (§19 USC 1337). This statute provides that:

> the following are unlawful, and when found by the Commission to exist shall be dealt with (...): 'Unfair methods of competition and unfair acts in the importation of articles (...) into the United States, or in the sale of such articles by the owner, importer, or consignee, the threat or effect of which is (i) to destroy or substantially injure an industry in the United States; (ii) to prevent the establishment of such an industry; or (iii) to restrain or monopolize trade and commerce in the United States'.

In the case of *TianRui Group*, the US Court of Appeals for the Federal Circuit ruled that the ITC was within its rights to apply section 337 in order to address a trade secret misappropriation that had occurred in China.[157] The Court determined that both the historical context and the literal interpretation of the statute supported a reversal of the presumption against extraterritoriality. By focusing on unfair acts 'in the importation', the legislature did not, the Court reasoned, have solely 'domestic concerns' in mind.[158] Nevertheless, this interpretation has been the subject of criticism. As Judge Kimberly Moore observed in her dissenting opinion, the language of section 337, which specifies that the unfair act must occur 'in the importation', could be interpreted to imply that it

155. *Ibid.*, 265-266.
156. *Cisco Systems, Inc. v. Huawei Technologies, Co., Ltd.*, 266 F. Supp. 2d 551 (E.D. Tex. 2003), 555.
157. *TianRui Group v. ITC*, 661 F. 3d 1322.
158. *Ibid.*, 1329.

applies only when the importation itself involves unfair conduct.[159] In this case, Judge Moore posited that 'there is nothing inherently unfair about the wheels or the process by which they are imported'.[160] In light of the potential limitations in its reasoning, the Court added that the conduct under sanction was not purely extraterritorial: the 'unfair' activity was deemed relevant only in that it culminated in the importation of goods.[161] Furthermore, the remedy is limited to the banning of the products concerned from the US market, which mitigates the risk of inferring with Chinese policy.[162]

In civil matters, the extraterritorial reach of US law has recently evolved with the introduction of the DTSA, a development that could have significant implications. The EEA, which has criminalized trade secret theft and misappropriation at the federal level since 1996, included an explicit extraterritorial provision. Specifically, 18 US Code §1837 states:

> This chapter also applies to conduct occurring outside the United States if –
> (1) the offender is a natural person who is a citizen or permanent resident alien of the United States, or an organization organized under the laws of the United States or a State or political subdivision thereof; or
> (2) an act in furtherance of the offense was committed in the United States.

In 2016, the EEA was amended with the introduction of the DTSA, expanding federal law to allow civil actions in cases of trade secret misappropriation. Under 18 US Code §1836, '[a]n owner of a trade secret that is misappropriated may bring a civil action under this subsection if the trade secret is related to a product or service used in, or intended for use in, interstate or foreign commerce'. Since this provision resides within the same chapter as §1837, the question arises as to whether the federal civil protection for trade secrets also supports an extraterritorial application. This question remained unresolved until recently, in part due to the fact that §1837 employs criminal terminology such as 'offence' or 'offender'.[163] However, in a recent ruling, the Court of Appeals for the Seventh Circuit provided comprehensive support for the extraterritorial application of the DTSA.[164] The case concerned Motorola, which alleged that its trade secrets had been misappropriated by Hytera, a Chinese company that had recruited three of Motorola's employees in Malaysia. In its decision, the Court of Appeals concurred with the District Court's reasoning:

> 'the clear indication of Congress in amend[ing] Chapter 90 of Title 18 of the US Code was to extend the extraterritorial provisions of Section 1837 to Section 1836, meaning Section 1836 may have extraterritorial reach subject to the restrictions in Section 1837. [...]

159. *See* above n 152.
160. *See* above n 157, 1338.
161. *Ibid.*, 1329.
162. *Ibid.*, 1332.
163. For a critical view toward such an extension, *see* Rochelle Dreyfuss & Linda Silberman, 'Misappropriation on a Global Scale: Extraterritoriality and Applicable Law in Transborder Trade Secrecy Cases' (2017) 8(2) *Cybaris, An Intellectual Property Law Journal* 265.
164. US Court of Appeals for the Federal Circuit, *Motorola Solutions INC SDN BHD v. Hytera Communications Corporation LTD (2024). Nos. 22-2370 & 22-2413.*

> The district court then rejected Hytera's alternative argument that section 1837(2)'s use of the word 'offense' limits its extraterritorial reach to criminal cases. The court explained that 'offense' could reach both criminal and civil violations, so that the extraterritorial provisions of section 1837 apply to civil claims under section 1836(b). [...]
>
> Because the DTSA rebuts the presumption against extraterritoriality, the only limits on its reach are 'the limits Congress has imposed on the statute's foreign application' in section 1837(2). [...] Section 1837(2) is satisfied if 'an act in furtherance of the offense was committed in the United States.' As the district court wrote: 'The offense, in the context of the DTSA private cause of action, is the misappropriation of a trade secret.' Motorola, 436 F. Supp. 3d at 1163. [...] The district court found that 'use' of the alleged trade secrets had occurred in the United States because Hytera had advertised, promoted, and marketed products embodying the stolen trade secrets at numerous trade shows in the United States. [...] We agree that Hytera's marketing of products embodying Motorola's stolen trade secrets constituted domestic 'use' of those trade secrets, amounting to completed acts of domestic 'misappropriation' under 18 USC. § 1839(5)(B). Hytera's completed domestic acts of misappropriation are sufficient to satisfy section 1837(2). We affirm the district court's holding that Hytera committed an act in furtherance of misappropriation of Motorola's trade secrets in the United States. Id. at 1166. The district court did not err by awarding Motorola relief based on Hytera's worldwide sales of products furthered by that misappropriation, regardless of where in the world the remainder of Hytera's illegal conduct occurred.

This decision indicates that the potential extraterritorial reach of US trade secret law is now fully established, with the only limiting factor being the necessity to demonstrate that an act was carried out 'in furtherance of the offense'. In practice, this is not a stringent requirement, as any use of the misappropriated trade secret within US territory - such as manufacturing goods that benefit from the violation - is typically considered sufficient. The implications of this approach are open to debate, particularly in relation to the question of respect for the sovereignty of other countries in establishing their own trade secret policies.

§5.04 THE CRIMINAL LAW

In the US, the criminal law also plays an important deterrent role. However, there were no statutory criminal provisions dealing with trade secrets at federal or state level in the US until the 1960s. Fetterley suggests that US technological pre-eminence then made the country a target for foreign industrial spies, many of whom had obtained training in the cold war secret arts. Some high-profile trade secrets cases apparently engendered a sense that American know-how was not sufficiently protected from the depredations of foreign companies.[165] Later, the same concerns would result in the enactment of a federal penal law, the *EEA*.[166] Foreign entities were easily able to evade civil lawsuits

165. In particular involving pharmaceuticals and Italian defendants. *See* Fetterley, above n 6, 1538.
166. *See* Michael L. Rustad, 'Negligent Enablement of Trade Secret Misappropriation' (2006) 22 *Santa Clara Computer and High Tech Law Journal* 455.

'because defendants had left the country or were judgment proof'.[167] The general criminal law proved equally ineffective because of the well-known difficulties of fitting theft of information into existing property offences. As a result, state legislatures began to amend laws to expressly accommodate trade secrets, the first to do so being New York, where the larceny provisions were amended in 1964 to provide that objects embodying trade secrets fell within the definition of property that could be the subject of larceny.[168] The state of New Jersey went a step further by introducing a new section, rather than amending an existing one, and defining trade secrets as secret and valuable scientific or technical information. Not only the theft or embezzlement of an article containing a trade secret but also copying the secret information was criminalized, if done with intent to deprive or withhold control or to misappropriate a trade secret. Interestingly enough, intent to return the article was expressly excluded as a defence.[169] According to Fetterley, this provision became a model for other states, quite a number of which followed suit. These provisions are similar to the penal protection still afforded to '*secrets de fabrique*' in France (even post-implementation of the EU Trade Secrets Directive in that country) and the penal provisions in the Law on Trade Secrets in Germany.[170]

However, prosecutions under state laws are few and far between and the penalties imposed tend to be mild, as we saw in Chapter 1. The same pattern has prevailed in relation to enforcement of the recently introduced federal law, the *EEA* (2006); prosecutions are also few. It should be noted that the Protecting American Intellectual Property Act of 2022 additionally imposes sanctions on certain foreign individuals and entities involved in the theft of trade secrets belonging to a US individual or entity. It also requires the US President to report periodically on foreign individuals and entities that have knowingly engaged in, benefited from, or assisted in theft of US trade secrets that materially contributed to a significant threat to US national security, foreign policy, or economic health.[171] Opinions are divided about the gravity of the issue of (foreign) industrial espionage. Rustad, for instance, argues that there is a serious problem and that the law should be further strengthened to give private parties a greater role. Bone, however, doubts that there is sufficient empirical evidence of an explosion of espionage and the consequential costs to business.[172] We saw in Chapter 1 that Moohr is of the same view. An important problem with the reporting of trade secrets misappropriation is that often another party may in fact have obtained

---

167. *See* above n 6, 1538.
168. *Ibid.*
169. *Ibid.*
170. On 26 April 2019, the German Trade Secrets Act (Geschäftsgeheimnisschutzgesetz, GeschGehG) entered into force in Germany. Article 23 of this Act subjects infringements of trade secrets provisions to criminal liability (previously such liability was based on n §§17-19 of the UWG).
171. Public Law No: 117-336 (1 May 2023). It is early days in terms of actual reporting by the President; for a more comprehensive review of foreign threats to trade secrets in the US, *see* United States Department of Justice, 'Department of Justice Report to Congress Pursuant to the Defend Trade Secrets Act' *United States Department of Justice* (online) 24 January 2022, https://www.justice.gov/criminal/iptf/page/file/1101901/dl?inline.
172. *See* above n 103, 530.

trade secrets by *legitimate* means like reverse engineering and independent invention. The fact alone that another party has the same information in their possession does not 'inevitably' indicate that it was stolen. Further, whether or not a misappropriation has occurred is often difficult to determine, such as in the standard case of a departing employee using knowledge acquired on the job – is there a theft of a trade secret or mere use of free know-how? Self-reporting of trade secrets misappropriation, one would suspect, would be on the very high side of what the law would actually recognize as such.[173]

The loss of trade secrets cannot simply be determined with the same certainty as the loss of a material possession, since there is no resulting absence of the good which indicates the loss. Bone simply argues that the existing empirical evidence is not sufficiently reliable to justify further strengthening of trade secrets law. He also makes the point that stronger protection against trade secrets theft may indeed be a deterrent, but it will also have downside effects. Most importantly, it could have a detrimental effect on innovation: 'secrecy impedes the diffusion of information. When one firm's stronger trade secrecy prevents other firms from building on the information, the pace of innovation is likely to slow with negative effects on economic productivity'.[174]

Be that as it may, the federal *EEA* is of interest exactly because it appears to cast such a wide net, but is, however, rarely enforced. Krotoski points out in an article published in 2009 that since 1996, there have been six cases approved for prosecution under paragraph 1831 of the EEA.[175] This paragraph applies to economic espionage, narrowly speaking, i.e., misappropriation of a trade secret with the intent of benefiting a foreign entity (government, instrumentality or agency). Paragraph 1382, however, covers any misappropriation of a trade secret with the intent to convert it to the economic benefit of anyone other than the owner and to injure its owner. Under this section, prosecutions are more frequent. The standards are similar to the UTSA in that trade secrets under the EEA are information concerning which reasonable protective measures have been taken and which derive independent economic value from not being publicly known. Conspiracy and attempt, as well as other offences, can be charged, for instance, involving mail fraud or data security.[176] A number of 'defences' can complicate the matters for prosecutors, such as the 'tool kit' defence (i.e., the information was the know-how of the employee); that the employee did not know something was a trade secret, although proof that the employee knew this is perhaps not expressly required; that the information was in the public domain or belonged to the defendant; that reverse engineering lay at the source of the disclosure to a different employer; and finally, that the provisions in the EEA are 'unconstitutionally vague', which argument has been aired (ultimately unsuccessfully) in a number of cases

173. *Ibid.*, 531.
174. *Ibid.*, 535.
175. Mark L. Krotoski, 'Common Issues and Challenges in Prosecuting Trade Secret and Economic Espionage Cases' (2009) 57(5) *United States Attorneys' Bulletin* 2. This whole issue is dedicated to Economic Espionage and Trade Secrets.
176. *See* Krotoski, above n 175, 17.

including *Hsu*.[177] Thus, prosecutions are not likely to be brought to a successful conclusion from the state's point of view in any but the most clearcut cases.[178]

§5.05 CONCLUSION

In the US, unfair competition and misappropriation have jockeyed for influence, and the law of trade secrets has oscillated between the two. Unfair competition can be seen as directed to the impropriety of the actions of the defendant – the unfairness means acting in disregard of the standards of proper behaviour that can be expected of an honest trader. This is the approach that has eventually won out because 'impropriety' is central to the UTSA and subsequently also in the DTSA. Alternatively, a purer unjust enrichment approach can be adopted, i.e., the unfairness lies simply in the unauthorized 'appropriation of trade values' of another.[179] This is a more objective approach that requires no moral judgment about the actions of a competitor. Such misappropriation can be seen as a form of unfair competition, as happened, for instance, in France and Germany prior to the EU Trade Secrets Directive, but alternatively, it can logically stand on its own feet as a separate tort 'of misappropriation'. If the anchor of a competitive relationship between the litigants is cast asunder, so that misappropriation is wrong even if the appropriator is not in competition with the complainant, then we approach something close to the old French concept of '*agissement parasitaires*'. Misappropriation here amounts to something akin to a common law default property regime, which recognizes that sometimes value is created by effort and ingenuity, which merits some form of protection as an incentive but that falls outside the existing statutory IP regimes. This is not in line with English law because the value and incentive thinking is absent, the focus being on maintaining trust and good faith in communications.

177. *United States v. Hsu*, 40 F Supp 2d 623 (ED Pa 1999). As related in Thomas Dougherty, 'Common Defences in Trade Secrets Cases' (2009) 57(5) *United States Attorneys' Bulletin* 27.
178. *See also* Office of Legal Education – Executive Office for United States, 'Prosecuting Intellectual Property Crimes' (4th ed.) *Chapter IV – Theft of Commercial Trade Secrets*, 155.
179. *See* Andrew Terry, 'Unfair Competition and Misappropriation of a Competitor's Trade Values' (1998) 51 *Modern Law Review* 296 https://doi.org/10.1111/j.1468-2230.1988.tb01758.x.

CHAPTER 6
The European Trade Secret Directive

§6.01 INTRODUCTION: CONTEXT OF THE DIRECTIVE AND INFLUENCE OF US LAW

In the EU, the legal framework has been profoundly modified with the enactment of Directive 2016/943 in 2016 on 'the protection of undisclosed know-how and business information (trade secrets) against their unlawful acquisition, use and disclosure' (TSD).[1] This Directive was adopted at the EU level to ensure a level and coherent playing field concerning the civil law protection of trade secrets within the internal market. It is a comprehensive piece of legislation which aims to regulate at European level both the definitional (Chapter I Directive), substantive (Chapter II Directive), enforcement and procedural (Chapter III Directive) aspects of protection. It concerns only civil and not criminal liability.

The Directive entered into force in June 2016, opening a two-year transposition period for the Member States to incorporate its content into their national law. As is usually the case, some States took more time to transpose it. For instance, Germany's transposition was not completed until 18 April 2019. The results of this process in France and Germany will be analysed in the following chapters.[2] For the sake of completeness, it should be noted that in 2016, the UK was still formally part of the EU and was therefore obliged to transpose the directive, which led to certain evolutions in UK law, covered in Chapter 4.[3]

If the Directive is one of the most detailed pieces of legislation devoted to the civil protection of trade secrets, it remains relatively recent, and its effects are only beginning to impact the concerned parties. Moreover, the development of a structured

1. European Commission, *Council Directive (EU) 2016/943 of the European Parliament and of the Council of 8 June 2016 on the Protection of Undisclosed Know-how and Business Information (Trade Secrets) Against Their Unlawful Acquisition, Use and Disclosure* [2016] OJ L157 1.
2. *See* Chapter 7 for the French and Chapter 8 for the German transposition.
3. *See* Chapter 4.

body of European case law to inform this legal framework is still in its infancy.[4] However, this case law could find significant support for its development in in the decisions of courts in the United States. As will be explained in more detail in this chapter, the drafters of the European Directive were highly influenced by the US legal framework and the Directive can therefore be regarded as a bridge between the two systems.

Before the Directive was introduced, the legal protection of trade secrets within the EU varied significantly among the Member States.[5] They not only relied on different legal instruments, but the nature of protection itself also differed between the different legal systems composing the European internal market.[6] A review of the chapters detailing the laws in the UK, Germany, and France prior to the Directive reveals the fragmented legal landscape faced by businesses operating across multiple EU Member States. In the UK, trade secrets were protected under a broad interpretation of the breach of confidence action within the English legal system.[7] In Germany, protection was rooted in specific provisions within the law on unfair competition.[8] Meanwhile, in France, trade secrets were primarily safeguarded through case law developed under unfair competition claims.[9] In contrast, Italy treated trade secrets as a form of IP under the Code on Industrial Property (former sections 98-99). These disparities raised concerns for the EU legislator, as they could hinder cross-border innovation and reduce the competitiveness of European firms within the internal market. This concern prompted the decision to move toward harmonization of this area in 2016.

The intensity of this need for harmonization resulted in the essential question of the justification for legal protection and the appropriate level of protection needed being almost undebated. Indeed, the preparatory work for the adoption of the Directive focused on demonstrating the divergences between national legislations and the risk they posed to the European economy to justify action at the European level.[10] Such a demonstration was indeed necessary because of the principle of subsidiarity, which prevails in the exercise of competences assigned to the EU (Article 5§3 Treaty on European Union (TEU)). The institutional importance of these questions, however, led

---

4. In this regard, *see* European Union Intellectual Property Office, *Trade Secrets Litigation Trends in the EU: IPR Enforcement Case Law Collection* (June 2023).
5. *See* the preparatory work undertaken by the European legislator prior to the adoption of the TSD, European Commission, *Impact Assessment Accompanying the Proposal for a Directive of the European Parliament and of the Council on the Protection of Undisclosed Know-How and Business Information (Trade Secrets) Against Their Unlawful Acquisition, Use and Disclosure* (online) 28 November 2013, https://www.eumonitor.eu/9353000/1/j9vvik7m1c3gyxp/vjfc6rhrlmyt; Hogan Lovells, *Report on Trade Secrets for the European Commission* (online) 23 September 2011, https://op.europa.eu/en/publication-detail/-/publication/068c999d-06d2-4c8e-a681-a4ee2eb0e116. *See also* Tanya Aplin, 'A Critical Evaluation of the Proposed EU Trade Secrets Directive' (2014) 4 *Intellectual Property Quarterly* 257, 258-260 https://doi.org/10.2139/ssrn.2467946.
6. In Germany, trade secrets protection was primarily regulated in ss 17-19 of the former Act against Unfair Competition; it was regulated within the Code on Industrial Property in Italy (former ss 98-99), and it was mainly the result of case law in France. *See* the conclusions of the European Commission in its Impact Assessment, above n 5, 19-27.
7. *See* Chapter 4.
8. *See* Chapter 8.
9. *See* Chapter 8.
10. *See* above n 5, 12-40.

to material questions regarding the type and intensity of protection needed being ignored.

This lack of engagement in an in-depth investigation of these issues had two consequences. First, despite its detailed nature, the Directive contains many grey areas that will need to be clarified by case law. Second, the European legislator's lack of certainty led to a more or less conscious copying of the protection system existing in the United States. Indeed, faced with the imperative of harmonizing trade secret legislation across Europe, the considerable disparities among Member States' existing laws and the absence of a robust theoretical framework, the EU legislator found substantial inspiration in the existing US system. This influence of North American law on European legislation can be explained by the fact that the latter's definition of trade secrets has served as a model for the definition contained in Article 39 of TRIPS in the first place, which in turn was highly influential for the EU harmonization process. Faced with the divergences between the legal orders of the EU Member States, this definition, contained in an international agreement to which all EU Member States were parties, appeared to the Commission as a 'common benchmark' for defining trade secrets and thus a starting point for harmonization.[11] By selecting this definition as a foundation for harmonization, the European legislator found it straightforward to adopt additional aspects of the US approach, such as with the definition of unlawful behaviours or concerning the enforcement modalities.

§6.02 EU COMPETENCY, LEGAL *INSTRUMENTARIUM* AND SCOPE OF THE DIRECTIVE

[A] EU Competency and Decision to Rely on a Directive

According to Articles 4(1) and 5 of the Treaty on the European Union, the EU can only act within the limits of the competencies conferred upon it by the Member States in the EU treaties (the so-called principle of conferral). Furthermore, even when the EU has competence in an area, its exercise is further framed by the principles of subsidiarity and proportionality. Subsidiarity requires the EU to act only when a given objective cannot be achieved at the level of the Member States, while proportionality limits the exercise of EU legislative competence to what is necessary.[12] These *constitutional principles* of EU law shed light on both the choice of the legal *instrumentarium* chosen by the EU legislator as well as its material scope.

For the adoption of the Trade Secrets Directive, the EU legislator finds its *competency* and legal basis in Article 114 of the Treaty on the Functioning of the

11. European Commission, *Study on Trade Secrets and Confidential Business Information in the Internal Market* (April 2013) 19. The authors of the preparatory study ordered by the Commission found that Art. 39 of the TRIPS Agreement represented 'a pillar for the protection of trade secrets among signatory countries' and that 'a general definition of "trade secrets" was provided by Article 39.2 of the TRIPS Agreement'.
12. *See* the *Treaty on European Union and Protocol (No 2) on the Application of the Principles of Subsidiarity and Proportionality* [2008] OJ C 115, Art. 5(3) and 5(4).

European Union (TFEU), which is the general legal provision allowing the EU to adopt '*measures for the approximation of the provisions laid down by law (...) which have as their object the establishment and functioning of the internal market*'. In this regard, the justifications for action at the European level were straightforward due to significant discrepancies in the protection of trade secrets among Member States. Recitals 8 and 9 of the Directive explain that:

> the differences in the legal protection of trade secrets provided for by the Member States imply that trade secrets do not enjoy an equivalent level of protection throughout the Union, thus leading to fragmentation of the internal market in this area and a weakening of the overall deterrent effect of the relevant rules. The internal market is affected in so far as such differences lower the incentives for businesses to undertake innovation-related cross-border economic activity, including research cooperation or production cooperation with partners, outsourcing or investment in other Member States, which depends on the use of information that enjoys protection as trade secrets. Cross-border network research and development, as well as innovation-related activities, including related production and subsequent cross-border trade, are rendered less attractive and more difficult within the Union, thus also resulting in Union-wide innovation-related inefficiencies. [...] In addition, there is a higher risk for businesses in Member States with comparatively lower levels of protection, due to the fact that trade secrets may be stolen or otherwise unlawfully acquired more easily.

Regarding the *instrumentarium* to achieve its harmonization, the EU legislator opted for a 'directive': a legislative act that is addressed to the Member States and which binds them as to the result to be achieved. This requires each state to transpose the directive into national law.[13] However, each country is free to decide on the appropriate measures within its legal order to achieve these objectives. The advantage of this approach is that it enables the integration of the new rules while respecting the legal traditions, coherence, logic and principles of each Member State. However, a potential drawback is that divergences may arise during the transposition stage, the legality of which depends on the freedom left by the Directive to the Member States.

This margin of freedom of the Member States hinges on at least three elements. First, it is necessary to consider the scope of harmonization of the directive. Any matter falling outside this scope is not subject to harmonization and remains within the competence of the Member States.[14] Second, and this time within the scope of the directive, the Member States may be afforded a margin of appreciation. Lastly, the level of detail of the directive itself plays an important role in determining the extent of freedom afforded to Member States: the greater the level of detail, the more limited the freedom of the Member States will be.[15] With regard to this final element, if directives were originally conceived as legislative instruments that should bind the Member

13. Regarding the justification of this choice in comparison to a Regulation, which would have been self-executing and would hence have applied without requiring any transposition, *see* above n 5, 66.
14. *See* in this respect the two paragraphs of this chapter concerning the lack of harmonization concerning the criminal law dimension of the protection and concerning the question of the legality of confidentiality or non-competition clauses.
15. *See* below §6.02[E].

States solely with regard to the 'results to be achieved', in practice, this instrument has been employed with increasing frequency for highly detailed legislation, effectively relegating the national legislator to the role of a mere transcriber of a European text into national law. The Trade Secrets Directive provides an illustrative case in point: in regard to the areas it regulates, its provisions present a high level of detail, leaving little freedom in their transposition.

[B] No Harmonization of Criminal Protection

Despite the considerable latitude offered by Article 114 TFEU, the European legislator decided to only harmonize the civil dimension of trade secrets protection, leaving the possibility of criminalization up to the Member States. The reasons advanced in the impact assessment to justify this choice is that the harmonization of the penal dimension of the protection 'would require the negotiation of two different legal instruments at the EU level', as well as 'changes in national criminal law which is at the heart of national sovereignty'[16] and finally that such protection would have created a discrepancy between the protection offered to trade secrets and IPRs at the European level.[17] The soundness of these arguments is questionable. While it is certainly true that criminal matters are more delicate to negotiate at the European level due to their political sensitivity, the risk of divergence between the protection of IP rights and trade secrets does not disappear by the matter being dealt with at the national level. On the contrary, the choice of the national level creates an additional risk of territorial divergences.

In reality, the main reason lies in political contingencies. As acknowledged in the Impact Assessment, the Commission's attempt to harmonize criminal sanctions for IP rights was until today.[18] Additionally, the European Parliament's rejection of the Anti-Counterfeiting Trade Agreement in 2012 clearly indicated its reluctance to endorse the enactment of criminal norms in this area.[19] Therefore, the EU legislator opted for a less ambitious approach by harmonizing only the civil protection of trade secrets, allowing Member States the discretion to implement additional criminal protections. Whereasin some countries criminal protection is rather anecdotal,[20] some countries have quite extensive criminal protections in place.[21]

16. *See* above n 5, 62.
17. *Ibid.*, 61-62.
18. *Ibid.*, 61.
19. *See* European Parliament, *Legislative Resolution on the Draft Council Decision on the Conclusion of the Anti-Counterfeiting Trade Agreement between the European Union and its Member States, Australia, Canada, Japan, the Republic of Korea, the United Mexican States, the Kingdom of Morocco, New Zealand, the Republic of Singapore, the Swiss Confederation and the United States of America* [2013] CE 349/552.
20. In France, this protection is governed by an old norm. Art. L-621-1 Code of Intellectual Property, which dates back to the 19th century, provides protection only to manufacturing secrets. For more details of this provision, *see* Luc Desaunettes-Barbaro, 'Employees, Trade Secrets and Restrictive Covenants in France' in Anselm Kamperman Sanders & Christopher Heath (eds), *Employees, Trade Secrets and Restrictive Covenants* (Kluwer Law International, 2016) 138-139.
21. *See* §23 German Law on the *Protection of Trade Secrets Act*.

[C] No harmonization of the Relationship Between Employer and Employee

The second issue that the European legislator chose to leave beyond the scope of the Directive – and therefore in principle in the hands of the national lawmakers – relates to employer-employee relationships. Specifically, Article 3 states, 'Nothing in this Directive shall be understood to offer any ground for restricting the mobility of employees. In particular, in relation to the exercise of such mobility, this Directive shall not offer any ground for: (...) (b) limiting employees' use of experience and skills honestly acquired in the normal course of their employment.' Recital 14 further clarifies that such experience and skills are carved out from the definition of trade secrets: 'The definition of trade secret excludes trivial information and the experience and skills gained by employees in the normal course of their employment, and also excludes information which is generally known among, or is readily accessible to, persons within the circles that normally deal with the kind of information in question.'

The Directive's structure is somewhat problematic. First, if employees' experience and skills were indeed intended to lie outside its harmonization scope, it is unclear why Recital 14 felt it necessary to explicitly exclude them from the trade secret definition. This negative limitation, moreover, is not reflected in Article 2 of the Directive, which provides the operative definition of trade secrets. Second, a systematic analysis of the text of the Directive reveals a certain circularity at this level. It refers to the determination of its scope to a standard of honesty concerning the acquisition of information, namely that only 'experience and skills honestly acquired in the normal course of their employment' are supposed to be outside of its scope. However, it is precisely the purpose of this Directive to regulate the conditions under which an acquisition should or should not be considered honest. Furthermore, although the Directive purports to leave the regulation of employer-employee relationships to the discretion of national lawmakers, the interpretation of Article 3 is a matter of European law. Consequently, since experiences and skills that have not been 'honestly acquired in the normal course of their employment' will, *a contrario*, fall under the regime of the Directive, it will be for the Court of Justice to interpret when a piece of information was honestly acquired in order to determine whether the Directive applies. This will, in turn, set the standard of honesty required in this context.

Similarly, the European legislator excluded from the remit of the Directive the questions pertaining to the validity and scope of confidentiality or non-competition clauses. According to Article 1(3): 'Nothing in this Directive shall be understood to offer any ground for restricting the mobility of employees. In particular, in relation to the exercise of such mobility, this Directive shall not offer any ground for: [...] (c) imposing any additional restrictions on employees in their employment contracts other than restrictions imposed in accordance with Union or national law.'[22]

During the drafting of the Directive, a possible harmonization of the conditions for the validity and scope of these clauses was considered but ultimately rejected. In its

22. *See also* Recital 13 of the Trade Secrets Directive.

Impact Assessment, the EC explained that it would be economically inefficient to impose uniform clauses at the European level, as it would not be possible to achieve the level of granularity permitted in *inter partes* agreements. Moreover, it would not increase the effectiveness of the protection of trade secrets, as such clauses would not be sufficient to prevent third parties from benefiting from the trade secrets.[23] These arguments are highly questionable and, in reality, hide a political reluctance on the part of the European legislator to intervene in areas of law - particularly employment law - where Member States are very protective of their prerogatives.[24] Contrary to the Commission's assumption, harmonizing the conditions for the legality of such clauses would not have required a prescriptive uniformization of their conditions. It would have been possible to impose only certain restrictions on the parties' freedom of contract.

Moreover, although harmonization of these clauses would not have increased the level of protection of trade secrets per se, it would have brought legal certainty to two key elements of the legal framework established by the Directive. First, at the level of the definition of a trade secret, the validity of these clauses is crucial to verify whether the information has been subject to 'reasonable steps [...] to keep the information secret' (Article 2(1)(c) of the Directive) - one of the three conditions for information to qualify as a trade secret. In the case of employees working with confidential information, contractual measures such as non-disclosure or post-contractual non-competition clauses are among the most effective mechanisms, especially for secrets that can be memorized. Second, and perhaps more importantly, the validity of these clauses is critical to the assessment of an infringement. As will be discussed in more detail below, the Directive not only prevents the unlawful acquisition of trade secrets but also considers it an infringement 'the use or disclosure of a trade secret [...] whenever carried out, without the consent of the trade secret holder, by a person who is found to meet any of the following conditions: [...] (b) being in breach of a confidentiality agreement or any other duty not to disclose the trade secret; (c) being in breach of a contractual or any other duty to limit the use of the trade secret' (Article 4). Thus, in order to establish unlawful use or disclosure as a result of a breach of contract, it is necessary to establish the validity of the breached clause in the first place.

This is exemplified under US law, which influenced the Directive's definition of what constitutes unlawful acquisition. For instance, the Restatement of Unfair Competition states that 'such agreements can reduce or eliminate potential competition, they are subject to the traditional rules governing contracts in restraint of trade and are accordingly enforceable only when ancillary to a valid transaction and otherwise reasonable'.[25] Thus, the current US federal challenge to most post-employment

23. *Ibid.*
24. Compare also Roland Knaak, Annette Kur & Reto Hilty, 'Comments of the Max Planck Institute for Innovation and Competition of 3 June 2014 on the Proposal of the European Commission for a Directive on the Protection of Undisclosed Know-How and Business Information Trade Secrets) Against Their Unlawful Acquisition, Use and Disclosure of 28 November 2013, COM (2013) 813 Final' (2014) 45(8) *International Review of Intellectual Property and Competition Law* 953, 955 https://doi.org/10.1007/s40319-014-0270-3.
25. American Law Institute, *Restatement of Unfair Competition (Third)*, 471 §41.

non-compete agreements between employers and their employees could potentially have a significant impact on the assessment of what may be considered a misappropriation of trade secrets.[26] The lack of harmonization of the standards of validity of these clauses in the EU will consequently lead to differences in the level of protection from one Member State to another and will oblige a new employer of a foreign employee to verify the applicable law in another Member State.[27]

[D] Minimum Harmonization and the (Limited) Potential for More Far-Reaching Protection

Regarding the margin of appreciation afforded to Member States within the Directive's material scope, it is important to note that it is based on a minimum harmonization logic. It means that the Directive establishes the minimum threshold of protection that national legislation must adhere to. Nevertheless, Member States are at liberty to exceed this minimal basis, should they so desire. This possibility is explicitly acknowledged in Article 1(1) of the Directive, which states: 'Member States may, in compliance with the provisions of the TFEU, provide for more far-reaching protection against the unlawful acquisition, use or disclosure of trade secrets than that required by this Directive.'[28]

Nevertheless, the possibility for Member States to provide more extensive protection is considerably constrained. Article 1(1) indeed restricts this freedom by obliging Member States to comply with several of the Directive's enumerated provisions (Articles 3, 5, 6, 7(1), 8, the second subparagraph of 9(1), 9(3) and (4), 10(2), 11, 13, and 15(3)). An analysis of this list reveals that the European legislator has made each provision of the directive aiming at limiting the scope of protection provided by the directive mandatory for Member States. In practice, with regard to the areas regulated by the Directive, the freedom of the Member States is, in reality, limited to the possibility of imposing additional criminal sanctions in case of violations.

[E] Overview of the National Transpositions

According to Article 19 of the Directive, EU Member States had until 9 June 2018 – two years after the Directive came into force – to transpose it into their national laws. As is often the case, some Member States encountered delays in meeting this deadline. For example, Germany only enacted its 'Law Implementing Directive (EU) 2016/943' in April 2019.

Member States employed varied strategies during the transposition process. Due to the level of specificity within the Directive, some opted for a sui generis legislation that largely mirrors its structure. Germany, for instance, elected to disassociate the

26. In this regard, *see* Chapter 5.
27. *See* Chapter 5. For detailed reports on the legal regimes in Germany, the Netherlands, France, Italy, and Spain, *see* Anselm Kamperman Sanders & Christopher Heath (eds), *Employees, Trade Secrets and Restrictive Covenants* (Kluwer Law International, 2016) 61-199.
28. *See also* Recital 10 of the Trade Secrets Directive.

protection of trade secrets from the framework of its Unfair Competition Law (UWG) by enacting a distinct legislative instrument. The German legislation now comprises four distinct parts: the first three transpose the Directive, while the fourth introduces criminal law provisions aimed at enhancing the protection of trade secrets. Spain,[29] Denmark,[30] Finland,[31] and Sweden[32] have also pursued comparable courses of action.

In contrast, the French legislator chose to incorporate the Directive into the French Code of Commerce (Articles L. 151-1 to L. 152-8) as part of a broader chapter on 'general trade', which regulates general principles of commercial law.[33] This decision is noteworthy in that the legislature could have chosen to incorporate the provisions into the French Code of Intellectual Property. The French legislator's decision to incorporate the Directive hence suggests an emphasis on the unfair competition aspect of trade secret protection.

Portugal chose conversely to transpose the Directive within its reformed Industrial Property Code.[34] However, this decision should not be interpreted as an indication that the Portuguese legislature views the new rules as establishing a new industrial property right. Notably, the protection of trade secrets is situated in Title III, titled 'Infractions', which encompasses unfair competition rules, rather than in Title II, 'Legal Regimes for Industrial Property.' Consequently, trade secrets remain conceptually aligned with unfair competition law.[35] In contrast, the Italian legislature has chosen to maintain trade secret protection within its Industrial Property Code, incorporating the Directive into Section VII of Chapter II, which covers the 'rules relating to the existence, scope, and exercise of industrial property rights'. This placement underscores, at least from a systematic perspective, Italy's classification of trade secrets as a form of property.[36]

It is also noteworthy to mention the approach taken by the UK in transposing the Directive.[37] At the time, the UK was still a member of the EU and was thus required to implement it. To this end, the UK adopted specific regulations to 'amend' its common law framework where necessary. This method allowed the UK to comply with the Directive while preserving its established legal logic and case law.

29. Ley N° 1/2019, de 20 de febrero de 2019, de Secretos Empresariales.
30. Lov om forretningshemmeligheder (Lov nr 309 af 25/4/2018).
31. Liikesalaisuuslaki, 10.8.2018/595.
32. Lag (2018:558) om företagshemligheter.
33. Loi n° 2018-670 du 30 juillet 2018 relative à la protection du secret des affaires.
34. Código da Propiedade Industrial (aprovado pelo Decreto-Lei n.° 110/2018 de 10 de dezembro de 2018 e alterado pelo Decreto-Lei n.° 9/2021 de 29 de janeiro de 2021).
35. *See also* with the same systematic reading of the new legislation Ana Nordberg & Bárbara Díaz Alaminos, 'Implementation of the Trade Secrets Directive into National Law: Portugal and Spain' in Jens Schovsbo, Timo Minssen & Thomas Riis (eds), *The Harmonization and Protection of Trade Secrets in the EU* (Edward Elgar Publishing, 2020) 129.
36. Attuazione della direttiva (UE) 2016/943 del Parlamento europeo e del Consiglio, dell'8 giugno 2016, sulla protezione del know-how riservato e delle informazioni commerciali riservate (segreti commerciali) contro l'acquisizione e la divulgazione illeciti.
37. *The Trade Secrets (Enforcement,* etc.*) Regulations 2018*, n°597.

These varied approaches illustrate that, despite the Directive's comprehensive provisions, numerous Member States perceived that they retained a degree of discretion in how to implement it. As a result, they sought to preserve the coherence of their existing legal systems while adjusting them to meet the Directive's requirements.

§6.03 SUBJECT MATTER: REPLICA OF THE TRIPS DEFINITION

[A] Origin, Logic and Impact

The first claimed added value of the Directive is to ensure a homogeneous definition of the subject matter to be protected.[38] Indeed, prior to the adoption of the Directive, EU Member States relied on different definitions.[39]

Article 2 (1) TSD adopts a harmonized definition:

> 'trade secret' means information which meets all of the following requirements:
>
> (a) it is secret in the sense that it is not, as a body or in the precise configuration and assembly of its components, generally known among or readily accessible to persons within the circles that normally deal with the kind of information in question;
> (b) it has commercial value because it is secret;
> (c) it has been subject to reasonable steps under the circumstances, by the person lawfully in control of the information, to keep it secret

This definition is merely a copy of the definition contained in Article 39(2) of the TRIPS Agreement. The first reason for this choice was pragmatic: since all EU Member States were parties to the TRIPS Agreement, the definition provided was considered a common benchmark, despite their regulatory differences and different definitions. By using the TRIPS, the European legislator was able to avoid a difficult discussion on the establishment of a common standard. However, as a result, some jurisdictions may consider, even in the presence of a textual amendment of their national law, that the material conditions of protection have remained unchanged.[40]

38. Recital 14 of the Trade Secrets Directive.
39. *See* Chapter 7 for France and for Germany 8.
40. In this regard, *see* European Union Intellectual Property Office, *Trade Secrets Litigation Trends in the EU* (2023) 115-116, where it is observed that in *KK. M., J. K., M. K. and BloomEst OÜ* (15 May 2020), 'the Supreme Court expanded on the definition of "trade secret" and, interestingly, observed that, although the proceedings had started in 2016 (i.e., before the Trade Secrets Directive was transposed into Estonian law), the definition of "trade secret" in the Directive was identical to the definition in Article 39(2) of the TRIPS Agreement, which had so far been used to define the concept of trade secret in Estonian jurisprudence'. On the other hand, making a strict distinction between the conditions applicable before the transposition law came into force in Germany and those applicable afterwards, *see* OLG Düsseldorf, *Urteil vom 11 March 2021-15 U 6/20 (LG Düsseldorf)*, §39 which states: 'Since Section 2 No. 1c) GeschGehG is a new or additional obligation of the trade secret holder compared to Section 17 (2) UWG (old version), which was not stipulated by law at the time of the disputed action in spring 2017, the protection of legitimate expectations and the prohibition of impermissible undue retroactive effect of laws requires that reasonable steps to maintain secrecy only be required from the date on which the

The second, less acceptable reason is that the EU legislator lacked a clear understanding of the policy role this definition should play. The need for a clear definition of trade secrets depends on the regulatory approach the legislator chooses to protect trade secrets. Under an unfair competition approach, which relies on the prohibition of conduct deemed unfair, the need for a definition of what is indirectly protected by the prohibitions is not imperative. Conversely, under a subjective rights approach, which recognizes a certain legal exclusivity of a person over an immaterial object, a precise definition of this object is essential to delineate the scope of the recognized prerogatives.[41] The Directive expressly claims to opt for the first option, stating that it 'does not create any exclusive right',[42] and the protection provided is indeed built around prohibitions addressed to third parties.[43] However, since the ultimate purpose of this framework remains the protection of an intangible asset – often considered and traded as a form of property by its holders – the European Directive presents a structure and logic that mirrors that of IP legislation. This explains why the legislator felt somewhat obliged to provide a definition of a trade secret. However, the uncertainty as to its true purpose is evident in Recital 14 of the Directive,[44] which states that '[i]t is important to establish a homogenous definition of a trade secret without restricting the subject matter to be protected against misappropriation'. The purpose of a subject matter legal definition is precisely to establish its limits. Therefore, if the definition does not seek to limit the information that qualifies as a trade secret, it would have no function.

Lastly, relying on the TRIPS definition had a further, more insidious effect: it serves as an entry gate for the US legal framework to influence the shaping of the rest of the European legislation. The definition in Article 39(2) of TRIPS was heavily influenced by §1.4 of the UTSA.[45] Consequently, adopting this definition as the foundation for harmonizing trade secret law in Europe led EU legislators to also embrace the solutions inherent in this legal order for other aspects of protection.[46]

GeschGehG came into force. The appropriate steps of protection must, therefore, have been in place without interruption from April 26, 2019, until today (OLG Stuttgart GRUR-RS 2020, 35613 – Schaumstoffsystem)'.

41. Luc Desaunettes-Barbaro, *Trade Secrets Legal Protection: From a Comparative Analysis of US and EU Law to a New Model of Understanding* (Springer, 1st ed., 2023) 25-27.
42. Recital 17 of the Trade Secrets Directive.
43. *See* Chapter II of the Directive.
44. In EU law, 'Recitals' are a part of the act explaining the reasons of its operative provision. In practice, Recitals play a fundamental role when it comes to interpreting the meaning of the operative part of the act.
45. Sharon Sandeen, 'The Limits of Trade Secret Law: Article 39 of the TRIPS Agreement and the Uniform Trade Secrets Act on Which It Is Based' in Rochelle Dreyfuss & Katherine Stranburg (eds), *The Law and Theory of Trade Secrecy: A Handbook of Contemporary Research* (Edward Elgar, 2011).
46. *See* below §6.04 and §6.05.

[B] Importance of Case Law and Implications of the Current Lack of CJEU Decisions

It was previously explained that in the US, the USTA definition was the result of crystallisation, in the form of *requirements*, of several *weighting factors* used by the US case law to identify protectable information.[47] This structuration process results in a definition the components of which rely on terminology with a certain degree of fuzziness and in which the independent *ratio* of each condition might be difficult to determine.[48] In the US, this criticism is tempered by the abundant case law that informs the concerned parties.[49] In theory, European judges could draw on the extensive case law developed by their US counterparts to inform their decisions. In practice, however, this influence is unlikely to materialize, especially with the UK now being outside the EU and the civil law tradition not being particularly receptive to case law from other jurisdictions. Therefore, and as is often the case with IP in the European context, the Court of Justice will be called upon in the future to play a fundamental role in clarifying the exact meaning to be given to the different conditions of this definition.[50] To date, the latter has not yet been called upon to interpret the Directive. As a result, and not surprisingly, early industry surveys indicate that there is still considerable uncertainty among market participants as to what information is likely to be considered a trade secret.[51]

Upcoming developments will therefore be based on the first decisions handed down by national courts. The impact and influence of the latter will have to be regarded with a certain degree of caution. First, the principle of stare decisis does not apply in civil law countries. Second, a decision handed down by a national court in a Member State is made primarily on the basis of its national law transposing the Directive, and it does therefore (in principle) not concern the interpretation of other national laws. Nonetheless, the impact of these decisions extends beyond mere national boundaries. Even when applying their own laws, national courts are bound by the EU principle of consistent interpretation. This principle requires that, when interpreting national transposition provisions, courts must ensure their interpretation aligns with the content of the Directive. As previously noted,[52] the Directive often leaves the Member States with limited discretion during transposition, meaning that interpreting a national

47. *See also* Chapter 5; Sharon Sandeen, 'The Evolution of Trade Secret Law and Why Courts Commit Error When They Do Not Follow the Uniform Trade Secrets Act' (2010) 33(3) *Hamline Law Review* 493.
48. *See* above n 41, 29-113.
49. *See* Chapter 5.
50. According to Art. 267 TFEU, a preliminary ruling mechanism allows (and sometimes even obliges) national courts to refer a question of interpretation of EU law to the CJEU. This 'dialogue' mechanism between national courts and their European counterparts is a fundamental feature of the EU legal system, designed to ensure a uniform interpretation of EU law.
51. European Innovation Council and SMEs Executive Agency (European Commission) et al., 'Study on the Legal Protection of Trade Secrets in the Context of the Data Economy: Final Report' (online) 2022, https://op.europa.eu/en/publication-detail/-/publication/c0335fd8-33db-11ed-8b77-01aa75ed71a1/language-en.
52. *See* below §6.02[D].

provision frequently equates to interpreting the Directive itself. In cases of uncertainty regarding how the Directive's provisions should be understood, national courts are obligated to refer questions to the Court of Justice for a preliminary ruling. Consequently, decisions from other national courts, particularly those from higher courts – even when they on their face aim only at interpreting national law –also shape the understanding of the Directive. When interpreting its own national provisions, a court faced with a prior decision from another Member State that clarifies the relevant Directive provision should not disregard it. If the court disagrees with the interpretation offered by the other Member State's court, it should seek guidance from the Court of Justice to ensure the uniform application of the Directive across the EU.

[C] Requirements

[1] Secrecy

The first requirement, concerning the secrecy of the information, provides only that the information, as a body or in the precise configuration and assembly of its components, should not be generally known or readily accessible to persons normally handling the type of information involved. The required level of secrecy remains as ambiguous as in the US under the UTSA, leaving ample room for interpretation.[53] The language of this provision makes it clear that absolute secrecy is not required.[54] However, while this sets an upper limit, it leaves the lower limit undefined. This ambiguity was evident during the transposition phase, and the French Parliament initially considered adopting a very low threshold that would grant protection once the information was inaccessible to a single person who typically handles this type of information.[55]

Probably aware of the need for greater clarity in the application of this condition, the Austrian *Oberster Gerichtshof*, in one of the first decisions by a national Supreme Court on the subject, took the time to devote several paragraphs to explaining in the abstract how this requirement should be applied. The case involved two former employees of a company that manufactured machinery for the construction of railroads who had founded their own competing company. As is often the case with trade secrets disputes, the two employees had collected data from their former employer before leaving the company, in particular, some design plans and drawings used as templates to produce some machines. The main issue was whether this information qualified as a trade secret. According to the court:

> 3.2. Information is not considered secret (26b para. 1 no. 1 UWG) only if it is absolutely new; rather, what is decisive is the practical accessibility of the information for a certain group of persons (*see Alexander* in *Köhler/Bornkamm/*

53. *See* above n 5, 261.
54. Also Austrian Oberster Gerichtshof, 26 January 2021, 4 Ob 188/20f, §31.
55. *See* French Assemblée Nationale, *Proposition de loi n°675 portant transposition de la directive du Parlement européen et du Conseil sur la protection des savoir-faire et des informations commerciales non divulgués contre l'obtention, l'utilisation et la divulgation illicites*, 28 March 2018, Art. 1.

Feddersen, dUWG § 2 GeschGehG Rz 31). The relevant group of persons is to be determined on the basis of an objective and normative standard specific to the information. In the case of information of a technical nature, the average professional groups must be taken into account (*Alexander* in *Köhler/Bornkamm/Feddersen*, dUWG § 2 GeschGehG Rz 33).

3.3. Information is generally known if it is part of the common knowledge of the general public or of an average person belonging to the relevant professional group (*Alexander* in *Köhler/Bornkamm/Feddersen*, dUWG § 2 GeschGehG Rz 35). Publications in relevant trade journals or in disclosed patent applications generally lead to information being considered generally known (*Harte-Bavendamm* in *Harte-Bavendamm/Ohly/Kalbfus*, GeschGehG, Sec. 2 para. 24; *Hofmarcher*, Das Geschäftsgeheimnis [2020] para. 2.20; *see also Beetz*, Geheimnisschutz und Patentrecht, ipCompetence 2019 H 21, 48).

3.4. Information is readily accessible if it is not generally known but a person in the relevant public can obtain it without considerable work and expenditure of time, effort, costs and/or skill by means that are otherwise fair (*Alexander* in *Köhler/Bornkamm/Feddersen*, dUWG§ 2 GeschGehG Rz 37; *Harte-Bavendamm* in *Harte-Bavendamm/Ohly/Kalbfus*, GeschGehG, § 2 Rz 30; *McGuire* in FS Harte-Bavendamm 367, 381 f). This restriction results, as *Hofmarcher* (Das Geschäftsgeheimnis [2020] Rz 2.21) convincingly explains, from the provision of § 26d para. 2 no. 2 UWG, which would be dispensable if the possibility of reverse engineering, which involves a great deal of effort, would already eliminate the secret character.

3.5. It is questionable whether information that belongs to the 'state of the art' is generally known or easily accessible. This is denied in parts of the literature (*Ohly*, Das neue Geschäftsgeheimnisgesetz im Überblick, GRUR 2019, 441 [446]; *Harte-Bavendamm* in *Harte-Bavendamm/Ohly/Kalbfus*, GeschGehG, § 2 Rz 32; *Alexander* in *Köhler/Bornkamm/Feddersen*, dUWG § 2 GeschGehG Rz 36), but affirmed by *Hofmarcher* (Das Geschäftsgeheimnis [2020] Rz 2.134 [FN 434]). In the decision 4 Ob 12/11k, *Rohrprodukte* (= ecolex 2012, 65 [*Horak*]), the Senate leaned towards the first view by examining the assertion that the information belonged to the state of the art as an objection of lawful alternative conduct and thus implicitly affirmed the existence of a trade secret.

3.6. On closer examination, however, a distinction must be made, especially since the term 'state of the art' defies a uniform interpretation (*see Saria*, Grundsätzliches zum 'Stand der Technik aus rechtswissenschaftlicher Sicht', in *Saria* [ed], Der 'Stand der Technik' 25 [32 ff]). On the one hand, the 'state of the art' is defined as the specialized knowledge that the 'average expert' has in the relevant field (RS0071399). If information is therefore part of the 'state of the art', it is generally known to the relevant circles of experts (*see also* Art 54 (2) EPC; Sec. 3 (1) PatG; Sec. 3 (1) GMG). On the other hand, certain product properties or manufacturing methods are also referred to as belonging to the 'state of the art'. However, this does not exclude the possibility that the necessary information in the sense of instructions or plans may be secret if the skilled person can only develop them with considerable effort (*see* BGH I ZR 118/16 = GRUR 2018, 1161).

3.7. The information must not be generally known or readily accessible 'either in its entirety or in the precise arrangement and composition of its components'. Section 26b (1) UWG thus protects complex information (*Thiele* in *Wiebe/Kodek*, UWG Section 26b Rz 11). Information consisting of known or readily accessible components is also to be considered secret as long as the specific composition and arrangement of these components is not yet known or easily accessible (*Hofmarcher*, Das Geschäftsgeheimnis [2020] Rz 2.23; *Kraft/Steinmair*, UWG[2], § 26b UWG Rz 4), i.e., can be determined without great expenditure of time or money (*Harte-Bavendamm* in *Harte-Bavendamm/Ohly/Kalbfus*, GeschGehG, § 2 Rz 34).

This part of the decision is interesting in several respects. First, it is notable that the Austrian Court frequently cites commentaries pertaining to the German legislation on trade secrets, which was enacted to transpose the Directive. Although the interconnections between these two legal systems have historically been robust, particularly due to their shared linguistic heritage, these cross-references can be viewed as an indicator of the emergence of a unified European standard.

Subsequently, the decision endeavours to elucidate the distinct conditions applicable to trade secrets and patents. Hence, the Court explains that it would be erroneous to equate the condition of confidentiality with absolute novelty as exists in the context of patents. Similarly, while the 'state of the art' criterion can provide information on the knowledge of the circle of persons working with the information in question, it is still necessary to analyse precisely what these persons know, for instance, about the implementation of a given solution.[56] In the present case, if 'the basic shapes of all three components belong to the state of the art. Particularly as they are derived from the publication of corresponding, expired patents, they were in any case generally known. However, additional information was obtained from the plaintiff's design drawings. Although an average designer could have obtained much of this information from public sources, he would have had to spend 40-50 working hours on the relevant drawings. The plaintiff's drawings saved him 25 hours'.[57] Ultimately, the court acknowledged that the information met the secrecy requirement for a trade secret.[58] However, it concluded that the information did not possess sufficient economic value to deserve protection as a trade secret.

Regarding complex information – i.e., information comprised of potentially known or readily accessible components but whose specific composition and arrangement are not known or easily accessible – the Austrian court clarified that the same standard applies as for simple or homogeneous secrets: it must not be possible to ascertain this information 'without great expenditure of time or money'. This alignment is logical because the distinction between complex and more conventional information, while useful in practice, is in fact rather artificial. Any information can be endlessly subdivided into smaller units or, conversely, combined with other units.[59] Similar to the US approach, the recognition that 'complex information' can also qualify for protection particularly ensures that some client lists can be protected as trade secrets.[60] In today's data-driven economy, it also allows for the protection of datasets that aggregate individual data – even if the individual data is public – provided that the

56. Compare also OLG Düsseldorf, 11 March 2021, 15 U 6/20, §26.
57. Austrian Oberster Gerichtshof, 26 January 2021, 4 Ob 188/20f, §42.
58. *Ibid.*, §43.
59. Jean Druey, *Information als Gegenstand des Rechts: Entwurf einer Grundlegung* (Schulthess Polygraphischer Verlag, 1995) 102-104.
60. *See* Kevlaer bv v K.D.V., Elano nv, Finance 4 You bv, S.V.D.L., Finaid bv, Business Court Brussels, (29 July 2020); German Regional Labour Court of Düsseldorf, docket No 12 SaGa 4/20 (3 June 2020).

aggregation imparts sufficient value and requires some effort to assemble.[61] Here, the overlap between the secrecy and economic value requirements becomes particularly evident.

[2] Economic Value

The second condition for the information to qualify as a trade secret is to have 'commercial value because it is secret'. Article 2(1) of the Directive does not specify the threshold for this value. In this regard, Recital 14 TSD proposes some criteria for evaluation:

> such know-how or information should have a commercial value, whether actual or potential. Such know-how or information should be considered to have a commercial value, for example, where its unlawful acquisition, use or disclosure is likely to harm the interests of the person lawfully controlling it, in that it undermines that person's scientific and technical potential, business or financial interests, strategic positions or ability to compete.

Nevertheless, these parameters for conducting a value evaluation do not offer more guidance concerning the threshold to be attained. Furthermore, this second condition establishes a causal relationship between the secrecy requirement and economic value. The information is said to have 'commercial value *because* it is secret'. This link raises doubts concerning the independence of these two conditions.[62] Should the information be considered to have sufficient value as soon as it reaches the secrecy required in the first condition? If some countries, like, for instance, France or the UK, have maintained two separate conditions,[63] the German legislator has elected to consolidate these two conditions into a single entity:

> 'For the purposes of this Act, a trade secret is information that a) is not generally known or readily available, either as a whole or in the precise arrangement and composition of its components, to persons in the circles that usually handle this type of information, and is *therefore* of economic value' (emphasis added).[64]

In the decision of the Austrian *Oberster Gerichtshof* previously mentioned, the Austrian judges again try to provide some further guidance:

> 4.1. Due to its secrecy, information has a commercial value (§ 26b paragraph 1 no. 2 UWG) if it has an actual or future commercial value or if its disclosure entails economic disadvantages for the owner of the trade secret (*Alexander* in *Köhler/Bornkamm/Feddersen*, dUWG § 2 GeschGehG Rz 40). In accordance with recital 14 of the Directive, trivial information should not be covered. A purely ideal value is not sufficient (*Thiele* in *Wiebe/Kodek*, UWG § 26b Rz 14). [...] *A certain*

61. *See* above n 51, 78-80.
62. *See*, for instance in the Supreme Court of Estonia, *K. M., J. K., M. K. and BloomEst OÜ* 15 May 2020, §40: 'In the view of the Chamber, the secrecy of the information and its commercial value are closely linked.'
63. For France, *see* Art. L. 151-1 new of the Commercial Code. For the United Kingdom, *see Trade Secrets (Enforcement,* etc.*) Regulations, 2018*, 2.
64. *See* s. 2 No 1(a) German Law on the Protection of Trade Secrets.

> *minimum value threshold does not have to be reached* (*Harte-Bavendamm* in *Harte-Bavendamm/Ohly/Kalbfus*, GeschGehG, Section 2 para. 36; *Hofmarcher*, Das Geschäftsgeheimnis [2020] para. 2. 28; *Heinzke*, Directive on the Protection of Trade Secrets, CCZ 2016, 179 [183]; *Namysłowska* in MüKomm zum UWG, Art 2 Geheimnisschutz-RL Rz 11; *Alexander* in *Köhler/Bornkamm/ Feddersen*, dUWG § 2 GeschGehG Rz 41).
>
> 4.2. Insofar as it is argued in the literature, with reference to recital 14 of the Directive, that a commercial value presupposes that the disclosure or exploitation of the information could negatively influence the competitive position of the company (*see Harte-Bavendamm/Ohly/Kalbfus*, GeschGehG, § 2 para. 32), this cannot be accepted without reservation. *Although the protection of trade secrets is located in the Unfair Competition Act, it does not require a competitive relationship or special effects on competition* (e.g., in the sense of the appreciability requirement in Section 1 para. 1 UWG; *see* RS0121680) (*Hofmarcher*, Das Geschäftsgeheimnis [2020] para. 2.4). Accordingly, according to recital 14, a commercial value is to be assumed if the unauthorized acquisition of the information or its unauthorized use or disclosure is likely to harm the 'the interests of the person lawfully controlling it, in that it undermines that person's scientific and technical potential, business or financial interests, strategic positions or ability to compete'. The impairment of competitiveness is therefore only one possible manifestation of commercial value, which is of equal importance to the financial interests of the owner.
>
> 4.3. For commercial value to exist, it is therefore sufficient that the financial interests are impaired without there having to be a noticeable impairment of the competitiveness of the owner of the secret. However, the focus should not be on a specific commercial value, but on whether the acquisition of knowledge or exploitation by third parties (in particular competitors) would impair the commercial interests of the owner in a relevant manner. There must therefore (as before) be an economic interest in maintaining secrecy (*Hofmarcher*, Das Geschäftsgeheimnis [2020] para. 2.31).

The Court first elaborates on the link between secrecy and economic value. It argues that this value explains the trade secret owner's interest in keeping the information secret (paragraph 4.3) and that the secrecy of the information is what enables it to have such value (paragraph 4.1). However, these arguments are almost tautological. It is obvious that if the information were public, the trade secret holder would have no control over it and the information would have no competitive value. Adopting such reasoning leads to the conclusion that the commercial value requirement lacks almost any normative significance compared to the secrecy condition.

The Court further seems to support an interpretation offering the commercial value requirement only little practical relevance when discussing the threshold. It explains that there is no minimum requirement for the economic value other than that it should not be trivial. While this interpretation is permissible under the text of the Directive, it reduces the importance of the economic requirement to its minimal possible reading. However, despite this general explanation, in the present case, the Court found that the requirement was not met because the defendant saved only approximately twenty-five hours of work by using the information.[65]

65. Austrian Oberster Gerichtshof, 26 January 2021, 4 Ob 188/20f, §42.

Given the importance of the interpretation of this requirement in resolving the case and the uncertainty as to its proper application, the attempt of the Austrian court to provide an important clarification is to be commended. However, it is regrettable that the Austrian court did not refer the matter to the Court of Justice for a more specific interpretation which would have been binding throughout the EU.

[3] Reasonable Protection Measures

The final requirement pertains to the reasonable steps taken by the trade secret holder to maintain its secrecy. Regarding the extent of these steps, Article 2(1) of the Directive mandates a proportionality assessment, requiring that protection measures be 'reasonable under the circumstances'. However, the Directive does not specify what constitutes 'reasonable' or what factors should be considered to define the 'circumstances'. As previously discussed in this book,[66] the normative function of the requirement for reasonable steps to be taken is a topic of debate in US law. Some legal scholars interpret, for instance, this requirement as having only an evidential role with regard to the fulfilment of the secrecy and economic value criteria. It is notable that Recital 14 of the Directive, which aims to clarify the definition of trade secrets, does not address this requirement. This omission indicates that the European legislator may have had limited clarity regarding the precise function of this requirement within the framework of the definition. In the absence of further guidance, the case law will be pivotal in determining the way this proportionality assessment should be conducted.

A stringent interpretation demanding the establishment of an impenetrable fortress is impractical and should be rejected. The very nature of a trade secret case involves a misappropriation claim, indicating that the secret has inevitably leaked beyond its original owner's control. If such situations were to invalidate trade secret status, the entire legal framework would be rendered ineffective. Emerging case law supports this pragmatic approach. For instance, a recent decision by the *Oberlandesgericht* Düsseldorf explicitly states that the law does not require 'optimal protection' or 'extreme security'.[67]

Once this hypothesis is rejected, the range of potential measures is significant, encompassing a variety of options from material securities to actions aimed at increasing awareness among those accessing the information and the use of contractual types of restraints. Two trends in the emerging case law become apparent. Initially, national judges appear to rely on case-specific analysis,[68] rather than conducting further theorization to construe this requirement. The *Oberlandesgericht* Düsseldorf, in the decision previously mentioned hence, points out that:

> Which steps of protection are appropriate in individual cases is determined on the basis of an objective standard (...). In this respect, the type of trade secret, the

66. *See* Chapter 5.
67. OLG Düsseldorf, 11 March 2021, 15 U 6/20, §38.
68. With this conclusion, *see* European Union Intellectual Property Office, *Trade Secrets Litigation Trends in the EU* (2023), 64.

specific circumstances of the use, the value of the trade secret and its development costs, the nature of the information, the importance for the company, the size of the company, the usual confidentiality measures in the company, the type of labeling of the information and agreed contractual arrangements with employees and business partners must be taken into account (OLG Stuttgart GRUR-RS 2020, 35613 - Schaumstoffsystem; LAG Düsseldorf GRUR-RS 2020, 23408 - PU-Schaum).

A second trend that is worthy of note is the growing emphasis on the need to identify with precision the information that should be regarded as a trade secret as part of the relevant measure. This is becoming increasingly evident in decisions handed down by courts of different national systems.[69] This identification was of particular significance when the individual in question was initially granted access to the relevant information by the trade secret owner but under the stipulations of a confidentiality agreement (e.g, in the context of an employment relationship). This development is noteworthy for several reasons. First, the obligation to accurately identify or particularize the information is not explicitly required by the Directive itself. However, the courts appear to be enforcing it as a measure to protect individuals who originally had lawful access to the information. This highlights one of the main weaknesses in terms of harmonization mentioned earlier in this chapter: the European framework does not aim to harmonize the legal treatment of employer-employee relationships, in particular with regard to the validity and scope of confidentiality or non-competition clauses. As this case trend shows, the terms of these contractual restrictions are highly relevant in determining whether certain information is sufficiently protected. Fortunately, national jurisdictions appear to be converging on this issue for the time being, although there is no legal obligation to do so.

In conclusion, almost a decade after the entry into force of the Directive, the trade secret definition still appears to be both particularly vague and potentially wide-ranging. Such a conclusion is not really surprising. The jurisprudence that has the task of clarifying the scope of this definition is only just beginning to emerge. This technique of normative 'co-construction', in which the legislature delegates part of its work to the judiciary, certainly has the advantage of a certain flexibility; however, it has the disadvantage of requiring a certain amount of time before a degree of legal certainty can be provided to the actors concerned. Moreover, as we have seen, the legislator wanted to establish a definition that would certainly harmonize the understanding of what should constitute a trade secret within the EU, but 'without restricting the subject matter to be protected against misappropriation'. It is therefore at the level of defining the acts constituting 'misappropriation' that one might expect the most telling clarification of the scope of protection. However, this is not the case.

69. *Ibid.*, 67. *See* for instance, Estonia Supreme Court, *K. M., J. K., M. K. and BloomEst OÜ* (15 May 2020) §41; German Regional Labour Court of Düsseldorf, 3 June 2020, 12 SaGa 4/20.

§6.04 MISAPPROPRIATION

[A] Direct Infringers: Unfair Competition Versus Proprietary Approaches

According to its Recital 16, 'the provisions of this Directive should not create any exclusive right to know-how or information protected as trade secrets'. The Directive thus appears to explicitly eschew a proprietary model of protection in favour of one based on unfair competition. In this regard, it is indeed exact that the European legislation does not afford trade secret owners an *erga omnes* exclusive right. This has the consequence that the same trade secret may be legally held by several persons without any of them being able to take legal action against the other regarding the use they make of the information protected.

This unfair competition logic is also reflected in the systematic legislation at the level of the definition of the acts constituting a violation.[70] The Directive is formally not structured around a subjective right that would enable the holder as a matter of principle to control any use made of the trade secret. Conversely, it adopts, in its Chapter II, devoted to the 'acquisition, use, and disclosure of trade secrets', an unfair competition logic based on prohibitions directed at other market participants regarding specific behaviours.

However, a closer look at the material content of the Directive reveals that the legislator's choice is less obvious, which once again illustrates uncertainty as to the type of protection required. The determination of what constitutes an infringement is organized in Articles 3 and 4 of the Directive. The drafting of these two provisions, which respectively prescribe which behaviours should be regarded as lawful or unlawful, was once again strongly influenced by the US framework, particularly the UTSA.[71]

Accordingly:

Article 3 Lawful acquisition, use and disclosure of trade secrets

1. The acquisition of a trade secret shall be considered lawful when the trade secret is obtained by any of the following means:
   (a) independent discovery or creation;
   (b) observation, study, disassembly or testing of a product or object that has been made available to the public or that is lawfully in the possession of the acquirer of the information who is free from any legally valid duty to limit the acquisition of the trade secret;
   (...)
   (d) any other practice which, under the circumstances, is in conformity with honest commercial practices.

70. Regarding the overall structure of the Directive, we previously pointed out that it reflects much more than one IPR. *See* §6.03[A].
71. *See* for an in-depth comparative analysis, *see* above n 41, 134.

Article 4 Unlawful acquisition, use and disclosure of trade secrets
(...)
2. The acquisition of a trade secret without the consent of the trade secret holder shall be considered unlawful, whenever carried out by:
   (a) unauthorised access to, appropriation of, or copying of any documents, objects, materials, substances or electronic files, lawfully under the control of the trade secret holder, containing the trade secret or from which the trade secret can be deduced;
   (b) any other conduct which, under the circumstances, is considered contrary to honest commercial practices.
3. The use or disclosure of a trade secret shall be considered unlawful whenever carried out, without the consent of the trade secret holder, by a person who is found to meet any of the following conditions:
   (a) having acquired the trade secret unlawfully;
   (b) being in breach of a confidentiality agreement or any other duty not to disclose the trade secret;
   (c) being in breach of a contractual or any other duty to limit the use of the trade secret.

A close analysis of these two norms reveals the potential for a broad definition of behaviours that could constitute a violation. Consequently, among the acts explicitly recognized as lawful, only the provision in Article 3(b) of the Directive, which clarifies the legality of reverse engineering, reflects a genuine policy decision that restricts the scope of protection. The acknowledgement of 'independent discovery' as a permissible act is contingent upon the decision not to bestow an *erga omnes* exclusive right over protected information. In contrast, regarding conduct explicitly recognized as unlawful, Article 4(2)(a) of the Directive deems any means of acquiring a trade secret from its holder without consent to be unlawful. Moreover, Article 4(3) expands this protection to encompass the utilization or disclosure of trade secrets, including scenarios that emerge from an unlawful acquisition or from breaches of contractual agreements that restrict the use or disclosure of particular trade secrets. In fact, the accumulation of these prohibitions reveals the (negative) contours of an IPR – albeit without *erga omnes* effect.

This impression is further reinforced by the fact that the European legislator has blurred the lines between what should be the principle in an unfair competition logic (i.e., free competition and the free circulation of information) and the exception (i.e., the exceptions to these). First, the lawmaker decided to dedicate a specific provision (Article 3) to specify the lawful behaviours. In the absence of recognition of a subjective right to the trade secret, the lawfulness of any acquisition not expressly identified as unlawful should be presumed. Following this logic, Article 3 should only be recognized as having a declaratory function, and its content could have been placed not in the operative part but in the recitals of the Directive. As a matter of comparison, equivalent considerations are, for instance, only included in the UTSA's comments.

Second, the wording of Article 3 also raises questions regarding the premise that trade secret acquisitions are, in principle, considered lawful. Indeed, rather than merely clarifying that two practices (independent discovery and reverse engineering) should be regarded as lawful, which could have been considered a mere clarification with no further normative implications, the EU legislator has additionally included a general clause in this article according to which 'any other practice which, under the circumstances, is in conformity with honest commercial practices' should also be regarded as a lawful means of acquisition. This general clause is the counterpart of Article 4(2)(d), which also imposes, in identical terms, a general clause regarding the conduct that should be considered unlawful. The parallel construction of the two articles in the operative part of the text of the Directive makes clear that the normative power of the two norms is identical and that neither should prevail. The alignment of the normative power of Article 3 and Article 4 yet disrupts the principle/exception logic that should prevail under the unfair competition approach. This alignment does not go so far as to overturn the unfair competition framework into a proprietary model; nevertheless, it brings the protection closer to an IPR logic.

From a pragmatic standpoint, the decision to rely on two general clauses is, from a legal security standpoint, an unsatisfactory one. A general clause can be seen as an element of flexibility within a legal system. However, the introduction of not one but two general Janus clauses renders the legal system much opaque regarding its doctrinal integrity and, consequently, the manner in which it should be enforced by courts. Therefore, if most of the Member States at the transposition stage have remained faithful to the text of the Directive,[72] some, such as France (Article L. 151-3 Code de commerce), Germany (§3 GeschGehG), or Italy (Article 99 Codice della proprietà industriale), have elected to exclude the general clause concerning conduct deemed lawful.

The final element that reinforces the impression of a proprietary logic at the level of the definition of the behaviours that constitute an infringement is the lack of consideration of the characteristics of the infringer: the latter is not required to possess certain subjective qualities, such as being a competitor or acting with a commercial purpose. In addition, the Directive adopts a strict liability regime in which the intent of the infringer is not a prerequisite for the characterization of the infringement.[73] This disregard for both the objective and intentional characteristics of the person to whom the prohibition applies further objectifies the regulation, which seems to focus more on the protection of an intangible asset than on the regulation of certain competitive behaviours.

[B] Third Parties and Infringing Goods

The European Directive extends protection beyond direct infringers, granting trade secret owners the right to take action against third parties – those who have not

72. This is for instance the case of Belgium (Art. 7 of the Loi relative à la protection des secrets d'affaires, 30 July 2018, Moniteur Belge, 14 August 2018, 64584-64594), Spain (Art. 2 of the Ley 1/2019, de 20 de febrero, de Secretos Empresariales, Boletín Oficial del Estado 45/2019, 21 February 2019, 16713-16727), Netherlands (Art. 3 of the Wet bescherming bedrijfsgeheimen, Staatsblad 369, 22 October 2018, 00001-00099).
73. In contrast, The UTSA, upon which the Directive is based, consistently requires proof that the infringer 'knows or has reason to know' that they are committing an infringement.

unlawfully acquired the information themselves nor breached any duty not to use or disclose the secret. This legal framework is outlined in the final two paragraphs of Article 4 of the Directive:

Art. 4 Unlawful acquisition, use and disclosure of trade secrets

4. The acquisition, use or disclosure of a trade secret shall also be considered unlawful whenever a person, at the time of the acquisition, use or disclosure, knew or ought, under the circumstances, to have known that the trade secret had been obtained directly or indirectly from another person who was using or disclosing the trade secret unlawfully within the meaning of paragraph 3.

5. The production, offering or placing on the market of infringing goods, or the importation, export or storage of infringing goods for those purposes, shall also be considered an unlawful use of a trade secret where the person carrying out such activities knew, or ought, under the circumstances, to have known that the trade secret was used unlawfully within the meaning of paragraph 3.

Article 4(4) extends the scope of protection to third parties but requires proof of the violator's intent, specifically that the individual 'knew or ought, under the circumstances, to have known' that the trade secret was misappropriated. This mechanism, which holds accountable those benefiting from a violation, is quite common and prevents bad faith beneficiaries of trade secret misappropriation from escaping liability.[74]

The European Directive introduces a more innovative approach by extending possible violations to include the commercialization of so-called infringing goods, defined in Article 2(4) as 'goods, the design, characteristics, functioning, production process or marketing of which significantly benefits from trade secrets unlawfully acquired, used, or disclosed'. While including behaviours concerning 'infringing goods' is typical in the context of IPRs – securing the *erga omnes* exclusivity these rights confer – it is more unusual to see such a mechanism implemented within an unfair competition framework, which traditionally focuses on prohibiting specific behaviours that disrupt fair competition. Notably, a similar rule does not exist under US law. This approach aims to enhance the effectiveness of European protection, particularly against foreign infringements. The provision holds limited significance if the marketing of the infringing goods occurs following a misappropriation within European borders. In such instances, it can be reasonably argued that these actions would already be covered by the prohibitions outlined in Article 4(4). It becomes much more relevant when a misappropriation, as defined by EU law, occurs outside the EU. Recital 28 of the Directive, which addresses 'infringing goods', explicitly connects the prohibition on the commercialization of such goods to the broader context of trade globalization: 'Considering the global nature of trade, it is also necessary that such measures include the prohibition of the importation of those goods into the Union or their storage for the purposes of offering or placing them on the market.' In an international constellation, the initial act may indeed be legal in the country where it took place. A strict application of the territoriality principle would thus suggest that no misappropriation has occurred,

74. *See* for other jurisdictions Chapters 7 and 8 of this book.

leaving the trade secret owner without any recourse against the commercialization of the infringing goods. By explicitly including within the Directive a provision that covers any commercial activities within the EU market involving products derived from unlawfully acquired information by reference to the European legal standard applied in an extra-European jurisdiction, the European legislator ensures that trade secret owners have a cause of action even when the initial violation occurs outside the EU legal framework.[75]

[C] Reverse Engineering: Lawfulness at the Mercy of Contract

In the previous section, we emphasized that among the acts explicitly recognized as lawful means of trade secret acquisition under Article 3 of the Directive, only the clarification regarding reverse engineering reflected a genuine policy decision that limits the scope of protection. Hence, according to Article 3(1)(b): 'The acquisition of a trade secret shall be considered lawful when the trade secret is obtained by (...) observation, study, disassembly or testing of a product or object that has been made available to the public or that is lawfully in the possession of the acquirer of the information who is free from any legally valid duty to limit the acquisition of the trade secret.'

This clarification is particularly significant in European law because, prior to the Directive, Member States had varying approaches to reverse engineering. Although the EC's preparatory documents suggest that reverse engineering was generally viewed as lawful,[76] some Member States had a more restrictive stance. In Germany, for instance, reverse engineering was deemed unlawful following a 1935 Reichsgericht decision,[77] while in France, case law on unfair competition developed parasitic copying claims that had a similar effect.[78] Faced with the need to harmonize the law across the EU, the European legislator chose again to align with the US framework, where the legality of reverse engineering was established not solely due to trade secret policy considerations but merely due because of the division of powers between the Federal and the federated states.[79]

Interestingly, the European legislator acknowledged its uncertainty regarding the best approach to adopt. This doubt, along with a call for further examination of the issue, is explicitly expressed in Recital 17 of the Directive:

---

75. In comparison, the same issue is solved under US law thanks to the acceptance of long-arm jurisdiction developed by some US jurisdictions, which allows the sanctioning of unfair behaviour, despite the fact that the latter took place outside US territory. *See TianRui Group v. ITC*, 661 F. 3d 1322.
76. *See* above n 5, 131 in footnote 396 that 'this practice [Reverse Engineering] is legitimate and in no way prohibited or legally restricted'.
77. German Reichsgericht (Zivilsenat), 22 November 1935, Stiefeleisenpresse, II 128/35, RGZ 149, 329, GRUR 1936, 183.
78. *See* for instance: French *Cour de Cassation*, chambre commerciale, 15 June 1983, *Sapin v. Cellier*, 81-15936, *Bul. civ. IV*, n°174. For a more in-depth presentation, *see* above n 71, 151.
79. *See Kewanee Oil Co v. Bicron Corp*, 416 US 470, 476 (1974) and Chapter 5.

> In some industry sectors, where creators and innovators cannot benefit from exclusive rights and where innovation has traditionally relied upon trade secrets, products can nowadays be easily reverse-engineered once in the market. In such cases, those creators and innovators can be victims of practices such as parasitic copying or slavish imitations that free-ride on their reputation and innovation efforts. Some national laws dealing with unfair competition address those practices. While this Directive does not aim to reform or harmonise the law on unfair competition in general, it would be appropriate that the Commission carefully examine the need for Union action in that area.

Ultimately, these doubts have led to a cautious yet unsatisfactory solution. The European legislator decided to condition the legality of reverse engineering on the acquirer being 'free from any legally valid duty to limit the acquisition of the trade secret'. Recital 16 further clarifies that this 'legal duty' can include contractual obligations: 'Reverse engineering of a lawfully acquired product should be considered as a lawful means of acquiring information, except when otherwise contractually agreed. The freedom to enter into such contractual arrangements can, however, be limited by law.'

This provision expressly allows trade secret owners to contractually circumvent the policy decision made by the legislator. The Recital itself reveals that the legislator was cautious in this regard, explicitly reserving the possibility to legally restrict such contractual freedom. However, as far as we know, no Member State has chosen to impose such restrictions during the transposition phase.

The first key issue that courts will need to address is whether the ability to limit reverse engineering practices should be confined to specific agreements, such as those with subcontractors or for products not freely released on the market (likely the scenario envisaged by the legislator). Alternatively, should trade secret owners be allowed to extend this limitation to any contractual arrangement, including general terms of sale for bulk products, given that such a restriction is not explicitly prohibited by the law? Although the directive seems to permit the use of contractual clauses to limit the legality of reverse engineering, this remains an exception to the overarching principle that reverse engineering is fundamentally lawful. Consequently, courts may interpret this exception narrowly, potentially restricting it to specific personal relationships, such as those based on *intuitu personae*. Following this rationale, a court might decline to extend the exception to broader contexts, like bulk product sales under standard terms and conditions, thus preventing trade secret owners from fully bypassing the policy choice set forth by the legislator.

The second crucial question is whether breaches of these agreements should be treated merely as conventional contractual violations, addressed through standard contract law remedies, or whether they should also be considered infringements of trade secrets under Article 4(2)(b) of the Directive, thereby triggering the full enforcement mechanisms provided by the Directive. At present, no relevant case law provides clear answers to these fundamental questions.

§6.05 ENFORCEMENT AND PROPORTIONALITY TEST

In Europe, the civil enforcement of IPRs is harmonized through the so-called Enforcement Directive.[80] However, when drafting the Trade Secrets Directive, the European legislator chose not to rely on this instrument for trade secret violations. Instead, a distinct enforcement regime was established in the third chapter of the Directive.

This choice stemmed from criticisms of the Enforcement Directive, which, even for traditional IPRs, is often viewed as one-sided – favouring rights holders and lacking sufficient flexibility. These characteristics were considered problematic when combined with the breadth and vagueness of both the subject matter and the scope of trade secret protection.[81] Instead, the European legislator wanted to ensure that the judge at the enforcement stage would be in a position to avoid the emergence of dysfunctional effects. In shaping this approach, the European system once again looked to the American model for guidance.

The enforcement tools available to European judges for protecting trade secrets are in the first place largely aligned with those traditionally recognized for IPRs. Article 12 of the Directive first allows judges to issue injunctions and corrective measures, including orders to cease or prohibit the use or disclosure of the trade secret (Article 12(1)(a)), to ban the production of infringing goods (Article 12(1)(b)), and to recall these goods from the market or destroy them (Article 12(2)(a), (c)). Article 14 TSD addresses damages, which are calculated using the same approach as the triple damages calculation commonly applied in IP cases. When setting the damages, the competent judicial authorities might therefore take into account either the 'negative economic consequences, including lost profits, which the injured party has suffered' or the 'unfair profits made by the infringer' or, as a third alternative, 'set the damages as a lump sum on the basis of elements such as, at a minimum, the amount of royalties or fees which would have been due had the infringer requested authorisation to use the trade secret'.[82]

The difference with the European IP enforcement regime lies in the proportionality assessment that must be carried out before any measure – especially injunctions – is taken. The latter is principally foreseen in Article 13(1):

> Member States shall ensure that, in considering an application for the adoption of the injunctions and corrective measures provided for in Article 12 and assessing their proportionality, the competent judicial authorities shall be required to take into account the specific circumstances of the case, including, where appropriate:
>
> (a) the value or other specific features of the trade secret;
> (b) the measures taken to protect the trade secret;
> (c) the conduct of the infringer in acquiring, using or disclosing the trade secret;
> (d) the impact of the unlawful use or disclosure of the trade secret;

---

80. European Commission, *Directive 2004/48/EC of the European Parliament and of the Council of 29 April 2004 on the Enforcement of Intellectual Property Rights* [2004] OJ L 157.
81. *See* above n 5, 266-268.
82. *See* above n 80, Art. 13.

(e) the legitimate interests of the parties and the impact which the granting or rejection of the measures could have on the parties;
(f) the legitimate interests of third parties;
(g) the public interest; and
(h) the safeguard of fundamental rights.

This provision is mandatory for both Member States, which are obligated to transpose it ('Member States *shall* ensure'), and for courts, which are required to conduct the assessment ('the competent judicial authorities *shall* be required'). It mandates judges to reassess all interests at stake, including those of the parties involved in the proceedings, as well as the interests of third parties and the broader public. Notably, the interests of the trade secret holder are not given priority over those of the infringer. Furthermore, judges are encouraged to re-evaluate factors previously considered at the substantive stage, such as the nature of the information and the conduct of the infringer.

Entrusting judges with such broad discretionary power, akin to the US balancing doctrine,[83] is generally foreign to the continental civil law tradition. This approach reflects yet another instance of European lawmakers drawing inspiration from the US legal framework. Article 13(1) closely mirrors §44(2) of the US Restatement (Third) of Unfair Competition, which aims to consolidate US case law on awarding injunctions in cases of trade secret violations.[84] Interestingly, albeit perhaps unintentionally, the EU legislator may have created a bridge between two distinct legal traditions.

However, the significance of this provision was not fully recognized by all Member States during the transposition stage. The German legislator clearly grasped the unique nature of the proportionality assessment, enacting a specific provision, §9 GeschGehG, which explicitly allows for the rejection of a claim if the measures sought are disproportionate and lists the factors outlined in the Trade Secrets Directive. In contrast, the French transposition seems to have overlooked this nuance. Article L. 152-3 of the French Commercial Code, mirroring the standard approach for IP rights, simply states that the 'judicial authority might (...) order any proportionate measure capable to stop or to avoid the violation'. The only measure of proportionality seems to be related to the ability of the measure to stop the infringement.

83. *Campbell v. Acuff-Rose Music* 510 US 569 (1994); *eBay v. MercExchange* 547 US 388 (2006).
84. *See* above n 71, 176-185.

CHAPTER 7

Civilian Approaches: France

§7.01 INTRODUCTION

[A] Historical Background

French law can be considered a pioneer in the legal protection of trade secrets in modern times. The first instance of such protection dates back to Napoleon and the enactment of the Criminal Code of 1810. Article 418 of this code already criminalized the violation of 'secrets de fabrique' (manufacturing secrets) to safeguard the French industry against foreign powers, notably England during the continental blockade.

Despite significant economic changes since the end of the Napoleonic empire, the legislative framework around trade secrets in France remained largely unchanged until the recent transposition of the EU Trade Secrets Directive. Article 418 of Napoleon's Criminal Code, with nearly identical wording for over two centuries, can now be found in Article L. 1227-1 of the French Labour Code.[1] However, this legislative longevity was more a result of the legislator's inertia than an indication of Napoleon's enduring legal ingenuity. In fact, the limited modifications in the legal framework can largely be attributed to the significant efforts of French jurisprudence. Over the years, courts have worked to extend the protection of trade secret holders in both civil and criminal contexts, filling gaps left by the legislature.

In recent years, the French legislator has begun to be more active in this area. Since 2012, several attempts have hence been made to expand the scope of trade secret protection, particularly in the realm of criminal law. However, none of these proposals successfully passed through the French Parliament. It was not until 2018 that significant changes were made to the civil legal framework with the transposition of the EU Directive, finally modernizing French trade secret law.

1. Article L. 1227-1 is also reproduced in Art. L. 621-1 French code of Intellectual Property.

[B] Some General Comments on the French System

Before the transposition of the European Trade Secrets Directive,[2] French law primarily relied on a mix of unfair competition, contract, labour, and criminal law to protect trade secrets. Although no distinct civil law regime existed specifically for trade secrets, holders were not entirely without legal recourse. French case law intervened to fill the gap, developing actions rooted in unfair competition. In this regard, the French approach accorded with TRIPS Article 39, as the principal civil remedy outside contract lies broadly in unfair competition law.

Prior to an in-depth examination of the French legal stance on trade secrets, it is essential to reiterate certain fundamental comparative considerations. In contrast with the general perception of civilian jurisdictions, case law plays a fundamental role in shaping the protection and civil protection regime for trade secrets in France, as in other countries with similar legal systems. In the absence of a specific legal regime, the judges inferred the possibility of an action for trade secret violation based on unfair competition. It is notable that such an action for unfair competition itself was not (and is still not) expressly provided for in the Civil Code. The entirety of unfair competition, including that pertaining to trade secrets, was thus derived on the basis of two brief sections of the Civil Code, which set forth the principles of tortious liability (*responsabilité civile*).

Second, the majority of court decisions are concise, comprising merely a cursory account of the legally pertinent facts and a statement of the pertinent legal principles. The most notable distinction from the common law is the absence of exhaustive explanations. This is particularly evident in the case of decisions by the highest court (the *Cour de Cassation*), where references to previous cases are minimal and attempts to align the reasoning in the present case with those precedents are scarce. This form of decision-making is open to criticism in certain respects, particularly in regard to its potential to obscure the reasons that led to the decision. Nevertheless, it is an assumed approach. In the words of Montesquieu, the judges should be the 'mouth of the law'. It is therefore the role of the court only to 'tell the law', which should in theory be found in its entirety in legislation. There should also be no major room for interpretation, as it would suggest that the judge would have to go beyond a simple reading and enforcement of the decision made by the democratically legitimated lawmaker. This reductionist interpretation of the judge's role seems particularly puzzling when viewed in conjunction with the discretionary authority they have assumed in certain domains, particularly those pertaining to unfair competition and trade secrets.

Third, the question of how to reconcile different judgments over time and identify the underlying unifying principles and policies is addressed by academic and professional authors in a variety of journals and publications. These commentators play an important role in unifying, developing and critiquing the law; however, there is no express reference to their writings in judgments. Despite this absence of express acknowledgement, they are regarded as exerting an unacknowledged influence on the

2. *See* Chapter 6.

judiciary. In this regard, it is not uncommon to find that there are two or more fundamentally different views or 'schools of thought' which contest for dominance in the commentaries and other forms of scholarship. This was particularly relevant in the context of trade secrets, given the contested nature of trade secrets law and, more broadly, the action for unfair competition in France, about which more is said further below. Interestingly, although in the common law, academic writings are generally said to have a lower status than judgments as sources of law, in fact, in such jurisdictions, express references to academic writings are more common than in civilian jurisdictions. In the latter, the status and influence of academic writings are traditionally said to be higher, although certainly, in France, they are never referred to in express terms by courts. Perhaps the truth is that academic writings are more influential in France because they constitute a more significant learning resource for lawyers and because they exert considerable but less openly acknowledged influence over judges.

§7.02 CIVIL LAW: EXTRA-CONTRACTUAL PROTECTION

[A] From the Praetorian Establishment of a Protection System Based on Unfair Competition ...

The French civil law framework was significantly impacted by the transposition of the Trade Secrets Directive through Law No 2018-670 of 30 July 2018. We will examine certain aspects of this law in detail. However, it remains worthwhile to explore the state of French law and its evolution prior to this transposition. These developments, along with the debates they sparked, are indicative of the tensions inherent in any attempt to protect trade secrets.

[1] Unfair Competition Law and the Law of 'Parasitic Misappropriation'

Before the transposition of the Directive, trade secrets – whether technical or commercial – were not expressly protected under French civil law. Some protection was available under criminal law, particularly concerning so-called secrets de fabrique, as discussed below. However, a legal claim emerged from case law to provide a civil remedy independent of criminal action.

From a theoretical perspective and according to French legal doctrine, French law does not recognize 'ownership' of trade secrets. Intangible goods ('biens immatériels') cannot be possessed or owned in the traditional sense. The central maxim 'les idées sont de libre parcours' underscores that ideas and information reside in the public domain and can only be subject to ownership if explicitly provided for by statute.[3] Authority over undisclosed information exists based on two key factors: that the

3. *See also*, CA Paris, 10 avril 1962, Ann. Propr. Ind. 1962: 'The fact of reproducing an article that is not protected by a patent or a registered trademark is but the exploitation of a right in the context of the freedom of commerce and industry.'

information is not in the public domain and that the party can prevent it from becoming public. French doctrine occasionally refers to 'détention légitime' to legally describe this control without ownership or legal possession, which is circumscribed and enforced by the remedies available for unfair competition. This concept of 'control' without formal legal characterization found its way in Article 2 of the European Directive, which defines a 'trade secret holder' as 'any natural or legal person lawfully controlling a trade secret'.

Thus, the starting principle of French law, akin to that in common law jurisdictions, holds that all knowledge or information not protected by an exclusive IPR is in the public domain and available for competitive use. Nonetheless, under certain circumstances, exploiting such information was considered a wrongdoing (or 'faute') that could engage civil liability ('responsabilité civile'). This type of tortious civil liability for fault is based on Article 1240 of the French Civil Code,[4] the foundational provision of French civil liability. It states: 'Any act whatever of man that causes damage to another obliges the one by whose fault it occurred to repair it.' This broad legal basis has enabled French judges to develop principles of fault and liability across various legal domains, leading to a flourishing case law, notably in the field of unfair competition.

It is under this action for unfair competition ('*action en concurrence déloyale*') – and more specifically, '*parasitisme*' – that civil law protections for trade secrets have emerged. '*Parasitisme*' between competitors can be defined as riding on the coattails of a competitor by profiting from his efforts and his reputation or that of his products. If this cause of action was rooted in unfair competition, it has then gradually expanded to encompass scenarios typically considered outside the traditional purview of this legal area. When unfair competition serves as the basis for liability, acquiring confidential information is not inherently wrongful, nor is unauthorized or improper disclosure itself. Instead, the focus is on the commercially dishonest nature of the competitive use or acquisition of information. French law has yet progressively evolved to first recognize liability for faults involving the misappropriation of a competitor's efforts under the action for '*concurrence parasitaire*'. The scope of this liability has further then broadened, eliminating the requirement for parties to be in a direct competitive relationship, a development now referred to as '*agissements parasitaires*'. Consequently, the *Cour de Cassation*, in 1996, declared that parasitic actions can constitute a fault in the sense of Article 1382 of the Code Civil '*même en l'absence de toute situation de concurrence*'.[5]

In the literature, the concept of parasitism tends to draw most debates in relation to slavish imitation, but the arguments developed also concerning misuse of '*savoir-faire*', trade secrets in the broad sense.

---

4. As a matter of clarification, the numbering of the French *Code civil* changed following a reform in 2016. Previously, Art. 1240 was designated as Art. 1382. Readers should not be surprised to encounter references to the former numbering in older judicial decisions.
5. Cass. Com. 30 janv. 1996, Bull. civ. IV, no 32.

Critics like Passa argue against the extension of unfair competition claims, emphasizing the centrality of IPRs.[6] He contends that by granting special proprietary rights to some forms of knowledge, the legislator has left others free, upholding the principle of freedom of industry and competition. Passa also highlights the ambiguity surrounding '*parasitisme économique*', noting that courts often hesitate in recognizing its validity.[7]

Izorche takes issue with this view and stresses that the fact that something is not expressly prohibited by the legislator does not equate to unrestrained or unlimited permission:

> il faut, bien entendu, assurer la liberté de la concurrence, mais cette liberté est bornée par le principe de la responsabilité. ... il n'est pas exact qu'en dehors des droits privatifs tout soit permis sans restriction, mais il n'est pas vrai non plus que tout soit interdit: la jurisprudence en témoigne abondamment, et d'ailleurs la doctrine n'a jamais adoptée une position aussi radicale.[8]

Izorche also stresses that providing a remedy against unfair competition in some circumstances is not to be equated with granting protection by exclusive proprietary rights. Rather, the remedy sanctions a *fault* and not a *right* – it operates *ex ante* and not *a priori* like a property right. From that perspective, Izorche argues that it would be illogical to protect certain kinds of dishonest conduct because of the notional existence of proprietary rights in contiguous material.[9] More generally, the law provides at the most fundamental level of principle that persons should be protected against the faults or wrongs of others that do them damage. Alternatively, others should be allowed to profit from the investments and technical advances of their competitors in the interests of freedom of competition and industry, but only in a manner that is not commercially dishonest.

Concerning the expansion of the action in the absence of a competitive relationship, Izorche considers it as a freestanding regime based directly on Article 1240 and not as a sub-category of the law of unfair competition. The underlying wrong is then no longer narrowly circumscribed as dishonest commercial conduct but parasitic behaviour per se, i.e., profiting from another's creative investment '*sans bourse délier*', without any expenditure of one's own.

Alternatively, the wrong can be conceptualized as not committed against one particular competitor but against the competitive market as a whole:

---

6. Jérôme Passa, '*Propos dissidents sur la sanction du parasitisme économique*' (200) *Recueil Dalloz* 297.
7. *See* Jérôme Passa, 'Pour ou contre la sanction du parasitisme? Divergences, confusions et contradictions' (2009) 30 Intellectual Property 109.
8. Marie-Laure Izorche, '*Concurrence déloyale et parasitisme économique*' in *La Concurrence déloyale, Thèmes et commentaires*, Yves Serra ed. (Dalloz 2000) 34: 'Absence of prohibition does not amount to permission without limits: the freedom of competition must indeed be safeguarded, but is limited by the principle of responsibility. In our view, it is not correct to say that outside proprietary rights everything is permitted, but it is also not right to say that everything is permitted: the caselaw bears ample witness to that, and furthermore scholarly writings have never adopted such a radical position.'
9. *See* Izorche, above n 8, 35.

> [the prejudice does not lie simply against a competitor] mais comprend aussi, ... le trouble causé à la concurrence, voire au bon fonctionnement du marché, ce qui comprend aussi les intérêts du consommateur: un tel 'trouble commercial', pour reprendre l'expression de la jurisprudence, est aussi bien le fait de l'agissement parasitaire, que celui de la concurrence parasitaire ou de la concurrence déloyale au sens strict.[10]

However, Article 1240 requires compensation for damages, meaning that without proof of damage, there can be no liability. In situations where the parties are not in a competitive relationship, it may be challenging to characterize or quantify the relevant damage. Furthermore, it is difficult to justify why a party in a dispute should receive individual compensation for harm that affects the market as a whole. A legal framework that imposes liability without requiring proof of damage is, in essence, similar to a property regime; remedies in the form of injunctions for patent, copyright, design, or trademark infringement are available as a matter of right.

Le Tourneau supports the logic of *parasitisme* and addresses the common concern about the excessive reach of actions for unfair competition in the light of the existence of proprietary IPR (*droits privatifs*) by stressing the subsidiarity of the action. Thus, the action is only available if the action is grounded on separate facts or if the applicant has no other recourse available, even if in the same action, some IPR is found inapplicable, or if the IPR has run its full term.[11]

[2] Notion of 'Savoir Faire' *and Fault Before the Transposition*

Since the action, in the form of '*concurrence parasitaire*' or '*agissements parasitaires*', was grounded in Article 1240 of the Code Civil, the victim was required to establish three key elements: fault, damage, and the causal connection between the two.

Regarding the protection of savoir-faire,[12] it was essential to first demonstrate that the asset was worthy of protection for its appropriation to constitute a fault. In this context, legal scholarship analysing case law has generally concluded that protection typically requires the knowledge to be technical in nature, provide an economic advantage, and be transmissible, as well as secret (and hence non-patented). The term 'technical' (technique) is employed in a broad sense, encompassing all practical

10. *See* Izorche, above n 8, 32, references omitted: 'includes also the interference with competition, viz with the proper functioning of the market, which also includes the interests of consumers: such a "commercial distortion," to use an expression found in the cases, occurs just as much in relation to parasitic actions, as in relation to parasitic competition or unfair competition in the strict sense'. *See also* in the same line Larrieu according to whom unfair competition has become more of an instrument in the fight against acts that disturb the proper functioning of the market, rather than a mean to resolve a conflict between two traders: Jacques Larrieu, '*Un an de concurrence déloyale*', Propriété industrielle No 6, juin 2009, chron. 5 at p. 2.
11. However, some authors noted that the requirement of a different factual basis for each action, which reflects different policy goals and legal categories, was in reality eroded in some of the *Cour de Cassation* decision. *See* above n 10, 2 and the decision Bollé: Cass. Cm., 12 juin 2007, No 05-17.349, Sté Bollé Protection, Propr. Industr. 2007, comm. 73, J. Larrieu.
12. Which would be referred to as trade secrets in the common law, since the literal translation 'know-how' has a narrower legal scope.

information, including commercial, management, and organizational knowledge. The criterion of transmissibility signifies that the information must be identifiable and communicable; in essence, savoir-faire must be distinguishable from individual experience (or know-how in the narrower common law sense). Furthermore, while the knowledge must be secret, this does not imply absolute secrecy; rather, it means that either as a collection or as individual pieces of information, it is not generally known or readily accessible.[13] The applicant was then expected to establish that the knowledge resulted from intellectual effort, involving a certain level of investment in the creation of the relevant intangibles - a criterion whose application entails a high degree of case-specific analysis and uncertainty.

The concretization of a fault was impacted by the debate on whether *parasitisme* constitutes a separate legal action or falls under unfair competition and has implications for confidential information. Accepting parasitism as a fault per se renders the search for a distinct legal wrong redundant. In cases of slavish copying, a typical form of parasitism, identifying another fault, such as public deception, is often straightforward, but this is less clear in trade secrets.

In some cases, the finding of fault was easier to identify when the acquisition, for instance, involves breaches of contractual duties of confidence. In some instances, the fault aroused from an ex-employee's violation of good faith, with liability for *parasitisme* justified by such breaches. Often, the fault was not further merely in appropriating another's investment but rather in the circumstances of the activity. This is termed 'usurpation de savoir-faire', indicating the illegal use of confidential information initially received with permission.[14] This principle extends to former employees who exploit information acquired during their employment; their breach of good faith establishes grounds for liability for *parasitisme*.

Identifying fault for the mere appropriation of another's efforts on this other side created tension with the foundational principles of industry freedom and competition. In such a case, it was, however, accepted that the fault could arise from the fact that the offending party benefited from the applicant's investments while avoiding the associated costs, thereby acting '*sans bourse délier*'. Interestingly, since no absolute right is recognized to discover and use whatever one wishes, even if the object in question is lawfully in one's possession, some authors have argued that the use of information obtained through reverse engineering may be restricted. Consequently, obtaining secret information through reverse engineering, despite being otherwise legitimate, may be actionable under principles of unfair competition or unjust enrichment ('*agissements parasitaires*').[15] As a result, French doctrine appears to diverge from the common law approach, aligning more closely with the existing framework in Germany.

13. *See* Marie Malaurie-Vignal, 'La protection des informations privilégiées et du savoir-faire' (1997) *Receuil Dalloz, 26ieme Cahier. Chronique*, 207 ('An original piece of information requiring an intellectual or financial investment').
14. *See* Propriétés industrielles, Avril 2006, no 19, 3. *Concurrence déloyale*, 227.
15. *See* above n 13, 208 ('Privileged information must be able to be protected, even if it is possible for a third party to discover it in a legitimate way, if he uses the investments of another to make a similar product. Privileged information, even if made available to the public, deserves to be protected if it is singular or original').

[3] Comparative Points Concerning the French Approach Prior to the Transposition of the Directive

The evolution of French case law regarding the protection of trade secrets through the concept of parasitism is from a comparative perspective noteworthy for several reasons. First, the expansion of the scope of action for economic parasitism was not an isolated phenomenon in Europe. In fact, many European and Eastern European countries have legislatively moved away from the requirement that parties must be in a direct competitive relationship.[16] This link between trade secret protection and parasitism was also perceived by the EC. Hence, during the preparatory work leading to the adoption of the European directive on trade secrets, the Commission considered harmonizing issues related to economic parasitism independently of trade secret violations. A comparative study was conducted in this regard;[17] however, this initiative was ultimately not pursued. The directive on trade secrets acknowledges in Recital 17 that:

> In some industry sectors (...) products can nowadays be easily reverse-engineered once in the market. In such cases, those creators and innovators can be victims of practices such as parasitic copying or slavish imitations that free-ride on their reputation and innovation efforts. Some national laws dealing with unfair competition address those practices. While this Directive does not aim to reform or harmonise the law on unfair competition in general, it would be appropriate that the Commission carefully examine the need for Union action in that area.

As discussed in the chapter that thoroughly analyses the European directive, the neglect of this issue has led to regulations that lack clarity regarding the legality of reverse engineering practices.

The broad concept of 'parasitisme économique' under French law can also be compared to the English legal tradition, where liability in equity is expansive, and disclosure or misuse is actionable per se. This broader theory posits that a wrongdoing (faute) occurs when one party, through sustained intellectual efforts and significant investment, creates something of economic value while another party unjustifiably diverts this value for its own benefit. This framework bears a resemblance to the principle of unjust enrichment in the common law tradition. It is also noteworthy that the debate within French scholarship regarding the expansion of the scope of action parallels the discussion on impropriety versus property in US legal scholarship. The expansionist view aligns with the property analysis put forth by some scholars, such as Lemley in US law (as discussed in Chapter 1), whereas the narrower perspective emphasizes impropriety as the governing principle.

16. *See* Yves Picod et al., Receuil Dalloz 2006, p. 2923, Receuil – Concurrence interdit – *Concurrence déloyale et parasitisme: panorama 2005-2006*, at p. 9 of 12. Legislation in Switzerland and, in particular, Spain is cited for its express rejection of this requirement in unfair competition cases.
17. *See* Hogan Lovells, *Report on Trade Secrets for the European Commission* (online) 23 September 2011, https://op.europa.eu/en/publication-detail/-/publication/068c999d-06d2-4c8e-a681-a4ee2eb0e116.

[B] ... to the Transposition of the European Directive

[1] Legal and Political Context of the 2018 Reform

The French legal framework for the civil protection of trade secrets has undergone significant changes due to the transposition of the EU Trade Secrets Directive. This comprehensive Directive, which is discussed in a specific chapter of this book,[18] left limited flexibility for national legislators. However, in areas not directly addressed by the Directive, national lawmakers had some discretion to shape local protections, particularly concerning the establishment of a criminal protection regime and the rules governing employer-employee relationships.

The transposition of the Directive hence provided an opportunity to revamp the entire French legal framework. Unfortunately, French legislators did not seize this opportunity. With Law No 2018-670 of 30 July 2018,[19] they simply implemented the European Directive into French law without addressing the issues that the European legislator left unresolved. The reluctance to take further action can be traced back to the political context surrounding the legislation. While the French lawmakers were required to transpose the Directive, there was significant opposition from journalists in France. They were concerned that legal protections for trade secrets could be misused to limit their freedom of expression. In this environment, the French government considered the introduction of criminal law provisions, alongside the civil protections outlined in the Directive, to be too controversial.

[2] Overview of the Transposition

The first notable aspect of the French transposition is the decision by the French lawmakers to integrate the content of the Directive into the Code of Commerce. A directive indeed allows Member States the flexibility to determine where to transpose its provisions, which is one of the key features of this legal instrument. This flexibility enables to respect national traditions, such as classification and general structure of the law, while also ensuring that the substantive law is harmonized at the European level. In this case, the French legislator could have chosen to incorporate the Directive into the French Code of Intellectual Property. However, they decided to include it in the French Code of Commerce, specifically in Articles L. 151-1 to L. 152-8. This choice of classification suggests that the French lawmakers view trade secret law not as part of IP but rather as closely related to general trade regulation and unfair competition.

The section of the Commercial Code dedicated to protecting trade secrets closely aligns with the European Directive in both structure and content. This section is divided into three chapters: the first addresses the objectives and conditions for protection; the second outlines the measures that a court may impose to prevent or remedy infringements; and the third discusses procedural issues.

18. *See* Chapter 6. On the transposition obligation, *see* §6.02[A] below.
19. LOI n° 2018-670 du 30 juillet 2018 relative à la protection du secret des affaires.

The definition of trade secrets is detailed in Article L. 151-1. This definition is consistent with Article 2(1) of the European Directive, with no significant changes.[20] Article L. 151-2 and L. 151-3 address the lawful acquisition and possession of trade secrets. As J.C. Galloux notes, the French legislator opted to use the term 'holder', which refers to someone who has control or possession of a trade secret, instead of 'titulary', which is reserved for the owner of a property right.[21]

Concerning legal acquisition, Article L. 151-3 2° transposed Article 3(1)b of the European Directive and prescribes the legality of reverse engineering practices, hence clarifying that this practice should be accepted under French law. It can also be noted that the French legislator decided not to include a general clause for lawful means of acquisition, in contrast to the European Directive, which featured two general mirror clauses: one addressing lawful acquisition (*see* Article 3(1)b) and another for unlawful acquisition (*see* Article 4(2)b). This dual wording led to confusion, as it did not provide judges with clear guidance on which clause to apply. By opting to include a clause only for unlawful acquisition (*see* Article L. 151-4(2)), the French legislator implies that acquisition or use is presumed lawful unless it is explicitly deemed unlawful or if it is demonstrated that the latter occurred as a result of conduct 'considered, in the circumstances, to be unfair and contrary to commercial practice'.

Article L. 151-4 to L. 151-6 define the acts that violate trade secrets in accordance with the European Directive. These violations can occur both during the acquisition of trade secrets and later in their use or disclosure. Article L. 151-6 specifies that a third party may be held liable for such violations if they 'knew, or ought to have known, in the circumstances, that the secret was obtained, directly or indirectly, from another person who was using or disclosing it unlawfully'. Additionally, Article L. 151-5 states that the commercialization or importation of infringing goods is also considered a violation of trade secrets.

Regarding the protection of journalists, French law extends beyond the mere transposition of the directive's exceptions found in Article L. 151-7 to L. 151-8. The French legislator has introduced an additional safeguard in the form of a civil fine, which judges can impose in cases of dilatory or abusive legal actions. According to Article L. 152-8:

> Any natural or legal person who engages in dilatory or abusive conduct under the provisions of this chapter may be ordered to pay a civil fine. This fine cannot exceed 20% of the damages claim. If there is no damages claim, the civil fine may not exceed €60,000. This civil fine can be imposed in addition to any damages awarded to the party harmed by the dilatory or abusive actions.

Even though the fines might be considered inadequate given their relative insignificance compared to the revenues of certain large companies, this mechanism remains interesting. Indeed, one of the primary concerns for journalists was the

20. Substantive developments to the conditions of this definition are offered in Chapter 6.
21. Jean-Christophe Galloux, 'La transposition de la directive sur les secrets d'affaires' (2018) 3 *RTDCom. Revue trimestrielle de droit commercial et de droit économique* 643.

potential misuse of trade secret protection laws against them through intimidation lawsuits.

[3] The Flawed Transposition of the Proportionality Test by the French Legislator

The main criticism of the French implementation of the Trade Secrets Directive concerns the transposition of proportionality control at the enforcement stage. Article 13 of the Directive includes a comprehensive requirement for proportionality, which mirrors the US balancing doctrine.[22] Notably, the European legislator chose not to reference the Enforcement Directive, which addresses this issue in the context of IPRs and instead provided a specific regime within the Trade Secrets Directive for this reason. In contrast, the French legislator did not include any specific provision explicitly requiring this proportionality assessment.

The only mention of a need for proportionality appears in Article L. 152-3 of the French Commercial Code, which states that the 'judicial authority may ... order any proportionate measure capable of stopping or avoiding the violation'.[23] The wording used here is the same as that found in the context of classical IPRs. Even interpreting this in a way consistent with the Directive is challenging, as the only benchmark for proportionality appears to be the ability of the measure to end the violation. The French legislator's lack of recognition of the specific control required by the Trade Secrets Directive is even more apparent when compared to the approach taken by the German legislator. Despite sharing a similar legal tradition, the German legislator deemed it necessary to enact a specific provision, §9 GeschGehG, which expressly provides for the dismissal of a claim in cases of disproportionality and outlines the factors involved in the Trade Secrets Directive.[24]

§7.03 CIVIL LAW: CONTRACTUAL PROTECTION OF TRADE SECRETS

[A] Transfer of *Savoir-Faire*

In the circumstances, contract is the most secure device for ensuring a remedy is available for unauthorized disclosure or use of '*savoir-faire*'. The starting principle in French law is that unless the ex-employee or contractual partner engages in acts of unfair competition or parasitism in the absence of a confidentiality or non-compete clause, he is free to use '*savoir-faire*' acquired during the contractual relationship. In other words, in the absence of proof of an actionable wrong in the use of *savoir-faire* that has been acquired normally in the course of employment or a contractual

22. *See* Chapter 6.
23. Article L. 152-3 of the French Commercial Code: 'Dans le cadre d'une action relative à la prévention ou la cessation d'une atteinte à un secret des affaires, la juridiction peut, sans préjudice de l'octroi de dommages et intérêts, prescrire, y compris sous astreinte, toute mesure proportionnée de nature à empêcher ou à faire cesser une telle atteinte'.
24. §9 GeschGehG 'Anspruchsausschluss bei Unverhältnismäßigkeit.'

relationship, there is no remedy against an ex-employee or other contractual partner who uses it.[25] Leaving aside the exceptional penal provision relating to '*secrets de fabrique*', in a legal landscape governed by the principle that *savoir-faire* is free, contract plays an exceptionally significant role in providing secure and targeted protection for specific trade secrets. As in other jurisdictions, the main contract questions in trade secrets law relate to provisions in employment contracts: confidentiality clauses and non-competes (restraint of trade) clauses. These are further considered below.

As property is a prerequisite for any contract of sale or licence, a party in possession of '*savoir-faire*' cannot grant a transfer or permission by way of such contracts. French legal theory does not accept property rights or ownership of '*savoir-faire*' but rather refers to '*réservation sans appropriation*' (reservation without appropriation).

Contracts granting the right to use confidential information must take the legal form of a '*contrat d'entreprise*', a contract for work (or 'for services').[26] Because contracts relating to '*savoir-faire*' are not expressly mentioned in the *Code Civil*, no specific formal requirements attach to such contracts, so that only the general requirements for a valid contract apply: '*cause*', '*objet*', '*capacité*' and '*consentement*'. If the information concerned is not secret but a party nonetheless offers consideration for '*savoir-faire*', the contract has neither '*objet*' nor '*cause*' and is not valid. The '*objet*' is what the contract requires the parties to perform (revealing a secret, paying compensation), and if information is not secret, then there is no revelation to perform. The '*cause*' is the immediate goal the party intends to achieve by engaging in the contract: the goal pursued by the receiving party (the revelation of the information) becomes meaningless if there is nothing to perform for his benefit by the other party.[27] The service offered by the contract is that of ending the secrecy and protecting the information concerned for the specific benefit of the co-contractant. The possessor (*détendeur*) of the information is paid to inform or teach the '*savoir-faire*'.

---

25. *See* Joanna Schmidt-Szalewski, Jean-Pierre Viennois, Propriété Industrielle, Revue mensuelle, LexisNexis Jurisclasseur, février 2005, No 15, pp. 34-36, '*Concurrence déloyale – Savoir Faire; Utilisation du savoir-faire acquis auprès de leur ancien employeur par des salariés*'. *See also* Cass. Com. 24 September 2013, K 12-22.413 (the employee may use savoir-faire learned during employment); Cass. Com. 10 September 2013, SA Serop Concept, 12-20.933. Here, we leave to one side the question of whether an ex-employer might have a claim to a patent deriving from some knowledge or idea developed by an employee.
26. *See* Cass. Civ. 3eme, 28 février 1984, No 82-15550: '*que les travaux d'ordre intellectuel ne sont pas exclus de la définition du contrat d'entreprise*'.
27. *See*, for instance, Cass. Com. 20 octobre 1998: '[the facts establish that the process concerned was the subject of numerous publications at the date of the contract and was therefore in the public domain which means that the contested contract did not give to its beneficiary the quiet enjoyment of the rights conceded;] *qu'en déduisant de ces constatations et appréciations, que le contrat n'avait ni cause, ni objet, des lors qu'il tendait a concéder un droit de propriété industrielle sur des procédés et formules qui ne pouvaient pas être protégés*', [the Court of Appeal was correct]'.

In this respect, it may be noted that neither the adoption of the European directive nor its transposition into French law has altered these aspects.[28] As explained by Passa: 'the provisions of the Commercial Code resulting from the reform of the Law of July 30, 2018 relate to the protection of business secrecy vis-à-vis third parties, outside contractual relation'.[29]

[B] Employment Contract and Confidentiality Clauses

The regulation of the relationship between employees and trade secrets is particularly sensitive, as it requires a balance between competitive freedom, the protection of employees' fundamental rights, and the safeguarding of business secrets. This area, however, largely remains outside the scope of the European Directive. Article 1(3) states that 'Nothing in this Directive shall be understood to offer any ground for restricting the mobility of employees. In particular, in relation to the exercise of such mobility, this Directive shall not offer any ground for: (b) limiting employees' use of experience and skills honestly acquired in the normal course of their employment; (c)imposing any additional restrictions on employees in their employment contracts other than restrictions imposed in accordance with Union or national law.' Additionally, Article 14(2) allows Member States to limit the awarding of damages when employees act in good faith. Beyond this, the European legislator has delegated to national legislators the matters related to obligations arising from employment contracts, including confidentiality or non-competition clauses that may be part of them.

In France, the task of defining this regime has been left to the courts, resulting in a jurisprudential system that governs the obligation of loyalty in employment contracts, as well as the regimes of confidentiality and non-competition clauses. This case law approach creates a system built on empirical evidence, reflecting the challenges courts have faced, but it still leaves many unresolved issues. The transposition of the Directive on trade secrets could have provided an opportunity to clarify this regime by codifying or rejecting specific solutions. However, this clarification has not occurred, and guidance on these issues must continue to be sought in jurisprudence.

[1] Legal Duty Inherent in the Employment Contract

Trade secrets might in the first place be protected by some confidentiality obligation imposed on employees. These obligations can originate from two sources: either from the employee's general duty of loyalty or from a specific clause in their employment contract.[30]

---

28. *See* Jérôme Passa, 'Le contrat de communication de secret d'affaires après la réforme' (2024) Dalloz IP/IT, 206.
29. *Ibid.*
30. For a detailed analysis of this regime in France, *see* Luc Desaunettes-Barbaro, 'Employees, Trade Secrets and Restrictive Covenants in France' in Anselm Kamperman Sanders & Christopher Heath (eds), *Employees, Trade Secrets and Restrictive Covenants* (Kluwer Law International, 2016) 135-155.

According to section L. 1222-1 of the Labour Code (LC), the employment contract must be executed in good faith, which creates an implicit obligation of loyalty and confidentiality for the employee.[31] While the existence of this obligation is well-established, both its material and temporal scope present significant ambiguities. From a material standpoint, the primary challenge is determining which information falls under this obligation based on its nature. Case law provides limited clarity, as the assessment of good faith is inherently context-dependent.[32] However, it is generally accepted that information of direct competitive significance, such as trade secrets, is included within this confidential framework.[33] Similarly, the temporal aspect of the obligation remains uncertain. It is clear that the obligation persists throughout the duration of the employment contract, but its applicability after termination raises questions. The French Court of Cassation has yet to address this issue conclusively.[34]

[2] *Express Confidentiality Clauses*

Regarding explicit confidentiality clauses in employment contracts, no legal provision specifically governs their regime. However, in an employee/employer relationship, the parties' contractual freedom is limited by section L. 1121-1 of the Labour Code, which states: 'No one can put the rights of persons and the individual and collective freedoms under restrictions which are not justified by the nature of the task to be accomplished and proportionate to the purpose intended.' Despite the broad nature of this rule, jurisprudence in this area is rather limited,[35] leaving uncertainty about the level of restrictions (both in scope and duration) that courts might deem proportionate, as well as whether financial compensation is necessary.

Because of this need to be proportionate, a confidentiality clause cannot, therefore, extend to the *totality* of information obtained during employment, and its subject matter cannot remain undefined. In other words, a valid clause requires a list identifying the particular information concerned.[36]

31. Antoine Latreille, 'Réflexion critique sur la confidentialité dans le contrat (1re partie)' (2006) 156 *Les Petites Affiches* §30; Del Sol, Lefranc-Hamoniaux, 'La protection de l'information confidentielle acquise par les salariés et leur représentants' (2008) 52 *JCP social* §2; Olivier Leclerc, 'Sur la validité des clauses de confidentialité en droit du travail' (2005) *Droit social* §1.
32. *Ibid.*, §30.
33. *Ibid.*, §4-7.
34. The majority of academics nonetheless consider that with the termination of the employment contract, the employee recovers - under the restriction not to commit an act of unfair competition - his complete freedom. *See* Stoffel-Munck, 'L'après-contrat' (2004) 1 *Revue des contrats* §14; Delphine Sassolas, 'La durée des clauses de confidentialité' (2015) *RTD com.* 625, 626. For an opposite view, *see* Marie Malaurie-Vignal, 'Le parasitisme des investissements et du travail d'autrui' (1996) *Receuil Dalloz* §3; above n 31, §113.
35. Describing the case law as 'as discreet as the obligation it aims to produce', *see* above n 34. Marie-Ange Moreau, 'La protection de l'entreprise par des clauses contractuelles de non-concurrence et de confidentialité' (1999) 69 *Droit et Patrimoine* 56.
36. This is the implication of the decision in the *Dassault* case, which held that the absence of a precise legal determination of the limits of the obligation of confidence of the employee did not mean the employer was entitled to unilaterally decide to what information the duty of an employee was to extend: *see* Malaurie-Vignal, above n 13.

Further, the contract principle of 'proportionality' (*proportionnalité*) requires that the clause is justifiable in terms of the particular employee's duties and proportionate to the goal of protecting trade secrets, and for that reason also, it must refer to specifically identified information. Not everything can be rubberstamped as confidential. More generally, confidentiality clauses must properly identify information intended to be kept secret; otherwise, the clause will fail because of the indeterminacy of its object (*indétermination de son objet*).[37]

A significant issue in jurisprudence is the legality of confidentiality clauses without a time limit under French law.[38] French legal scholars are divided on this topic.[39] Section L. 121-1 of the Labour Code does not require a temporal limit for these clauses. Therefore, a confidentiality clause that pertains to very specific, potentially technical information but lacks a time restriction could be seen as necessary and proportional in limiting an employee's freedom of speech.[40] However, some scholars contend that such an unlimited clause may contradict the general prohibition against perpetual agreements. However it is debatable if a confidentiality clause without a defined duration is considered perpetual, as it could be argued that such an agreement is inherently limited to the point at which the information becomes public.[41]

A last issue concerning confidentiality clauses for a period exceeding the employment contracts was whether financial compensation was required for the validity of the agreement. Here, the Court of Cassation has clarified that financial compensation is only necessary when the confidentiality clause significantly restricts the employee's ability to perform their professional duties, similar to a non-compete clause.[42]

[3] Use of Information after Termination of the Contractual Relationship

As indicated at the outset, absent a confidentiality clause in a contract, '*savoir-faire*' acquired by a party, such as an employee, is in principle free for him or her to use. Any disclosure that leads to the acquisition of '*savoir-faire*' by an employee in France is thus at the confidor's own risk in the employment context. This is because *savoir-faire* cannot be unlearned and becomes part of the person, and it is difficult to distinguish between what comes from the employer and what stems from the personal knowledge and abilities of the employee. However, *savoir-faire* here is analogous to the common law concept of know-how, as distinct from genuine trade secrets. Thus, a cour d'appel in an older decision held as follows:

> aucune atteinte ne saurait être portée au droit d'un salarié, fut-il cadre et haut placé dans la hiérarchie, de mettre son savoir-faire, même acquis au cours d'une longue

37. *See* Marie Malaurie-Vignal, 'Réflexions sur la protection du patrimoine informationnel de l'entreprise contre le piratage économique', (2012) *Recueil Dalloz*, D 2012, 1415 at para. 26.
38. *See* above n 34, 628.
39. For a detailed presentation, *see* above n 30, 142.
40. For a different view, *see* above n 34, 631.
41. *See* above n 31, §111.
42. Supreme Court, 15 October 2014, 13-11524, *Adex*; obs.: Garinot, 'Validité de la clause de confidentialité dépourvue de contrepartie financière' (2014) 345 *Gazette du Palais* 9-11.

> carrière, au service d'un employeur concurrent, dont il est régulièrement devenu l'employé, des lors qu'il ne révèle ni n'exploite en sa faveur les secrets industriels ou commerciaux de son précédent employeur.[43]

It is often said in cases that an ex-employee can use what they learned, as long as they have not taken documents and the like belonging to their ex-employer. Naturally, if they do take documents, they may find themselves on the wrong side of the criminal law, as explained below. Against this background, trade secret owner might be tempted to rely on non-compete or restrictive covenants to further protect their secrets.

[C] Non-competes

[1] General Regime

The starting point for any consideration of non-competes in employment contracts is the fundamental freedom to work. In a constitutional sense, this present-day freedom is rooted in Article 7 of the famous *Décret d'Allarde* of 2 and 7 March 1791, which consecrated the principles of freedom of work and of industry.[44] With this decree and the subsequent '*loi Le Chapelier*', '*tout frein au libre déploiement de l'industrie est désormais rejeté*' (any brake on free enterprise is henceforth rejected).[45] As Damy and Pelli point out, most European Constitutions recognize the freedom to work as fundamental; in France, the preamble to the Constitution of 4 November 1950 states that every person has the duty (*devoir*) to work and the right to obtain employment.[46] This means any person has the right to take up new work immediately upon termination of a contract of employment.

The non-compete clause or restraint of trade is not referred to in any statute or legislation, unlike in other European jurisdictions like Germany. The Labour (Law) Code (*Code du travail*) is silent on the matter. However, as is the case in relation to confidential information, an abundant case law has evolved over the years into a comprehensive regulatory structure. This case law has many parallels with the law that has developed since *Nordenfelt* in England and other comparable jurisdictions.

A non-compete clause derogates from the freedom to work, but nonetheless, courts recognize the validity of such clauses, as well as the right of employees to seek to invalidate the clause for reason of its incursion upon the freedom to work. In the period up to 2002, the courts were not interventionist, emphasizing freedom of

---

43. *See* CA Paris, 17 mars 1967, D. 1967, Jur. P. 437; as cited in Marie Malaurie-Vignal, 'La protection des informations privilegiées et du savoir-faire', (1997) *Recueil Dalloz*, 26ieme Cahier. Chronique, para. 7: 'there is no restriction on the right of an employee, be he a manager or highly placed in the hierarchy, to use his savoir-faire, even if acquired during a long career, in the service of a competing employer, with which he became properly engaged, as long as he does not reveal then commercial or industrial secrets of his previous employer'.
44. '*il sera libre a toute personne de faire tel négoce, ou d'exercer tel profession, art out métier qu'elle trouvera bon*' (any person is free to engage in any trade, profession, art or craft they *see* fit).
45. *See* Gregory Damy & Sabrina Pelli, '*La clause de non-concurrence dans les relations du travail*', La semaine juridique entreprise et affaires, No 1, 3 janvier 2008, 133, para. 2.
46. *Ibid.*, para. 5.

contract.[47] The *Cour de Cassation* held in 1969 that even an employee who was wrongfully dismissed could be held to the non-compete clause in the employment contract. In essence, during this period, the autonomy of the parties came first: the fact that the employee agreed validly to the clause was paramount – Article 1134 al. 1 of the *Code Civil* asserts the binding force of contracts.

However, this situation where freedom to contract trumped the right to work, and open competition did not persist. The position that non-compete clauses were *ipso facto* valid was abandoned by the *Cour de Cassation* in 1992 when their validity was made subject to the condition that they should be indispensable in light of the legitimate interests of the firm,[48] the onus being on the employer to establish this. The *Godissart* decision concerned a window-cleaner, and the court held that given the fact that he was in a lowly position and had no access to confidential information that could affect legitimate competition, a non-compete was invalid. The employer is not free to prevent an employee from working within his area of competence and experience in the absence of an identifiable risk of unfair competition that justifies the clause, such as the misuse of trade secrets or existing clients. If no legitimate interest can be established, the clause is void.

The case law has applied the general contract principle of proportionality between the restriction on the freedom to work and the protectable interests of the employer.[49] It is up to the employer to determine carefully whether the firm has an interest in particular trade secrets to protect, for which purpose a non-compete is indispensable, and the extent of the restraint necessary to safeguard it.[50] The other recognized interest is in protecting existing clients against '*détournement*' by the ex-employee – the term can be translated as diversion or misappropriation, in this context meaning wrongfully capturing known clients. The latter subject is not under particular consideration here, as the relevance of the law concerning non-competes in the present context derives from the fact that it is the most significant legal tool available to protect trade secrets.

As well as requiring a demonstrable and legitimate interest, the cases have also developed a condition of spatial and temporal limitation. By virtue of a 1992 decision of the *Cour de Cassation*, the requirements of legitimate interest and limited extent in time and space are cumulative, and it is within the discretion of the court to determine whether the limitation is excessive in light of the freedom to work.[51] Geographically, the clause should not extend beyond an area where the ex-employee would be competing with the employer but for the restraint clause. The courts thus engage in a balancing act expressed more in terms of fundamental rights and interests but not fundamentally much different from the exercise common law judges engage in.

47. *See* Marc Gomy, 'L'autonomie de la clause de non-concurrence post-contractuelle en droit du travail', in *Etudes sur le droit de la concurrence et quelques thèmes fondamentaux. Mélanges en l'honneur d'Yves Serra* (Dalloz 2006), at p. 199.
48. By virtue of the *Godissart* decision, Cass. Soc. 14 mai 1992. *See* above n 45, paras 17-23.
49. *See* above n 45, paras 24-27.
50. *See* Arnaud Teissier, '*La clause de non-concurrence en droit du travail: loyauté renforcée ou forcée?*', La Semaine Juridique Social No 5, 26 juillet 2005, 1085, para. 4.
51. Cass. Soc., 10 juillet 2002, No 00-45.387: JurisData No 2002-015270.

However, since the right to work constitutes one side of the balance, in France, the clause must be adapted to the particular characteristics of individuals' employment and not place limitations that extend beyond these to prohibit them from exercising their own profession *entirely*. The particular training and experience of the employee are also relevant factors. According to Damy and Pelli, a clause that excludes an employee from activities he or she has performed over many years, accumulating long experience, will be invalid. Teissier explains that if an employee can establish that his seniority (years of service) and expertise in a particular pursuit means that he has become an expert in his particular field of engagement, a non-compete that prohibits his participation in that field may be void. His long experience in a very specific field means he has no other particular competences, and therefore, the prohibition fully denies him the right to work.[52] Teissier gives examples of employees of 15 and 22 years standing in a particular type of work, general maintenance in one case.[53]

He also points out that here, again the employer must act in good faith. The employee might have broad competence and ability upon his engagement when the clause is signed, which would allow him to work in different fields upon termination. But if the employer then effectuates his specialization over the years in a particular field, 'boxes him in' in a particular specialization, he cannot then prohibit him from exercising his specialized skills post-termination because that would effectively take away his ability to work at all.[54] The non-compete must not impose an excessive restraint on the freedom to work.

In the case of an employee with a general training which allows him or her to exercise many different functions, the prohibition will have to be precise and extend to specific duties to be held valid. What is determinative in the French approach, and in this, it appears more mindful of the rights of employees, is the remaining scope for exercising a profession in line with his or her particular skills, training and experience.[55] Therefore, in one case, a clause that had the effect that a person who had always worked in radiology lost the benefit of fifteen years of experience and had to go abroad to work was found void.[56] In another case (Go Sport), a clause that prohibited work for one year in any enterprise that engaged in clothing and sports retail as a primary or secondary activity was held void, as it did not leave the employee any possibility of finding work in line with his professional experience.[57]

In this respect, French law disapproves of restraints that do not enable the employee to find any work in line with his or her particular competences – the complete prohibitions regularly upheld in the common law go beyond this standard. The main goal of the courts is to find a balance between protecting the legitimate

52. *See* above n 50, para. 12.
53. *Ibid.*
54. *See* above n 50, para. 13: '*l'employeur ne peut "enfermer" professionnellement un salarié dans une spécialité et lui interdire par la suite de l'exercer en dehors de l'entreprise*'.
55. *See* above n 45, §29: '*Tout dépendra de la possibilité laissée au salarie d'exercer une activité conforme a ses compétences*'.
56. Cass. Soc. 28 October 1997: RJS 12/1997, No 1369.
57. Cass. Soc., 18 September 2002, No 00-42.904: JurisData No 2002-015505; *see* above n 45, para. 35.

interests of the employer and the freedom to work for the employee. Further, we shall see below that the French courts also impose a strict requirement that there be separate consideration for a non-compete clause.

On the application of the employee (the old and new employer have no standing in this regard), a clause that is disproportionate is held null and void by the court. Only a clause the employee has validly agreed to can ever be enforced, and an employer cannot, by virtue of a clause in the employment contract, reserve for itself the option to impose a restraint or not after termination or reserve the right to extend the scope of a clause after termination. It is relevant in this context that French law has a strict requirement that an employee be paid consideration for observing the clause, separately and post-employment. Nonetheless, the parties can enter into a restraint clause as part of a separation agreement or deed.[58]

The court can declare the clause null and void, but alternatively, where the restraint is excessive, it can reduce its scope to achieve the equilibrium referred to above, but naturally only where there is a legitimate interest to protect in evidence. Even where there is such an interest, the courts can reduce the scope of the clause in time, space or the restrained activities concerned. In particular, a court will so act where the restraint does not allow the employee to engage in any activity in line with his training and professional experience. In other words, the court can remould the clause so that the individual can still engage in some relevant work. That may take the form of limiting the restraint to a prohibition on solicitation of clients of the ex-employer.[59] Teissier points out that although reframing the time and place restraints is an acceptable adaptation of the terms of the agreement to the intention of the parties (so-called *réfaction*, sometimes referred to as '*réécriture*', a well-established practice even before the decision of the *Cour de Cassation* of 18 September 2002)[60] and one which was well established, where the re-writing concerns the field of activity, the judge becomes a creative actor who substitutes himself for the parties in the contractual bargain. This Teissier considers a step too far.[61]

Damy and Pelli also, and rightly, draw attention to the risks inherent in French courts' far-reaching power to refashion the non-compete clause in the interests of re-establishing proportionality in the contract: this '*laisse le salarié dans l'incertitude sur l'étendue de ses obligations et empêche de lutter efficacement contre les abus des clauses excessives*'.[62] In other words, as we have noted elsewhere, the judicial power to reconfigure a restraint encourages employers to include excessively wide restraints that act *in terrorem* against employees contemplating leaving, or who have left and are considering challenging the restraint in their own interest. Canut calls for the nullity of excessive clauses, rather than re-writing, precisely for this reason: '*seule, la nullité de*

58. *See* above n 45, paras 38-39.
59. *See*, for instance, the *Gan Vie* case: Cass. Soc., 18 octobre 2002: D 2002, p. 3229, note Y. Serra; as cited by Damy & Pelli, above n 45, para. 43.
60. *See* Florence Canut, '*Clause de non-concurrence illicite et responsabilité civile de l'employeur*', La Semaine Juridique Social, no 29, 18 juillet 2006, 1575, para. 12.
61. *See* above n 50, para. 15.
62. *See* above n 45, para. 44: 'leaves employees in a state of uncertainty about the extent of their obligations and prevents an effective fight against the abuse of excessive clauses'.

la clause a un effet réellement dissuasive pour l'employeur, qui sera ainsi amené a rédiger des clauses en adéquation avec ce qu'exige l'intérêt légitime de l'entreprise'.[63] Whereas the courts no longer prioritize individual autonomy, freedom of contract and the sanctity of the bargain to the extent they once did (*see* above), their greater intervention may thus not have the desired effect. Perhaps a situation where the employee must carefully consider the restraint at the time of negotiating the contract of employment, because more or less certain to be held to its terms, might encourage more resistance at that point, or more effective collective action.

In comparison with the French position, the traditional common law 'all or nothing' approach presents a clear policy alternative.[64] Damy and Pelli also note that there is a fine line between applying the contract law principle of 'proportionality' and simply remaking the parties' contract for the sake of fair and just equilibrium between their respective obligations, and that in the light of their primary capacity as willing partners to a private agreement.[65] However, Teissier raises a different point that the power of the court to rewrite the clause forces the ex-employee to act in good faith, as is required in relation to every contractual obligation under French law. The employee who immediately starts work with a competitor or who works in the immediate vicinity of the ex-employer will be found to have acted in bad faith when he tries to rely on the unlimited term or excessive geographical extent of the non-compete to argue it is null and void and not binding upon him.[66] This is an interesting departure from the norm in common law jurisdictions, where the clear public policy interest prevails over any concern that the employee may be acting rather deviously in entering into a restraint with eyes wide open, then to turn around and claim its nullity after employment has terminated.

Naturally, the ex-employer can also bring an action in unfair competition before the Labour Tribunal and against the new employer before the commercial court. The nullity of the clause is no obstacle to an action in unfair competition either against the employee or the new employer.[67]

---

63. *See* above n 60, para. 13. She supplies further legal-technical arguments against the power to rewrite and in favour of nullity as sanction at paras 14, 15, 16.
64. Note that in Australia the *Restraint of Trade Act* (NSW) gives the court the power to rewrite, but a clause will still be struck down if it is apparent that there was no genuine attempt on the part of the employer to fashion reasonable terms.
65. *See* above n 45, para. 45.
66. *See* above n 50, 8 citing Cass. Soc., 27 September 1989; RJS 10/89, No 762; Cass. Soc., 2 fevr. 1994: RJS 3/94, No 252; Cass. Soc., 29 avr. 1980; Cass. Soc. 29 avr. 1980, V, No 373; Cass. Soc., 13 janv. 1982: Bull. Civ. 1982, V, No 8; Cass. Soc., 19 November 1997, No 95-41.912, J. *Campione c/ Ste Samse*, inedit; CA Toulouse, 21 November 2002: RJS 5/03, No 696.
67. *See* Guillaume Blanc-Jouvan, '*L'expiration d'une clause de non-concurrence ne constitue pas un obstacle a une action en concurrence déloyale contre le nouvel employeur*', La Semaine Juridique Social No 11, 10 mars 2009, 1115. *See also* Malo Depincé, '*La nullité d'une clause de non-concurrence au regard du droit du travail ne fait pas obstacle a la condamnation de l'ancien salarie pour concurrence déloyale*', La Semaine Juridique Entreprise et Affaires No 40, 6 Octobre 2005, 1463.

[2] *The Requirement of Consideration*

In French jurisprudence, a non-compete clause without separate consideration is null and void. A valid agreement requires consideration (or '*cause*', *see* above), i.e., a countervailing obligation. In the common law, there is no requirement for separate consideration for this individual obligation in a contract that contains many other terms and conditions. In France as well, the *Cour de Cassation* long considered that the '*cause*' for the non-compete clause lay in the totality of benefits the employment contract bestows on the employee. However, then the focus turned to the fact that for sometimes long periods, employees are unable to exercise their profession and their fundamental right to work without any reciprocal obligation on the part of the ex-employer at that time.[68] Specific and separate financial consideration became a critical requirement by virtue of three decisions handed down on 10 July 2002.[69] The change wrought by the *Cour de Cassation* in 2002, requiring separate consideration, has been variously described as a 'tsunami' or a 'storm' coming over the non-compete clause, in part because of its subsequently upheld retroactive effect: in other words, the lack of consideration operated to invalidate clauses entered into before the change to the law, which was brought about purely by the courts, not the legislator.[70] The requirement and the presence of consideration do not affect the court's power to invalidate non-compete clauses for other reasons (extent of term, space, duties).[71]

In 2006, the same court held that derisory or symbolic financial consideration was not sufficient and rendered such a clause null and void.[72] Later judgments then reinforced the principle that the consideration was for the prohibition the employee must observe and should, therefore, be proportionate with the restrictions suffered. The amount could therefore not be determined by reference to the employee's seniority;[73] rather, relevant considerations are the length and extent of the restraint and the options for employment left open for the employee.

In the same decision, the court laid down the rule that the consideration must be paid during the period of restraint and could not be incorporated or reflected in salary during employment - the latter being what is often presumed to be the relevant consideration in the common law. Damy and Pelli indicate that consideration fluctuates between one-fourth and two-thirds of gross salary, with half being a common

68. *See* above n 45, paras 49-51.
69. Cass. Soc., 10 juill. 2002, No 99-43.334-99-43.336.
70. *See* above n 60, para. 1; *see also* Brigitte Reynes, '*La renonciation à la clause de non-concurrence à la portée du revirement jurisprudentiel de 2002*', Receuil Dalloz Entreprises, 2004, no 22, 1543; Frederic Chautard and Loic Le Berre, '*Contrat de travail: Comment gérer les clauses de non-concurrence depuis les arrêts du 10 juillet 2002?*', JCP - La Semaine Juridique Entreprises et Affaires, no 52-52, 2046.
71. *See* above n 60, para. 7. *See also* Danielle Corignon-Carsin, '*Conditions cumulatives de validité d'une clause de non-concurrence*', JCP - La Semaine Juridique Entreprises et Affaires, no 42, 17 octobre 2002, 1679.
72. Cass. Soc., 15 November 2006, 04-46.721: JurisData No 2006-035916; Bull. Civ. 2006, V, No 341; JCP S 2007, 1057, I. Beyneix.
73. Cass. Soc., 7 mars 2007 No 05-45.511; JurisData No 2007-037811; JSL 3/2007, No 208, p 18, note H.-C. Haller.

norm.[74] In fact, the *Cour de Cassation* decided that the payment for the purposes of social security, leave, etc., was to be considered salary.[75] In this sense, there is little to distinguish this situation from garden leave in the common law, except for the fact that employees might have scope for other work in line with their abilities and that not the whole but a fraction of the salary only is payable. The amount must be determined in the employment contract and not in an external instrument, such as a collective bargaining agreement only. Interestingly enough, as the payment constitutes salary, the court does not permit refashioning of the financial consideration, and therefore, the clause is null and void if it is held to fall short.

Given the financial implications, an employer may be tempted to renounce the clause, which he has a right to do, but only immediately after termination or within the term stipulated in the contract.[76] Alternatively, an unpaid ex-employee has the choice of ignoring the restraint and working for a competitor or respecting it and demanding payment of the sum due in consideration under the contract. However, in French contract law, the employer is held to a general duty of good faith in executing the contract. If the employer acts in bad faith, the nullification of the non-compete clauses can be combined with the grant of damages.[77] Because of the gravity of the fact of interference with the fundamental freedom to work, the employee is *ipso facto* entitled to damages.[78]

When the employee breaches the restraint, the consideration is no longer payable, although it remains due for the period during which the restraint was observed. The employer can also file an action with the specialized Labour Tribunal (*conseil de prud'hommes*) for damages in case of breach. A contractual clause (*clause pénale*) specifying the amount due in case of breach is valid and enforceable.[79]

As was indicated above in the context of the action for unfair competition, a new employer who knowingly engages an employee who is in breach of a non-compete clause may be civilly liable to compensate the ex-employer.[80] Without knowledge, the new employee cannot be liable, but whenever he becomes aware that the employee is still subject to a restraint, he is obliged to terminate the employment contract; otherwise, again, damages will be due. The court can even order the termination of the new employment contract, according to Damy and Pelli.[81] There is some doubt as to whether the onus is on the ex-employer to prove the knowledge of the new employer

74. *See* above n 45, para. 63.
75. Cass. Soc., 26 September 2002, No 00-40.461; JurisData No 2002-015599.
76. *See* Carole Lefranc-Hamoniaux, '*Clause de non-concurrence: quand la contrepartie financière doit-elle être versé?*' Receuil Dalloz 2007, 1708. *See also* Jocelyne Sechier-Dechevrens, '*Vers un déséquilibre contractuel de la clause de non-concurrence*', Receuil Dalloz 2006, 1357.
77. *See* above n 50, para. 7.
78. *See* above n 60, para. 27; the *Cour de Cassation* has held that the infringement of the fundamental freedom to engage in a profession is so grave, that '*le respect par le salarié d'une clause de non-concurrence illicite lui cause nécessairement un préjudice*'. The difficulty of proof is said to partly underlie this approach.
79. *See* above n 45, paras 72, 73.
80. *See also* Yves Chagny, '*Débauchage de salarié, nullité de la clause de non-concurrence: une prise de possession du droit du travail par le droit commercial*', Revue de Droit du Travail, Juillet-Aout 2008, 453.
81. *See* above n 45, para. 77.

or that the new employer is under an obligation to ascertain whether the new employee is under a non-compete obligation. Damy and Pelli indicate that the judicial tendency is towards stricter application of principles of fault under Article 1382, and therefore, the first position is now preferred.[82] It should be noted that a new employer has no standing in relation to the validity of a non-compete clause.[83]

For employers, non-compete clauses have obvious drawbacks in France, not least the obligation to pay quite substantial compensation. In that light, an alternative protection against direct competition by an ex-employee has developed in the form of the non-solicitation clause. This term can of course apply to a clause prohibiting ex-employees from approaching the clients of their previous employer. However, broad non-solicitation clauses of that kind might be viewed as a restraint of trade and therefore subject to the conditions discussed above for non-competition clauses. A more interesting alternative for employers is the commonly used non-solicitation clause between a business *and a client*, prohibiting the latter not only from soliciting but also from hiring an employee who works for the client, particularly in positions of secondment or detachment.[84] In France, the prohibition can be validly made to persist after the end of the contract between employer and client. Normally, the resulting restriction on the employee's freedom of work is limited because he or she is not bound by the contract and can find work with any other firm. According to Benilsi, the courts therefore treat this type of non-solicitation clause quite liberally, as their impact on the right to work is slight and they differ in crucial respects from non-competition clauses. Quite unlimited non-solicitation clauses have been held valid.[85] An action for breach of contract lies against a new employer who hires an employee in breach of the non-solicitation agreement. If the employee signs the employment contract in the knowledge that his new employer was bound by a non-solicitation agreement with his previous employer, he may be liable for third-party complicity to the breach.[86]

But in some cases, the employer might bind all potential future employers in a region with such clauses, so that the effect of multiple non-solicitation clauses is equivalent to that of a non-compete clause but without the need for compensation. Employers within a sector and region could also agree on a network of such clauses which effectively prohibit movement of employees between them. In such cases, the employee might have recourse to contractual remedies or an action in delict.[87] However, these are issues that are too far removed from the consideration of the indirect protection of know-how and trade secrets by way of non-competes to warrant further attention here.

82. *Ibid.*, para. 78.
83. *See* Isabelle Beyneix, *Nullité de la clause de non-concurrence et tierce opposition*, La Semaine Juridique Social No 40, 2 Octobre 2007, 1747.
84. *See* Stéphanie Benilsi, '*La clause de non-sollicitation*', La Semaine Juridique Social No 51, 18 décembre 2007, 1976, at para. 2. *See also* Jacques Mestre and Bertrand Fages, *La singularité … et la validité de la clause de non-sollicitation*, RTD Civ. 2007, 111, Dalloz.
85. *Ibid.*, para. 10.
86. *Ibid.*, paras 18, 19.
87. *Ibid.*, paras 21-37.

§7.04 CRIMINAL PROTECTION

[A] Secrets de Fabrique

As mentioned earlier, the only provision explicitly addressing a category of trade secrets is Article 1227-1 of the Code du Travail, which concerns 'secrets de fabrique' (literally, 'factory secrets' or 'manufacturing secrets'). Historically, this offence dates back to the Napoleonic Penal Code of 1810. It was introduced to protect French industry from foreign powers, particularly England, during the Continental Blockade. During the Industrial Revolution, key innovations that provided competitive advantages were primarily technological and required substantial capital investments, which were often beyond the reach of most employees. This historical context is significant because the provision still retains its 1810 wording,[88] resulting in a scope of protection that mirrors the concerns prevalent during the Industrial Revolution.

The scope of this provision indeed is very narrow. The term is not defined in the statutory provision, but the following elements have been advanced in the '*doctrine*'.[89] It applies only to an original production process that provides a practical or commercial advantage, has been applied industrially and has been kept secret from competitors who were thus not aware of it prior to its wrongful disclosure. Methods, processes and materials used are included, but commercial secrets such as client lists and details are not. The '*secrets de fabrique*' are only a narrow category, and by itself, the provision is not sufficient to comply with the requirements concerning 'undisclosed information' of Article 39 TRIPS. For that to be achieved, it is complemented by the general criminal law and civil action for unfair competition.

The standard of secrecy of Article 1227-1 is high, and therefore, protection does not extend to know-how more generally. Malaurie-Vignal points out that the information must not be publicly known so that any publication, even in a specialist journal, will render it ineligible for protection.[90] The standard of secrecy is higher than the relative requirement of English breach of confidence, for instance. Nonetheless, although 'originality' is required, the process need not be patentable; in fact, whether a proprietary right may or may not extend to it (in the form of a patent) is of no consequence.[91] Nonetheless, the fact that the process is known or used by a number of other firms does not necessarily mean it will not qualify as a '*secret de fabrique*'. Schmidt-Zalewski points out that the critical requirement is that the process is kept hidden from its competitors.[92]

Further, liability only attaches to directors and employees and only where the information concerned is *communicated* in an unauthorized manner (*divulgué*), not where it is used or exploited for personal gain by the employee or director concerned.

88. *See* s. 418 Napoleonic Criminal Code.
89. By which is meant the writings of academics applying the underlying theories and principles upon which French law is based and reconciling these with the decisions of the courts.
90. *See* Malaurie-Vignal, '*Réflexions* ...', above n 37, at para. 12.
91. *See* Joanna Schmidt-Zalewski, '*La révélation d'un secret industriel peut être un délit pénal*', Propriété Industrielle No 2, février 2007, comm. 15, 3.
92. *Ibid.*

In this aspect, it is similar to the penal provision applying to employees in Germany. Liability attaches not only if the communication occurs during the term of employment but also if the information concerned was acquired during and as an incident of employment and if it is communicated to a third party (divulgation) after the employment is terminated (which is different from the situation in Germany). An ex-employee handing over a secret process to a new firm he establishes after termination may suffer criminal liability, as would passing on the information to a new employer or exploiting it in one's capacity as an employee of a firm newly joined.[93] It is also possible that in a situation where an ex-employee, for example, uses a hitherto secret process of the ex-employer in a new venture, the general criminal law concerning receiving *(le recel)* might in some cases apply. Although simply drawing a commercial advantage from the criminal disclosure does not render a person an accomplice (*see* below), by virtue of the general criminal law, liability for receiving may result from knowingly benefiting from another's criminal offence.[94]

The provision is, thus, squarely aimed at a gross breach of trust by an employee who passes on a genuinely secret production process kept deliberately hidden in the factory to a third party.[95] Passing on the information is sufficient to ground liability, with actual exploitation in competition not being required. In terms of *mens rea*, the act must be intentional in the sense that a person who did not know or could not know of the secret nature of the information passed on cannot be held criminally liable.[96] Attempt is equally punishable as actual commission of the offence, so that a director travelling overseas after contacting competitors of the employer was found guilty by that fact alone in one instance.[97] Liability can also extend to an accomplice who takes an active part in the commission of the offence, for instance, by hiring an employee from a competitor and offering him the means to apply the secret process.[98]

[B] General Criminal Law: Theft of Information 'as Such'?

As a result of the very limited protection offered by the 'secret de fabrique' incrimination, courts are sometimes tempted to rely on general offences to provide trade secrets owners with better protection, such as theft, receiving (or handling), and fraudulent breaches of trust *(abus de confiance)*. Most commonly, criminal prosecutions concern employees or ex-employees who have removed records containing valuable information from the possession of their employers and then turned the information to their own account or divulged it to third parties, either during or after the term of employment. In general, there is no difficulty in relation to the application of the law concerning theft or receiving of physical records such as documents, computer disks,

93. *Ibid.*
94. *Code Penal* (Criminal Code) (France) Art. 321-1, 2.
95. *See* Malaurie-Vignal, '*Réflexions …*', above n 37, at para. 12.
96. So-called *intention délictueuse,* in casu '*dol général*', i.e., general rather than specific criminal intent.
97. Although this is an old case: Cass. Crim., 4 juill. 1903, *Sté Franchomme et Faucheville c/ Smeets*: Sirey 1904, 105.
98. *See* above n 91, 4.

and memory sticks. That the real reason they have been taken from the employer is not the value of the thing itself but of the information contained within which does not make any difference to the question of criminal liability for the appropriation of the physical record. In this regard, the legal position is no different from that which is attained in common law jurisdictions.

The more relevant question is whether the taking of information *as such* might constitute theft or an allied offence. Here, the preponderance of the case law and longstanding principle holds that information cannot be the object of theft. Nonetheless, in a number of higher decisions, the concept of theft of information as such is, at the very least, *not clearly dismissed* by the court. Thus, for instance, the decision of the *Cour de Cassation* in the *Bourquin* case rejected the appeal against a decision finding two employees guilty of theft of the *'contenu informationel'* of two diskettes for the time necessary to copy their content.[99] In the *Antoniolli* decision, the *Cour de Cassation* also upheld a decision of the *cour d'appel* (Court of Appeal) where that court had referred to information being legally the property of the accused's employer. A commentator considers that the accompanying theft of documents used by the employee to copy information for a third party justified rejecting the appeal in any case and that the *Cour de Cassation* should not be taken to have generally approved of information being property and thus capable of being stolen per se.

The most illuminating statement of the law is probably to be found in this passage from a *cour d'appel* of Paris decision of 2 May 2001:

> le salarié d'une entreprise qui, détenant matériellement certains documents appartenant a son employeur, en fait des copies a des fins personnelles, a l'insu et contre le gré de leur propriétaire, et qui, ainsi, appréhende frauduleusement ces documents pendant le temps nécessaire a leur reproduction, se rend coupable de vol.[100]

In the *Code, Pénal* theft is defined as *'la soustraction frauduleuse de la chose d'autrui'* (the fraudulent 'subtraction' (perhaps best translated as '"dispossession") of another's thing'; Article 311-1), and, therefore, has a broader field of operation than the same offence in the common law tradition. The essence of the cited passage is that the temporary detention by an employee of a document for the purpose of making unauthorized copies of it is sufficient to constitute a 'fraudulent dispossession', as the definition of theft (*vol)* requires. It should be noted that the relevant section refers to *'chose'* and not *'bien'*, i.e., thing and not 'good'. Although it could be characterized as a 'good', IP as such is clearly not a thing. Malaurie-Vignal considers that courts are

99. Bourquin: Cass crim. 12 janv. 1989: Bull. Crim. No 14; for the comments referred to in text, *see* Propriétés intellectuelles, avril 2004, No 11, 687-689 (Chroniques, No7 *'Vol d'informations?'*: concerning Cass. Crim., 9 septembre 2003, pourvoi No 02-87098). However, as the commentator points out, if the theft only concerned that limited period, it would not really apply to the information but more relevantly to the diskettes themselves.

100. Com. Com. Electr. October 2001, actu. P4. Rappr. CA Paris, 9 November 2000: Dr penal mai 2001, comm. 57, obs. M. Veron, 688.

generally very weary of the concept of theft of information, as is illustrated by consistent refusal to recognize criminal conversion of information.[101]

Nonetheless, as well as the occasional decision which appears to recognize the possibility of theft of information as such, there is also a scholarly school of thought which supports this approach. As indicated, the difficulty is that the statutory definition of theft refers to *things* which information is most definitely not. Nonetheless, scholars point to certain decisions and stress that it cannot be denied that sometimes *'l'information est assurément protégée en elle-même et pour elle-même'*.[102] However, the large majority of such decisions concern cases where there is a close association between theft of a record and the intent to appropriate information contained or to turn it to the accused persons account. Further, decisions of the *Cour de Cassation* to this effect are said to be difficult to interpret or understand, and they continue to fall short of a firm decision 'of principle' in favour of theft of information as such. There is, however, a sense that lower courts are nonetheless well disposed towards a future evolution in the direction of theft of information as such; as Beaussonie puts it, *'leur existence n'en reste pas moins un appel ostensible a une évolution du droit'* – the existence of the decisions favouring this approach is a 'call for' development of the law in that direction.[103] It should be kept in mind that the French definition of theft, making reference as it does to fraudulent appropriation, leaves perhaps more latitude for theft without full recognition of information as property. The common law requiring permanent dispossession as it does, perhaps, sets a higher bar.

Sometimes, the fact that the legislator has created specific offences which clearly protect an informational interest is advanced as an argument against accepting theft of information under the general criminal law. Such offences relate, for instance, to misuse of electronic databases (hacking) as referred to above or to disclosure of 'privileged' information. In the final analysis, however, information does not fit properly into the juridical theory of goods. Nor does it in fact make sense, as is recognized by commentators, to penally create a property right in secret information in the face of the existence of clear *'droits privatifs'* (private property rights) in IP created by statute – most relevantly here, patents. Notwithstanding all these arguments and the difficulties with the case law, in some quarters, there is support for the application of the general criminal law to secret information. It remains to be seen what the effect of the *Loi Carayon*, if it passes into law, would be on this movement. It would undoubtedly deprive it of much of the oxygen it presently enjoys because its field of application by comparison with the present provision relating to *'secrets de fabrique'* would be so broad.

101. *See* Malaurie-Vignal, *'Réflexions ...'* above n 37, at para. 16.
102. 'It is sometimes affirmed that information is most assuredly protected as such.': Guillaume Beaussonie, *'La protection penale de la propriete sur l'information'*, Droit pénal No 9, septembre 2008, étude 19 (Jurisclasseur). This article makes a sustained case for recognizing theft of information per se.
103. More literally translated as 'The existence (of the Appeal or lower court decisions) is nonetheless a clear call to evolve the law (in the direction of recognition of theft of information).'

[C] Receiving and Handling Stolen Information?

Article 321-1 of the Criminal Code (*Code Pénal*) provides that it is an offence to hide, retain or transmit a thing or to be an intermediary for that purpose, knowing that the thing comes from an offence. Equally knowingly benefiting in any way from the product of an offence is itself a criminal offence.[104] Here again, the '*doctrine*' is divided as to whether information per se can be the object dealt with. De Jacobet de Nombel ('De Jacobet') points out that the case law also '*ne cesse de tergiverser sur ce point*' continues to procrastinate on this point.[105] The author cites a case where a person who made a punch in accordance with a recipe which had been passed on to him in breach of rights in a '*secret de fabrique*' offended against Article 321-1. Another case resulting in a conviction concerned a person who knowingly performed stock exchange transactions with the benefit of '*information privilégiée*'.[106] Subsequently, the question of whether the offence applies to the use of information as such or whether it only concerns the underlying physical record (a thing) has been the subject of a number of changes in direction. In 2007, the *Cour de Cassation* held, at least by implication, that criminal liability could only attach to the documents themselves containing the information, as opposed to the information per se.[107] Perhaps the correct answer to the question lies in the second limb of the Article. As de Jacobet says, because of its immaterial nature, information is not a thing in the sense of the first limb. But the second limb provides that to benefit from the product of a crime is also punishable. De Jacobet maintains that this extends to *anything* that results from an offence and that its material or immaterial nature is of no consequence. In other words, deriving a benefit from the theft of a thing such as a memory stick, by knowingly turning the information so provided to one's own account, attracts criminal liability on this view.[108] This view is not without its detractors, according to De Jacobet, but he nonetheless reiterates that this particular offence, in particular in its 2nd limb, the '*recel-profit*', no longer requires the retention of a material thing to attract criminal liability. On a final note, the author points out that the courts are rather more reluctant to extend this offence to information where the press is concerned.

104. '(1st limb): *Le recel est le fait de dissimuler, de détenir ou de transmettre une chose, ou de faire office d'intermédiaire afin de la transmettre, en sachant que cette chose provient d'un crime ou d'un délit. (2nd limb): Constitue également un recel le fait, en connaissance de cause, de bénéficier, par tout moyen, du produit d'un crime ou d'un délit*'. (Receiving is the concealment, retention or transfer a thing, or acting as an intermediary in its transfer, knowing that that thing was obtained by a felony or misdemeanour. Receiving is also the act of knowingly benefiting in any manner from the product of a felony or misdemeanour: translation at legifrance.gov.fr.).
105. Or better: 'Constantly procrastinates on this point'. *See* Camille de Jacobet de Nombel, '*Le recel d'information*', Droit Pénal No 9, septembre 2008, étude 21, para. 2.
106. *Ibid.*
107. Cass crim., 12 juin 2007, No 06-87.361; *see* note 9 in de Jacobet de Nombel, '*Le recel* ...' above n 105.
108. *See* above n 105, para. 7.

[D] Abus de Confiance

According to Article 314-1 of the Criminal Code, the diverting (*détourner)* by a person of funds, valuable goods or any good that has been transferred to that person and accepted with an obligation to return them, to offer them or to make a particular use of them, to the detriment of another person, is an offence.[109] Note that the term used here is '*bien*' (good) rather than '*chose*' (thing), as is found in the Article concerning theft. The notion is broader, and in one case cited by Malaurie-Vignal, an employee was found guilty under this Article for having used information obtained in the context of his duties to encourage clients to turn to a competing company, without any diverting (misappropriating) of documents. However, she also points out that other decisions have opposed this approach.

[E] The Reform Projects Aimed at Adopting Transversal Criminal Protection

It is clear from the above that at present, the application of the criminal law to secret information is only uncontroversial in relation to '*secrets de fabrique*', where the scope for criminal liability is, however, very narrow, and criminal prosecutions rare. The application of the general criminal law to secret information is problematic; information is not generally regarded as property for this purpose; and in most successful prosecutions under the general law, there is in fact such a close association between the information and the physical thing on which it was recorded that the question of criminal liability relating to information per se is always clouded. The case law is inconsistent and differing schools of thought compete in the scholarly literature. Confronted with a criminal norm that is often criticized for being outdated and with questionable efforts by the criminal courts to expand the scope of other offences in order to provide greater protection for trade secret holders, it is not surprising that lawmakers have occasionally contemplated the introduction of a comprehensive criminal offence. So far, these attempts have not been successful. The most notable of these proposals is the Carayon proposal, which has been widely debated but has never been formally adopted. More recently, but still unsuccessfully, the transposition of the directive has seen the debate resurface, but again without success.

[1] The 'Projet De Loi Carayon'

Critics of the state of the law in France cite the absence of a unitary concept of trade secrets, comprising both the technical and commercial, the illogicality of a single express criminal provision narrowly defined, and the uncertainty of the various civil remedies as unsatisfactory in the modern internationally competitive commercial

109. *'L'abus de confiance est le fait par une personne de détourner, au préjudice d'autrui, des fonds, des valeurs ou un bien quelconque qui lui ont été remis et qu'elle a acceptée à charge de les rendre, de les représenter ou d'en faire un usage determine.'*

environment. The 'Projet De Loi Carayon'[110] sought therefore to expand criminal liability in France regarding the protection of trade secrets by following a comprehensive approach similar to the US EEA. The proposed bill, which passed the lower house on 24 January 2012, however, never made its way to the Senate.

The proposal provided fora higher level of protection, introducing a unitary concept of trade secret protection, and usefully adopting an approach akin to the *EEA* in the United States. However, supporters of the status quo, maintained that the existing law, although disparate and fractured, is in fact adequate. They also criticize the *Loi Carayon* for being too far-reaching and ignoring the interests of openness, freedom of information and competition in favour of overbearing protection, about which further below; suffice it to note here that the US law on which the *Loi Carayon* is said to be based (although with significant differences in fact) has itself come in for considerable criticism, as discussed in Chapter 1.

The *Loi Carayon* would have provided direct protection for trade secrets rather than indirectly by way of unfair competition or breaches of various specific obligations of good faith and confidentiality. According to Malaurie-Vignal, the *Loi Carayon* elevates '*secrets d'affaires*', literally 'business secrets' but closely analogous to 'trade secrets', to a class of goods (*biens*) that merit the protection of the law, i.e., not IP law but criminal law.[111] The subject matter of protection was, however, very extensive and amorphous, certainly for a penal statute.[112] The standard of secrecy was also less high or more relative than attached to '*secrets de fabrique*' but is more analogous to what is required in the common law. Le Stanc also emphasizes the difficult interaction between the proposed law and patent grant as protection for new technical products and processes. If a firm benefits from such apparently broad penal protection for its secrets, why then apply for a patent, with all its attendant detriments of publicity and limitation in term? Importantly, patents have a social contract element – they encourage disclosure, diffusion and further innovation and improvement, although within the confines of the patentee's rights. Trade secrets protection, however, is anathema from this perspective.

[2] The Reform Attempt During the Transposition of the Directive

The last attempt to establish a criminal law system for trade secrets occurred during the transposition of the European directive. It is important to note that the directive did not require criminal law protection; rather, it allowed Member States the option to include it. In France, during parliamentary discussions, there was consideration of aligning criminal protection with the new civil law framework. The French Senate proposed adding Article L. 314-4-1 to the French Penal Code, which would criminalize the misappropriation of trade secrets as defined under civil law. This proposal specifically

110. Proposal for a Law No 3985, Registered with the Presidency of the National Assembly on 22 November 2011, to punish violations of trade secret.
111. *See* Malaurie-Vignal, '*Réflexions* …', above n 37, at 36.
112. *See* Malaurie-Vignal, '*Réflexions* …', above n 37, at 37; Christian Le Stanc, '*Une protection pénale du secret des affaires?*', Propriété Industrielle no 10, octobre 2009, repère 9.

targeted acts committed with the intent to circumvent the protective measures of trade secret owners for economic gain.[113]

Ultimately, this proposal was rejected by the Commission mixte paritaire (joint mixed committee), which cited the need for a more thorough examination of whether such alignment was necessary and how it should be implemented.[114] While there was a timeline for transposing the directive, the proposal's rejection was likely influenced by journalists' opposition to the legal protection of trade secrets, especially regarding any form of criminalization. This resistance made it politically challenging to adopt the proposal.

Although aligning the criminal offence with the civil standard would have ensured consistency, it also would have transferred the uncertainties surrounding trade secret protection in civil law to the criminal context. While such uncertainties may be manageable under civil law, they raise significant concerns in criminal law, which demands precise definitions to meet constitutional standards.[115]

§7.05 CONCLUSIONS

The evolution of French law serves as a reflection of broader global trends in trade secret law. Although the Napoleonic Code included a criminal provision for trade secrets from the beginning, the protection framework has mainly developed within civil law over time, primarily through case law related to unfair competition. This area of law has gradually expanded to include behaviours known as 'parasitic misappropriation', which goes beyond traditional unfair competition. It emphasizes the importance of protecting trade secrets as intangible assets that deserve safeguarding, regardless of whether there is a direct competitive relationship. This jurisprudential development has given rise to much debate in the French academic world. As is often the case when it comes to trade secrets, the main task of legal scholars in the meandering jurisprudence has been to try to identify a general logic for determining what is protected and how. The transposition of the European Directive has significantly impacted these jurisprudential developments, aligning French civil law more closely with US law, from which the Directive drew considerable inspiration. This

113. *See* French Senate, *Proposition de loi relative à la protection du secret des affaires, texte n°95*, 18 April 2018, Art. 1er quater: 'Art. 314-4-1. – Le fait d'obtenir, d'utiliser ou de divulguer de façon illicite une information protégée au titre du secret des affaires en application du chapitre Ier du titre V du livre Ier du code de commerce, en contournant sciemment les mesures de protection mises en place par son détenteur légitime, afin d'en retirer un avantage de nature exclusivement économique, est puni de trois ans d'emprisonnement et de 375 000 € d'amende'.

114. French Parliament, Commission Mixte Paritaire, Comptes rendus sur la proposition de loi relative à la protection du secret des affaires, 24 May 2018.

115. *See* in this regard, the reticence of the French Conseil d'Etat regarding the instauration of a criminal regime based upon the civilian framework: French Conseil d'Etat (Assemblée générale), *Avis sur la proposition de loi portant transposition de la directive du Parlement européen et du Conseil sur la protection des savoir-faire et des informations commerciales non divulgués contre l'obtention, l'utilisation et la divulgation illicites*, 15 March 2018, N° 394422, para. 8; in contrary *see* the rejection by US Court of this critic regarding the EEA: US District Court for the Eastern District of Pennsylvania, 11 March 1999, *United States v. Hsu*, 40 F. Supp. 2d 623 and US Court of Appeals for the Sixth Circuit, 26 July 2001, *United States v. Krumrei*, 258 F.3d 535.

transposition introduces new questions for French law, many of which will now need resolution at the European level by the Court of Justice. In terms of criminal protection, French law remains fragmented despite efforts to bolster legal measures in this domain. In France, as in other countries, there is a growing tendency to enhance the protection of trade secrets – often motivated by a desire to shield national industries from foreign interference – without fully acknowledging the potential drawbacks of over-protection.

CHAPTER 8

Civilian Approaches: Germany

§8.01 INTRODUCTION

The central economic value of trade secrets is often stressed by German commentators.[1] They also stress the vulnerability of trade secrets because publication destroys their value even if it is unlawful.[2] Hence, the high cost of industrial espionage is emphasized by Piper/Ohly/Sosnitza,[3] who contend that from an economic (rather than juridical) perspective, trade secrets are IP ('*Immaterialgueter*') because they have economic value and their possessor can exclude others and they can exploit them personally or by licence. They are, nonetheless, not the object of the normal gamut of IPRs as they do not provide exclusivity but only protection against particular forms of 'attack'.[4]

Historically, German law has approached the issue of protecting trade secrets through criminal law. Hence, betrayal of trade secrets by employees dated back to the UWG of 1896 and Industrial espionage was criminalized by the '*2. Gesetz zur Bekämpfung der Wirtschaftskriminalität*' of 1986.[5] Despite the early attention from legislators, it will become clear that, as in many legal systems, case law has played a pivotal role in shaping the legal protection of trade secrets. Jurisprudence has been crucial in defining which secrets can be protected and in establishing the civil conditions for their protection. The 2019 transposition of the European Directive significantly altered this legal framework. However, key elements of the previous

1. Ansgar Ohly & Olaf Sosnitza, Kommentar, *Gesetz gegen den unlauteren Wettbewerb* (Beck München, 2023) (available online at beck-online.beck.de), GeschGehG,Vorbemerkungen RN 2-4 according to whom: Trade secrets are 'often more valuable than industrial property rights and are often the most significant asset of the firm'.
2. Ohly & Sosnitza, above n 1.
3. *Ibid.*
4. *Ibid.*
5. Law on Combatting Economic Crimes (2. WiKG).

framework persist and are still reflected in sections of the *'Gesetz zum Schutz von Geschäftsgeheimnissen'* (GeschGeG).

§8.02 SITUATION UNDER THE UNFAIR COMPETITION LAW (UWG) BEFORE THE TRANSPOSITION OF THE EUROPEAN DIRECTIVE

[A] Generalities and Comparative Elements

Before the transposition of the European Directive, the law of trade secrets in Germany was significantly different from English common law in terms of legal sources and doctrinal framework. Similar to French law, it was based on liability for unfair competition or commercial practices rather than on breaches of confidence and trust. Although, like its French counterpart, it lacked a coherent, unitary character and was considered fragmented and disordered (*'zersplittert und unübersichtlich'*),[6] it had a substantial statutory foundation, at least as far as criminal liability was concerned. In this regard, the protection of trade secrets in Germany diverged from the path taken by France. While in France, the origin of trade secret protection was also rooted in criminal law, the importance of the latter eventually diminished as civil law assumed a more prominent role. Conversely, in Germany, civil protection became feasible by building on the existing criminal standards despite the absence of a specific legal framework dedicated to trade secrets until the transposition of the European Directive.

In Germany, trade secret protection was indeed primarily governed by two penal provisions – Articles 17 and 18 of the *'Gesetz gegen den unlauteren Wettbewerb'* (UWG; Law Against Unfair Competition).[7] One advantage of this penal approach was the greater ability of authorities to gather information and evidence when a trade secret breach was suspected, compared to private litigants.[8] The same argument was made regarding the introduction of the EEA in the United States.

[B] Subject Matter: A Definition Forged by Case Law

As in the United States, prior to the transposition of the European directive, the definition of trade secrets was left to case law. Articles 17 and 18 of the old UWG offered protection for commercial and technical secrets (*'Geschäfts – und Betriebsgeheimnissen'*). Piper/Ohly/Sosnitza pointed out that the first category concerned commercial secrets, such as client and supplier data, financial and contractual documents,

6. Piper, Ohly & Sosnitza (hereinafter 'POS 2010'), *Gesetz gegen den unlauteren Wettbewerb, Kommentar* (Beck München, 2010) (available online at beck-online.beck.de); *Vorbemerkungen* (Vor) 17 at RN 9. In this regard, *see also* Mary-Rose McGuire, Bjorn Joachim & Jens Kuenzel.,'Der Schutz von Geschäftsgeheimnissen durch Rechte des Geistigen Eigentums und durch das Recht des unlauteren Wettbewerbs (Q215)', (2010) GRUR Int., Heft 10, 829 at 831, referring to trade secrets law as the *'Stiefkind des geistigen Eigentums'* – The 'stepchild' of intellectual property law.
7. To avoid any confusion between the new and old regimes governing trade secrets, we will use the abbreviation 'UWG_old' when referring to the texts that prevailed prior to transposition of the directive.
8. *See* McGuire et al., above n 6, at 833.

and the latter technical information, such as construction plans and production processes, but that it was neither necessary nor desirable to try to strictly separate the two categories as nothing turns on the classification.[9] The European Directive reflects a hint of this dichotomy in its title: 'On the Protection of Undisclosed Know-How and Business Information (Trade Secrets).' However, similar to former German law, this semantic distinction does not influence the uniformly applicable framework. In fact, it completely disappears in the Directive's operational provisions.[10]

The terms '*Geschäfts- und Betriebsgeheimnisse*' were not explicitly defined in the UWG. However, case law progressively established four conditions that needed to be met for information to qualify as a trade secret under Articles 17 and 18 of the old UWG: (1) the information had to be related to the business ('*Unternehmensbezogenheit*'); (2) it must not have been in the public domain ('*fehlende Offenkundigkeit*'); (3) the owner had to have the intention to keep it secret ('*Geheimhaltungswille*'); and (4) the owner had to have an interest in keeping it secret ('*Geheimhaltungsinteresse*').

The level of secrecy required under the '*fehlende Offenkundigkeit*' condition was relatively low and can be ultimately said to align with the new standards set by the European directive[11] (which, as a reminder, follows the international standard as set in Article 39 of the TRIPS Agreement). Hence, information was in the public domain if it was 'generally known in the relevant professional circles or easily accessible'.[12] The requirement for the owner to have had a legitimate interest in keeping the information secret ('*Geheimhaltungsinteresse*') served the function of excluding arbitrary or capricious insistence on secrecy ('*Willkürsausschluss*').[13] In conjunction with the requirement of a real connection with the business, it also met the standard of Article 39(2)(b) TRIPS, requiring economic value.[14] 'Legitimate' in this context meant legally significant or recognized, rather than suggesting that the information should not have concerned something illegal. However, the question of whether the requisite secrecy interest could have resided in information about illegality or impropriety was contested.[15] Whether disclosure in a given case might have been justified because it served higher-order interests of third parties was yet to be determined by virtue of paragraph 34 of the *Strafgesetzbuch* (StGB) concerning justification ('*Rechtfertigung*').

The most interesting aspect of the old German definition was that it contained elements that were related not to the information *as such* but to its relationship with its owner. This aspect underlined the fact that protection was rooted more in a logic of unfair competition. Hence, the condition for information to genuinely connect to a

9. *See* POS 2010, above n 6, at para. 17 RN 1. *See also* McGuire et al., above n 6, at 829, where the authors also suggest the compendious term '*Wirtschaftsgeheimnisse*' or 'economic secrets'.
10. *See* Chapter 6 of this Book.
11. Piper, Ohly & Sosnitza were for instance explaining that the information was in the public domain if it was 'generally known in the relevant professional circles or easily accessible': *See* POS 2010, above n 6, at para. 17 RN 7.
12. *See* POS 2010, above n 6, at para. 17 RN 7; McGuire et al. said that information is in the public domain if it can be generally obtained in a normal manner ('*auf normalem weg*'): *see* McGuire et al., above n 6, at 829.
13. *See* POS 2010, above n 6, at para. 17 RN 6.
14. *See* McGuire et al., above n 6, at 830.
15. *Ibid.*

business (*Unternehmensbezogenheit)* reflected the purpose of the protection to allow a specific business to operate competitively without disturbance.[16] The key prerequisite here was that the information could be ascribed to a *particular* business and the connection was not so loose that the information could be said to belong to the market as a whole or to all competitors. McGuire et al. maintained that the protected object of rights under the old UWG was not the information as such but precisely its connection with a particular business. The fact alone that a certain business used a particular process could thus be considered a trade secret, even if the process itself was in the public domain.[17] The intention to maintain secrecy (*'Geheimhaltungswille'*) followed the same logic, distinguishing a legally protected trade secret from information that merely happens to be unknown to the public (*'bloßen Unbekanntsein einer Tatsache'*).[18] Although this conceptual approach theoretically allowed for limiting the scope of the definition, in practice, it proved largely ineffective. As such intent is challenging to establish, it was often presumed to exist, leading some commentators to refer to it as a legal fiction.[19]

Despite the numerous loopholes and uncertainties inherent in the old German definition – particularly problematic for a criminal standard – it remains noteworthy. First, it highlights that the definition in Article 39 of TRIPS, which is increasingly becoming a global standard (and which is not significantly more precise), is merely one of many possible definitions. Second, the old definition illustrates that the object of protection can be defined not only based on intrinsic characteristics (such as value or degree of secrecy) but also in terms of its connection to its holder. This approach hence focuses less on the object itself and more on maintaining fairness in the competitive process.

[C] Criminal Protection under Articles 17 and 18 of Former UWG

The relevant criminal provisions were specific and limited in scope. Article 17 of the old UWG addressed two main forms of conduct. First, Article 17(1) criminalized the unauthorized disclosure of trade secrets (referred to as *'Verrat'* or literally 'betrayal') by current employees. Second, Article 17(2) prohibited certain types of industrial espionage committed by any individual. This included the unauthorized acquisition or securing of trade secrets, as well as the exploitation of those trade secrets – whether by the individual who acquired them or by someone else – and the communication of such secrets to a third party. Additionally, Article 18 of the old UWG also addressed trade secrets but was more specific; it imposed criminal liability for the misuse of prototypes, models, plans, and similar items that had been entrusted to an individual.

16. POS 2010, above n 6, at para. 17 RN 2.
17. *See* McGuire et al., above n 6, at 829.
18. Harte-Bavendamm & Frauke Henning-Bodewig, *Gesetz gegen den unlauteren Wettbewerb* (UWG), *Kommentar*, 3. Auflage (Beck, München, 2013) (available online at beck-online.beck.de), para. 17 RN 3.
19. *See* POS 2010, above n 6, at para. 17 RN 11.

Regarding Article 17(1) of the old UWG, employees were not subject to criminal liability for using or disclosing trade secrets or know-how after their employment ended. This lack of liability placed a significant responsibility on employers to include contractual provisions for the protection of trade secrets after termination. The criminal offence itself involved unauthorized communication (referred to as '*unbefugte Mitteilung*'), whether in written or oral form, during the term of the employment relationship. Since all employees are bound by an implied duty of confidentiality (known as '*Schweigepflicht*'), any communication to third parties that was not legally justified – such as through express permission, statutory obligation during testimony, or in the case of an emergency – was considered unauthorized.[20]

Article 17(2) former UWG had the purpose of protecting trade secrets against *particular methods* of industrial espionage. This provision extended criminal liability to any person in relation to any trade secret, not just employees or information in the hands of an employer. Under Article 17(2)(1), the conditions that determined criminal liability were the securing or obtaining of a trade secret through impugned methods in the absence of authorization. The impugned methods were specifically, although broadly, described: use of technical means ('*Anwendung technischer Mittel*'); making a physical record of the information ('*Herstellung einer verkörperten Wiedergabe*'); or removing an article incorporating the secret ('*Wegnahme einer Sache, in der das Geheimnis verkörpert ist*'). Harte-Bavendamm et al. described the methods targeted as 'typical and particularly dangerous forms of economic espionage' whose use to secure information was therefore made criminal per se, irrespective of whether the information concerned was further communicated or exploited.[21] Liability extended to a person who, without authorization, acquired ('*sich-Verschaffen*') or secured ('*Sichern*') the trade secret by one of the methods described.[22] This meant that a person could be liable even if they already knew the trade secret.

Besides actual spying, criminal liability also extended according to Article 17(2)(2) old UWG to what was compendiously referred to as '*Geheimnisverwertung*' or '*Geheimnishehlerei*' (i.e., unauthorized communication and/or 'exploitation' of a trade secret) and hence to any person who without authorization used or communicated a trade secret that has been obtained by virtue of a breach of Article 17(1) by an employee, or by way of his own industrial espionage or that of another person (Article 17(2)(1)), or acquired for himself or secured without authority by any other means.

Article 18 old UWG was lastly a more limited provision. It dated back to 1909 and has remained largely unchanged since then and imposed criminal sanctions for the unauthorized exploitation or communication of templates ('*Vorlagen*') or technical specifications or instructions ('*Vorschriften*') in particular (architectural and technical) drawings, models, sketches, patterns.[23] The section was predicated upon the possessor

20. *Ibid.*, at para. 17 RN 10.
21. *Ibid.*, at para. 17 RN 18.
22. A possible description is that the first equates to taking cognizance of, the second to securing for future use, certain information; *see also* McGuire et al., above n 6, at 832.
23. *See* POS 2010, above n 6, at para. 18 RN 1.

handing a specified item over for one purpose and the recipient then taking unauthorized advantage of the know-how it incorporates.

A final aspect resulting from the criminal nature of these provisions is the need to demonstrate not only *actus reus* but also *mens rea (subjektiver Tatbestand)*. In terms of the latter, it was required that the criminal act be done *'zu Zwecken des Wettbewerbs, aus Eigennutz, zugunsten eines Dritten oder in der Absicht, dem Inhaber des Unternehmens Schaden zuzufügen'*, i.e., for the purpose of competition; for personal gain; for gain of a third party; or with the intention of causing harm to the business owner. The perpetrator had to know that the information was a trade secret, or the element of intention would be absent. Additionally, at least one of the four forms of subjective intent had to be present but need not have been the sole motivating factor. Any act that had the purpose and tendency to advance competition by the employee or third parties to the detriment of the employer fell within the first category. The second category was fulfilled if the perpetrator wanted to obtain some direct or indirect material or immaterial (but analogous to material) advantage for himself. The third category had been added to the law in 1986 and could apply where an employee acted with the motive, for instance, of assisting a foreign state, without seeking a competitive or material advantage but for ideological reasons. Harte-Bavendamm et al. pointed out that this was thought necessary in light of the damage suffered by German industry from foreign industrial or state espionage. In terms of the fourth category, the intention to see actual damage occur to the employer had to be present, but the term damage was to be understood widely and could include interference with other legally recognized interests or good standing and reputation.[24] Although the criminal law provisions were significantly modified following the adoption of the GeschGehG, the German legislator nonetheless maintained these elements at the stage of criminal law protection provided in the new legislation.

[D] Civil Protection under Article 3 UWG and 823, 826 BGB

By contrast with the penal provisions of the UWG, there were no civil law statutory provisions dealing with trade secrets misuse. Convictions under Articles 17 & 18 UWG triggered liability for compensation. Still, some acts were not covered by those provisions and could only be addressed under civil law, such as post-contractual (particularly employment) duty of confidence (*'Verschwiegenheistpflicht'*) or the area of liability and damages for *negligent* betrayal of trade secrets (as the penal provisions only cover intentional acts). These questions were addressed under Article 3(1) UWG, according to which 'Unfair business practices are prohibited' and under 823 and 826 of the Civil Code (BGB). For liability to arise under Article 826, it was necessary to establish that the person acted with the intention of causing harm to the trade secret's owner and in a manner contrary to public policy, whereas Article 823 imposed a duty to compensate for any damage caused unlawfully either by negligence or intentionally.

24. *Ibid.*, at para. 17 RN 17. *See also Ibid.*, at para. 17 RN 25.

Hence, although exercising the freedom to exploit properly acquired trade secrets, an ex-employee could nonetheless offend against the ex-employer's subjective right to trade secrets (*'Bei dem subjektiven Recht am Unternehmensgeheimnis'*). However, civil liability could only be imposed where factors other than mere exploitation or transmission of the trade secret were present and only after a judicial evaluation of competing interests.[25] Similarly, in exceptional circumstances, doing so could also amount to a breach of competition law (Article 3 UWG; i.e., other than Article 17, which did not apply post-employment). Differently put, although a use was not constitutive of a trade secret violation under Article 17 or 18 UWG, *exceptional additional facts* could lead a court to hold that what ex-employees did nonetheless amounted to unfair competition or wrongful conduct under the BGB.[26] The literature stressed that the courts needed here to engage in a careful weighing up of competing interests in the particular circumstances of the case (*'sorgfältigen Güter- und Interessenabwägung aufgrund aller Umstände des Einzelfalls'*),[27] as the constitutional rights and interests of the parties were colliding.[28] Thus, it was, for instance, necessary to examine whether the particular trade secret was *realistically* required for the ex-employee's advancement rather than to simply presume this to be the case. Further factors that were thrown into the balance were: the centrality of the trade secret to the ex-employer's business; the importance of the employee's erstwhile position and their level of access to secret information; the preparations for a future competing undertaking the ex-employee might have engaged in while still employed; whether the employee made any contribution to the development of the trade secret; if he was specifically remunerated for the work resulting in the trade secret; and whether the employee was only briefly employed or not. Whether the ex-employee encouraged others to leave their employment may also be relevant. This was obviously a difficult area of law and practice, where differing views were propounded in the literature and the case law was very fact-based and thus not entirely predictable. This area of residual civil liability, especially in relation to the use of trade secrets in post-employment, was hence an uncertain area, all the more so since the concept of a trade secret was wide, encompassing unimportant information as well as critical technical secrets.[29] Hence, even in the presence of a fairly elaborate system of criminal sanction, non-competes were very significant, and they were accepted but regulated to a considerable extent by statute.[30] We will revisit these points later in this chapter, as the *GeschGehG* did not alter the legal regime of these clauses.

25. *Ibid.*, at Zivil. RN 49.
26. McGuire et al. state that only if *'ganz besonderen Umstände'*, 'very unusual circumstances' exist can the use of properly acquired information post-employment be a breach of the general clause of the UWG, or of provisions of the BGB; *see* McGuire et al., above n 6, at 832.
27. *See* Harte-Bavendamm et al. (2013), above n 18, at Deliktsrecht RN 48, for quoted passage.
28. *Ibid.*
29. *Ibid.*, at para. 17 RN 1.
30. An action for breach of contract will be available even though an employee is strictly speaking free to use the trade secret to which it relates. In other words, a factually secret piece of information can be made a valid subject of a contractual obligation, even though according to principle, the employee would otherwise have been free to use it. Naturally, the use of a trade

A further interesting point in the old law was the legal regime devoted to reverse engineering practices. By contrast to the common law approach, in Germany, reverse engineering was only permissible if it was relatively easy to do; if great technical or financial efforts were required to discover the information hidden in an article or machine, then reverse engineering could constitute a breach of the law. We will revisit this system in greater detail, which was overturned with the implementation of the *GeschGeG*.[31] However, it can already be said that the dividing line between acceptable and illegal reverse engineering was difficult to draw.

§8.03 THE TRADE SECRET ACT (*GESCHGEHG*) AND TRANSPOSITION OF THE EUROPEAN DIRECTIVE

[A] The 2019 Trade Secret Act: Context and Generality

In Germany, the implementation of the European Directive was delayed. Member States had until 9 June 2018 – two years after the directive entered into force – to adopt it.[32] However, it was nearly a year past this deadline when the '*Gesetz zur Umsetzung der Richtlinie (EU) 2016/943 zum Schutz von Geschäftsgeheimnissen vor rechtswidrigem Erwerb sowie rechtswidriger Nutzung und Offenlegung*' (the Trade Secrets Act, abbreviated as *GeschGehG*) came into force on 18 April 2019. This delay was not due to reluctance on the part of the German government but rather stemmed from a political vacuum created by challenging negotiations to form a federal government following the 2017 legislative elections.[33] As a result, Germany was technically in breach of its European obligations, necessitating a swift transition. Similar to the situation in France, this transition phase was characterized by intense lobbying from journalists who were concerned about the potential impact of the new law on investigative journalism.[34]

Perhaps the most remarkable aspect of the law, from a systemic perspective, is the removal of trade secrets from the general law on unfair competition (UWG) and the establishment of a separate legal framework for them. The reasons for this decision are primarily pragmatic. Integrating the Directive into the UWG would have disrupted its balance, as approximately half of its articles would be devoted to trade secrets. However, this decision also carries an interesting symbolic dimension. By being separated from the UWG, trade secrets are accorded their own status, emphasizing their unique importance. While not recognized as a standalone property right, trade secrets are now distinguished from the realm of unfair competition.

---

secret by an ex-employee may in the natural course of events result in its disclosure to others; in such a case, the ex-employer has no further recourse under the UWG.

31. *See* §8.03[D].
32. *See* Art. 19(1) of the EU Directive.
33. Ronny Hauck, *Münchener Kommentar zum Lauterkeitsrecht (MüKoUWG* hereafter) (Beck München, 3rd ed., 2022), GeschGehG before §1 RN 1.
34. *See* Ohly, 'Germany: The Trade Secrets Protection Act of 2019' in Jens Schovsbo, Timo Minssen & Thomas Riis (eds), *The Harmonization and Protection of Trade Secrets in the EU: An Appraisal of the EU Directive*, 104; Hauck, MüKoUWG, above n 33, GeschGehG §2, RN 4.

The *GeschGehG* largely mirrors the structure of the Directive. It begins with a 'General' section, which defines trade secrets, outlines their scope of protection, and specifies exceptions. Section 2 is devoted to remedies, while section 3 is devoted to procedural matters. Lastly, the criminal provisions previously found in the UWG have been consolidated into a single provision in the new law, located in section 4. Since the European Directive is covered in a specific chapter of this book, we will focus here only on aspects of German law that hold particular interest.

[B] The Definition of Trade Secrets in Article 2 *GeschGehG*: A German Recipe

The first impact of the directive's transposition into German law was the introduction of a statutory written definition of trade secrets. Hauck characterizes this change as a paradigm shift, as it removes the responsibility from the case law to define this standard.[35] This definition is notable for not simply reiterating the European Directive. Instead, the German legislator has exercised some creativity in its formulation. However, the overall result is questionable regarding both the added value of these modifications and their compatibility with the text of the European directive.

Hence, according to the Article 2(1) *GeschGehG*:

> A trade secret is information
>
> a) which is not generally known or readily accessible, either as a whole or in the precise arrangement and composition of its components, to persons in the circles that normally deal with this type of information and is therefore of commercial value, and
> b) which is subject to measures of secrecy appropriate in the circumstances by its rightful owner, and
> c) for which there is a legitimate interest in confidentiality.

The definition first merges the Directive's initial two requirements: secrecy and commercial value. This choice was guided by the Directive's wording, which establishes a causal link between these two elements. According to Article 2(1)(b) of the Directive, information is supposed to have 'commercial value *because it is secret*' (emphasis added).[36] Therefore, the German legislator felt it was coherent not to separate these conditions in the legal text, as they are not materially independent.[37] Ironically, this systematic interpretation aligns the German definition more closely with that of the United States as set out in the UTSA.[38] By contrast, the UTSA definition was slightly modified specifically by separating these two requirements and incorporated

35. Hauck, MüKoUWG, above n 33, GeschGehG before §1, RN 13.
36. On this *see* Chapter 6 of this book. *See also* Hauck, MüKoUWG, above n 33, GeschGehG §2, RN 13.
37. Desaunettes, Hilty, Knaack & Kur, *MPI Stellungnahme zum Referentenentwurf eines Gesetzes zur Umsetzung der Richtlinie (EU) 2016/943 zum Schutz von Geschäftsgeheimnissen vor rechtswidrigem Erwerb sowie rechtwidriger Nutzung und Offenlegung vom*, 17 April 2018, RN 4-6.
38. Ohly & Sosnitza, above n 1, GeschGehG RN 1.

into Article 39 of TRIPS before being included in the European Directive. However, this return to the original source ultimately sets the German definition apart from other definitions in Europe following the transposition.[39]

The more problematic change involves adding a final requirement that the owner must have 'a legitimate interest in confidentiality', a condition absent from the Directive's definition. This addition can be viewed as a concession to journalists. The condition of a legitimate interest can be interpreted to exclude information regarding illegal activities from protection, right from the definition stage.[40] This justification can be inferred from the *Bundestag* (the German federal parliament) documents, although it is not explicitly conceded. According to the law proposal's justification:

> According to recital 14 of Directive (EU) 2016/943, the definition of a trade secret is based on the fact that it covers know-how, business information and technological information for which there is both a legitimate interest in its confidentiality and a legitimate expectation that this confidentiality will be maintained. This is in line with previous case law on the concept of trade secrets, according to which information is protected if the legal entity has a legitimate interest in not disclosing it.[41]

As noted by Ohly and Harte-Bavendamm, this justification is unsatisfactory.[42] Recital 14 of the Directive indeed explains that '[i]t is important to establish a homogenous definition of a trade secret without restricting the subject matter to be protected against misappropriation. Such definition should therefore be constructed so as definition should therefore be constructed so as to cover know-how, business information and technological information *where there is both a legitimate interest in keeping them confidential and a legitimate expectation that such confidentiality will be preserved*' (emphasis added). The emphasized part of the second sentence, which the German legislator referred to, might indicate a limitation for secrets lacking a 'legitimate expectation' or 'interest.' If this interpretation were correct, it could exclude, for instance, secrecy about illegal conduct, which Ohly suggests is the aim of the third condition in the German definition. However, this reading contradicts the first sentence of Recital 14, which stresses the need to 'establish a homogenous definition of a trade secret without restricting the subject matter to be protected against misappropriation'. The first sentence indicates two things: first, the EU legislator's intent for a single standard regarding trade secret definitions in the EU. This assertion alone challenges the German decision to add further conditions. Second, the final part of this sentence clarifies that the subject matter should not be limited in terms of the information's

39. *See* Ohly, 'Germany: The Trade Secrets Protection Act of 2019', above 34, p. 105, considering the latter 'legally unproblematic and only inconvenient, as it makes the comparison with the legislation in other EU member states and the discussion of future CJEU judgement more difficult'.
40. *Ibid.*, p. 109.
41. Deutscher Bundestag, Drucksache 19/4724, 4 October 2018, p. 24.
42. *See* Ohly, 'Germany: The Trade Secrets Protection Act of 2019', above n 34, p. 109; Harte-Bavendamm & Frauke Henning-Bodewig, *Gesetz gegen den unlauteren Wettbewerb* (UWG), *Kommentar*, 5 Auflage (Beck, München, 2021) (available online at beck-online.beck.de), GeschGehG, RN 36.

nature ('without restricting the subject matter to be protected'). It should indeed 'cover know-how, business information, and technological information', as an interest in maintaining their confidentiality might exist regardless of their nature. Since Article 1(1) envisages hormonization by the imposition of a universal minimum standard, prohibiting Member States from restricting the Directive's protection scope, the addition appears potentially inconsistent with the Directive.[43]

Some scholars, such as Hauck, however, argue that considering the Directive's purpose, it should yet be assumed that unlawful information cannot constitute a trade secret.[44] Indeed, the Directive aims only to protect the competitiveness of innovative companies. Furthermore, the protection of unlawful information would also be incompatible with the requirement of an inherently consistent legal system: a coherent system could not offer legal protection to information about departures from its legal provisions.[45] If this interpretation prevails under the Directive, then unlawful information should be regarded as not fulfilling the commercial value requirement under the Directive. In that case, the German condition would be superfluous.[46]

[C] Definition of Lawful and Unlawful Behaviour: Transposition of the Directive with Minimal Adjustments

The *GeschGehG* marks a significant change in German civil law protection for trade secrets. Previously, civil protection was secondary to criminal law under the UWG, but with the transposition of the Directive, it is now logically prioritized.[47] Unlike the definition on which the German legislator put its stamp for a somewhat dubious result, the latter adopted a much more lenient attitude when it came to defining the actions that were to constitute a breach of trade secrets. The provisions of the *GeshGehG* concerning the scope of protection align well with the Directive. Specifically, Article 3 covers 'Permitted Actions', Article 4 addresses 'Prohibitions', and Article 5 discusses 'Exceptions', all of which closely follow the structure and concepts outlined in the Directive. We will not revisit these concepts here and invite the reader to consult the Chapter devoted to the European directive, where they are elaborated upon in detail.[48]

Concerning the divergences, the German lawmaker (as did its French counterpart)[49] chose not to include a general clause on permitted acts in Article 3 *GeschGehG*.[50] As will be recalled, the Directive was structured around two parallel general clauses, both at the level of lawful and unlawful behaviours. This Janus-faced structure was explained as problematic as it could lead to the two general clauses not being interpreted in a complementary manner.[51] This in turn could lead either to the creation

43. *Ibid.*
44. *See* Hauck, MüKoUWG, above n 33, GeschGehG §2, Nr. 66.
45. *Ibid.*, §2, Nr. 68.
46. Ohly, 'Germany: The Trade Secrets Protection Act of 2019', above n 34, p. 109.
47. Ohly & Sosnitza, above n 1, GeschGehG Vorbemerkungen RN 15.
48. *See* Chapter 6 of this book.
49. *See* Chapter 7 of this book.
50. Desaunettes, Hilty, Knaack & Kur, above n 37, RN 14.
51. *See* Chapter 6 of this book.

of a grey area that is not covered by either of the two general clauses or to an overlap of their areas of application. To avoid this pitfall, the German legislator has chosen to transpose only the general clause for unlawful behaviours (in Article 4 *GeschGehG*).

[D] The Lawfulness of Reverse Engineering: A Paradigm Shift

The most significant change to German law following the transposition is the legalization of reverse engineering practices as outlined in Article 3(1) No 2 of the *GeschGehG*. According to this article:

> A trade secret may be obtained in particular by observing, examining, disassembling or testing a product or item that
>
> a) has been made publicly available or
> b) is in the lawful possession of the observer, investigator, dismantler or tester and the latter is not subject to any obligation to restrict the acquisition of the trade secret;

Before this change, German law was based on a decision from the *Reichsgericht* (the erstwhile German Supreme Court) in 1935.[52] This case involved a producer of iron presses whose patent had expired over thirty years prior. A company that already owned one press considered the plaintiff's price for a second press too high and therefore hired a third party (the defendant) to disassemble its existing press to create a copy. In its ruling, the German Supreme Court, overturning the lower court's decision, held that reverse engineering as a method of acquisition violated 'the moral standards of competition'.[53] Despite facing criticism – particularly regarding the Court's reasoning[54] – this decision established the legal framework in Germany for nearly a century,[55] setting it apart from most other legal systems. In much of the theoretical analysis of trade secret protection (*see* Chapters 1 and 2), the right to reverse engineer has been considered absolute, regardless of the methods or efforts involved. The only limitation was the prohibition against infringing statutory or contractual rights during reverse engineering (e.g., infringing copyright by decompiling a computer program). In contrast, under German law, reverse engineering was only permissible if it could be conducted relatively easily. If significant technical or financial efforts were necessary to uncover the information hidden within an article or machine, reverse engineering could be considered a legal breach and potentially unfair competition. As a result, the law governing trade secrets in Germany was somewhat less 'porous' than commonly portrayed by common law scholars. However, the boundary between

52. German Reichsgericht (zivilsenat), 22 November 1935, Stiefeleisenpresse, II 128/35, RGZ 149, 329, GRUR 1936, 183. *See* on this Hauck, MüKoUWG, above n 33, GeschGehG §3, RN 9.
53. 'Guten Sitten des Wettbewerbs': *Ibid.*, 187.
54. For an analysis *see* Desaunettes-Barbero, *Trade Secrets Legal Protection*, pp. 130-132.
55. BGH, 12 February 1980, *Pankreaplex* II, KZR 7/79, GRUR 1980, 750, 752; OLG Hambourg, 3 October 2000, *Reglers für Warmwasserbereitung*, 3 U 191/98, GRUR-RR 2001, 137; OLG Karlsruhe, 29 January 2016, *Kartensperre eines Mobiltelefons*, 2(6) ss 318/15, NstZ-RR 2016, 258.

acceptable and illegal reverse engineering was often difficult to define. More recently, there was a gradual liberalization in judicial attitudes toward reverse engineering, leading to it being deemed unfair less frequently.

This change was welcomed in the literature.[56] It aligned German law more closely with the majority of other legal systems. Ohly noted that the prohibition of reverse engineering was 'hardly reconcilable with the practice in many areas of industry, where reverse engineering is common'.[57] The German approach to contractual restrictions is also noteworthy. As noted, the potential to bypass the Directive's policy decision to allow reverse engineering by the imposition of contractual restrictions was highlighted as a key weakness.[58] In response, German lawmakers explicitly distinguished between two scenarios: on the one hand, if the product is publicly available, contractual restrictions seem not to be permitted – or at least their violation would not constitute a trade secret breach.[59] On the other hand, where the goods are not freely available in the market but are lawfully in the observer's possession, contractual restrictions that could lead to a breach of trade secrets are permissible. According to Kamlah, an object should then be considered publicly available if it is offered for purchase or otherwise made available to an unlimited group of persons and these persons are actually able to 'get their hands on' the object.[60]

[E] Enforcement and Proportionally: The German Approach to the Balancing Test of the European Directive

We have explained that the European Directive includes proportionality control at the enforcement stage, which is directly inspired by the North American balancing test.[61] We also pointed out that the French legislator overlooked this fundamental element, which allows judges to prevent dysfunctional effects arising from over-protection at the enforcement stage.[62] In contrast, the German legislator recognized the significance of this control.[63] Like many continental legal systems, German law generally does not differentiate between the violation of a right and the granting of remedies; once a

56. Piper/Ohly/Sosnitza had for instance doubts that there is a clear persuasive basis for the old approach. According to them, in the absence of patent protection, the product would otherwise be freely reproducible, and the use of information obtained by reverse engineering can thus not really be seen as unauthorized ('*Verwendung der so gewonnen Erkentinisse nicht als "unbefugt" gelten*'). *See* POS 2010, above n 6, at para. 17 RN 10.
57. Ohly, 'Germany: The Trade Secrets Protection Act of 2019', above n 34, p. 114.
58. *See* Chapter 6 of this book.
59. The validity of this clause from a civil law perspective remains uncertain: Dietrich Kamlah, *Münchener Kommentar zum Lauterkeitsrecht (MüKoUWG* hereafter) (Beck München, 3rd ed., 2022), GeschGehG §3 RN 13-15, also Ohly, 'Germany: The Trade Secrets Protection Act of 2019', above n 34, p. 115.
60. Kamlah, *Ibid.*, GeschGehG §3 RN 10.
61. *See* Chapter 6 of this book.
62. *See* Chapter 7 of this book.
63. *See* on the specificity of this rule: Franz Hofmann, *'Equity' im deutschen Lauterkeitsrecht? Der 'Unterlassungsanspruch' nach der Geschäftsgeheimnis-RL* (WRP 2018), 1; Tochtermann, *'Zur Unverhältnismäßigkeit' einer Rechtsfolge nach dem neuen GeschGehG: Versuch einer Maßstabsbildung* (WRP 2019), 688.

violation is established, a remedy automatically follows.[64] This logic is notably reflected in the section title, which is labelled 'Claims in the Event of Infringements' rather than 'Remedies'.

The German legislator aimed to incorporate the proportionality control required by the Directive while maintaining the systematic nature of the German legal framework. This is why Article 9 is structured not as a general rule but as a defence that the infringing party can invoke.[65] This provision is entitled '§ 9 Exclusion of Claims in the Event of Disproportionality' and states:

> The claims pursuant to §§ 6 to 8 (1) are excluded if fulfillment would be disproportionate in the individual case, taking into account in particular
> 1. the value or another specific characteristic of the trade secret,
> 2. the confidentiality measures taken,
> 3. the behavior of the infringer in obtaining, use or disclosure of the trade secret,
> 4. the consequences of the unlawful use or disclosure of the trade secret disclosure of the trade secret,
> 5. the legitimate interests of the trade secret holder and the of the trade secret and the infringer as well as the effects that the fulfillment of the claims could have for both,
> 6. the legitimate interests of third parties or
> 7. the public interest.

The legality of this modification, particularly regarding its compatibility with the Directive, is questionable, as it may shift the burden of proof.[66] However, as noted in the literature, this change is unlikely to have significant practical implications because it is typically the defendant's responsibility to provide reasons to the court as to why proportionality is not present.[67] Ultimately, the German proposal emphasizes the importance and specificity of the proportionality test outlined in the Directive, further highlighting the oversight of the French legislator.

[F] Criminal Law: Reshaping to Ensure Coherence with the Civil Law Framework

The European Directive allowed Member States the option of 'providing for more far-reaching protection against the unlawful acquisition, use or disclosure of trade secrets' (Article 1 No 1). The primary aim of this provision was to give Member States the freedom to maintain or introduce criminal protection for trade secrets, as the European legislator chose not to address this area.

As we explain above, before the transposition of the Directive, the German protection regime was primarily centred around the criminal law provisions in Articles

---

64. Hofmann, *'Equity' im deutschen Lauterkeitsrecht*, above n 63, p. 30.
65. Clemens Krbetschek, *Münchener Kommentar zum Lauterkeitsrecht (MüKoUWG* hereafter) (Beck München, 3rd ed., 2022), GeschGehG §9 RN 1-5; Ohly, 'Germany: The Trade Secrets Protection Act of 2019', above n 34, p. 118.
66. Desaunettes, Hilty, Knaack & Kur, above n 37, RN 114.
67. Harte-Bavendamm et al. (2021), above n 42, GeschGehG, RN 36, Ohly, 'Germany: The Trade Secrets Protection Act of 2019', above n 34, pp. 118-119.

17 and 18 of the UWG.[68] In theory, the German legislator could have left these rules unchanged. However, for the sake of consistency, it chose to align the criminal provisions with the civil provisions of the Directive. Consequently, Articles 17 and 18 were replaced by a new, single but comprehensive standard, articulated in Article 23 of the *GeschGehG*:

> (1) A custodial sentence not exceeding three years or a monetary penalty shall be imposed on any person who, in order to promote his own or third-party competition, for his own benefit, for the benefit of a third party or with the intention of causing damage to the owner of a company
>   1. obtains a trade secret contrary to Section 4(1) Nr.1,
>   2. uses or discloses a trade secret contrary to Section 4(2) Nr.1(a), or
>   3. discloses a trade secret that has been entrusted to him or has become accessible to him in the context of the employment relationship during the term of the employment relationship, contrary to Section 4 Nr.2 number 3.
>
> (2) Likewise, anyone who uses or discloses a trade secret which he has obtained through a third-party act pursuant to subsection 1 Nr. 2 or Nr. 3 in order to promote his own or third-party competition, for his own benefit, for the benefit of a third party or with the intention of causing damage to the owner of a company shall be punished.
>
> (3) A custodial sentence not exceeding two years or a monetary penalty shall be imposed on any person who, in order to promote his own competition or that of a third party or for his own benefit, uses or discloses a trade secret which is a secret template or technical instruction entrusted to him in the course of business, contrary to section 4 (2) Nr. 2 or Nr. 3.
>
> [...]

This integration work pursued several objectives. First, it aimed to ensure that existing criminal law protection was not weakened. The new Article 23 hence extends criminal protection while retaining specific provisions, such as the protection of template (Article 23 Nr.3), which has no equivalent in the civil measures established under the Directive.[69] This reflects a broader trend where harmonization efforts almost systematically result in the strengthening of legal frameworks through an upward alignment of protection regimes. Second, the provision is designed to ensure overall coherence by aligning criminal protection with civil protection. This alignment involves numerous references to concepts from civil law, such as the definition of secrets and the conditions that constitute a violation. This cross-referencing, which is common in German legislation, strengthens general consistency but may make the texts less accessible at first glance. Lastly, the German legislator has made some effort to acknowledge the specificities of the penal framework, which constitutionally requires a precise definition of prohibited acts. This necessity prompted the German legislator to distinguish among the behaviours that constituted a violation of trade secrets from a civil law perspective, identifying those that could be criminalized. As a result, Article 23 does not criminalize breaches of trade secrecy as according to Article 4(1) No 2,

68. *See* Harte-Bavendamm et al. (2021), above n 42, GeschGehG, RN 203, according to whom: 'The Trade Secrets Directive has freed the protection of trade secrets from the shackles of criminal law.'
69. Harte-Bavendamm et al. (2021), above n 42, GeschGehG, RN 203.

which entails the general clause stating that 'any other conduct which, under the circumstances, does not comply with the principle of good faith and fair market practice' also constitutes a civil breach. This general clause is considered too vague to adequately define the *actus reus* of a penal norm.

Overall, this leads to a broader range of protections. Article 23 prohibits 'unlawful acquisition, use, or disclosure' in its first paragraph, addresses the 'use or disclosure of secrets obtained from third parties' in the second, and prohibits the 'use or disclosure of trusted documents' in the third. The personal scope of these provisions is general and is no longer confined to employee relationships. Additionally, paragraph 4 increases penalties in specific cases, particularly when the disclosure or use of secrets involves a foreign country or when espionage practices occur as part of a systematic operation rather than isolated incidents. Finally, it is worth noting that the German legislator has retained the requirement for qualified criminal intent, stipulating that the acts must have been committed 'to promote one's own or third-party competition, for personal gain, for the benefit of a third party, or with the intent to harm the owner of a company'.

Despite the precautions taken, §23 has faced significant criticism in the literature for its general lack of precision, which seems to conflict with the principle of legality in criminal law that requires clarity (Article 103(2) German Constitution).[70] This criticism previously targeted the criminal provisions of the UWG, which as noted even lacked a legal definition of trade secrets. However, it was often argued that this uncertainty was lessened by jurisprudence that clarified these norms. The same cannot be said for the new provisions of the *GeschGehG*, as many of its concepts still require clarification. Until this happens, the constitutional legality of this article remains precarious.[71]

The challenges faced by German law illustrate the difficulties of using criminal law to protect trade secrets. Because trade secrets are inherently fragile – lacking *erga omnes* protection and being easily compromised upon disclosure – resorting to criminal law, the ultima ratio of the legal arsenal might seem advantageous. However, criminal law requires that the object of protection be clearly defined to ensure individuals receive the fundamental guarantees required when the state leverages this tool. As discussed throughout this book, trade secret law often resists such precision. This ambiguity can be seen as both a strength, allowing for adaptability to technological and economic changes, and a weakness resulting from an absence of clarity concerning the precise goal of the protection. This tension is further exemplified by the paradox that trade secrets are not classified as IPRs, yet, due to the inadequacy of their civil protections, they receive reinforcement from a criminal framework – a protection not extended to IP.

70. Ohly, 'Germany: The Trade Secrets Protection Act of 2019', above n 34, p. 122.
71. Ohly & Sosnitza, above n 1, GeschGehG §23, RN 2.

§8.04 EMPLOYMENT AND NON-COMPETES: REMAINING AREAS OF NATIONAL LAW

[A] Employment and Extra-contractual Protection of Trade Secrets

As already stressed in the chapter dedicated to the European Directive, one of the main weaknesses of this piece of legislation is to leave unharmonized the question of the divulgation or use of trade secrets by former employees.[72] According to Article 1 Nr. 3(b): 'Nothing in this Directive shall be understood to offer any ground for restricting the mobility of employees. In particular, in relation to the exercise of such mobility, this Directive shall not offer any ground for (...) limiting employees' use of experience and skills honestly acquired in the normal course of their employment.'

Ohly explains that this article 'has not been explicitly implemented into German law. But since this principle was already applied under the old law (...) there is no doubt that it applies'.[73] In fact, the *GeschGehG* did not result in any substantial changes to the protection of secrets in the employment relationship.[74] In this regard, it was explained that German law, as it has developed on the basis of the general clause of the UWG and Articles 823 and 826 of the BGB, is a field presenting many uncertainties. In its theoretical insistence that an ex-employee is free to use any information, including a trade secret properly acquired, in her otherwise legitimate pursuits post-termination, the German law indeed stands apart from other legal systems here considered. Harte-Bavendamm et al. also point out that the distinction between free know-how in the common law sense and trade secrets properly so-called (the *Faccenda* distinction) has not been adopted in German jurisprudence, even though it has been advanced in the literature. Nonetheless, the authors maintain that although the 'separation theory' ('*Trennbarkeitstheorie*') is formally rejected, the alternative approach of weighing up all the circumstances in a given case in practice has regard to very similar factors.[75] Thus, if there are clearly and obviously abusive circumstances, the use of a trade secret properly so-called may nonetheless be restrained by a labour court. However, beyond these theoretical considerations, distinguishing between the knowledge an employee can freely use and what is likely to breach trade secrets has proven to be complex.[76]

In fact, the German lawmaker was not obligated to transpose Article 1 of the Directive, which merely clarifies its scope. This means that aspects outside its scope are left within the imperium of the Member States. However, as explained in the European Chapter, defining the scope of the Directive is a matter of European law. By stating that the Directive does not provide grounds for limiting 'employees' use of experience and skills honestly acquired in the normal course of their employment', it paradoxically 'Europeanized' the concept of 'employees' experience and skills honestly acquired'. As

72. *See* Chapter 6 of this book.
73. Ohly, 'Germany: The Trade Secrets Protection Act of 2019', above n 34, p. 112.
74. Ulrich Preis & Stefan Greiner, *Erfurter Kommentar zum Arbeitsrecht*, 25. Auflage (2025), BGB §611a RN 811.
75. Harte-Bavendamm et al. (2013), above n 18, at para. 17 RN 1.
76. Ohly, 'Germany: The Trade Secrets Protection Act of 2019', above n 34, p. 113.

a result, it is likely that the Court of Justice of the European Union will eventually need to interpret these terms, which could subsequently influence national case law.

[B] Contractual Obligations During and after Employment

Due to the uncertainty surrounding the protection of trade secrets in employment relationships, contract law is often relied upon for support. Leaving aside the context of NDAs or other provisions in commercial contracts, where employment is concerned, contractual obligation can take two forms: on the basis of an express term in the employment contract that binds the employee to secrecy even after the termination of the employment; and on the basis of a continuing operation of the duty of secrecy of the employment contract (*'Nachwirken von arbeitsvertragliche Geheimhaltungspflichten'*). It should be kept in mind that, as a matter of principle, employees are free to use properly learned secrets after termination – hence, the most effective protection against them doing so is to include a continuing confidentiality clause in the employment contract. If such a clause amounts to a restraint of trade or non-compete, then the statutory requirements for enforceability must be met – *see* further below. However, even in the absence of a confidentiality clause, the employer is not necessarily without a contractual remedy, notwithstanding the above-mentioned principle. In Germany, the employer can also submit that the duty of confidence (or of 'silence' or discretion, '*Schweigepflicht*') inherent in the employment relationship has some degree of continuing operation even after termination. However, as Piper/Ohly/Sosnitza point out, this is an area of some legal uncertainty (*'Rechtsunsicherheit'*).[77]

Concerning first the nature of an employee's obligations during employment, German law approximates common law and other systems: employees have a general contractual duty of fidelity (*'Treuepflicht'*), which requires them to keep quiet about and not exploit for themselves any information whose confidentiality is in the firm's interest.[78] Employees are also under a general duty to do what they can to prevent breaches of confidence by their colleagues, in particular in their own work environment,[79] although the extent of that obligation increases with the seniority of the employee. The implied contractual duty (*'vertragliche Nebenpflicht'*) of confidence (*'Verschwiegenheitspflicht'*) can be confirmed and strengthened by an express contractual clause but must not be so broad as to prevent the employee from pursuing his own legitimate interests.[80]

Harte-Bavendamm et al. point out that the contractual duty of confidence (*'Geheimhaltungspflicht'*) continues to bind employees after termination 'within specific limits that must be carefully circumscribed' (*'in gewissen, sorgfältig abzussteckenden Grenzen'*).[81] In effect, the treatment of any such contractual post-termination claim will proceed by way of a balancing of competing interests very similar to the one

77. *See* POS 2010, above n 6, at Zivil. RN 38.
78. Preis & Greiner, *Erfurter Kommentar zum Arbeitsrecht*, above n 74, §611a RN 811.
79. *See* Harte-Bavendamm et al. (2013), above n 18, at Deliktsrecht RN 51.
80. Preis & Greiner, *Erfurter Kommentar zum Arbeitsrecht*, above n 74, §611a RN 817.
81. Harte-Bavendamm et al. (2013), above n 18, at Deliktsrecht. RN 52.

that existed under Article 3 UWG or Articles 823 and 826 BGB. The authors stress that the actual imposition and scope of this duty depend on the facts of the specific case. However, the duty of confidence does weaken with termination, and the authors stress that the BGH has emphasized the narrow scope of its continuing operation.[82]

In balance is the importance of the particular secret to the ex-employer's business versus the significance it realistically has to the ability of the employee to advance his career ('*seinem Fortkommen*'). According to Harte-Bavendamm et al., the jurisprudence of the *Bundesarbeitsgericht* (BAG, the Federal labour and employment court) has adopted a similar approach to the BGH, although without going so far as to effectively impose an obligation not to compete. The authors point out that an ex-employee is free to rely on his knowledge of clients and their requirements as long as he does not rely on retained documented client lists, whereas the BAG sees the right to use and, in particular, to communicate specified core trade secrets of the ex-employer as limited. According to Piper/Ohly/Soznitza, the BAG's jurisprudence holds that the post-contractual duty of good faith (confidence) means that the ex-employee can only make use of know-how ('*berufliches Erfahrungswissen*') and not of actual trade secrets, but the authors refer to this distinction as difficult to make in practice.[83] Interestingly enough, Harte-Bavendamm et al. maintain that this tendency to draw a distinction between what would be referred to as 'know-how' ('*Erfahrungswissen*') in English law and core trade secrets ('*bedeutende konkrete Betriebsgeheimnisse*') has come in for considerable criticism.[84] Nonetheless, they point out that making this distinction is difficult to avoid and something analogous is in fact arrived at by way of the balancing of competing interests adopted in relation to the BGB and which has found its way into the jurisprudence of the BAG.[85]

Piper/Ohly/Sosnitza's position is that in principle the ex-employee is free to use properly acquired trade secrets, but that in an exceptional case, a post-contractual duty of confidence exists. To determine whether it does in any given case requires an evaluation of the Constitutional right of an employer to safeguard his trade secrets (by virtue of Article 14 of the Constitution) and the Constitutional right of the employee to professional advancement (guaranteed by Article 22). Relevant criteria listed by Piper/Ohly/Soznitza are the importance of the secret for the employee's advancement; his previous position and salary; the duration of his employment; the reason for the termination; the existence and scope of possible contractual confidentiality clauses and non-competes; and the way the knowledge was acquired.[86] The distinction, which by itself they consider insufficient, between a genuine trade secret and know-how can also be included as one of the relevant factors.

82. *Ibid.*, RN 53.
83. *See* POS 2010, above n 6, at Zivil. RN 40.
84. *See* Harte-Bavendamm et al. (2013), above n 18, at Deliktsrecht RN 55, referring to Krasser GRUR 1977, 177, 186 and POS 2010, above n 6, para. 17 RN 40.
85. *Ibid.*
86. *See* POS 2010, above n 6, at Zivil. RN 40.

In any case, this area of the law in Germany is beset by the same difficulties and fine judgments as in the common law world and France.[87] In the end, important principles collide and the courts are careful to assess the facts and strike a reasonable balance between freedom of employment and enterprise and a firm's right to secure its operational trade secrets. The implication is the same in Germany as elsewhere that the employer is well advised to clarify and strengthen, within the bounds the law will allow, its position vis-à-vis trade secrets by express contractual provisions. However, such contractual terms must be carefully drafted in Germany not only for the same reasons as apply elsewhere but also because non-compete clauses are regulated by statute. An expansion of the operation of confidentiality clauses thus risks undermining the statutory regulation of non-competes. This regulation, by virtue of Article 74 ff. of the HGB (*Handelsgesetzbuch), inter alia,* imposes restrictions on time, area and scope of a valid non-compete clause and is further considered below. As in the common law, therefore, it is in Germany important to draft confidentiality clauses with concrete reference to particular significant trade secrets rather than in abstract omnibus terms. However, unlike in the common law, the distinction between a genuine trade secret and know-how, difficult as it is, is not the sole determining factor of post-employment liability – a broader evaluation of the circumstances is called for, and this perhaps would please some of the American commentators.[88]

[C] Non-compete Agreements in German Law

In German law, ex-employees are in principles free to use all knowledge properly acquired during previous employment, which also means that they are free to use it to compete with their previous employer. As indicated above, they can, for instance, deal with clients who have become known to them in previous employment or use know-how acquired. Even properly learned actual trade secrets are open to them, subject to the limitations addressed in the previous passages. No aspect of the general law is thus to be regarded as amounting to a prohibition on competition with the ex-employer: not, for instance, Articles 241(2) and 242 of the BGB (obligation of good faith and of respect for the rights of the other party in contractual performance). This results from the fundamental freedom of enterprise and the freedom of professional advancement (*'Fortkommen'*). But it is also implicit in the fact that the Commercial Code (HGB) regulates employment non-compete agreements by imposing particular statutory requirements on them. In the circumstances it would defy logic and practicality to find a non-compete obligation could emerge from the general law that is not subject to these statutory requirements.

87. On this point *see* for a detailed presentation of protection in France, Chapter 7 of this book, and Chapter 9 for a comparative analysis of the issues raised by the protection of trade secrets vis-à-vis employees.
88. Third party liability seems to be a question of the criminal law. Harte-Bavendamm says nothing about the civil liability of third parties, either in terms of individual recipients of information, nor of the civil liability of the new employer. The *'Interessenabwägung'* approach does not apparently leave any room for it.

Article 74 HGB ('*Vertragliches Wettbewerbsverbot*') provides that the validity of a contractual non-compete agreement between employer and employee is subject to a number of conditions: that it be in writing; that a separate document signed by the employer and setting out its terms be provided to the employee; that the employer pay compensation for each year of the non-compete term at a minimum rate of 50% of the employees' final remuneration. It also prescribes that a non-compete concluded with a minor is null and void, as is also the case in some other circumstances. It contains more specific rules concerning payment of the consideration required (*see* Article 74b and 74c). A maximum term of two years is prescribed.

Most relevant in the present context is that by virtue of Article 74a(1), a non-compete is unenforceable in so far as it does not serve to protect a legitimate economic *interest* of the employer. The most interesting issue here is to what extent the protection of company trade secrets is such a legitimate economic interest, which is considered below. Article 74a(1) further provides that the non-compete is also unenforceable to the extent that, in light of the consideration granted, the area, time or extent of the restraint constitutes an undue restriction on the employee's professional advancement ('*eine unbillige Erschwerung des Fortkommens des Gehilfen*').

In terms of the legitimate interests of the firm, the BAG has held that a non-compete in an industry without particular secrets is not enforceable.[89] In a case example provided by Bauer/Diller, the employee concerned was a driving instructor, an industry in which no fixed client base exists for any particular firm.[90] If the only effect is to prevent competition for *future* clients, there is also no secret to protect. Another example provided by Bauer/Diller is that of a top-chef against whom a non-compete was not enforceable as it was not concerned with protection of trade secrets but rather with the elimination of a potential rival.[91] A non-compete will also not be enforceable if the employee can establish that he had no exposure to (the relevant) trade secrets during his employment, which is more likely if the employment relationship was short-term. If the ex-employee questions whether there are trade secrets worthy of protection, the employer will have to identify these sufficiently for the court to understand what is being protected by the non-compete.[92]

The legitimate interest in protecting a trade secret by way of a non-compete also disappears when it becomes public or when it has become irrelevant to the employer, outdated, no longer used, or the employer's business has relevantly changed.[93] According to Bauer/Diller, it is not correct to say that there is no legitimate interest in protecting a trade secret where statutory or contractual obligations of confidentiality suffice.[94]

In a general sense, the law of non-competes is quite extensively regulated, unlike in the other countries considered in this work. In particular, it also differs from the

89. BAG 21/3/1964 AP 15 zu para. 133f GewO.
90. *See* Jobst-Hubertus Bauer & Martin Diller, *Wettbewerbsverbote* (Beck, 9. ed., 2022), RN 312.
91. *See Ibid.*
92. *See* Bauer/Diller, above n 90, at RN 322.
93. *See Ibid.*, at RN 323.
94. *See Ibid.*, at 324, disagreeing with Gaul on this point.

common law countries in that separate consideration is required, and a statutory maximum term is imposed. However, in terms of some of the core judgments required, as to whether a legitimate interest is present and warrants a restraint of a certain term and reach, it is similar to the other jurisdictions and relies on the courts to fill out the law. It seems that the court has quite extensive power to rewrite or limit the clauses; we need to check this. As in other countries, it is often the outcome of the interim or interlocutory application for a temporary injunction that is decisive in matters of enforcement of non-competes, as Kicker illustrates in relation to the famous 'Lopez-scenario'.[95]

§8.05 CONCLUSION

German law stood apart in a number of respects: the definition of trade secret; the statutory regulation of non-competes; the freedom-in-principle of ex-employees to use both know-how and properly acquired trade secrets of their previous employer; the limits on reverse engineering; and the extensive but circumscribed reach of the criminal law. In contrast, civil liability in Germany was not governed by statute in any great detail, relying on what are in effect broad statements of principle elaborated by the courts.

These specificities have partly disappeared with the enactment of the *GeschGehG* due to the harmonization imposed by the European directive, notably as regards the definition of trade secrets, the legalization of reverse engineering practices and, more profoundly, the establishment of a much more detailed civil framework. The German legislator has decided to go further than what was imposed by the Directive, bringing criminal law into line with the civil system to ensure the overall coherence of the German legal framework. In general, the consequences of these changes have brought protection under German law very significantly closer to that existing under American law without the German legislator having sought such a rapprochement.

German law has nonetheless retained several specific features, particularly regarding the definition of trade secrets. The German legislator has maintained a condition of legitimate interest, which was established by case law prior to the European Directive. Similarly, when it comes to regulating employee-employer relations concerning trade secrets, German law has – for the time being, as far as extra-contractual protection is concerned – not been affected by European law. The '*Interessenabwägung*' in the post-employment phase is as complex and fact-specific as the common law approaches the conflict between ex-employee and ex-employer. Therefore, in this crucial area of law, the greater prescription and clarity so often associated with the German legal system is absent. However, employers who are prepared to pay proper consideration for it can bind their departing employees effectively with a properly drafted and statutorily compliant non-compete. Due to the

95. *See* Jürgen Kicker, *Festschrift fur Henning Piper* (Beck, 1996) '*Problematik des Beschäftigungsverbot als Nachlese zum "Lopez-Szenario"*'.

more regulated approach to the latter, they are probably more robust than their equivalents in some of the common law jurisdictions.

Overall, comparing French and German law after the transposition of the European Directive highlights both the strengths and weaknesses of this regulatory instrument. While the Directive has indeed facilitated significant harmonization of the civil legal framework, it has overlooked critical areas of protection, such as how employee-related issues are addressed, and the intermeshing with criminal law. The former oversight is particularly blameworthy, as the regulation of the post-employment constellation in particular is fundamental for ensuring the free movement of workers, a signature ambition of the European single market. Finally, although the choice of a directive aims to respect the legislative traditions of Member States, it has the drawback of allowing divergences to arise during the transposition process. This is where the European Court of Justice could play a fundamental role in further enhancing the level of harmonization between legal system, in particular given that the provisions of the Directive are broad.

CHAPTER 9

Trade Secrets and Employees

§9.01 INTRODUCTION

In our society, knowledge and information are most often shared within firms and organizations, in other words, by employees. Unsurprisingly, therefore, this is where most conflicts arise and where trade secrets law is most important: 'Firms whose profits depend upon trade secrets typically consider their workers a potential threat to the firm's interests. Indeed, one would not be wrong in concluding that the historical impetus for trade secret law was to restrain employees from competing with their employers.'[1] However, during employment, the civil liability of employees is governed more by the express or implied contractual duty of fidelity and sometimes more extensive fiduciary-type obligations. These are more employment law-related issues, although the criminal law of trade secrets may also play a role in relation to existing employees (e.g., the offence of '*Verrat*' of a manufacturing or trade secret under the Swiss Criminal Code section 162).

By contrast, after an employment contract terminates, the general law of trade secrets governs the use of knowledge and information. However, at that time, its operation was modulated by the universally recognized freedom of individuals to work where, how and for whom they choose and also to compete with their previous employers. This basic freedom is expressed in various forms in the jurisdictions here considered: freedom of personal advancement ('*Fortkommen*') in Germany, the freedom first guaranteed by the *Décret d'Allarde* in France, and the freedom to compete recognized more instrumentally in longstanding common law decisions.

Freedom of employment is of course less meaningful if the employee is not allowed to draw on the knowledge, know-how and experience acquired on the job. Various IP regimes affect this control or conversely the ability of individuals to freely

1. *See* Geraldine Szott Moohr, 'The Problematic Role of Criminal Law in Regulating the Use of Information: the Case of the Economic Espionage Act' (2002) 80 *North Carolina Law Review* 853, 903.

draw on all their 'knowledge assets'. Statutory rules concerning ownership of proprietary knowledge (copyright, designs, patents) are very important,[2] but the default rules of trade secrets law are also very significant and concern not only recorded information but also knowledge 'in the mind' of employees.

Although the general law plays an important role post-employment, in reality, contract law is often determinative, most significantly, not only through the medium of non-compete clauses in employment contracts but also through express confidentiality clauses or settlement deeds which have intended application post-termination.

As was explained above, trade secrets law differs considerably from country to country, as civilian jurisdictions traditionally relied on 'unfair competition' torts or statutes, whereas common law countries adopt an equitable (England) or misappropriation (US) method. The latter method has now been adopted by the EU in its Trade Secrets Directive and consequently in EU countries. And yet the law *universally* strives to strike a balance between the interests of a former employer in protecting its commercial interests by upholding a degree of secrecy and the freedom of employees to find work and use all their knowledge, skills and experience, whether in competition with their previous employer or not. This chapter explores the very significant complex of rules that apply to post-termination use of knowledge acquired during employment, with a particular focus on the common law jurisdictions. Aspects of the relevant law relating to the civilian jurisdictions are dealt with more extensively in the chapters relating to German and French law, respectively. The EU Trade Secrets Directive did not address this area of law expressly.

The traditional motivation for restricting the reach of general trade secrets law and the law of contracts in the post-termination phase lies in basic rights and freedoms: the freedom to work; the freedom of enterprise and competition; the right to personal advancement and self-realization; and the freedom of communication. But the policy interest can also be explained in instrumental terms: workers who cannot use knowledge previously acquired may not be able to generate the income to support themselves and their families; they will not be as able to accumulate skill and knowledge to the benefit of themselves and the productivity of society; they will be less attractive to prospective employers; and their investment in knowledge acquisition and training will be rendered unproductive. In any case, whereas employers might gain from restricting their departing employees from using all they have learned, they will also suffer from those restrictions when hiring new employees from other firms, so in the balance, there might be little gained from an approach that is too restrictive. Democratic societies with free markets value the free circulation and diffusion of knowledge, both for its own sake and because this freedom supports social, commercial, scientific and technological advances. In this context, firms are learning environments within which individual employees interact to both transfer knowledge to others

2. *See, e.g.*, the debate concerning ownership of academic inventions, recently enlivened by the Australian decisions in *University of Western Australia v. Gray (No 20)* [2008] FCA 498 (French J); *University of Western Australia v. Gray* [2009] FCAFC 116 (Lindgren, Finn and Bennett JJ).

and receive it from them.[3] These transfers happen not only by the exchange of documented information but also the mobility between organizations of employees with knowledge. Firms who hire new people acquire new knowledge, and conversely, employees who leave diminish the knowledge stock of the firm.

However, the axiomatic principle that firms cannot control employees' movements could act as a disincentive for investment in R&D and accumulation of knowledge, as the latter potentially migrates freely with departing employees.[4] It could also result in excessive secrecy and restraints on the sharing of information within firms. Thus, the law of trade secrets gives firms a necessary level of control in relation to knowledge and information in the possession of departing employees, as does the law of contract relating to confidentiality clauses and non-competes. The nexus between the latter and trade secrets lies in the fact that courts universally accept reasonable non-competes only if the employer can establish a legitimate interest to protect, one of which is the integrity of trade secrets the employee may have come across. It should be noted that although the law tends to enforce reasonable non-competes, there is an international trend later discussed towards further restricting non-competes by legislative intervention.

§9.02 RELEVANT AREAS OF LAW AND THE USE OF KNOWLEDGE AFTER TERMINATION

Multiple legal regimes impact the right to use information post-termination. Apart from the ownership rules of the proprietary regimes,[5] the relevant areas are trade secrets or unfair competition law, contract law, the law relating to non-compete (or 'restraint of

3. In the firm, employees not only part-bargain for the privilege of learning from the employer (i.e., from other employees) but also contribute to the firm environment as 'teachers' of knowledge or know how. The fact that employees in firms are bound by duties of fidelity and confidentiality encourages them to be open and unrestrained in their exchanges.
4. *See, e.g.*, Jarle Moen, 'Is Mobility of Technical Personnel a Source of R&D Spillovers?' (2005) 23(1) *Journal of Labour Economics* 81 https://doi.org/10.1086/425434; Rajshree Agarwal, Martin Ganco & Rosemarie H. Ziedonis, 'Reputations for Toughness in Patent Enforcement: Implications for Knowledge Spillovers via Inventor Mobility' (2009) 30(13) *Strategic Management Journal* 1349 https://doi.org/10.1002/smj.792. The question of the effect of physical proximity on innovation also emerges in the literature on clustering for innovation: *see, e.g.*, Christopher Arup, 'Split Entitlements? Intellectual Property Policy for Clusters and Networks' in Christopher Arup & William van Caenegem (eds), *Intellectual Property Policy Reform: Fostering Innovation and Development* (Edward Elgar, 2009) 285. In countries with a rigid labour market innovation seems to suffer: *see* William van Caenegem, 'Inventions in Russia: From Public Good to Private Property' (1993) 4 *Australian Intellectual Property Journal* 232. This difficulty was identified by Arrow who saw labour mobility as a source of information diffusion in the context of an analysis of the public-good qualities of knowledge: *see* Kenneth J. Arrow, 'Economic Welfare and the Allocation of Resources for Invention' in Richard R. Nelson (ed.), *The Rate and Direction of Inventive Activity* (Princeton University Press, 1962).
5. The rules concerning ownership of IPR's are also a less harmonized aspect of IP law. *See* R. Merges, 'The Law and Economics of Employee Inventions' (1999) 13(1) *Harvard Journal of Law and Technology* 2; in relation to universities, *see* Ann Monotti & Sam Ricketson, *Universities and Intellectual Property: Ownership and Exploitation* (Oxford University Press, 2003).

trade' clauses), and labour law.[6] However, the criminal law also plays a role in many jurisdictions, as does corporations law, as it determines the duties of company officers and employees in some places.[7] There is no great uniformity in either the mix or structure of the legal regimes for trade secrets in general or in relation to the specific post-employment phase: the non-contractual obligations of former employees are governed by equity in the UK and Australia;[8] mostly by statutory misappropriation provisions in the US;[9] by unfair competition law and the civil codes in many civil law jurisdictions;[10] and sometimes by sui generis regimes.[11] Within some countries, such as the US or Australia, the law varies between states, provinces or other sub-national levels. Nor does a common civilian heritage guarantee uniformity of approach. Some jurisdictions are hybrid in character.[12] In certain jurisdictions, employment or commercial law plays a greater role than in others, either by direct regulation or because it

6. Restraints of trade attract a distinct kind of public policy intervention in contractual bargains. *See, e.g.*, Alan Hyde, *Working in Silicon Valley: Economic and Legal Analysis of a High-Velocity Labor Market* (ME Sharpe, 2003); Michael V. Risch, 'Comments on Trade Secrets in High Velocity Labor Markets' (2009) 12(2) *Employee Rights and Employment Policy Journal* 339.
7. For example, in Australia, *see Corporations Law 2001* (Cth) s.183: *Use of Information – Directors, Other Officers and Employees*; s. 184: *Good faith, Use of Position and Use of Information – Criminal Offences*. Corporate law is not further considered in this book.
8. And other countries with a similar legal heritage, such as New Zealand. On the wide range of approaches *see, e.g.*, Kelly Irene Phair, 'Enabling American High-tech Companies to Protect Their Trade Secrets Abroad: A Comparative Analysis of Irish and American Trade Secret Regulation' (2001) 24(3) *Hastings International and Comparative Law Review* 507. As to common law jurisdictions in general *see* Allison Coleman, *The Legal Protection of Trade Secrets* (Sweet & Maxwell, 1992); Francis Gurry, *Breach of Confidence* (Clarendon, revised ed., 1993); Robert Dean, *The Law of Trade Secrets and Personal Secrets* (Lawbook Company, 2002); more specifically also Robert Dean, *Employers, Ex-employees and Trade Secrets* (Lawbook Company, 2004). For general comparative studies *see* Herman Cohen Jehoram (ed.), *The Protection of Know-how in 13 Countries* (Kluwer, 1972); Richard Schloetter, *Der Schutz von Betriebs- und Geschaftsgeheimnissen und die Abwerbung von Arbeitnehmern, Eine rechtsvergleichende Untersuchung des englischen, franzosichen und deutschen rechts* (Carl Heymans Verlag, Koln, 1997); & François Dessemontet, *Protection of Trade Secrets and Confidential Information* (1998) http://www.unil.ch/webdav/site/cedidac/shared/Articles/Protection%20Trade%20Secrets.pdf.
9. *See* the *UTSA*, now adopted by 45 of the states of the US. This Act is only concerned with civil liability, and not criminal offences; *see* in relation to criminal law, for the US, the *Economic Espionage Act* (1996) (18 USC. §1831-1839), a federal statute; and state laws, as discussed in Chapter 5.
10. For instance in Holland, *see* Feer Verkade D.W., *Ongeoorloofde mededinging* (1978), Tjeenk Willink Zwolle, Chapter X: 'Afhandig maken van personeel, know-how en vaste clientele'; in Germany, *see* Harte-Bavendamm & Henning-Bodewig, *Gesetz gegen den unlauteren Wettbewerb* (2. Aufl, Beck, 2009), in particular concerning *UWG* §17 Abs 1, *Verrat von Geschäfts- und Betriebsgeheimnissen*; *see also* Chapter 7. This work also contains extensive commentary on the law of other EU member countries (*see* pp. 275ff.); in Belgium, *see* Mireille Buydens, *Droits des brevets d'invention et protection du savoir faire* (Larcier, 1999) (in particular Chapitre II *'Protection du savoir-faire et des secrets de fabrique')*; and in France, *see* Yves Serra (ed.), *La Concurrence Déloyale, Permanence et Devenir, Thèmes et Commentaires* (Dalloz, 2001); Philippe Le Tourneau, *Le Parasitisme: Notion, prévention, protections* (Litec, 1998); Chapter 6.
11. As for instance in Sweden, *see* the *Act on the Protection of Business Secrets* (FHL), at present under review by the Swedish parliament: *see Förstärkt skydd för företagshemligheter*, SOU 2008:63 http://www.sweden.gov.se/sb/d/10025/a/106952.
12. *See* for instance, as to the situation in South Africa, Johann Knobel, 'Wrongfulness of Trade Secret Misappropriation; and Trade Secrets as Objects of Subjective Rights' (2000) *Acta Juridica* 196. The law in South Africa invokes the Roman *lex Aquilia*, which relates to commercial

governs relevant aspects of the contract of employment. Thus, the treatment of non-compete clauses is affected by labour law and commercial law statutes in some countries and in others by collective bargains.[13] Although in many, it remains purely case-based, recent developments in the US, the UK and Australia have seen a tendency towards statutory intervention to limit contractual restraints on employee mobility.[14]

This all adds up to a complex and unsettled legal picture in relation to post-termination trade secrets cases and contracts. [A] The Use of Information during Employment Penal trade secrets provisions apply to existing employees in all jurisdictions here considered other than the traditional common law countries such as England and Australia. However, in terms of civil liability, the relevant duties of employees are classified more as labour law and contract than trade secrets law.[15] During employment, the contract of employment is the primary source of employees' obligations. Implicit contractual duties of fidelity or good faith circumscribe the use of *any* information that is of relevance to the employer, not just trade secrets. Their duties are thus broader and of a different character than those governed by trade secrets law, which persists in its effect after termination. How the duty of good faith affects the use of information is intimately linked with the right of any given employee to undertake other work or compete with their employer.[16] Whereas employees are universally subject to a broad contractual duty of fidelity, some employees with general management positions may be held to a higher standard of loyalty to their employer,

conduct; *see also* as to the situation in Quebec, Julie A. Thornton & Keith G. Fairbairn, *Law of Confidential Business Information* (Law Book Co, 2010) 4.

13. My thanks to Prof Reinhold Fahlbeck of Lund University for comments concerning collective bargaining and non-competes in Sweden, during a seminar held at Lund University. In Germany Arts 74 and 75 of the Commercial Code (HGB) contains mandatory rules; *see Bauer*, Jobst-Hubertus & *Diller*, Martin, *Wettbewerbsverbote* (Beck, 5th ed., 2009). And *see* Chapter 7; for Holland and Belgium *see* Jeroen P. Quist, *Het concurrentiebeding nader beschouwd* (Boom, Den Haag, 2004).
14. Although on the whole employment law is more concerned with the obligations of employees during employment, in fact, certain forms of conduct while employed may have legal repercussions after termination. For instance, a surreptitious gathering of information during employment may be the kind of breach of a duty of fidelity or fiduciary duty that founds a remedy against a former employee for misuse of the confidential information concerned; *see also* in Germany, the persistence of some aspects of the contractual duty of fidelity, *see* Chapter 7. As for statutory intervention in non-competes law, in the United States, *see* Federal Trade Commission, 'Non-compete Clause Rule' *Federal Register* (online) 5 July 2024, https://www.federalregister.gov/documents/2024/05/07/2024-09171/non-compete-clause-rule. In the United Kingdom *see* United Kingdom Department of Business & Trade, 'Non-compete Clauses: Response to the Government Consultation on Measures to Reform Post-termination Non-compete Clauses in Contracts of Employment' *United Kingdom Government* (online) 12 May 2023, https://assets.publishing.service.gov.uk/media/645e27612c06a30013c05c57/non-compete-government-response.pdf. In Australia, *see* Australian Government Treasury, 'Worker Non-compete Clauses and Other Restraints' *The Treasury* (online) 2024, https://treasury.gov.au/consultation/c2024-514668.
15. However, a strict demarcation is not always observed since some breaches of specified fiduciary duties or obligations of fidelity committed during employment can found remedies awarded when a former employee is sued after termination. *See* the discussion in this regard in *Del Casale & Ors v. Artedomus (Aust) Pty Limited* [2007] NSWCA 172.
16. A useful volume for comparative information concerning employees' obligations during employment is *Comparative Labor Law and Policy Journal* (1999) 20(2) 'The Duty of Loyalty' with articles on many countries.

sometimes referred to as 'fiduciary' in common law countries, which further limits their ability to do other work, compete with the employer, benefit personally from information received professionally, or divert certain opportunities to their own advantage.[17] Implicitly, this limits the scope of permitted use of any information obtained or generated during employment.

After termination, the employee is either no longer bound by implied contractual duties or, to a much lesser extent.[18] The legal rights of the employer become much more narrowly based. Any remedy for misuse of information post-termination will be based either on the general law applying to trade secrets, the specific provisions of some criminal laws, or contractual provisions expressly drafted to be enforceable after termination, principally confidentiality and non-compete clauses. Employees acquire a great deal of knowledge from the firm that they can turn to their own or other firms' advantage after termination: what are the limitations on them doing so? Can a former employer reach in and restrain a former employee from using some knowledge or information she has allegedly acquired while with the firm? Alternatively, can a former employer impede a new *employer's* right to draw on all the knowledge a new employee has brought with her?

Courts are generally on guard against actions which invoke protection of trade secrets with an actual intention to do no more than prevent competition by former employees.[19] Any limitation on workers' freedom to pursue their own interests, choose work and deploy *all* their talents and experience *to the full* is perceived as only justified by a clear interest of an employer to protect an important trade secret.[20]

In most jurisdictions, this will require the court at some point to draw a line between trade secrets which 'belong' to the firm and the general knowledge, know-how and experience any employee unavoidably accumulates. Differentiating between 'trade secrets' and 'know-how' is the traditional approach in common law-based jurisdictions. Because information is seamless and interconnected, and what is learned

---

17. Although in UK, Canadian and Australian case law (and perhaps elsewhere) a distinction is made between the contractual (implied) duty of fidelity owed by every employee, and the higher level fiduciary duty owed by professional or high level employees, some scholars argue that there is only one undivided fiduciary duty, of which the so-called duty of fidelity is but a subspecies. *See* Robert Flannigan, 'The (Fiduciary) Duty of Fidelity' (2008) 124 *Law Quarterly Review* 274 (*see also* other writings by the same author, e.g., 'The Fiduciary Duty of Departing Employees' (2009) 14 *Canadian Labour & Employment Law Journal* 356). *See also* Matthew Conaglen, *Fiduciary Loyalty* (Hart, 2010). It is perhaps the case that some employees owe particular fiduciary duties which may be individually pleaded, rather than a general fiduciary duty.
18. In Germany for instance, there is a degree of persistence of the contractual duty of fidelity after termination: *see* Chapter 7.
19. In *Industrial Rollformers Pty Ltd & v. Ingersoll-Rand (Australia) Ltd* [2001] NSWCA 111 Giles JA put it as follows:

    > A restraint is not unreasonable in the interests of the public simply because part of its operation protects the promisee against competition, although a restraint which does no more than protect against competition will not be upheld [citations omitted].

20. *See* Joellen Riley, 'Commodifying Sheer Talent: Perverse Developments in the Law's Enforcement of Restrictive Covenants' in Christopher Arup & William van Caenegem (eds), *Intellectual Property Policy Reform: Fostering Innovation and Development* (Edward Elgar, 2009) 267.

cannot be unlearned, this is often a difficult task. Evidentiary hurdles are high where the information or knowledge concerned is not in a recorded form, where there is no document, file, data storage device or the like allegedly in the possession of a former employee. Courts tend to favour employees where information is mixed because they rate the freedom to work so highly, and they are reluctant to restrain former employees from using an alleged trade secret that will have the effect of also restraining the use of other 'free' knowledge or information. They are, therefore, usually not satisfied by ambit claims based on abstract descriptors ('the trade secrets', the 'confidential information', etc.) of the trade secrets claimed. Nor is it the case that because information is unique to an employer, it is necessarily a trade secret to the standard of the law. Its uniqueness can be coincidental, irrelevant or unidentified by an employer at the time, and a court will not be sympathetic to a claimant who nonetheless, *ex post*, decides that it was a significant trade secret a former employee should not be able to use. Hence, the significance of being able to demonstrate reasonable measures to maintain the secrecy of particular information.

In the civilian jurisdictions here considered the situation is somewhat different. In Germany, the principle is that a former employee is free to use all acquired knowledge, including real trade secrets of the previous employer. Some other civilian jurisdictions, such as the Netherlands, are also favourably disposed towards the employee: there is only a very narrow category of actionable cases.[21] Nonetheless, the relevant Law on Unfair Competition and Civil Code provisions might have the effect of rendering the use or imparting of particular trade secrets actionable; this is a matter for individuals weighing up in any given case, as addressed in the relevant chapter. In France also, there is controversy about the practicability of a strict 'separation approach', and the issue of use of a trade secret post-termination is considered, taking into account all the circumstances so as to determine whether or not it amounts to unfair competition.

§9.03 KNOW-HOW AND TRADE SECRETS IN THE ENGLISH LAW TRADITION

In the English common law, which relies on the concept of 'confidential information', the term 'trade secret' is not a general term of art to whose protection special conditions attach.[22] However, there is one context in which the term 'trade secret' does amount to a term of art, and that is in the case of an action against a former employee. A distinction is here drawn between a trade secret on the one hand, protected in the hands of the employer, and 'know-how' on the other, which 'belongs' to the employee. One of the main tasks of a court in such cases is to draw this line and decide whether certain information is a trade secret or mere know-how that falls outside the scope of

21. *See* above n 10.
22. Although in one context this is perhaps not quite the case, where 'trade secrets' are in the employment context contrasted to 'know-how', the latter 'belonging' to the employee.

a former employer's control. However, in the civilian tradition, know-how (or '*savoir faire*') is a term used to designate information that may be protected as a trade secret – in other words, it is what falls within and not outside the *patrimonium* of the employer. Certainly, in common law jurisdictions, the requirements that: the alleged trade secrets are properly particularized; the private nature of each individual item is established; the measures taken to defend them are proven; and legal obligations are made clear to the employee at the time, mean that it is not easy for an employer to prove that some information is not just free know-how.[23] Often, courts either openly or surreptitiously have recourse to a rule of thumb, which is of dubious doctrinal stature but has been present in the English law since *Robb v. Green*:[24] if the employee cannot be shown to have made a deliberate and surreptitious effort to acquire information in recorded form, there is a good likelihood that she will be able to continue to use all she has learned. Be that as it may, separating trade secrets from know-how is inherently fraught with conceptual and practical difficulties. In the US, where the same distinction is made, these difficulties are augmented by differences between states and the additional federal layer. As a result, trade secrets litigation is high risk and high cost in any case, but most certainly if it is against former employees.[25] Further, time is often of the essence, so that as proceedings become more drawn out they become less and less fruitful.

To determine whether a former employee or their new employer has engaged in unfair competition or triggered statutory or general civil liability, courts everywhere have to tread a fine line between competing basic rights and interests. Therefore, a whole series of circumstantial factors will be considered to determine every instance on a case-by-case basis. The deliberation with which an employee has acted to record or collect information before departing will be considered: an employee using knowledge naturally acquired to further their career after termination does not normally act in bad faith.[26] But this is only one relevant factor: others are whether it is more in the nature of a distinct trade secret or general skill and know-how: its importance to the previous employer, the level of appointment of the employee, the real need to use a particular trade secret in new employment, the duration of previous employment, etc. The outcome of such cases, where freedom of work and competition and the right to protect business assets clash, is always difficult to predict.

In any case, courts tend to be reluctant to impose an injunction where prohibiting the use of some particular item of knowledge would have a deleterious effect on the individual's ability to pursue a career because it is inextricably linked to 'free'

23. *GlaxoSmithKline Australia Pty Ltd v. Ritchie* [2008] VSC 164.
24. [1895] 2 QB 315.
25. In this regard *see, e.g.*, Wendi S. Lazar, 'Employment Agreements and Cross Border Employment: Confidentiality, Trade Secret, and Other Restrictive Covenants in a Global Economy' (2008-2009) 24 *The Labor Lawyer* 195.
26. This sometimes takes the form of warning that if too much scope is given to unfair competition concepts such as '*parasitisme*', the concept of IPRs may be undermined: for instance, Larrieu points out that the concept of '*parasitisme*' in cases of alleged misuse of know-how must be treated with care because if taken too far it undermines the whole edifice of IPR's. *See* Jacques Larrieu, '*Un an de concurrence déloyale*', Chronique, Propriété Industrielle No 6, Juin 2009, chron. 5.

know-how. Courts do not like injunctions that are in practice embarrassing or unworkable, a point made in civilian jurisdictions as well, as knowledge cannot be unlearned.[27] Nonetheless, it may also be that in light of the unfair competition approach, the subsequent employer, rather than a former employee, is more often the proper respondent. This is particularly the case in France, but seemingly not in Germany. This was not on the basis of knowing third-party participation in the breach,[28] but because competing by taking unfair advantage of trade secrets obtained from a new recruit may be considered to fall below the standards of honest trade the new employer should observe. The clearest cases involve deliberately hiring them with a view to obtaining valuable information from them, and that is where a competitive situation exists between the two employers. The European Directive was not intended to regulate aspects relating to employees. However, following the American example, it has imposed liability on third parties who have knowledge of the infringement. In the future, it will be interesting to see whether legal systems such as France will maintain the specificity of a special wrong implying 'direct' liability on the part of the new employer in previously mentioned cases or will align their case law towards responsibility by 'ricochet'.

27. *See* for example the Dutch decision *Gerechtshof te Arnhem, Eerste Kamer*, Nr 65, 14 Juli 1982 (*Vredestein Doetinchem v. Dam, Siemes & Thijssen*), in *Bijblad Industriele Eigendom*, 16 juni 1983, 179. This striking passage is illustrative: '*Die know-how, die mede bevatte hetgeen [the respondent ex-employees] zelf in appellante's dienst hadden ontwikkeld, was in hun persoon belichaamd, en zij mochten die know-how, nu geen concurrentiebeding noch een geheimhoudingsplicht gold, hetzij voor zichzelf hetzij voor een nieuwe werkgever aanwenden, ook al zou die know-how gedurende de tijd dat zij bij appellante werkzaam waren kunnen worden aangemerkt als know-how van appellante. Het zou onredelijk zijn … te vergen dat zij niet de huns inziens meest juiste en/of efficiente werkwijze zouden blijven toepassen, ook al is hun die werkwijze bekend geworden in hun werkkring bij appellante.*' (p. 182) In translation: '*That know-how which included things [the respondents] had themselves developed, was incorporated in their own person, and they were entitled, as there is no non-compete or confidentiality clause, to use this know-how either for themselves or for a new employer, even though this know-how could have been considered as belonging to the appellant [ex-employer] during the period they were employed there. It would be unreasonable to demand that they should not continue to use the most correct and/or efficient methods, even accepting that these methods came to be known by them in their working environment with the appellant*'. In an analogous statement, the Court of Appeal of Paris, said: *qu'une société qui prend le risque de se séparer de techniciens éminents et qui ne leur impose pas une obligation de non concurrence n'est pas fondée a se plaindre qu'ils n'aient pas été atteints d'amnésie et qu'ils utilisent, hors de tout secret de fabrique ou de toute formule confidentielle constituant un savoir-faire, leurs connaissances personnelles*. In translation: '*That a company that risks termination of eminent technicians and does not bind them by a non-compete has no basis for a complaint that they were not struck by amnesia and that they use their personal knowledge, no including genuine trade secrets*'. *See Propriété Industrielle*, Février 2005, pp. 34, 35, CA Paris, 4ieme ch., s. A, 5 Mai 2004, Rexam c MT Packaging (with comment by Schmidt-Szalewski and Viennois).
28. Knowing participation is the basis for third party liability in the common law; i.e., actual or constructive knowledge that the information was passed on in breach of an obligation of confidence. If a restraint exists, a new employer may also be held liable for inducement of contract breach by a former employee. *See* further below.

As a result, actions against former employees based on the general law, whether in breach of confidence, misappropriation or unfair competition, are often unappealing. Strong countervailing policy goals and legal complexities combine with evidentiary difficulties to augment cost, risk and uncertainty. That does not mean that astute and well-resourced employers will not be able to use trade secret-invoking letters of demand, interim applications, etc., to effectively deter former employees from competing. Employers can also improve their chances markedly by having appropriate strategies and policies in place, such as monitoring circulation of secret information, controlling access, requiring confidentiality undertakings in writing, reviewing contracts, documenting trade secrets as codicils to employment contracts, etc. Properly documenting and identifying information is important not only for the sake of establishing that certain information is indeed a trade secret but also because a putative injunction will have to be framed in terms that are precise enough to be observed. The person under restraint must know with precision and certainty what information can or cannot be used. Courts are astute to ensure that any order they make is clear and certain, and therefore a former employer who cannot exactly particularize the information concerned will face considerable difficulties convincing a court to grant an injunction.

In these circumstances, contractual provisions are a more attractive option for employers, and these fall into two main categories: confidentiality clauses and non-competes (restraints of trade). Above all, the latter approach is favoured by employers because its potential ambit is much broader than just preventing the use of specific information. But everywhere, non-competes come under considerable judicial scrutiny, and a large body of case law has arisen. In civilian jurisdictions, the law also tends towards a more regulatory and prescriptive approach, in particular, in Germany. Non-solicitation clauses, non-poaching clauses and the like are here considered sub-categories of non-competes.

§9.04 CONTRACTUAL DEVICES

[A] Confidentiality Clauses

Confidentiality clauses seek to identify, clarify, or contractually extend (beyond the default general law position) the information classified as a trade secret and introduce express legal obligations for employees during employment, but more relevantly, also after termination.

Such clauses can be effective where the firm has clearly identifiable secrets at the time of engagement, the details of which can be particularized in (or attached to) the contract of employment, or a separate deed. They are an important indicator to a court that an employer has *treated* information as a trade secret, as the law tends to require. But it can be challenging to document as yet unidentifiable information that may be generated during the future course of employment with sufficient particularity and also to amend confidentiality clauses in line with the changing duties and responsibilities of an employee. Most employees' duties or positions evolve during the course of their employment, but tracking, amendment and documentation of changing legal obligations is often incomplete.

Choosing abstract terms ('the trade secrets', 'confidential information', etc.) as contractual descriptors does little to relieve the difficulties described above of properly identifying trade secrets, showing they have been effectively guarded, and distinguishing them from free know-how or public domain information. A further problem with abstract descriptors is that they may be so broad as to amount to an illegal and unenforceable restraint of trade or competition because they tend to cover the use of an employee's ordinary stock of knowledge.[29] In civilian jurisdictions as well, a very broad confidentiality clause might be considered a non-compete agreement and, therefore, will be governed by the prescriptions that apply to such agreements. It is also not possible to turn public domain information into a trade secret that must be kept confidential by contractual *fiat*.[30]

As a result, there may be little difference between attempting to enforce a confidentiality clause expressed in broad and abstract terms and bringing an action for misuse or misappropriation of a trade secret. That at least is true in terms of the elements of the action, even if there may be relevant differences in terms of the remedies sought and awarded.

[B] Non-compete Clauses

The main alternative for firms is to protect their position by binding employees with a non-compete clause (sometimes referred to as a restraint of trade in the English context, although particular rules attach to restraints of trade in the employment context). These are a contractual device common to all jurisdictions, but are attended with difficulties because they are hostile to the public interest. The drafting, adoption and enforcement of non-compete clauses is everywhere constrained by a dense thicket of laws, whether statute or case-based. More recently, the topic has attracted considerable academic and policy interest and reform, not least in the US; this is a topic further addressed below. The law relating to non-compete clauses in France and Germany is dealt with in the relevant chapters, and the passages below, therefore, mostly focus on the common law jurisdictions.[31]

Although an individual employee may consider the signing of a non-compete to be in his or her own interest, the proliferation of such agreements would clearly be detrimental to the public interest in freedom of competition and employment. Whether or not the employee fully realizes it at the time of signing, they also stunt the development of an individual's skill and knowledge and risk leaving him or her with a

29. *See Electrolux Ltd v. Hudson* [1977] FSR 312. The 'restraint of trade' doctrine prima facie invalidates *any* restraint of trade, not just ones in employment contracts, as pointed out in Linda Tompkins, 'Confidentiality Agreements in a Commercial Setting: Are They Necessary?' (2008) 27(2) *Australian Resources and Energy Law Journal* 198.
30. *See Maggbury Pty Ltd v. Hafele Aust Pty Ltd* [2001] HCA 70; 210 CLR 181 and its consideration of this issue in an analogous context.
31. For more detail concerning the law in France *see* Chapter 6; the law in Germany Chapter 7.

reduced career and income potential.[32] Therefore, they are everywhere subject to close judicial oversight. In England, Lord Denning nicely explained a principle that goes back to the crucial case of *Nordenfelt:*[33]

> Every member of the community is entitled to carry on any trade or business he chooses and in such manner as he thinks most desirable in his own interests, so long as he does nothing unlawful: with the consequence that any contract which interferes with the free exercise of his trade or business, by restricting him in the work he may do for others, or the arrangements which he may make with others, is a contract in restraint of trade. It is invalid unless it is reasonable as between the parties and not injurious to the public interest.[34]

Although this is changing in the US, all countries here considered have allowed non-competes but only under relatively strict conditions. In some countries, these conditions or limitations are crafted by the courts acting as guardians of the public interest (or 'public policy grounds'), whereas in others, statutory conditions are also attached to the enforcement of non-competes, and the interests at stake are considered more in terms of fundamental human rights.

It is important to realize that the difficulty with enforcement of contractual non-competes does not lie in the quality of the bargain – duress, deceit, unconscionability, etc., are not the problem. Courts will intervene in what otherwise are perfectly valid agreements. They do not do so in the individual's interest (he or she might have gained a lot from signing up for the restraint and/or done it perfectly willingly or knowingly) but in the public interest.[35] This judicial willingness to override contractual autonomy is perhaps more surprising in common law countries, given their traditional reluctance to police clauses arrived at by competent autonomous parties and not affected by specific vitiating factors.[36] But nonetheless. it is well established there and rarely comes under serious principled attack.[37]

---

32. *See* however, for an original alternative approach, which considers this topic in terms of alienability of human capital, and the restraints which the law imposes on it, Stewart E. Sterk, 'Restraints on Alienation of Human Capital' (1993) 79 *Virginia Law Review* 383 https://doi.org/10.2307/1073417. Not only is the law reluctant to enforce non-compete clauses, it also refuses generally to order specific performance of employment contracts.
33. *Nordenfelt v. Maxim Nordenfelt Guns and Ammunition Co* [1894] AC 535.
34. *See Petrofina (Great Britain) Ltd v. Martin* [1966] Ch 146, at 169.
35. *See* concerning Belgium and Holland, above n 13. Concerning Germany *see* Günter Schaub et al., *Arbeitsrechts-Handbuch* (Beck, München, 2007), §58 '*Wettbewerbsbeschränkungen nach beendigung des Arbeitsverhältnisses*' and Bauer & Diller, above n 13. In France, Marc Gomy, 'L'autonomie de la clause de non-concurrence post-contractuelle en droit du travail', in *Etudes sur le droit de la concurrence et quelques themes fondamentaux, Melanges en l'honneur d'Yves Serra* (Dalloz, 2006).
36. Sanctity of contract and contractual autonomy are traditional mainstays of common law contract theory. Normally the courts do not upset the bargain unless it is vitiated by unconscionability, duress, fraud or the like. However, the courts do vary or strike down unreasonable restraints even though the bargaining parties are capable and well advised. *See* Maureen B. Callahan, Comment, 'Post-Employment Restraint Agreements: A Reassessment' (1985) 52 *University of Chicago Law Review* 703 https://doi.org/10.2307/1599633.
37. The comments of Callinan J in *Maggbury Pty Ltd v. Hafele Aust Pty Ltd* [2001] HCA 70; 210 CLR 181; 185 ALR 152; 76 ALJR 246, [93] notwithstanding; in particular, [94]: '*People who enter into agreements intended to be legally binding cannot credibly be heard to say that they did so relying*

A significant rule is that a non-compete will not be enforced if there is no valid interest to protect – an interest going beyond mere protection against competition. The two valid interests recognized universally are the securing of genuine trade secrets and 'client connection', although the so-called stability of the workforce is also an acceptable reason to enforce reasonably adapted restraints in many jurisdictions.[38] That trade secrets can justify enforcement of a non-compete is what provides the critical link between non-competes and trade secrets law. Of course, the willingness to enforce non-competes only in cases where there are real trade secrets to protect is in some ways surprising because in such a case a former employer could in any case rely on the default law of trade secrets. Implicit in the enforceability is recognition of some of the difficulties an employer faces with such actions. It also reflects the fact that there is a penumbra of information, perhaps not strictly a trade secret, for which an employer is arguably entitled to protection if he has taken care to provide for it contractually by way of a non-compete. The law also sees a benefit in the increased clarity a contract can bring. But in fact the effect of non-competes is to extend control to all information and knowledge an employee has post-termination, if only for a limited term.

In this context, California used to be the stand-out jurisdiction, now followed by the US in general because of federal (Federal Trade Commission) intervention. The Californian state legislature had already prohibited non-compete clauses outright, as the FTC has now purported to do. Some have maintained that this had a positive effect on the Californian economy, with its innovation culture and successful digital industries being partly explained by the ease of movement of employees.[39] This has triggered calls to ban or severely restrict the enforceability of non-compete clauses in other jurisdictions. These calls were earlier heeded in some of the US states and have now also been heard federally.[40] Nonetheless, where non-competes are outlawed, employers are of course not without recourse because they can still sue for post-termination

on, or conscious of, the existence of the doctrine of restraint of trade in its current form to relieve them of their obligations of performance'.

38. Although some other interests have sometimes been recognized, for instance, 'the adequacy and stability of their respective complements of employees' in *Kores Manufacturing Co Ltd v. Kolok Manufacturing Co Ltd* [1959] Ch 108 (CA), 127 (Jenkins LJ). Note the analogy with the tort of '*désorganisation*' in French jurisprudence. *See, e.g.*, Davy Labarthette, *Le débauchage de personnel, parent pauvre de l'action en concurrence déloyale* (Receuil Dalloz 2005), 1231. *See also* Christopher Arup et al., 'Restraints of Trade: The Legal Practice' (2013) 36(1) *University of New South Wales Law Journal* 1; Hui Chia & Ian Ramsay, 'Employment Restraints of Trade: An Empirical Study of Australian Court Judgements' (2016) 29(3) *Australian Journal of Labour Law* 283; William Van Caenegem & Caitlyn Douglas, Submission to the Australian Commonwealth Treasury, *Competition Review of Non-compete Clauses and Other Restraints* (31 May 2024).
39. As for the California experience, *see* Bruce Fallick, Charles A. Fleischmann, & James B Rebitzer, 'Job-Hopping in Silicon Valley: Some Evidence Concerning the Micro-Foundations of a High Technology Cluster' (2006) 88(3) *The Review of Economics and Statistics* 472 https://doi.org/10.3386/w11710. *See also* the well-known article by Ronald Gilson, 'The Legal Infrastructure of High Technology Industrial Districts: Silicon Valley, Route 128, and Covenants not to Compete' (1999) 74 *New York University Law Review* 575 https://doi.org/10.2139/ssrn.124508.
40. *See, e.g.*, for a roundup of states' initiatives to ban non-competes: The State of Non-Compete Bans: Legislation Trends to Watch; For businesses, the evolving landscape of non-compete agreement legislation carries significant implications that warrant careful consideration and strategic planning; Published: 29 March 2024, D'Mia Lamar and Josh Baca, available at https://www.sixfifty.com/blog/state-of-non-compete-bans/.

trade secret misuse or misappropriation. It may be that the unenforceability of non-competes will increase the frequency and willingness to bring such actions.

In that large majority of jurisdictions that still allow reasonable restraints on competition, the difficulty lies in predicting what courts will find reasonable in terms of geographical reach, term and scope of prohibition to protect trade secrets or other recognized interests. It should be noted that the courts view restraints of trade (the broad denomination used to encompass non-competes) with particular disfavour in employment contracts and less so in contracts concerning the transfer of goodwill. That is the case notwithstanding the fact that the latter restraints also restrict employment and effective use of knowledge and experience. But clearly, a contract for transfer of goodwill attaching to an individual's name will not be effective, if the individual concerned cannot be restrained from continuing to do the same work under his or her own name. The same applies to contracts for the assignment of trade secrets, where the assignor can validly agree not to use the information concerned: in France, that is seen as the basis of validity of such transfers (i.e., a licence to use combined with a non-compete undertaking) since in the absence of any property rights in trade secrets, there can be no real assignment.

The case law provides little useful guidance, the difficulty being that courts generally require that non-competes are properly and reasonably adapted to the *particular circumstances* of an individual employee. Boilerplate provisions which employers insert into all contracts of employment without proper adaptation to individual employees' circumstances will often fall short. In Germany, the law is more prescriptive, but really only with limited effect: for instance, a maximum term of two years is statutorily prescribed. In that country, separate consideration paid to the employee is also required by statute (in France as well but based only on case law) and certain guarantees relevant to informed consent are imposed (e.g., minimum age at which an employee can validly enter into a restraint).[41] In other countries, certain aspects of restraints have been the subject of a collective accord between unions and the government, such as in Sweden, although the present status and observance of the accord there is in some doubt. But the central difficulty of predicting what is reasonable in the given circumstances of a particular case remains in all jurisdictions. Naturally, this question is most easily resolved by giving the power to courts to rewrite the bargain on the basis of what they consider reasonable. But traditionally, in the common law countries, courts are reluctant to do this; they take an all-or-nothing approach. However, some have by legislation given this power expressly to courts; thus, in New South Wales (Australia), the *Restraints of Trade Act 1976* (NSW) allows judges to read down restraints to a reasonableness standard instead of holding them wholly invalid and without effect if unreasonable.[42] Other Australian states have no such statute.[43]

41. As to the situation in Germany and France and England, *see* Chapters 4, 6 and 7.
42. That is, if the clause does not fail for other reasons, such as lack of clarity, no protectable interest, or uncertain intent.
43. In common law jurisdictions employers attempt to secure the same outcome by relying on cascading clauses, which invite a court to hold a restraint enforceable at a level it finds

However, courts in other common law jurisdictions have accommodated and enforced cascading or step-wise clauses.[44]

Despite the uncertainty about what is a reasonable restraint, non-competes remain more attractive from an employer's perspective than relying on a patchwork of other contractual provisions (i.e., confidentiality clauses) and general trade secrets law that is uncertain in its effect. In terms of proof, the employer need only establish that the employee has or threatens to work in the prohibited field and place. That information may be fairly readily obtained from public sources. The employer need not show that the employee has misused any trade secrets during their new employment. Discovering and proving actual misuse of confidential information, which is much more difficult, is not necessary. In this regard, it is relevant to point out that most courts do not accept the 'inevitable disclosure' doctrine.[45] It may also be that the uncertainty concerning enforceability of non-competes generally favours employers: employees are less likely to challenge a non-compete or persist in the face of a letter of demand. Employees may stay in their present employment rather than carry their knowledge to new employment elsewhere because they know they are restrained by a non-compete. The uncertainty of the law may encourage firms to advance a case in the initial stages of court proceedings that is apparently arguable, at least sufficiently so, to deter a former employee.[46] Conversely, the negative repercussions of a 'gung-ho' approach to a trade secrets claim for well-resourced employers may be slight,[47] while the deterrent effect vis-à-vis other employees is considerable. There is little to discourage employers from inserting quite onerous non-compete clauses if they can, and employees are unlikely to take issue with such clauses at the time of engagement. In any case in the

reasonable. A cascading clause is one that starts with a certain level of restraint in terms of area and term; then gives a (number of) lesser alternative(s) if the more extensive restraint should be unenforceable.

44. That is not to say there are no legal problems with such clauses, such as possible unenforceability for uncertainty. *See, e.g., Cedar Hill Flowers & Foilage P/L & Anor v. Spierenburg & Ors* [2002] QCA 348. As further considered in Law Council of Australia, Submission to the Australian Commonwealth Treasury, *Competition Review of Non-compete Clauses and Other Restraints* (6 June 2024) https://lawcouncil.au/publicassets/5b085dba-2734-ef11-94a1-005056be13b5/4546%20-%20S%20-%20Worker%20non-compete%20clauses%20and%20other%20restraints.pdf.

45. *See* Michele B. Fagin, 'Non-Compete by Non-Disclosure: The Doctrine of Inevitable Disclosure' (1999) 28 *Columbia Law Review* 73. *See also* Christopher Heer, 'Employees and Trade Secrets: How the Concept of Inevitable Disclosure May Fit into Canadian Law' (2006) 19 *Intellectual Property Journal* 323. *See also* above, Chapter 5 at §5.03[F].

46. This may also enable firms to agitate against competition by former employees under the guise of a trade secrets claim.

47. Although courts do have the power to make adverse cost orders, e.g., on an indemnity basis: *see* for instance, *GlaxoSmithKline Australia Pty Ltd v. Ritchie & Anor (No 2)* [2009] VSC 25 at VSC [87]: '*Here, each offer, if accepted, would have had that result. For the reasons expressed above, however, this was not a case where the litigation, looked at in the broad, gave rise to clearly arguable issues. Only a tiny fraction of the areas of dispute fell into that category. When these are set against GSK's initial and repeated refusal to negotiate, and against the importance of a former employer not allowing concerns about competition to sway its judgment when seeking to protect its confidential information, the refusal to accept the Calderbank offers can be seen in its true light – as unreasonable*'.

civil law jurisdictions, they can at least be confident to receive significant compensation during the period of restraint.

Nonetheless, it is a fact that uncertainty remains in relation to enforceability of non-competes. Therefore, employers also look for other alternatives to protect sensitive information and trade secrets and in the process limit competition from former employees.[48] They use such devices also in jurisdictions where non-competes are not enforceable. Garden-leave clauses are one such device[49] whose adoption seems to be on the rise in the English-speaking world.[50]

Garden-leave clauses effectively amount to a long notice provision (e.g., six months to a year) during which an employee is not required to come to work but stays at home without contacting clients or colleagues. An employer can develop existing client contacts with alternative staff and ensure that trade secrets an employee may have accessed are stale before he or she starts work for a competitor. Such provisions have been tested in the courts in a number of places. Certainly, in the UK, where they originated, they have been relatively well received by the courts. The picture in Australia and the US is a developing one.[51] The main reason they are better regarded than non-competes is that the employee receives proper consideration while not working and is thus not left without an income for the restraint period. An employee on garden leave is therefore similar to a former employee in the non-compete phase in civil law countries because most of these require proof of separate consideration for a non-compete. Courts in common law countries do not require separate consideration to be established for a valid non-compete.

48. For instance, it can sometimes be discerned from the cases that employers have acted on advice to properly document and inventory trade secrets, control the circulation and distribution of sensitive information, and mark documents clearly as confidential. This assists them both in identifying exactly what is secret information, and proving that it has been dealt with as such within the firm.
49. Although this is not by any means the only legal strategy being adopted: the inclusion of liquidated damages clauses in employment contracts is also of interest. *See* for instance *Purcell v. Tullett Prebon (Aust) Pty Ltd* [2010] NSWCA 150 (28 September 2010) where the Court of Appeal upheld a decision to award liquidated damages of some AUD 500,000 against an employee broker who had terminated his contract of employment early and gone over to a competitor. Nothing further will be said about these developments here. *See also* Amanda Coulthard, 'Garden Leave, The Right to Work, and Restraints on Trade' (2009) 22(1) *Australian Journal of Labour Law* 87.
50. *See* Greg T. Lembrich, 'Garden Leave: A Possible Solution to the Uncertain Enforceability of Restrictive Employment Covenants' (2002) 102 *Columbia Law Review* 2291 Note https://doi.org/10.2307/1123728. *See also* Amanda Coulthard, 'Garden Leave, The Right to Work and Restraints on Trade' (2009) 22(1) *Australian Journal of Labour Law* 879; *BearingPoint Australia Pty Ltd v. Hillard* [2008] VSC 115; *Tullet Prebon (Australia) Pty Ltd v. Simon Purcell* [2008] NSWSC 852.
51. *See* in relation to the US, Howard J. Rubin & Gregg A. Gilman, 'Will Garden Leaves Blossom in the States?' (2007) 33(2) *Employee Relations Law Journal* 1. In relation to Australia, *see* above n 49.

§9.05 ASSESSMENT AND REFORM OF THE LAW

Commentators in all jurisdictions here considered stress the importance in terms of public policy of the operation of trade secrets law in the post-employment period. Most litigation in relation to trade secrets arises during this period; fundamental rights and interests are at stake and come into conflict. It is here that trade secrets law seems to have the greatest implications for the competitive functioning of the economy. A reasonable, efficient and fair balance is required between the competing interests of employees (who should be free to move with all they know) and employers whose investment in knowledge production and accumulation should be protected to a reasonable degree. Employer should be encouraged by the law to share useful knowledge within the confines of their organization. From a different perspective, this is where freedom of competition is most acutely threatened under the guise of trade secrets protection, and fair and unfair competition is most difficult to separate.

The key question is whether the present settings of the law achieve a defensible balance or not. However, it is difficult to see how the law of trade secrets itself can be made more effective by statutory intervention. More clarity may be achieved by the US and the new European statutory and prescriptive approaches, but the difficult judgments and distinctions of fact that are required at present will remain. The difficulties remain, whether they are struck along the lines of the common law – by distinguishing between real trade secrets and know-how – or along unfair competition lines – legitimate use of information versus taking unfair competitive advantage of something learned from the previous employer. Nonetheless, there is one area where the English common law remains at odds with other jurisdictions, that being the absence of criminal liability in general and in relation to employees either during or post-employment in particular. Naturally further consideration might be given to introducing penal provisions, but there is no universal support for this approach among commentators.

Despite its clear significance, the area of trade secrets misuse by former employees is not expressly addressed by the statutory provisions of the UTSA, the DTSA, the EU Trade Secrets Directive or the implementing legislation in the Member States.[52]

Equally significant and now a fertile ground for reform is the whole area of non-competes law. Significantly, some authors and now also legislators favour limiting or entirely prohibiting non-compete clauses with a view to improving the free flow of knowledge and information and thus innovation.[53] Some have very influentially drawn connections between the prohibition on non-competes in California and innovation productivity in high-tech industries there. Others have presented various more theoretical arguments that favour outlawing or at least greatly restricting non-competes

52. *See* Chapter 6 concerning the European Directive.
53. As is already the case in California, as mentioned above; *see, e.g.*, Karin Hoisl, *A Study of Inventors: Incentives, Productivity and Mobility* (DUV Gabler, 2007). *See also* Matt Marx, Deborah Strumsky & Lee Fleming, 'Mobility, Skills, and the Michigan Non-compete Experiment' (2009) 55(6) *Management Science* 875 https://doi.org/10.1287/mnsc.1080.0985; M. Motta & T. Rønde, 'Trade Secret Laws, Labor Mobility, and Innovation' (Working Paper, No 08-2002, Copenhagen Business School, Department of Economics).

with sufficient cogency to trigger law reform initiatives. Previously, this happened in some of the US states, for example, in the state of Massachusetts, but now it has also occurred at the federal level in the US.[54] Federal prohibition will overcome the problem of knowledgeable and inventive employees migrating to states or jurisdictions where restraints are either already outlawed or only enforced in very limited cases or to a very limited extent. Regulatory competition in this regard, in relation to attracting talent, investment and developing innovation pools and clusters is stopped dead in its tracks by the FTC's new universal rule.[55]

The law relating to non-competes is quite complex and uncertain, lacking clear a *priori* fence-posts in most jurisdictions as to what is a reasonable restraint. 'Reasonableness' depends on the specific situation of every individual (ex-)employee. The prescriptions in civilian jurisdictions do not have much direct effect on this particular question. One option, therefore, is to reduce uncertainty by imposing by statute some mandatory rules. It may be that imposing statutory maxima *qua* term, rules about reading down restraints, requirements as to consideration and consent, and clarity concerning available remedies would be most conducive to an adequate balance between the interests of the firm in a degree of predictability and the public interest in employee mobility. In this regard, the tendency of civil law jurisdictions to regulate non-competes more thoroughly by statute has some considerable merit, although the approach among those jurisdictions is not uniform or systematic. It might also be possible to introduce mandatory processes, perhaps before specialist courts or tribunals, which allow non-compete claims to be resolved more efficiently.[56] There again, the tendency of civilian courts to deal with cases more quickly and cheaply has some benefits.

However, extensive regulation can have perverse or unexpected effects and always gives rise to additional questions of interpretation and application of laws. Therefore, it may be simpler, following the Californian example, to ban non-competes altogether, as is now happening in the US. It should not be forgotten that a former employer would not be entirely without legal redress against misuse of trade secrets by former employees if that occurred. A firm is still 'protected' by the general default trade secrets law, whether the action lies in statute (as in the US and now the EU Member States), in equity (as in the UK (to a degree) and Australia), or in unfair competition (as in the pre-EU Trade Secrets Directive civilian tradition).

---

54. The law reform initiative in Massachusetts found strong support in the work of academics Matt Marx of MIT and Lee Fleming of the Harvard Business School. *See* above n 48.
55. *See* above at n 14. The Noncompete Rule promulgated by the FTC can be found at https://www.ftc.gov/legal-library/browse/rules/noncompete-rule. The Rule is now subject to serious legal challenges; *see*, for instance, Daniel Pasternak & Laura Lawless, 'Federal Court Enjoins Federal Trade Commission's Rule Prohibiting Non-Competition Agreements (US)' *Squire Patton Boggs* (online) 3 July 2024, https://www.employmentlawworldview.com/federal-court-enjoins-federal-trade-commissions-rule-prohibiting-non-competition-agreements-us/#: ~ :text = Among%20the%20arguments%20advanced%20by,the%20FTC's%20actions%20constituted%20an.
56. *See* William van Caenegem, 'Knowledge Mobility, Trade Secrets and Non-competes: Lessons From the Common Law Tradition' in Niklas Bruun & Marja-Leena Mansala (eds), *Research Handbook on Intellectual Property and Employment Law* (Edward Elgar Publishing, 2021) 361-96.

Thus, prohibition of non-compete clauses may well generate more clarity – and fewer opportunities for employers to strategize in the shadow of uncertain law. However, we see in other areas of the law that prohibition generates attempts at circumvention.[57] Legally robust alternatives may emerge, such as 'garden leave' or liquidated damages clauses,[58] which are not necessarily less inimical to freedom of information or less necessary to protect genuine commercial interests in real trade secrets. It may also be that the total absence of non-competes disincentivizes internal knowledge sharing in organizations and employer investment in employee training and development.[59]

[A] Non-competes: To Regulate or Not?

In relation to non-competes, in most common law jurisdictions, the courts want to keep their hands free and do not formulate generally applicable standards. In the common law jurisdictions, as well as judicial resistance to formulating *a priori* standards, there is notable legislative resistance to formulating prescriptive rules: they are few or non-existent in most such countries. This remains an area dominated by case law. In the common law world, courts are reluctant to give comfort to parties in relation to a contractual clause which is prima facie against public policy and void, by appearing to formulate *a priori* rules or principles of acceptability. They do not insist on distinct consideration because to accept that with consideration a non-compete is valid would give encouragement to the practice and would ignore the public policy detriment inherent in such encouragement. The English common law takes a blind man's bluff approach, where the courts review every clause on its merits in the particular factual circumstances, saying only that the restraint must be 'reasonable' without setting a priori principles, e.g., relating to length of time or level of (separate) remuneration.

Given the critical significance of this area of law, is the unregulated approach of the common law countries satisfactory or short of prohibiting non-competes should the legislator intervene prescriptively? The powers of the court could be clarified (as, for instance, done in the Australian state of New South Wales);[60] clearer standards for valid acceptance of restraints could be set, as exist to some degree in civil law countries; separate remuneration could be prescribed; and maximum terms set.

[B] Judicial Power to Rewrite Non-compete Clauses?

In the majority of jurisdictions, the employer's difficulties are twofold. First, predicting what courts will find reasonable in terms of geographical reach, term and scope of

57. The development and rejection of the 'inevitable disclosure'-doctrine in Californian law is an interesting example of this dynamic. *See* Jay L. Koh, 'From Hoops to Hard Drives: An Accession Law Approach to the Inevitable Misappropriation of Trade Secrets' (1998) 48(2) *American University Law Review* 271. *See also* above n 48.
58. *See* above nn 52, 53, 54; nothing further will be said about these developments here.
59. As canvassed by van Caenegem & Douglas above n 38.
60. *See* above n 46.

prohibition to protect a recognized legitimate interest in the case of a specific and unique employee. The case law provides little firm guidance other than formulating rather abstract legal principles which it is difficult to apply predictably to each employee's particular circumstances. Second, the cost of tailoring non-competes to the specific circumstances of every single employee. This usually requires the assistance of counsel, as courts are notoriously unimpressed by boilerplate clauses. Those are standard clauses included in all employment contracts without much regard to the individual characteristics of each employee.

Therefore, employers will be tempted to invite the court to rewrite, 'blue pencil', sever, or otherwise limit or adapt the operation of a non-compete. In effect, this amounts to shifting the burden of a proper investigation and adaptation of the clause from the pre-contractual phase to the enforcement phase, from the parties (principally of course the employer) to the court.

The question that concerns us here is whether it is desirable to give this power to the courts. The traditional common law position is, generally speaking, rather adverse: the courts refuse to do the job the parties should have done – they will resist shaping the bargain themselves. This of course increases the risk of total failure of the employer's case – which may well impact upon the desirability of litigation. The traditional hostility of the common law to invitations to interfere (that interference taking the form of severance) with the terms of a non-compete, as opposed to either upholding it or striking it down as a whole, is explained by Lord Moulton in *Mason v. Provident Clothing and Supply Co Ltd*:

> It would, in my opinion, be pessimi exempli if when an employer had extracted a covenant deliberately framed in unreasonably wide terms, the courts were to come to his assistance and by applying their ingenuity and knowledge of the law, carve out of this void covenant the maximum of what he might validly have required. It must be remembered that the real sanction at the back of these covenants is the terror and expense of litigation, in which the servant is usually at a great disadvantage, in view of the longer purse of his master.[61]

Justice Dodds-Streeton in *I.F. Asia Pacific v. Galbally* supported an approach that:

> cautions against curial disentanglement of unreasonably wide clauses, recognising that they may act in terrorem by exposing employees to the threat of litigation. Undue judicial readiness to save such clauses by severance reduces the sanction of invalidity otherwise applicable to employers who attempt to impose unjustifiably wide restraints.[62]

The point about the actions *in terrorem* by employers is well made and significant.[63] Employers try to make it more acceptable for courts to intervene nonetheless, by inclusion of so-called cascading or laddered non-compete clauses, inviting the court to

---

61. [1913] AC at 724 at 745; as approved of by Younger J in his noted judgment in *Attwood v. Lamont* [1920] All ER 55; and more recently, for instance in Australia by Dodds-Streeton J in *IF Asia Pacific Pty Ltd v. Galbally* [2003] VSC 192; and Hargrave J in *Integrated Group Limited v. Dillon* [2009] VSC 361.
62. *See* above n 61 at VSC [201].
63. Note that it is also the case that such clauses may still fail for other reasons.

exercise a choice while at the same time limiting uncertainty.[64] As indicated above, courts have been reasonably accommodating of this type of clause. The main difficulty with them is first, that from a contract law perspective, they may be too uncertain and leave employees in the dark as to what the precise extent of their obligation is. Second, from a policy perspective, they encourage employers to draft wide restraints. This strengthens their hand when litigation looms between parties and detracts from a key requirement that a non-compete's anti-competitive effect should be mitigated by insisting on specific adaptation to the circumstances of a particular employee and to the actual trade secrets or other legitimate interests of a former employer.

The Australian state of New South Wales provides an interesting example of a jurisdiction where the legislator has intervened to allow the courts a more active role in adapting non-competes than the traditional all-or-nothing common law position would permit. The *Restraints of Trade Act 1976* (NSW) allows judges to read down restraints to a reasonableness standard instead of holding them wholly invalid and without effect if unreasonable.[65] Other Australian states have no such law, but some of the American states either have such provisions or have them under consideration.

Justice McLelland identified the intention behind the New South Wales Act:

> The mischief or defect [inherent in the common law position] was that in determining the validity of a restraint, the courts were bound to consider all possible breaches within its terms (after any permissible severance) and determine whether public policy was infringed by the restraint of all such breaches, rather than by the actual or threatened breaches provided in the particular case.[66]

This is the issue addressed by section 4(1) of the Act, which provides:

> 'A restraint of trade is valid to the extent, to which it is not against public policy, whether it is in severable form or not'. The effect of this provision is that the courts, when deciding whether to grant relief under a non-compete, only have to consider whether the restraint in its application to the particular breach would be contrary to public policy. They do not need to 'consider its purported operation in other conceivable sets of circumstances'.[67]

In particular, the restraint need not necessarily be considered at its furthest point of application in time (and/or space).

However, there are of course still significant restrictions on what the court can do. It cannot save a restraint that is otherwise invalid, for instance, because there is no legitimate interest to protect, nor does section 4(1) enable a court 'to create a valid restraint out of an invalid one unless that can be done by a reading down process'.[68] As

64. *See* Christopher Arup, 'What/Whose Knowledge? Restraints of Trade and Concepts of Knowledge' (2012) 36(2) *Melbourne University Law Review* 369; and Chris Dent, 'Unpacking Post-Employment Restraint of Trade Decisions: The Motivators of the Key Players' (2014) 26(1) *Bond Law Review* 1 https://doi.org/10.53300/001c.5620.
65. That is, if the clause does not fail for other reasons, such as lack of clarity, no protectable interest, or uncertain intent.
66. In *Orton v. Melman* [1981] 1 NSWLR 583, 587.
67. *Ibid.*, at 588.
68. *See A Buckle & Son Pty Ltd v. McAllister* (1986) 4 NSWLR 426, 434.

Stewart says: 's 4(1) is … very useful to convenantees in permitting them to enforce "stripped back" versions of their restraints in circumstances where the common law might otherwise have considered the covenants in question too wide at their outer limit'.[69]

From a policy perspective, the difficulty with a provision such as section 4(1) standing alone is that it does nothing to encourage employers to keep restraints within reasonable limits. An employer may as well insert a very broad or oppressive clause, which either will be observed by the employee who has neither the courage nor the means to challenge it or will be rewritten to be valid by a court under the Act. The employer is encouraged to go well beyond what is required to protect trade secrets.

However, the New South Wales Act in section 4(3)[70] tries to meet this concern by providing that courts have a broad discretion not only to invalidate a restraint but also to rewrite it to whatever extent they see fit where there is a 'manifest failure' by the employer to attempt to make the restraint a reasonable one.[71] This imposes some limitations on the power of the court.[72] Nonetheless, it is not clear that section 4(3) really operates to ameliorate the chilling effect of a law which enables an employer to ask a court to make a restraint work.[73]

[C] Prescriptive Statutory Standards

In Germany, there is a specific statutory requirement that a former employee be paid distinct compensation for the duration of the restraint period. The payment must also be adequate. Further, a non-compete entered into by a minor will be void, and there are also other conditions specified in the relevant code, including formal requirements (a document in writing must be handed to the employee). By statute, a provision will also not be enforceable if there is no legitimate business interest to protect. There are also further grounds of unenforceability provided for in the law.[74] In France, the situation is

69. Andrew Stewart, 'Drafting and Enforcing Post-employment Restraints' (1997) 10 *Australian Journal of Labour Law* 181, 212.
70. Section 4(3) of the *Restraint of Trade Act 1976* reads: '*Where, on application by a person subject to the restraint, it appears to the Supreme Court that a restraint of trade is, as regards its application to the applicant, against public policy to any extent by reason of, or partly by reason of, a manifest failure by a person who created or joined in creating the restraint to attempt to make the restraint a reasonable restraint, the Court, having regard to the circumstances in which the restraint was created, may, on such terms as the Court thinks fit, order that the restraint be, as regards its application to the applicant, altogether invalid or valid to such extent only (not exceeding the extent to which the restraint is not against public policy) as the Court thinks fit and any such order shall, notwithstanding sub-section (1), have effect on and from such date (not being a date earlier than the date on which the order was made) as is specified in the order.*'
71. *See* above n 68, 212.
72. *See* Andrew Fell & Elizabeth Rudz, 'Employee Non-compete Restraints: Resolving Uncertainty' (2023) 46(4) *UNSW Law Journal* 1252.
73. In this context, it is interesting to note a pre-FTC development in the US State of Georgia, where recent amendments had increased the 'blue-penciling' power of the courts. *See* Shogun J. Khadye, 'An Uncertain Future: Georgia's Policy on Restrictive Covenants in Employment Contracts' (2009) 2 *John Marshall Law Journal* 208, 228-231 (concerning the provisions of House Bill 173).
74. *See* Bauer & Diller, above n 13, 45-60.

similar though largely based on the cases. As indicated above, in the common law, consideration is not a strict requirement. Apart from not wanting to legitimize restraints by indicating that they are acceptable if paid for, which is against the principle in *Nordenfeldt* that they are prima facie illegal, courts are often not in a position to know whether or to what extent overall remuneration in an employment package relates to, or what is specific consideration for entering into a post-employment restraint.

Courts also do not want to be in a position where they are effectively allowing employers to purchase more protection against competition than is necessary.[75] This goes back to the critical point that it is irrelevant that an employee has entered into the restraint with full understanding of the consequences and properly advised - it is the danger to the public interest and not to the private interests of the employee that the courts are concerned with. Enforcement is thus not simply governed by a weighing of the benefits and disadvantages to the employee concerned.

Further, in some countries, upper time limits are prescribed across the board for restraints of trade: as indicated above, in Germany, any restraint beyond two years is not enforceable for that period.[76] As noted above, in the UK, a statutory maximum term limit of three months is proposed.[77] In yet other countries, such as Sweden, certain aspects of restraints have been the subject of a collective accord.

The advantage of this type of regulatory approach is that some increased certainty about enforceability may be achieved: restraints that do not meet the statutory standards are clearly void. It is also true that the requirement of remuneration or some form of consideration meets one of the principal policy concerns recognized in common law countries: that the employee is left with insufficient or no means for support during the term of the restraint, if he or she is neither remunerated nor able to take employment in the area of his or her skills and experience.

If the legislation imposes other substantive and restrictive requirements as well as remuneration and certain formal requirements (such as unenforceability against minors, or trainees, or persons who have been sacked without cause), it may be a different matter. From this perspective, the German statute law is interesting, since it expressly includes the key requirement that the employer demonstrate a legitimate interest of the employer. Other issues such as term and extent are seen through that lens - for instance, it would be a rare case, according to Bauer/Diller, where the employer would have a legitimate interest to protect for anything like the two-year maximum term.[78]

In conclusion, it may be that the kind of regulation found in some civil law jurisdictions meets concerns about the weak bargaining position of employees, the chilling effect of restraints and the unfairness and personal detriment that can attach to them. But to some extent, prescriptive regulation actually encourages non-competes, and if, in the final analysis, the latter are against the public interest because they stymie

75. *See JA Mont (UK) Ltd v. Mills* [1993] IRLR 172.
76. *See* Bauer & Diller, above n 13, 139.
77. *See* above n 14.
78. *See* Bauer & Diller, above n 13, 128.

free flow of information in a manner not really necessary to protect trade secrets (given the existence of the default law and other measures), it is important to consider the 'Californian alternative': total prohibition on the enforcement of non-competes. The longstanding 'California experiment' is now joined by the new 'US experiment'.

[D] Rendering Non-competes Unenforceable by Statute?

California famously adopted a fairly unique approach in relation to non-competes a long time ago. The legislator intervened and prohibited non-compete clauses outright since the 1940s. Californian innovation productivity, particularly in digital industries, has drawn attention to the connection between non-competes and innovation, which is seen as being aided by free circulation of talent, knowledge and experience.[79] This spawned the call for a federal ban on non-compete clauses which has now been effected.[80]

This anti-noncompete 'movement' has been overtly inspired by a pro-diffusion, 'freedom of information' policy rationale, even though some commentators doubt that it is possible to state with any certainty that the particularity of this area of the law has had a significant impact on innovation productivity in Californian digital industries. Underlying this policy choice must be a conviction that the general law of trade secrets is sufficient to protect employers' interests in controlling commercially and technically significant secrets. Of course, it is not the case that in the absence of non-competes, employees jump ship without a second thought. There are many other factors that influence employees to remain with present employers and thus not shift their knowledge to others. One aspiration of prohibition is that it encourages employers to provide more stimulating workplaces where employees' ideas and innovations are given greater deference, encouraging them to stay. It remains to be seen what will transpire in the United States, as the FTC prohibition is under challenge on multiple fronts; whether it has the desired pro-competitive, pro-innovation effect emerges will also be demonstrated by future indicators of economic growth. It will remain challenging to isolate the effect of non-compete prohibition in terms of innovation performance and dynamics in the economy, however.

In terms of trade secrets, a relevant consideration in relation to abolition is the adequacy of the default law. Is it in fact adequate to protect the interests of employers in securing their trade secrets in the absence of the contractual self-help measure of the non-compete? Conversely, the more effective the default law and confidentiality clauses are at protecting employer interests in secret information, the weaker the case against prohibition of non-competes is. One risk that has been identified in relation to prohibition is that it might encourage 'strengthening' of trade secrets law and remedies (for instance, making the 'inevitable disclosure' approach more palatable).

79. *See* Fallick, Fleischmann & Rebitzer, as well as Gilson, both above n 39. *See also* William van Caenegem, 'The Mobility of Creative Individuality, Trade Secrets and Restraints of Trade' (2007) 14(2) *Murdoch University E Law Journal* 265.
80. *See* the call for such amendments in Massachusetts, above n 48.

Although the position of employers vis-à-vis departed employees is perhaps weak, more recently, some of the evidentiary difficulties they face have been alleviated. Much evidence of post-employment misuse is more readily available by way of emails, internet use, laptops, mobile phone records and the like. Such devices and facilities are commonly put at the disposal of employees by their employers, who nonetheless retain ownership and control of them. It appears that greater contractual rights are now also commonly built into employment contracts to facilitate employer access to all these devices, although the degree of access the law allows an employer will vary from jurisdiction to jurisdiction, taking privacy regulation into account.

Further, there are multiple other restraining factors on employees intending to pass on trade secrets. Corporations law imposes duties on employees and directors concerning use of company information. Legislation such as the *EEA*, at the Federal level in the US, now imposes criminal penalties on misuse of trade secrets, something that has been well established in civil law jurisdictions, with particular application to employees (*see* Chapter 4 on criminal law). There is also increasing legislation concerning misuse of computers and communications devices, in part providing for criminal penalties.

None of these developments is individually determinative of the debate. But the trends and developments in the default law concerning secret information arguably seem to benefit employers more. It may be that they provide support for the new US approach, following the Californian example.

[E] Strict Adherence to Principle?

Keeping in mind that the interests of employers in their trade secrets are already protected by way of the general law of trade secrets, non-competes are, therefore, an *additional* tool in the armoury of the employer. This fact reinforces the argument that strict judicial adherence to principles intended to safeguard the public interest in free competition and communication remains crucially important. Importantly, it is not only an employee's private interest in exercising his freedom to work to the full that is at stake but also the broader interest in keeping the economy free from a web of artificial restraints. Justice Callinan in the High Court of Australia case of *Maggbury v. Hafele*[81] sought to elevate freedom of contract above the public interest in free competition and flow of information:

> The law should seek to uphold bargains and enforce restraints other than those which are clearly and demonstrably against the public interest. In other words, a person who wants to break a restrictive covenant should be obliged to show that enforcement of it would substantially reduce competition within a marketplace, result in price fixing, or otherwise cause the public some real and discernible economic detriment of an anti-competitive nature. No less should be required to justify a unique interference with freedom of contract or the giving of a judicial

81. [2001] HCA 70; 210 CLR 181; 185 ALR 152; 76 ALJR 246.

> imprimatur to what would otherwise be a flagrant breach of contract when one party decides that he or she has had enough of it.[82]

But his Honour had insufficient regard for the fact that to meet his standard in each individual *employment* case would naturally be very difficult, so that a proliferation of non-competes would inevitably become a dead hand on the economy. His statement also does not admit the fact that not all restraints but only *unreasonable* restraints will in fact be struck down on the demand of the affected employee.[83]

Justice Callinan clearly states the opposing, freedom of contract view: a well-advised employee who deliberately chooses to enter into a non-compete should not be able to get escape its strictures 'on a technicality'. But the reality is that the courts, in all jurisdictions here considered, continue to apply tests to non-competes that blend regard for private and public interests. In particular, they require a protectable interest and restrictions that are reasonable and properly adapted to the particular circumstances of the employee concerned. In this context, the detail of the law counts, as the following passages are intended to illustrate.

[F] Legitimate or Protectable Interests

A significant issue in terms of 'holding the line' in relation to non-competes is the nature of the protectable interest that an employer must establish and the threshold of proof required. As indicated above, it is fairly universal that the law insists that a non-compete can only be justified if it serves to protect a recognized 'legitimate interest' of the employer. In Germany, this requirement is made expressly in the relevant statutory provision (*see* Article 74a of the HGB).

Trade secrets 'belonging' to the employers are the legitimate interest that is most relevant here, as they provide the counterpoint to the public policy goal of free circulation of ideas, knowledge, and information, and unimpeded competition. Requiring cogent evidence of particularized and real trade secrets is one way in which courts strike a balance between these interests and the interest of the employer to maintain the secrecy of certain information that is vital or significant for the operation and development of the business.[84]

Two significant legal issues arise here, as opposed to the more discretionary question of whether a restraint is 'reasonable': first, *the scope and extent* of the categories of protectable interests; and second, the *character* of the confidential or secret information 'belonging' to the employer which justifies 'protection' by way of a non-compete. These are explored below by reference to the traditional common law position.[85] But the decisions referred to will not appear unusual to lawyers from other jurisdictions, where much the same issues arise although in different guises.

82. *Maggbury Pty Ltd v. Hafele Aust Pty Ltd* [2001] HCA 70, 91.
83. Some comfort can be drawn from the fact that the majority of the court in this case did not agree with Callinan's J views.
84. This recognized that legitimate interest in protecting trade secrets is often accompanied by a conjoint interest in protecting client connection.
85. Focusing, in particular, on English and Australian cases.

As to the first issue, courts and legislation in most jurisdictions permit enforcement of restraints that are reasonably adapted to protect both genuine trade secrets and/or so-called client connection. About the status of these two interests, there appears to be little controversy. Additionally, 'stability of the workforce' is also recognized at times as a legitimate interest;[86] in French jurisprudence, this is referred to as protection against '*désorganisation*'.[87] Recognition of this interest appears to be more solid and longstanding in some civilian jurisdictions than it is in the common law, where it is nonetheless not unknown.[88]

Notwithstanding the prominence and acceptance of client connection and trade secrets as relevant interests, the courts occasionally insist that the categories of protected interests are in fact not closed. Courts sometimes invite employers to advance new interests, reiterating statements of the kind found, for example, in *Dawnay Day & Co Ltd v. D'Alphen,* where Evans LJ said:[89] 'the established categories are not rigid, and they are not exclusive. Rather, the covenant may be enforced when the covenantee has a legitimate interest, of whatever kind, to protect, and when the covenant is no wider than is necessary to protect that interest'.[90]

A recent example of approval of this permissive approach is the high-profile Australian case of *Seven Network (Operations) Limited v. James Warburton (No 2),* where Pembroke J said:

> In the United Kingdom, the English Court of Appeal held in Dawnay Day & Co Ltd v D'Alphen [1997] EWCA Civ 1753; [1997] EWCA Civ 1753; [1998] ICR 1068 that an agreement entered into between the plaintiffs and the first three defendants for the development of a joint venture company, and the contribution of capital for its

86. Whether there is indeed room for two views is to be doubted, since they do not seem compatible. In any case it seems to be now – perhaps unfortunately in the light of the Hong Kong Court of Appeal's point of view expressed above, that there an employer has a legitimate interest in the stability of its workforce, and can in principle protect this interest by a covenant restraining a former employee from enticing away former colleagues. In the UK, the conflicting positions taken by Dillon and Nolan LJJ in *Hanover Insurance Brokers Ltd v. Shapiro* [1994] IRLR 82 (no requisite interest) and Leggatt and Russell LJJ in *Ingham v. ABC Contract Services Ltd* [1993] UKCA Civ 1336 (legitimate interest in maintaining a stable and trained workforce) were resolved in favour of the latter in *Dawnay Day & Co v. D'Alphen* [1998] ICR 1069; [1997] IRLR 442 in a judgment of Evans LJ with whom Ward and Nourse LJJ agreed. An Australian case that has taken the same view as to legitimate interest is *Allison & Anor v. BDO (NSW-Vic) Pty Ltd & Ors* [2010] VSC 35.
87. *See* above n 41.
88. Nonetheless, in the common law world, *see* for instance reference to 'the adequacy and stability of their respective complements of employees', per Jenkins LJ in *Kores Manufacturing Co Ltd v. Kolok Manufacturing Co Ltd* [1959] Ch 108 (CA), 127. This issue is further considered below.
89. [1998] ICR 1068, 1107-1108.
90. This type of statement draws on the apparently very broad formulation in *Herbert Morris Ltd v. Saxelby* [1916] 1 AC 688, where it is said that a contract in restraint of trade is prima facie void, but can be enforced if: (1) the contract is reasonable as between the parties; and (2) it is consistent with the interests of the public: *see* [1916] 1 AC 688, 708. The judgment goes on to specify that to satisfy (2), the contract must be in no way injurious to the public interest. As to (1), the clause must not afford anything more than adequate protection, in relation to which the court examines against what the protection was required and why it was so required.

> business, provided a clear commercial interest that justified the plaintiffs safeguarding themselves against competition by obtaining restraints from the defendants for the agreed restraint period. In particular, the Court held that the categories of case in which covenants in restraint of trade are enforceable are neither rigid nor exclusive. They included, the Court said, any case where the covenantee has a legitimate interest of whatever kind to protect and where the covenant is no wider than necessary to protect that interest.[91]

However, this statement appears to ignore the crucial distinction between restraints of trade in general, where the courts are generally more lenient, and restraints of trade in employment contracts, where the courts by longstanding precedent have taken a much stricter approach – and legitimately so, given the particular rights and policy interests that attach to freedom of individual employment and of information. It also equates a legitimate interest with a 'clear commercial interest' (or, further in the case, 'a legitimate financial interest'). Of course, it will always be in the covenantor's commercial and financial interest to restrain competition by a former employee or his or her new employer. But that is not to the point: rather, what is important is that an employer should have some reasonable protection for his trade secrets by way of a non-compete protection, which might otherwise be difficult to effectuate on a pro-active basis. There is in fact little evidence from the cases that in the employment context, other interests have been recognized as warranting a restraint, except for the above-mentioned 'stability of the workforce'. In practice, in such cases, the categories of legitimate interest are not treated as being 'at large'. The balance is better struck by adhering to existing categories of recognized legitimate interests.

[G] Know-How as a Category of Information Protectable by a Restraint?

As to the second issue, there is a significant question as to the characteristics of the information that an employer can refer to when arguing that a legitimate interest exists that justifies the adoption of a non-compete. Mummery J in this passage from *FSS Travel* identifies just two classes of information or knowledge:

> The critical question is whether the employer has trade secrets which can be fairly regarded as his property, as distinct from the skill, experience, know-how, and general knowledge which can fairly be regarded as the property of the employee to use without restraint for his own benefit or in the service of a competitor. This distinction necessitates examination of all the evidence relating to the nature of employment, the character of the information, the restrictions imposed on its dissemination, the extent of use in the public domain and the damage likely to be cause by its use and disclosure in competition to the employer.[92]

But in other cases, a trend has emerged favouring a three-way categorization by drawing a distinction between two classes of confidential information: a category

91. [2011] NSWSC 386, 68.
92. *See FSS Travel and Leisure Systems Ltd v. Johnson* [1998] IRLR 382, [31]-[33].

which a former employee can use *unless* there is a valid contractual restraint (sometimes called 'Faccenda Class 2 information'),[93] and a category which a former employee is not entitled to use after termination: the latter being a trade secret in the narrow sense, which would attract protection by way of an action for breach of confidence. That Faccenda Class 2 information, although not protectable in equity, is nonetheless considered a legitimate interest protectable by a restrictive covenant.[94] Examples of such information are special information pertaining to company accounts[95] or costs and prices of certain products.[96] Very recently, this three-way split was affirmed in Australia by the Court of Appeal of New South Wales:

> However, in applying these general equitable principles to the particular case of post-employment use, by an ex-employee, of the confidential information of an employer obtained during employment, there are particular considerations which tend to qualify their operation. They are that very often an employee will necessarily through employment come to have knowledge which the employer would prefer not to have generally known, that often such knowledge will become part of the employee's know-how (which the employee should be able to use after employment ceases), that very often it is difficult or impossible to isolate from the employee's general know-how particular pieces of confidential information which the employee is not permitted to use while otherwise being free to use know-how generally, and that competition should not be prevented by preventing ex-employees using their know-how.[38] Considerations such as these have led to a distinction being drawn, in cases such as Faccenda Chickens and Wright v. Gasweld (1991) 22 NSWLR 317, between two classes of confidential information, one of which an ex-employee cannot use (even in the absence of contractual restrictions), and the other of which an ex-employee can use, at least unless there is a valid contractual restraint. There is some variation in the naming of these two classes. For example, there is a question whether both are properly called trade secrets, with the latter being a particular class of trade secrets which is also given the appellation 'know-how'; or whether only the former class should be called trade secrets. In either event, the latter class is often called 'know-how'.[97]

This passage is perhaps illustrative of the terminological confusion that follows from this distinction between two forms of confidential information. The term 'know-how' becomes alternatively used for two different categories of knowledge or information, depending on its context. In the more recent case of *Genesys Wealth Advisers Ltd v. Miles*, Palmer J makes a further attempt at explaining why the distinction between the two forms of confidential information is drawn and in what circumstances:

> It is important to bear in mind at the outset that there are two categories of confidential information which the Courts will protect at the suit of a former

93. After *Faccenda Chicken Ltd v. Fowler* [1987] Ch 117, *see* further below.
94. As held for instance in *see Herbert Morris Ltd v. Saxelby* [1916] 1 AC 688; *Littlewoods Organization Ltd v. Harris* [1977] 1 ELR 1472 at 1479 (CA) per Lord Denning MR; *Wright v. Gasweld Pty Ltd* (1991) 22 NSWLR 317.
95. *Evitt v. Price* (1827) 1 Sim 483; 57 ER 659.
96. *Thomas Marshall v. Guinle* [1978] 3 All ER 193; *Herbert Morris* (above n 90); *Half Court Tennis Pty Ltd v. Seymour* (1980) 53 FLR 240.
97. *See Del Casale v. Artedomus (Australia) Pty Ltd* (2007) 73 IPR 326 at 335 (cited with approval by Palmer J in *Genesys Wealth Advisers Ltd v. Miles* [2008] NSWSC 802).

employer: first, information which is of its nature so confidential or secret that the ex-employee cannot use it even if not bound by any contractual restraint; second, information which is to a degree confidential but, because it is closely linked to the know-how and experience which an employee acquires in the course of employment in a particular field, it will not be protected by the Court except where there is a valid contractual restraint on the employee. On the other hand, information which has no confidentiality, because of its triviality or because it is in the public domain, will not be protected by the Court even if it expressly described as confidential in a contractual restraint: *see* Del Casale v Artedomus (Aust) Pty Ltd [2007] NSWCA 172, at [37]-[38] per Hodgson JA; Wright v Gasweld Pty Ltd [1991] 22 NSWLR 317 at 333E-334A, 339E.[98]

The Court of Appeal generally agreed with Palmer J.[99] The judge in *Genesys* concluded that there was sufficiently identified confidential information to warrant the restraint.

Finally, and perhaps most illustrative of the difficulties of the more lenient approach towards allowing mere know-how as a protectable interest is this passage from *Cactus Imaging Pty Ltd v.Peters*:[100]

> An employer has an interest in its confidential information, which it may legitimately protect by a restraint of trade, even if the information is not in the nature of a trade secret such as to attract equitable protection in the absence of any contractual agreement [Wright v Gasweld Pty Ltd (1991) 22 NSWLR 317, 326F, 333G-334E, 341G]. [...] [13] And as Lord Denning said in Littlewoods Organisation Limited v Harris [1977] 1 WLR 1472, 1479, experience has shown that it is unsatisfactory simply to have a covenant against disclosing confidential information, because it is difficult to draw the line between information which is confidential and information which is not, and very difficult to prove a breach when the information is of such a character that an employee can carry it away in his or her head, so that the only practicable solution is to take a covenant from the employee by which he or she undertakes not to work for a trade rival. The permissibility of such restraints for that purpose is well established [Kone Elevators Pty Limited v McNay (1997) ATPR 41-564, 43,834; Woolworths Limited v Olson, [38], [67]; Lindner v Murdock's Garage, 650 (Fullagar J); Portal Software Pty Ltd v Bodsworth [2005] NSWSC 1179, [83]].

In this passage from *Cactus*, we see the three-categories orthodoxy stated in its most succinct and confident form. However, arguably, the information described above is exactly of a kind that should *not* warrant a restraint. In other words, it is the kind of valuable knowledge the employee should be *free to use* both in his own interest and to maintain a competitive market where skills and information circulate freely. In *TV Shopping Network v. Scutt*, Young J did not accept the threefold division, but his note of justifiable scepticism has not carried decisive weight in subsequent cases. As he said:

> Is that then confidential information? Almost all information is useful for some purposes, but that of itself does not make it confidential. The standard test of what

98. [2008] NSWSC 802, [45].
99. *Miles v. Genesys Wealth Advisers Ltd* [2009] NSWCA 25, [22].
100. (2006) 71 NSWLR 9; [2006] NSWSC 717, [12]-[13].

> is confidential information comes from what was said by Megarry J in Coco v A N Clark (Engineers) Ltd (1968) 1A IPR 587, 590. His Lordship said that ordinarily one looks for three elements: (i) that the information imparted a confidence; (ii) that it was imparted in circumstances importing an obligation of confidence, and that it was then necessary to prove (iii), that there was a threat to breach the confidence. A lot of what employees absorb during the course of their employment is very useful information and gives them a greater capacity to be employed. This information, insofar as it is know-how or general business skills, becomes part of the property of the employee and it is not a matter which the employer can restrain the employee from using. Examples of this type of knowledge are given in Printers & Finishers Ltd v Holloway [1965] 1 WLR 1 at 6.[101]

This is a much simpler proposition and should be adhered to. 'Know-how' so defined should not be protectable either in equity (by an action for breach of confidence) or in contract (by an action for breach of a non-compete clause). A restrictive approach should be taken to expand the categories of existing legitimate interests. It should be kept in mind that the starting point is that restraints of trade are against public policy and therefore void. They restrict information flows, limit competition, and disable employees. In any case, there is no proprietary interest at stake where this lesser category is concerned, since it is information that can neither be 'unlearned' nor adequately separated out. This principle is of universal application – restricting justification for a non-compete to cases where there is clear evidence of a genuine trade secret 'belonging to' the employer is clearly the right policy position, whatever the jurisdiction might be.

On a final note concerning protectable interest, as well as being required to warrant enforcement of a non-compete, it will also be a significant controlling factor where the reasonableness of the particular restraint is considered: the courts ask whether the restraint goes no further than required to protect the interest identified.

§9.06 CONCLUSION

The law surrounding the post-employment phase is perhaps the most significant part of the law of trade secrets. It certainly attracts a great proportion of the litigation in trade secrets cases. It is also the most common scenario to enliven the criminal law where such applies to trade secrets. But the vagaries of the law and the countervailing policy forces make trade secrets actions against former employees problematic. The law in most jurisdictions has thus accepted that trade secrets can be protected by way of non-competes, something otherwise against the public interest. Employers prefer to rely on these, and they are a most significant instrument for the protection of trade secrets and confidential information. Nonetheless, they must be policed carefully because they do more than just protect secrets, which in any case can benefit from the default law. They also prohibit competition of the most effective kind and interrupt the normal and beneficial flow of information and knowledge by way of mobile employees. It may well be that there is a good case for adopting the Californian approach, as the US

101. *TV Shopping Network v. Scutt* (1998) 43 IPR 451, 459.

has now done at the federal level, given that there are other factors at work strengthening the position of employers in relation to confidences, as discussed above. However, to prove empirically that the abolition of non-competes has a positive economic effect will remain very challenging.

In the debate concerning the level of protection afforded trade secrets by way of non-competes, it is important to keep in mind the 'swings and roundabouts' of commerce and hiring and firing. In other words, where it may become more difficult for an employer to retain an employee and all the knowledge and know-how that employee has if non-competes are restricted or prohibited, it also becomes easier to attract new or replacement employees. The firm may suffer and benefit from the new situation in equal measure. Logically, it also be encouraged to improve employment conditions so as to retain knowledgeable employees.

It should be remembered that when a non-compete is enforced, in the current climate of rapid technological change and innovation, even a very short period of inactivity and lack of participation can be a critical setback in terms of innovation and in terms of an individual's ability to absorb new information, knowledge, ideas, concepts and applications.

Even if the law does not everywhere go down the road of prohibition or restriction to very short maximum terms, what remains really important is that non-competes are subject to very close judicial scrutiny: of the real protected interest; the actual work sphere and sphere of experience of the particular employee; the time really required for a firm to secure its secrets; and anchoring all these things to real and cogent evidence.

CHAPTER 10
Conclusions: Global Convergence or Global Confusion?

§10.01 A GLOBAL DOCTRINAL PATCHWORK

Although there has been some degree of convergence or harmonization of trade secrets law since the first edition of this book was published, doctrinal divergence still marks this area of law. It is significant that in the decade between the two editions of this book, the fundamental question of why trade secrets should be legally protected remains not only unanswered but still appears to be marginalized in legal doctrine. This situation is troubling, as a clear understanding of this issue should take precedence in discussions regarding the legal protection of any intangible asset. In the context of trade secrets, the uncertainties surrounding this question are glaring and are reflected in the choices made regarding the preferred legal instruments for their protection – such as unfair competition laws, property rights, or sui generis tools. In practice, protection systems have often developed incrementally through case law, lacking a comprehensive legal framework. As a result, legal scholars have themselves engaged in a form of 'reverse engineering'. They attempt not to first justify the need for protection and then deduce themselves which approach should be adopted. Instead, they often look to correlate various elements – whether identified or not – within different existing national regimes to specific legal approaches.

There is, for instance, ongoing disagreement as to whether trade secrets are a form of IP at all. It is the 'property' rather than the 'intellectual' that causes doubt because, generally speaking, trade secrets are considered to be secret information whose commercial value derives at least in part from some intellectual effort uniquely contributed by their possessor. This value need not be high but then nor does the value of IP such as a patent or a copyright. Trade secrets law in many countries actually conceives of the value as resulting at least in part from exclusive control, and the evidentiary burden of proving some commercial utility is usually minor. In no jurisdiction does the law actually establish property rights in secret information – although it often focuses on misappropriation as the relevant wrong.

In any case, in terms of *property,* a critical difficulty is that the 'owner' has less than full control over trade secrets: any person can destroy the legal status of a trade secret by independent discovery or development of the same information or through reverse engineering, which is almost universally considered legal. Its very existence as a potential object of rights is outside the individual 'owner's control. The 'owner' thus does not have property rights in the information that operates *erga omnes*, but rather a contingent right of action against parties with whom the information is shared or to whom it is disclosed, or who access or use it in an improper manner.

The main alternative to the proprietary approach around the world sees the problem that trade secrets law addresses as being unfair of some kind: either offending against a relationship of trust or acting in a commercially dishonest manner. From this perspective, the cause of action relating to trade secrets neither lies in IP law nor in some other separate regime but is part of a broader remedial doctrine, equity in the English law and delictual liability in the civilian systems, the particular delict or wrong being 'unfair competition'. The relevant law is in both cases *adapted* to the particular circumstances of trade secrets cases rather than having been *specifically developed* for that purpose.

The above refers to civil rather than penal actions. Obviously, if a property approach is taken to trade secrets, then it is easier to allocate a role to the criminal law, since if a trade secret is property, it can conceivably be 'stolen'. The difficulty is an absence of deprivation which is normally a part of the law of theft and embezzlement and which does not easily apply to information. A penal approach does not conceptually fit well with an unfair competition rationale, although there is a possible analogy with dishonesty offences such as fraud. However, demonstrating how thin, or perhaps confused,[1] the conceptual foundations of trade secrets law are, the erstwhile German trade secrets law fell both within its Law on Unfair Competition while at the same time providing criminal sanctions for some conduct. More generally, criminalization, where it is a more longstanding feature of the law, tends to focus on deliberate dishonesty of employees; more recently, it is associated in particular with transnational industrial espionage, in particular relating to technical secrets.

Within the broader 'honesty' family of trade secrets law, the English breach of confidence approach is in origin based on vindicating obligations of trust, good faith and reliance that result from the particular characteristics of people's relationships. It has the broad aim of preserving certain standards of honesty and good faith in communications (in the sense of giving access to information) between parties and across the board and not just in relation to commercially relevant exchanges. Because, in origin, it has this communications-based rationale, it struggles doctrinally with industrial espionage cases, as there is no communication within a trustful relationship between parties to vindicate by the grant of a remedy in such circumstances. Instead,

---

1. Kung-Chung Liu, 'The Problem with Trade Secrets Protection/Overprotection in Asia' (2022) 53(1) *International Review of Intellectual Property and Competition Law* 94 https://doi.org/10.1007/s40319-021-01136-9.

there is unilateral action by one party to acquire another's trade secret. But because breach of confidence forms part of the flexible doctrinal structure of equity, it has managed to adapt to these types of scenarios: it is a virtue of equity that is not wedded to particular doctrinal stringencies. The central tenet of English law is thus that the determinant of illegality is the purpose of the communication. Because it does not focus only on commerce, the relevant English law of equity stands completely apart from the other jurisdictions considered here.[2] Schloetter importantly points out one of the implications of the English approach: third-party liability, has been extended quite readily in the context of breach of confidence in England, whereas in France and Germany, this requires proof of unfair competition or a delictual wrong committed by a third party.[3] In England, only knowledge of the breach ('knowing participation') needs to be established.

The honesty rationale is also present in the unfair competition approach to trade secrets law, which is longstanding, as recognized in TRIPS, where it says that 'In the course of ensuring effective protection against unfair competition as provided in Article 10bis of the Paris Convention (1967), Members shall protect undisclosed information [...]'. Fairness/unfairness is obviously a challenging standard to employ as it is inherently vague. The way it is 'firmed up' is usually by making reference to the standards of an honest trader. What exactly this standard would require can in theory be addressed by evidence that is adduced by the parties.

The US uniform trade secrets law, which has recently been influential through the adoption of its provisions in the EU TSD and the UMCA, is in effect a 'mixed bag' as it has proprietary characteristics but also focuses on bad faith or dishonesty. It uses the concept of misappropriation but with an emphasis on the 'mis' rather than on the 'appropriation'. In other words, *unauthorized* appropriation of the valuable knowledge or information discovered or accumulated by another *in itself* does not warrant a remedy. The acquisition must be *improper*, i.e., fall below some standard of honesty and fair conduct in commercial matters. In the process of regulating conduct US law also vindicates ownership to a limited degree, as the information protected must be properly identified; secret enough; subject to secrecy measures; and have some (not well defined) commercial value. The US approach is a hybrid: an ethical conduct rationale combined with a limited and conditional protection for effort or ingenuity in devising uniquely held knowledge. This rather cobbled-together approach, which we have argued lacks a coherent rationale, is, nonetheless, through TRIPS and the more recent multi-jurisdictional adoptions, making progress in global terms.

The rationale of the civilian unfair competition approach emphasizes the dynamic role of secret information in competition. Its starting point is that competition is distorted by certain practices that traders would consider dishonest but that do not fall

2. Schloetter also points out that protection is connected with a competitive advantage in France and Germany but not in England. Whereas, in Germany, a potential competitive advantage is enough in France an actual commercial value is according to him advanced as a requirement by scholars in France. *See* R. Schloetter, *Der Schutz von Betriebs- und Geschaftsgeheimnissen und die Abwerbung von Arbeitnehmern, Eine rechtsvergleichende Untersuchung des englischen, franzosichen und deutschen rechts* (Carl Heymans Verlag, Koln, 1997).
3. *Ibid.*, 232.

within a particular proprietary IP regime. Unfair competition law operates as a safety net, which interestingly enough some jurisdictions actually locate within their IP laws or codes, whereas others see it as separate. *Unauthorized* use of confidential information is not per se actionable as it is in the English system. Rather, it is actionable because taken together with other aspects of a competitor's behaviour, it amounts to the kind of intolerable commercial dishonesty that distorts competition. This rationale has more regard for the public interest in a properly operating competitive market than for the public interest in truth and honesty in human interactions. However, in essence, there is perhaps little difference between the flexible approaches of equity and that of unfair competition law. Both regimes primarily police conduct that is dishonest, a breach of faith, a breach of trust, etc., – i.e., that meets with a degree of moral opprobrium which is considered sufficient to warrant a legal remedy. It is interesting in this regard that the French terms for unfair competition are '*concurrence déloyale*', literally 'disloyal' rather than unfair competition. In civilian jurisdictions, market participants owe a duty to act in a manner that is honest (as that concept is recognized in a particular commercial sphere), and only honest competition is effective competition that serves the public interest. Thus, although the English law rejects a tort of unfair competition because of its vagueness, it is not reluctant to impose equally broad and unspecified obligations of good conduct through the medium of equity and the action for breach of confidence in particular.

Is trade secrets protection actually required to achieve any of these goals? As Bone has pointed out, there are numerous other contiguous remedies available, such as patent protection, the general criminal law, and labour law. Arguably, there is a sufficient case for some form of legal protection beyond obligations that exist because of a pre-existing relationship (e.g., between solicitor and client or doctor and patient) and ones that stretch beyond the privity of contractual relationships. It is more effective to *imply* obligations from certain circumstances than to require them to be conferred by some contract, and, in any case, contract cannot deal with industrial espionage scenarios. Some form of general obligation relating to confidential information will grease the wheels of commerce, by encouraging parties to share their confidential data in the knowledge that its use for uncontemplated purposes can be restrained. Alternatively, an enforceable obligation to maintain confidence encourages the sharing of information in a manner which is both commercially and technically efficient. The English tradition of the common law is not based on or conceived of as reflecting and balancing a catalogue of basic or human rights and freedoms. Rather, there is a 'system' – in fact, not systematic but incidentally grown – of individual causes of action. Thus, this area of law is not impacted by the legal recognition of a right to privacy, freedom of speech, free enterprise, professional advancement or right to respect for property, freedom of employment, freedom to work, freedom of competition, etc.: the constellation of basic rights that is the bedrock of civilian law. The area of privacy illustrates this difference between common law and civilian approaches well.

But the other sphere in which this traditional distinction is most relevant is in the post-employment phase: in the common law tradition, the rights of former employees to confidential information are not constructed on the basis of a contest between competing basic rights – freedom of work, of enterprise, of competition versus right to business assets, etc. The question is rather resolved on the basis of an instrumentalist approach reflected in so-called public policy: the desirability of free competitive labour markets versus the public interest in confidences being protected at law. The issues are the same, but the framework is different. Interestingly enough, in any practical sense, the effects are very similar: the courts are concerned with ensuring that trade secrets law and non-compete clauses do not go so far as to unduly restrain the competitive operation of a market and interfere with a person's freedom to deploy their knowledge and abilities to their greatest extent. They weigh up these competing demands in the light of the particular factual circumstances of each case.[4]

§10.02 PERSISTENT FUNDAMENTAL DIFFERENCES AT THE GLOBAL LEVEL DESPITE EVIDENCE OF RAPPROCHEMENT

Travelling beyond the jurisdictions we considered in more detail in earlier chapters, we see that in China as well, trade secrets protection fits within the confines of the broader Anti-Unfair Competition Law (1993 but substantially amended since).[5] This Act relates to misappropriation of trade secrets, which is 'defined as being disclosed to, acquired by, or used by others (including third parties who know or ought to know of the misappropriation) in a manner contrary to honest commercial practices (i.e., breach of duty of confidence, theft, inducement)'.[6] Progressive amendments to the Act made under pressure from the United States, as documented by Chen, have resulted in a regime showing considerable American characteristics.[7] The Chinese system also provides criminal penalties and administrative measures to protect trade secrets law, as does the Japanese Unfair Competition Prevention Act (UCPA).[8] The UCPA operates by prescribing 16 acts of unfair competition,[9] 7 of which relate to trade secrets, centring on acts of 'wrongful acquisition'. Acquisition by wrongful means refers not only to acts of illegality such as theft but also 'to the use of means that contravenes public policy and social norms'.[10]

---

4. *Ibid.*, 742.
5. *See* Ivy Liang, 'How to Protect Your Trade Secrets in South East Asian Countries and China' *Gowling WLG* (online) 18 January 2023, https://gowlingwlg.com/en/insights-resources/articles/2023/trade-secret-protection-in-sea-and-china.
6. *See* Yang Chen, 'Development of China's Trade Secrets Law in the US' Shadow: Negative Consequences for China and Suggestions' (2022) 17(1) *Asian Law Review* 138, 153.
7. *Ibid.*
8. Further details in Joe Raffetto & Dr Anna-Katharina Friese, 'Trade Secrets Global Guide' *Hogan Lovells* (online) 10 October 2022, https://www.hoganlovells.com/-/media/hogan-lovells/pdf/2022-pdfs/2022_10_10_global-trade-secrets-guide.pdf; Guanyang Yao & Ran Wang, 'Enforcement Strategy – Litigation vs Administrative Actions' *Managing IP* (online) 11 April 2023, https://www.managingip.com/article/2bhoso752z5oo1dlne2o0/sponsored-content/enforcement-strategy-litigation-vs-administrative-actions#:~:text=For%20example%2C%20the%20civil%20litigation,manufacturers%20or%20original%20equipment%20manufacturers.
9. *Ibid.*
10. *See* Thomas Landman, 'Trade Secret Protection in Japan and the United States: Comparison and Recommendations' (2019) 44(2) *Brooklyn Journal of International Law* 714.

Administrative measures as a distinct layer of regulatory intervention in IP matters are not confined to China and Japan: for example, in Mexico, an administrative IP infringement can give rise to a fine; in Vietnam, the law provides for administrative violations and sanctions.[11] The TRIPS agreement imposes certain equivalency requirements where administrative measures or procedures are provided for by the law of a Member State.[12] Thus, in some countries, trade secrets are the subject of administrative measures just as other forms of IP are; in others, it is a matter only of either civil judicial remedies or criminal law.

By contrast with China and Japan, which have a civilian and thus unavoidably statute-based system, in many countries with a common law tradition, such as India, for instance, there is no specific statute on trade secrets law and the matter is governed by breach of confidence principles in equity as in England.[13] Cases from the latter jurisdiction may still be called in aid in India.[14] The same can be said for Singapore,[15] Malaysia, Australia and New Zealand, but no longer Canada, which although a common law jurisdiction has now adopted trade secrets law in accordance with its obligations under the UMCA. In some of these jurisdictions where there has been little domestic evolution, the law of trade secrets is sometimes said to be 'underdeveloped'; cases decided by the courts can be few and far between.[16] However, Liu, in an insightful piece, points to the disadvantages of the 'overprotection' of trade secrets that may come with moving to a more 'modern' approach, with increased criminalization,

11. Vinh Le Quang, 'Enforcement of Intellectual Property Rights by Administrative Measures in Vietnam' *Lexology* (online) 8 July 2020, https://www.lexology.com/library/detail.aspx?g=3cf55080-1c5d-44eb-a6d7-ffb7a9de9ee7.
12. *See* Art. 49 Administrative Procedures: 'To the extent that any civil remedy can be ordered as a result of administrative procedures on the merits of a case, such procedures shall conform to principles equivalent in substance to those set forth in this Section.'
13. The TRIPS requirements concerning 'undisclosed information' are so general as to lend themselves to many different national approaches, which is well illustrated by the situation in Asia. For instance, the ASEAN countries have a typically varied patchwork of approaches. In Indonesia; Trade Secret Law No 30 of 2000 Regarding Trade Secret, providing civil remedies and criminal penalties; in Singapore, Malaysia, Brunei: the common law of confidence (equity) along English equity lines; in Thailand, Trade Secrets Act B.E. 2545 (2002)20; in Laos, the recently introduced modernizing Law on Intellectual Property No 50/NA of 2023 still lacks a dedicated legal framework for trade secret protection and enforcement; in the Philippines, trade secrets protection is dealt with in the Intellectual Property Code – Republic Act No 8293; and in Cambodia and Myanmar, no trade secrets laws apply as yet. An overview of trade secrets laws around the world is provided in Melvin F. Jager, Heinz Goddar & Melanie Müller, *Trade Secrets Throughout the World* (Clark Boardman Callaghan, 2023). In relation to India, *see* Lekhana Padmanabhan, 'Trade Secret Laws in India and Germany: A Comparative Analysis of Developed and Developing Nations' (2023) *SSRN Electronic Journal*.
14. *See* Mark Schultz & Douglas Lippoldt, *Approaches to Protection of Undisclosed Information (Trade Secrets)* (OECD Trade Policy Papers, No 162, OECD Publishing).
15. *See* above n 1. For Australia, *see* Dean; for New Zealand *see* [Sumpter]; for Malaysia confirming the application of the principles in *Coco v. Clark*, *see* https://taypartners.com.my/wp-content/uploads/LegalTaps/legalTAPS_Q4-2023.pdf. *See also* Kung-Chung Liu & Reto Hilty, *Trade Secret Protection: Asia at a Crossroads* (Kluwer Law International, 2021).
16. For instance, in Thailand, between 2004 and 2014, there were only 66 trade secrets cases in the Supreme Court. *See* Rati Kerdpu, 'Thailand's Trade Secrets Act: Understanding the Law and Prevailing in Disputes' *Tilleke & Gibbins* (online) 26 February 2016, https://www.tilleke.com/insights/thailands-trade-secret-act-understanding-law-and-prevailing-disputes/62/.

over-emphasis on property-like characteristics, sham use of trade secrets enforcement, reduction in positive externalities and removal from public oversight by the secret conducting, or redacting of matters involving trade secrets.[17] In some countries, change has come about through external influences more than internal dynamics: as mentioned above, in China, the law was amended because of US pressure.[18] It may further develop in the future as Asian and SEA countries seek greater alignment with the global trading and commercial system.

The TRIPS requirements concerning 'undisclosed information' are so general as to lend themselves to many different national approaches, which is in fact well illustrated by the situation in Asia more broadly. For instance, the ASEAN countries present a typically varied patchwork: in Indonesia: Trade Secret Law No 30 of 2000 Regarding Trade Secret, providing civil remedies and criminal penalties;[19] in Singapore, Malaysia, Brunei: the common law of confidence (equity) along English equity lines; in Thailand: Trade Secrets Act B.E. 2545 (2002);[20] in Laos: the recently introduced modernizing *Law on Intellectual Property No 50/NA of 2023* which still lacks a dedicated legal framework for trade secret protection and enforcement;[21] in the Philippines: trade secrets protection as dealt with in the Intellectual Property Code – Republic Act No 8293; and in Cambodia and Myanmar: no trade secrets laws at all as yet.

The African continent provides a rather similar picture of disparity and uncertainty. Some African countries take a breach of confidence approach, the law being based in the cases, whereas others have introduced trade secrets legislation. The former is the case, for instance, in Zimbabwe,[22] and the latter in Uganda.[23] In South Africa, there is no trade secrets legislation, but courts require that information is capable of application in trade or industry, is secret or confidential, requires some proof of diligence to protect the secret, and must have some economic value. Unlawful use

---

17. *See* above n 1.
18. *See also* Christine Yiu, 'Protecting Your Valuable Trade Secrets in China' *Bird & Bird* (online) 4 April 2023, https://www.twobirds.com/en/insights/2023/china/protecting-your-valuable-trade-secrets-in-china; Christine Yiu, 'A Comparison Between the EU Trade Secrets Directive and the Chinese Trade Secret Protection Regime' *Bird & Bird* (online) 11 June 2020, https://www.twobirds.com/en/insights/2020/global/a-comparison-between-the-eu-trade-secrets-directive-and-the-chinese-trade-secret-protection-regime.
19. *See* 'Law No. 30 of 2000 Regarding Trade Secret, Indonesia' *World Intellectual Property Organization* (online), https://www.wipo.int/wipolex/en/legislation/details/2258.
20. 'Trade Secret Act B.E. 2545' *IP Thailand* (online), https://www.ipthailand.go.th/images/781/______2_1.pdf.
21. *See* Nguyen Vu Quan, Do Thi Phan & Hoang Thi Tuyet Hong, 'Laos Unveils New IP Law 2023: 5 Burning Questions Every Business Should Ask' *Lexology* (online) 30 July 2024, https://www.lexology.com/library/detail.aspx?g=db6fe766-a1e0-48b1-a21a-15edf342c3ad.
22. *See* Munguma Christopher, 'The Protection of Trade Secrets in Zimbabwe' (2018) 3(1) *African Journal of Intellectual Property* 12.
23. Anthony Conrad Kakooza, 'Trade Secret Protection in East Africa: The Case Study of Uganda' in D.J Bakibinga & R Kakungulu-Mayambala (eds), *Intellectual Property Law in East Africa* (LawAfrica Publishing, 2022).

and acquisition of trade secrets is seen as a form of unlawful competition.[24] In Tanzania and Kenya, protection of trade secrets also relies on the common law and equity, and thus on case law rather than statute. As in many other jurisdictions, decided cases are, however, quite scarce.

This brief tour d'horizon is not intended to be comprehensive - merely to illustrate that unlike other areas of IP, trade secrets law continues to be approached in quite distinct ways, to some extent due to the varying influence around the world of the common law and civilian traditions and has commonly attracted only modest attention from legislators and courts. Again, because the WTO TRIPS standard is broad and non-specific in terms of legal instruments, many countries simply continue to rely on case law, whereas others apply broad principles of unfair competition. Some have introduced legislation which tends to mirror the TRIPS standards and rely on mixed concepts of misappropriation and unfair or disloyal conduct. Despite the trade-related harmonizations in North America and Europe, and despite endless assertions by practitioners that trade secrets protection is one if not the most important forms of legal protections, there are still many jurisdictions where trade secrets have received little attention or experienced any legislative intervention. This is interesting in light of the TRIPS related debate we address in Chapter 3 which pitted developing countries against the rich economies in relation to the need for and benefits from stricter standards of protection for trade secrets.[25]

§10.03 DOES HARMONIZING MEAN STRENGTHENING TRADE SECRETS PROTECTION?

There, thus, remain important differences in approach between jurisdictions. The question arises whether in those circumstances greater harmonization of trade secrets law is necessary and desirable, and if so, to what standard? Such harmonization will not now occur at the WTO level, and although the EU has now taken a major multi-jurisdictional step, there are few developments in that direction elsewhere except for North America. Economically developed nations seem to have the greatest appetite for harmonization and 'strengthening' of trade secrets law.

In any case, it is already proving difficult enough to make progress harmonizing other areas of IP law: to tackle an area with such radically different approaches in general presents much greater challenges again. The great disparity in regimes may appear to be a good reason *not* to attempt harmonization, but it may equally be *the best* reason to do so; in other words, although in one sense perhaps too difficult, the disharmony is arguably so great that some effort at harmonization is urgently needed in the interest of promoting cross-border commerce. That is one goal of the EU Trade Secrets Directive. Trade secrets law is often said to be the most critical part of IP law for corporations, and differences in the law certainly present practical challenges for

24. World Intellectual Property Organization, 'Overview of National and Regional Trade Secret Systems: South Africa' *World Intellectual Property Organization* (online), https://www.wipo.int/documents/d/trade-secrets/docs-overview-country-sheets-south-africa-final.pdf.
25. *See* below, Chapter 3.

transnational businesses and investment, and tech transfer. This is particularly true in their dealings with employees in various countries. However, although perhaps the post-employment phase is where the law of trade secrets is of most critical importance, it is also where harmonization is most difficult. Fundamental principles clash and divergent policy goals are most challenging to reconcile. Traditionally contract law steps into the breach, by way of non-competes and confidentiality clauses. It is interesting to note here that the European harmonization did not touch expressly on important issues such as the defining line between free know-how and real trade secrets post-employment. Another context where controversy and divergence are perhaps too great is in relation to criminal offences and liability. In some countries, the law of trade secrets is entirely left alone by the criminal law, whereas in others, penal sanctions figure prominently. Again, one of the most significant differences relates to employees and when and how passing on trade secrets without authorization should amount to a criminal offence (during and post-employment).

Furthermore, the discussion on the need for greater harmonization of trade secrets inherently raises the question of the appropriate standard of protection to adopt. Recent efforts toward harmonization have consistently led to enhanced protection. Countries often aim to align with the highest standards available to safeguard their national industries and corporations. This trend was particularly evident during the adoption of the European Directive, which brought European law in line with the civil protection standard established in US law. As a result, Germany revised its criminal law to ensure it was consistent with the new civil framework. This pursuit of stronger protection is influenced by the current economic environment. Traditional IP tools may seem increasingly outdated due to digitalization. Trade secrets, with their immediacy, flexibility, and wide applicability, have become a primary legal and practical means for managing data and algorithms. However, the rise of digitalization has also made trade secrets – related or not to the data-driven economy – more susceptible to misappropriation, especially through cyberattacks that can occur from great distances. While the growing importance and apparent vulnerability of trade secrets may motivate legislators to enhance their protection, it is essential to recognize that these increased protections are not neutral; they can affect the fundamental and competing freedoms of various stakeholders. In this context, it is questionable whether it is desirable to continually strengthen the protection of these assets without properly clarifying underlying purposes and objectives.

In the end, there are many open questions still in trade secrets law. For instance, in terms of possible criminal liability, what are the clearly defined elements of *actus reus* and *mens rea;* in terms of civil liability, whether reverse engineering should be entirely free or not; what rights employees should have post-termination; whether client lists are trade secrets; how far liability can be extended by contract; what interests trade secrets law really protects, etc. Arguably, in practical and public policy terms, however, the regulation of non-competes is the most critical issue, and it is interesting to note that finally, the regulators in a number of jurisdictions (the US, UK, Australia) have taken a genuine interest in the issue.

Whatever the scope and forum of any harmonization or reform of trade secrets law might be, its starting point should remain that the public interest demands free circulation of information and of the individuals who possess it. Adopting this as a starting principle accords with notions of democracy, freedom of speech, and competitive market economies that prevail in industrialized nations. From that starting point, the question then is what limitations should be imposed to enable society to function most effectively. If we accept that a universal recognition of privacy will develop (particularly in England and related jurisdictions), which regulates society's dealings with confidential information in the private sphere, what is the proper basis for imposing limitations on the free circulation of information in the commercial and corporate context? Taking into account that companies can use contract, what residual rules are required for companies to protect their legitimate interests in commercial secrets? The public interest is certainly served by encouraging the revealing of information to others on a limited-use basis, a critical benefit of legal protection of commercial secrets. This enhances efficiency and avoids excessive secrecy, which hampers cooperation and causes duplication of research efforts. But being able to maintain secrecy to some degree is critical for dynamic competition also. How to strike the balance optimally remains a critical question.

Index

A

Abus de confiance, 203, 207
Acquisition, 24, 26, 34, 46, 48, 51, 67, 69, 97-101, 106, 120, 130, 131, 136, 138, 151, 156, 157, 158, 166, 167, 170-175, 182, 185, 188, 193, 214, 222, 224, 226, 236, 269, 271, 274

B

Breach of confidence, 1, 3, 7, 8, 10, 11, 13, 14, 16, 22, 24, 34, 52-54, 61, 67, 69, 74-77, 79, 80, 84, 86, 87, 89-91, 93, 95-101, 103-112, 114, 115, 117, 118, 124, 126, 134, 137-139, 143, 152, 202, 244, 263, 265, 268-270, 272, 273
Business information, 33, 151, 213, 220, 221

C

Civil remedy, 74, 180, 181
Collection, 48, 185
Commercial information, 53, 79
Competency, 153-155
Competition, 123-130, 170-172, 181-186, 212-218
Confidentiality (agreements, clauses), 1, 102, 136, 139, 157, 169, 171, 190-194, 228-230, 236, 237, 244-245, 249, 258, 275
Contractual clauses, restriction, 175, 200, 228, 253
Cost, 5, 28, 29, 36-41, 48-50, 57, 112, 129, 134, 143, 148, 164, 169, 185, 211, 242, 244, 254, 263
Criminal (law, protection, offences), 16, 81-83, 98, 99, 111-113, 147-150, 155, 202-209, 214-216, 224-226, 275
Customer lists, 132

D

Definition (of trade secrets), 131-132, 219-221
Damages, 16, 25, 53, 93, 96, 98, 128, 176, 182-184, 188, 191, 200, 216, 225, 253. 262
Defence, 32, 40, 72, 75, 98, 133, 148, 149, 224
Discovery, 5, 27, 36, 55, 67, 119, 125, 137, 170, 171, 268
Disclosure, 139-141
Directive, 71-73, 99-101, 151-177, 186-189, 208-209, 212-226
DTSA (Defend Trade Secrets Act), 33, 121, 122, 130, 135, 139-142, 144, 146, 147, 150, 251

Duty of confidence, 52, 94, 120, 126, 216, 228, 229, 271

E

Economics, 23, 27-41, 44, 50
Economic Espionage Act (EEA), 25, 26, 59, 77, 81, 82, 113, 121, 146, 147, 148, 149, 208, 212, 259
Economic value, 21, 38, 68, 84, 111, 130-132, 142, 149, 165-168, 186, 211, 213, 273
Elements of the action, 75, 94, 109, 245
Employee, 156-158, 235-266
Employment, 191-194, 227-232
Enforcement, 99-101, 176-177, 223-224
Equity, 76-77, 79
Equitable remedies, 8, 77, 89, 91, 117, 118
Evidence, 26, 39, 55, 84, 106, 121, 133-136, 139, 140, 148, 149, 191, 197, 212, 259, 260, 262, 265, 266, 269, 271-274
Exceptions, 12, 27, 40, 50, 68, 75, 94, 119, 125, 171, 172, 175, 188, 190, 217, 219, 221, 229
Extraterritoriality, 143-147

F

Factors, 51, 77, 79, 83, 87, 97, 101, 108, 110, 116, 122, 131, 132, 134, 135, 143, 147, 162, 168, 177, 181, 189, 196, 216, 217, 227, 229, 230, 242, 246, 258, 259, 265, 266
Fiduciary duties, 7, 53
Foreign infringement, 173
Fraud, 43, 52, 65, 69, 72, 82, 103, 112, 113, 149, 203-205, 268
Freedom of competition, to compete, 14, 57, 109, 183, 245, 251, 270
Freedom of expression, 10, 74, 100, 187

G

Generally known, 63, 68, 131, 135, 156, 160, 163-166, 185, 213, 219, 263
Good faith, 8, 13, 19, 22-24, 34, 44, 47, 48, 51, 53, 59, 76, 79, 84, 85, 91, 92, 97, 98, 100, 102, 104, 106, 108, 110, 117, 120, 122, 133, 136, 140, 150, 185, 191, 192, 196, 198, 200, 208, 226, 229, 230, 239, 268
Gross negligence, 67, 69

H

Harmonization, 8-10, 155-158

I

Illegality, 54, 104-107, 109, 137, 213, 269, 271
Impropriety, 39, 43, 52, 69, 84, 104-110, 115, 121, 131, 136-139, 150, 186, 213
Information, 21-25, 62-63, 132-134, 193-194, 203-206, 262-265
Inevitable disclosure (doctrine), 139-141, 249
Infringer, 170-172, 176, 177, 224
Infringement, 25, 45-47, 53, 58, 67, 93, 94, 100, 157, 170, 172, 173, 175, 177, 184, 187, 224, 243, 272
Infringing good, 101, 106, 172-174, 176, 188
Injunction / Injunctive relief, 11, 47, 67, 77, 91-93, 96, 98, 101, 109, 114, 118, 119, 139-141, 143, 145, 176, 177, 184, 232, 242-244
Interlocutory injunction, 11, 232

K

Know-how, 241-244, 262-265
Knowledge (mobility of), 9, 16

L

Legitimate interest, 177, 195, 197, 213, 219, 220, 224, 228, 231, 232, 237, 254, 255, 257, 260-263, 265, 276
Loss, 5, 25, 45, 81, 96, 111, 149

M

Misappropriation, 129-130, 170-175, 181-184
Mobility, 9, 15-17, 24, 32, 41, 58, 156, 191, 227, 237, 239, 252

N

Negligence, 65, 216
Non-compete (agreements), 1, 9, 55, 70, 126, 158, 230-232, 245
Novelty, 68, 85, 96, 110, 133, 165

O

Owner, 2, 26, 33, 35-37, 39, 57-59, 70, 72, 84, 103-105, 113, 118, 120, 123, 134, 137, 141, 142, 144-146, 149, 166, 167, 169, 170, 172, 174, 175, 188, 194, 203, 213, 216, 209, 219, 220, 225, 226, 268

P

Parasitism, 182-186, 189
Patents, 3-6, 12, 14, 27, 29, 30, 32-34, 46, 48-50, 59, 68, 85, 91, 92, 95, 118-122, 125, 129, 132, 133, 164, 165, 184, 202, 205, 208, 222, 267, 270
Penal, 13, 15, 16, 78, 147, 148, 155, 190, 202, 203, 208, 212, 216, 225, 226, 239, 251, 268, 275
Personal information, 10, 41, 47, 54, 75, 90, 99, 106, 107, 114
Policy, 19-60
Privacy, 53-55
Preliminary (injunction), 11, 114, 143, 145
Proof, 2, 24, 83, 86, 99, 139, 145, 148, 149, 173, 184, 189, 224, 249, 250, 260, 269, 273
Property, 19-60, 83-85
Proportionality, 101, 107, 153, 168, 176-177, 189, 193, 195, 197, 198, 223, 224
Propriety, 24, 28, 31, 32, 42, 46, 59, 106
Protective measures, 25, 39, 136, 149, 209
Proportionality, 101, 107, 153, 168, 176-177, 189, 193, 195, 197, 198, 223, 224
Public domain, 85, 86, 89, 96, 101, 119, 122, 134, 144, 149, 181, 182, 213, 214, 245, 262, 264
Public interest, 14, 23, 24, 74, 75, 97, 100, 107, 140, 177, 224, 245, 246, 252, 257, 259, 260, 265, 270, 271, 276

R

Reasonable efforts, measures, steps (of protection), 39, 111, 132
Relative secrecy, 17, 32, 39, 46, 51, 68, 133-135, 139, 141, 143, 151, 202, 208, 213
Remedies, 44-47
Restatement, 52, 84, 111, 113, 115, 121, 123, 124, 126, 127, 130-133, 135, 142, 157, 177
Restraint of trade, 86, 117, 119, 140, 157, 190, 194, 201, 228, 245, 246, 255, 262, 264

Restrictive covenants, 194, 259, 263
Reverse engineering, 174-175, 222-223

S

Savoir Faire, 184-185, 189-191, 193
Secrets de fabrique, 82, 83, 148, 179, 181, 190, 202-203, 205, 207, 208
Secrecy requirement, 32, 68, 69, 135, 165, 166
Springboard doctrine, 101, 138

T

Technical Information, 4, 29, 55, 119, 132, 148, 193, 213
Third party, 172-174
Theft, 203-205
Transposition, 158-160, 184-189, 208-209, 212-226
TRIPS, 61-70, 160-169

U

Unauthorized (use, disclosure), 43, 71, 94, 109, 113, 127, 138, 167, 189, 214, 270
Undisclosed information, 4, 8, 61-67, 72, 181, 202, 269, 273
Unjust enrichment, 7, 19, 32, 58, 76, 95, 103, 129, 150, 185, 186
Unfair competition, 123-130, 170-172, 181-186, 212-218
Unlawful (act, means), 99-101, 106, 124, 137, 145, 151, 153, 154, 157, 166, 170-174, 176, 188, 211, 216, 221-222, 224, 226, 246, 273, 274
UTSA, 130-132

W

Whistleblowers, 14, 55
WTO, 4, 64, 73, 274

www.ingramcontent.com/pod-product-compliance
Lightning Source LLC
LaVergne TN
LVHW020642300926
849161LV00004B/782
* 9 7 8 9 0 4 1 1 8 6 6 4 5 *